THE GERMAN STURM UND DRANG

1. GOETHE, 1774 OR 1775
From Lavater's 'Physiognomische Fragmente'

THE GERMAN
STURM UND DRANG

by

ROY PASCAL

*Professor of German in the
University of Birmingham*

MANCHESTER UNIVERSITY PRESS

© Roy Pascal, 1953
Published by the University of Manchester at
THE UNIVERSITY PRESS
316–324, Oxford Road, Manchester, 13

First published, 1953
Reprinted, with minor corrections, 1959, 1967

GB SBN 7190 0194 3

ACKNOWLEDGMENT

I WISH GRATEFULLY to acknowledge a debt to colleagues in several British Universities for encouragement and criticism, and particularly to Mr. R. Hinton Thomas of my own Department. Miss L. Besag has given most valuable technical assistance. To the University Press of Manchester I am indebted for advice as well as for its readiness to publish this work, and to my own University for contributing to the cost. In dedicating the book to my wife, I wish to express my gratefulness for her constant help and advice.

ROY PASCAL.

1951.

v

NOTE

IN ORDER to make the material as accessible as possible to readers who know no German, quotations from German prose and verse sources are given in English. Verse passages have been rendered in a form which reproduces as nearly as may be the characteristics of the originals, but for obvious reasons the original verses are given as well. The translation even of prose passages offered many difficulties, for nearly all the works of the Stürmer und Dränger are eccentric in vocabulary, style, and punctuation, and there are many obscurities, particularly in diaries and letters. I have deliberately preserved these idiosyncrasies in my translations, though at times simplification and interpretation were forced on me. Where translation was so imperfect as to be misleading, I have added the original German word in square brackets.

I have used throughout the terms 'Sturm und Drang' and 'Stürmer und Dränger' for the movement and the men, as recognised and convenient labels. Where the title of a work gives a significant clue to its contents, it has been translated into English—though here again difficulties arise, as in the case of Goethe's *Dichtung und Wahrheit* ('Poetry and Truth'), where 'Dichtung' means both 'fiction' and 'poetry'. Works well known in English translation are mentioned by their English title, such as *The Sorrows of Young Werther*, but translation of other titles seemed clumsy and unprofitable.

Numerous notes were necessary. They are almost all confined to documentation, and in order to facilitate the reading of the book they have been placed at the end. I was frequently tempted to engage in polemics with other writers on this period, but for reasons of space have had to refrain, except in one or two instances.

CONTENTS

ix

Contents

ILLUSTRATIONS

INTRODUCTION

THE STANDPOINT

THE LITERARY movement known as the Sturm und Drang has an individuality and importance that have long been recognised, including as it does the early work of Herder and Goethe. Its quality and significance are, however, often obscured, partly because it may be treated as a mere phase in the lives of its members, and partly because its separate aspects may be isolated from one another for the purposes of special study. Taken as a whole, it is a movement of wide scope, whose multiple achievement springs from the same impulse, and whose various aspects reflect and sustain one another. It is an underlying principle of this study that only by grasping the totality of its range can we understand how it came about that this generation of young Germans found, for the first time since the Lutheran period, an original and profound interpretation of the world, which has exercised the deepest influence not only on German, but also on European culture. The distinctive characteristics of the Sturm und Drang are most easily and frequently discerned in its poetry, but its poetry is embedded in new principles of personal relationships, a new standard of evaluation of social life and history, a new attitude to thinking and to nature, as well as a new appreciation of poetry. Indebted in innumerable ways to British and French thinkers and poets, the Sturm und Drang reveals in its achievements, its problems, and its failures, the lineaments of a new cultural age, the bourgeois successor to the culture of ' polite society ' ; it is the harbinger of nineteenth-century romanticism and realism.

That so great a change should have found its first decisive formulations in Germany seems strange. Split into numerous states and free cities, the country was governed by absolute princes and hereditary oligarchies. It participated scarcely at all in the economic development so characteristic of France and Britain, and its middle class was traditionalist and subordinate. The expansion of Prussian power, the most signifi-

cant political process of the century, was unattended by any
new social principle, by any awakening of public opinion or
public conscience.   There were, however, intellectual stirrings
in the Protestant North, in which a rigid ecclesiastical control
prevented the Catholic South from participating.   In response
to philosophical trends abroad, men began to subject accepted
authority in Church and State to the test of reason, and
though with Christian Wolff and Gottsched reason chiefly
served to bolster up authority, the generation of Kant and
Lessing began to criticise dogmatic intolerance and political
despotism in the name of human well-being.   Within the
Protestant Church itself, loose groupings of Pietists existed in
many places, who sought to share religious experience outside
the limits of dogma and cult.   But the only public forum was
the theatre, the only medium of public discussion was literature,
and till the Sturm und Drang most literary works commended
the contentment of the confined round of burgher life and
sentimentalised its virtues, preached an abstract morality, or
indulged in rococo trivialities.   Only in Lessing's plays are the
problems of German life presented in their concrete and serious
reality ; but, while the Stürmer und Dränger acknowledged
their debt to him, they were repelled by his cool reasonableness.
In poetry, Klopstock discovered themes and a language arising
from the depths of personal experience, and he can be considered to be a forerunner of the Sturm und Drang ; but the
ideal and religious content of his *Messias* and his odes seemed
often to fail to link on to the actuality of living, sensuous
experience.

By contrast, vast developments had been taking place during
the preceding two centuries in the political, social, and intellectual life of Britain and France.   Feudalism had given way
to the unified state, the nobility was losing ground to the
mercantile and industrial bourgeoisie.   In Britain a revolution
had shattered the notion of divine right, and the categories
of dogma were being replaced by rational principles.   Empiricists and sensualists were inverting the traditional view
of the relationship of thought and being.   This mighty movement towards a secular, humanistic outlook was arrested by
all sorts of hesitations and questionings, all sorts of com-
promise with traditional powers, such as may be observed in

thinkers as bold as Hume or Voltaire, but it was in general inspired by an unmistakable confidence in the widening range of the middle class, in its moral worth and its energy. In literature the tone was still set by the ' polite society ' in which the aristocracy dominated. But here again writers were seeking in novels and plays for a new content and new forms appropriate to middle-class existence. And beneath the surface, a new response to Shakespeare and folksong, to wild nature and grandiose feelings, to melancholy and mystery, was shaking the serenity of classical poise. If in Locke, Hume, Voltaire, Diderot and the *Encyclopédie*, Richardson, Lillo, and Fielding, the intellectual challenge to traditional thought and values became explicit, in Young, Gray, the Wartons, Sterne, in Percy we see a groping after a new type of feeling. Rousseau summed up in its most provocative form the problematic of the new man, at loggerheads with his times, capable of new raptures and tortured by new, obscure desires.

The leading personalities of the Sturm und Drang—Hamann, Herder, Goethe, Merck, Lenz, Klinger—were nurtured in this European movement. A glance at Goethe's autobiography or Herder's *Journal of my Voyage* of 1769 will show the debt they owed it. The boldness of their aims and their thoughts is comparable with that of the *Encyclopédie* and Rousseau rather than any German predecessor. But, as contrasted with many earlier generations of Germans who had sought to transplant French ideas or cultural forms into Germany, they remained true to their native experience and circumstances and successfully absorbed the European movement into their own substance. They undertook this task with all the ardour of youth, for in 1770, when the Sturm und Drang began first to take shape, they were young men ; and they often fell into errors and absurdities. Members of burgher families, the rigidity of the German class-structure, and the Frenchified culture of the aristocracy, encouraged them to respond whole-heartedly to the revolt against polite society and its literary conventions. Their youth and inexperience, even more the motionlessness of German society, prevented them from reaching new principles of social or political organisation, but, following Rousseau, they inaugurated a new type of political thinking, which judged society against the measure of personal life and inner need.   Wrestling with all the major trends of contemporary thought, they applied a new criterion to theory, valuing it only in so far as it corresponded with experience, heightened their consciousness of being vital, sentient beings, and contributed to valuable activity.   In poetical works of startlingly new form they, and above all Goethe, found intense expression for their specific experience and their new values.

It was not possible, within the scope of the present work, to analyse the poetic qualities of the imaginative works of the Sturm und Drang.   To this task I hope to devote a separate volume.   Here I have confined myself to the exposition of the fundamental principles underlying their new values, as they emerge in the complex encounters of experience and idea, practice and theory.   It is not an analysis of a completed system, but the description of a process and a search ; we are dealing here with a Faustian ' obscure urge ', rather than serene clarity.   The best of the Stürmer und Dränger grew out of their Sturm und Drang, and it was necessary to indicate in what ways Herder and Goethe changed as they grew older.   It should be stressed, however, that the very principles which forced them to burst the husk of the Sturm und Drang are themselves a vital element within the Sturm und Drang.   One may apply to the movement as a whole what Goethe wrote in his old age about *Faust* : ' It is like the history of the world and man, in which the solution of every problem gives rise to a new problem which needs to be solved.'

CHAPTER I

THE PERSONALITIES

Hast du's nicht alles selbst vollendet
Heilig glühend Herz ?—GOETHE.

IN THE exact sense, the men who make up the Sturm und
Drang are Merck, Herder, Goethe, Lenz, Klinger, Friedrich (Maler) Müller, H. L. Wagner and Leisewitz ; but the
last three are peripheral and dependent figures with whom
we need to be concerned only here and there. We must add
to the group Herder's mentor and friend, Hamann, whose
personality and works were of great and direct importance
for the group. The position of Schiller is peculiar. The
Sturm und Drang took shape about the year 1770, and came
to an end by about 1778 ; but Schiller's first play was finished
only in 1781. He was much younger than the others, and at
this time knew none of them personally. Though he is
traditionally and with some justice reckoned as one of them,
we shall find that in several essential respects he differs from
the other Stürmer und Dränger.

While our attention must in the main be directed to this
group, many German contemporaries came into sympathetic
touch with it and to some extent participated in it. These
men must be mentioned in the appropriate context, but they
cannot claim an equal attention. Some, like Klopstock,
Justus Möser, or Gerstenberg, may be ranked as precursors
of the Sturm und Drang. In his younger days Klopstock was
temperamentally akin to the Stürmer und Dränger, but his
habit of soaring away in sublime flights was something they
felt they had to restrain in themselves. Möser, a high administrative official in the tiny state of Osnabrück, gave the younger
generation confidence in the worth of their own personality
and their country ; but, a responsible statesman with great
practical acumen, he was the very reverse of them in temperament. Gerstenberg, a German in Danish military service,
stimulated Herder and Goethe through his enthusiasm for
Shakespeare, for the Edda and the modern ' Bardic ' poetry.

But he was a vain and shallow person, and he faded away into insignificance after 1770.[1]

Other writers, closer contemporaries of the Stürmer und Dränger, made only temporary or partial contact with them. Of all of these, the Swiss clergyman Lavater had the closest affinity with Herder and Goethe. His correspondence with Herder began in 1772, that with Goethe after the publication of *Götz von Berlichingen* in 1773. He visited Goethe in 1774, being accompanied by him on a journey to Ems, and receiving visits from Goethe in exchange. His undogmatic religious enthusiasm, his delight in the discussion of religious experience, his lavish goodness of heart, the unaffectedness and independence of his character, brought him for a time very close to Goethe, whom he did not despair of converting to Christian tenets ; and at the same time his own mind was broadened by his sympathy for young men whose hearts were as rich as his own, and as greedy for communication. Between 1774 and 1776 Goethe, Merck, Herder, and Lenz contributed to Lavater's physiognomical work, the most secular and humanistic of his many enterprises. But Lavater's increasing parochial responsibilities in Zürich and his inveterate speculation about matters beyond the range of earthly experience took him out of the Sturm und Drang : Goethe's later comment defines the hindrance to their closer sympathy : ' His mysticism prevented his soaring to the heights his genius might well have reached.' [2]

Heinrich Jung, known as Jung-Stilling, was one of those pietists who came close to Goethe, and his only important work, the autobiographical *Heinrich Stillings Jugend*, was written at the suggestion of Goethe whom he met when they were both students at Strassburg. His clumsy unworldliness, his childlike candour, and his unquestioning trust in his own intimations, which he ascribed to the direct influence of God, appealed strongly to Goethe, who helped him in several ways. These qualities turned into intolerant self-righteousness as he grew older and socially successful, and he fades out of our picture. F. H. Jacobi reports an amusing and characteristic remark of Goethe's, which sums up his charm and his weakness : ' The queer fellow believes he only needs to throw the dice, and God will see that they fall out well.' [3]

Fritz Jacobi himself, who remained in friendly correspondence with Goethe all his life, made a similar ' electric ' but brief contact with the Sturm und Drang. A little older than Goethe, and on the way to a distinguished career as an administrator in the tiny state of Berg, Jacobi met Goethe and Lavater in 1774 and entered immediately into the most intimate and enthusiastic relations with them. In their uninhibited trust in feeling, in the spontaneity of their relations, their freedom from fixed formulas, he found for a time the answer to his own quest for a philosophy based on intuitive truth. By the end of 1775 however he was already troubled by the apparent irresponsibility of Goethe, by the threat of Sturm und Drang individualism to family life and social forms. A violent quarrel with Goethe in 1779 was bridged over, but Jacobi's later development as a systematic philosopher took him away from the Sturm und Drang, even though his main thesis was the reality of intuitive knowledge. The writer Heinse too may be reckoned among these temporary associates of the Sturm und Drang. He was a protégé of Wieland and Gleim, then of Fritz Jacobi and his brother Georg, whose *Iris*, a literary periodical for ladies, he edited from 1775 to 1776. His own works were strongly influenced at first by the playful eroticism of Wieland, which the Stürmer und Dränger, particularly Lenz, found most unpalatable ; his contact with Goethe, Herder, and Klinger brought an almost savage intensity into his sensualism and individualism, most marked in his novel *Ardinghello*. Reckless and feckless in his ideas, he had something in common with the Stürmer und Dränger ; but he was a creature of theory, and even his sensuality was the product of inexperience and innocence, as he told Wieland.[4] It was his theoretical, innocent ' lasciviousness ' that repelled Goethe ; and Fritz Jacobi, who often sympathised with his temperamental excesses, was justified in saying that he had ' no heart '—' his soul is in his blood '.[5]

It was quite a different sort of kinship that bound the Stürmer und Dränger for a time to the short-lived school of poets known as the ' Göttinger Hainbund '. These young poets, Hölty, Voss, the brothers Stolberg, were at one in their admiration of Klopstock, and cultivated lofty feelings of pure love, nature, and patriotism. Their innocence was too deliberate and their idealism too sublime for the Stürmer und Dränger. Goethe contributed poems to their periodical, Boie's *Musenalmanach*, but the only Göttingen poet to show any comparable earthy vigour was Bürger. Bürger was the only one of them who fully shared in the new appreciation of Shakespeare and folksong, but his affectation of a popular style, the coarseness of his perceptions and expressions, prevented any intimacy with Herder or Goethe. The ardour of the young Imperial Counts Stolberg captivated Goethe for a time, and they went on a famous trip to Switzerland together. Even on the journey, however, Goethe was somewhat sceptical of their exalted worship of the natural life and their abstract republicanism ; and very soon their ostentatious idealism was to lead them indignantly to repudiate what they considered to be Goethe's lack of morals ; they were to find in institutional religion the expression of all their spiritual needs.

All these temporary and partial associates of the Sturm und Drang were urged on by the desire to live according to instinctive feeling, to fashion their lives according to intuition and ' revelation ', not social norms and practical reasonableness. They express in various ways and degrees responses to the movement towards the liberation of feeling, sense, and imagination which had found its foremost exponents in France and Britain. Their divergence from the Sturm und Drang occurs at the point where the conflicts caused by the new values become explicit, and their repudiation of the Sturm und Drang is the measure of their failure to face up to the complexity of real life. A trait common to them all is temperamental instability, which was justified in their eyes by their belief in the truth of intense feeling. In Germany, where intellectual life possessed no homogeneous social leadership, this type of temperament was less inhibited than in England or France, though the ultimate conflict with the religious or social community, with Christian tenets or reason, could not be avoided. In the Stürmer und Dränger we find the same instability and individualism ; but they do not fit themselves, as the implications of their ' dunkler Drang ' become plain, into traditional patterns of existence and thought, but fight through to the formulation of new principles of personality as of poetry.

The central group of the Stürmer und Dränger were allies
in the fullest sense ; that is, they were bound not only by a
common outlook but also by close personal ties. The oldest
of them, Merck, was 29 in 1770 ; Herder was 26, Goethe 21,
Lenz 19, and Klinger 18. They were all university men,
trained or training for the learned professions. During 1772
Merck, Goethe, and Herder directed a critical review, the
Frankfurter Gelehrte Anzeigen, and gave it a character of its
own. By 1773 Nicolai identified them as a literary group and
complained that they wrote for one another, and not for the
general public, the characteristic complaint of a literary
pundit against young rivals.[6] The notebooks of the scientist
Lichtenberg were in these years full of disparaging references
to the ' Frankfurters ', as he calls them.[7] In 1774 Wieland
devoted the main part of an article in his *Teutscher Merkur* to
this ' sect '. For all his dislike of the obscurity and fanaticism
of its leaders, Hamann and Herder, he credits Goethe with
the reformation of German tragedy and Lenz with that of
German comedy.[8]

Goethe and Herder met in Strassburg in the winter 1770–1
when the one was completing his legal studies and the other
undergoing an (unsuccessful) operation to his eye, and the
long talks they had in Herder's sick-room were of decisive
importance for Goethe's future development. As Hamann
was Herder's mentor, so Herder was Goethe's : Goethe wrote
some months after Herder's departure : ' If I am destined
to be your planet, I will be it, be it gladly, faithfully. A
friendly moon to the earth.'[9] They saw one another rarely
until 1776, when Goethe managed to get Herder appointed
as superintendent clergyman at Weimar, but their correspondence, though desultory, did not lapse in the intervening years.
Merck and Goethe met in 1771 and immediately struck up a
most cordial friendship ; and as they lived close to one another, the one at Darmstadt and the other at Frankfurt, they
visited one another frequently. Goethe's *Götz von Berlichingen*
was published by them jointly. After Goethe went to Weimar
in 1775, Merck was frequently there as an honoured guest of
the ducal family. Klinger was a native of Frankfurt and
formed one of Goethe's intimate circle of friends there.
His studies at the near-by Giessen did not interrupt their

friendship. Lenz arrived at Strassburg from East Prussia just after Herder's departure, immediately became a close associate of Goethe, and soon entered into correspondence with Goethe's circle, Herder, Lavater, and the rest. He was visited by them when they passed through Strassburg, and in 1776 came up north to visit Klinger, and both of them stayed with Goethe in Weimar for some weeks. H. L. Wagner knew Lenz at Strassburg, and joined in Goethe's circle when he began to practise as a lawyer in Frankfurt. The others had much more slender associations with the group, and enjoyed no such intimacy. Leisewitz had indeed no personal contact with Herder or Goethe. Goethe was the only one of them all with private means, and it is characteristic of him, as of the degree of their cohesion, that he gave direct or indirect financial help to Jung-Stilling, Lenz, Klinger, Heinse, and Maler Müller ; he was directly responsible for Herder's appointment at Weimar ; and later, when Merck fell on evil days, he arranged for him too to receive substantial help.

The members of the group, bound by close personal ties, were at one in their dissatisfaction with their occupation or profession, which they felt to be confined, tedious, and arid. But, with the exception of Goethe, they could not dispense with a profession. It was at that time impossible to live by writing. There was no law of copyright, literary piracy was an established custom, and the honoraria paid for original works and articles were necessarily poor enough. Even such a tremendous success as *The Sorrows of Werther* brought Goethe very little profit ; *Götz* was a loss. Lenz was indeed so touchy that, sorely as he needed money, he thought it an indignity to receive an honorarium.[10] Thus, with the exception of Goethe, whose means made him independent, all of them depended on patronage. Aristocratic patronage weighed most heavily, no doubt, when they were forced to take private tutorships, the drawbacks of which were drastically described in Lenz's *Hofmeister*. But nearly all posts in the Church, the universities, and the bureaucracies were decided by the goodwill of the prince who, in such small states and tiny capitals, could keep a personal look-out on the behaviour of his subjects. In Weimar the names of citizens passing through the city gates were reported to the prince ; and when Schiller fled from Stuttgart he had to exercise the greatest ingenuity to get safely out of the town. All the circumstances of life seemed to conspire to intensify that temperamental restlessness that is common to the Stürmer und Dränger ; and, in these circumstances, this restlessness gained a wider, social, and philosophical significance, it may well be regarded as a typical expression of the malaise of the individual in modern society.

HAMANN

Hamann, born in 1730, belongs to the generation of Kant, Klopstock, and Lessing ; but in temperament and outlook he is closer to the Stürmer und Dränger. His father, a medical practitioner without academic qualifications, was a much-respected citizen of Königsberg, a thriving commercial city whose intellectual life was stimulated by its close connections with England and Russia. The father seems to have exerted an oppressive influence on his two sons, both of whom were hypochondriacs. They were kept in tight leading-strings even as young men, while their imagination and feelings were over-cultivated by devotional reading and practices.[11] Johann Georg developed a heavy stutter and from early life was completely unpractical, a characteristic that turned later into an invincible repugnance for public affairs and social conventions. But the home was sociable and Hamann had many friends ; he had indeed an unusual need and gift for friendship, and won the devoted affection of Königsberg friends and of men farther afield like Lavater, F. H. Jacobi, and F. L. Stolberg.

He studied at Königsberg University for five years, but his insatiable intellectual curiosity would not submit to the discipline necessary to take a degree. He devoured books at extraordinary speed, and read everything he could lay hands on, in Hebrew, Greek, Latin, English, French, and German. After some years as a private tutor he tried his hand at business with his friend Behrens, a well-to-do and ambitious merchant who thought so highly of him as to send him in 1757 on a confidential mission to London. What this mission was is unclear ; but it was a failure, and probably doomed from the first ; and if Behrens hoped it would contribute to Hamann's political and economic education he was disappointed in this too. Hamann frittered away his time in London, made debts, and became heavily oppressed by his failure. Lonely and in despair, he found refuge in reading the Bible ; it is, as he describes it in *Thoughts on my Life*, the decisive crisis of his life. He returned to Königsberg in a mood of remorse and defiance. When Behrens and Kant tried to persuade him to turn to practical life again, he refused, and his first important work, *Socratic Memorabilia*, opposes to the uncertainties of reason and common sense the certainties of intuitive belief. It was his first attack on all ' political arithmetic ', in which he uses the arguments of sceptics and empiricists, Socrates, Bacon, Locke, and Hume, to undermine the confidence of practical reason. Its whimsical, ' sybilline ' style earned for him the title of ' the Magus of the North ', given him by F. C. von Moser.

He now settled down in the home of his father, reading and writing, giving occasional lessons and apparently ready to become the permanent guest of his father and brother. But his brother became incapable of work and rapidly turned into an incurable melancholic. On the death of his father Hamann had to become the bread-winner, and for ten years, from 1767, he held a subordinate post as clerk and translator in the Prussian excise at Königsberg. He felt his work to be real forced labour, all the more distasteful since he served a state and king he detested, and was the subordinate of the French officials Frederick the Great had appointed. Throughout his life he kept up a running fire against the Prussian king and state-service. But this hatred was not political in character, however much it was fed by the provincialism of Königsberg. It took the form of a repudiation of the claims of all political and social organisation, an expression of his conviction that only religious faith, and the private life in which religious belief can be fostered, have real value. This is the principle of all his writings, which, mainly polemical, are directed against the authority of all impersonal forces, whether of state or of metaphysics, against all formalism in religion and secular life. His positive doctrine is harder to define. At times he seems to proclaim a literal faith in the Bible, at times to be the most orthodox of Lutherans, at times an eccentric

heretic, ' incomprehensibly queer ' [12] to his friends and to his
enemies. His style is of a piece with his themes. All his
writings are short, most of them are mere pamphlets, and
all seem to be intended to disprove the possibility of clear
rational statement of the fundamental values of existence.
So he piles allusion on allusion, image on image, quotes from
here, there, and everywhere, and mixes the language of argument with prophecy, irony, ridicule, and farce. As Hegel
wrote in his review of Hamann's collected works, his style is
' full of subjective particularities, self-complacent conceits,
and obscure, far-fetched references, together with a good deal
of noisy abuse and caricaturistic, even farcical ingredients '.
But, unsystematic and confusing as his works are, their significance was not lost on his contemporaries ; in direct and
shrewd opposition to his times he stood for subjective convictions, for a religious attitude which allowed him independent
thought and which expressed, as Hegel said, ' the energy of
living, individual, present experience '.[13]

His life bore out his convictions. He entered on a liaison
with his father's maid, and to the consternation of his acquaintance lived with her for the rest of his life, defying the formalism
of Church and State. Extremely indulgent to his daughters,
who feared his occasional violent gusts of anger, he devoted
himself utterly to his son's education, making him at an early
age a philological prodigy. In 1777 he was given a post
in the customs which was almost a sinecure, and from then
could indulge to the full his taste for reading and talking ;
in spite of his comfortable, though modest income, he still
showed complete obliviousness to conventional manners and
dress.

This man, in his defiance of accepted modes of thought and
norms of behaviour, in his restless unease within society, in
his devotion to inner convictions, is the starting-point of the
Sturm und Drang. As a young man, Herder was his pupil
and the two remained for many years in intimate correspondence. Goethe, who never met him and who admitted that he
often did not understand his writings, summed up his debt to
him in *Poetry and Truth* : ' The principle behind all Hamann's
utterances is this : " Everything that man undertakes, whether
it be produced in action or word or anything else, must spring

from his whole united powers ; all separation of powers is to be repudiated." ' [14]

Goethe's statement fairly accurately defines the debt of the Sturm und Drang to Hamann. As a judgment of the latter's work it is obviously inadequate. It is in one sense far too generous, for in fact Hamann failed to reach this wholeness of which Goethe speaks. He failed to combine effective action with thought, and his doctrine, like his life, asserts the significance only of the receptive powers of sense and imagination ; social and scientific activity finds no place in his scheme of things. He decried all intellectual discipline, and was himself subject to hypochondria, at the mercy, as he wrote, of an imagination ' more frightened of shadows than the horse of Alexander '.[15] But his revolt against social norms and rationalistic abstractions was immensely helpful to the younger generation, and even late in life, in his critique of Mendelssohn and Kant, he contributed to the Sturm und Drang through his attack on the divorce of religion and reason from experience.

This revolt led him himself into nebulous regions of subjectivism and ultimately, in the company of Princess Gallitzin, to dubious eschatological cogitations. Here his way parted from that of Herder, and their intellectual intimacy weakened noticeably as time passed ; in his last years Hamann came particularly close to Fritz Jacobi, whose subjectivism led him steadily further and further away from the Sturm und Drang. It is not surprising that Kierkegaard found in Hamann a kindred soul, and he quotes in the concluding paragraph of his *The Concept of Dread* words of Hamann's which are deeply characteristic of the older man :

I have nothing to do nor any responsibilities . . . and, with the strongest propensity for work and enjoyment, can come to neither, and can only rock to and fro like Noah in his Ark. This anguish [' Angst '] in the world is however the only proof of our heterogeneity. . . . This impertinent restlessness, this holy hypochondria is perhaps the fire in which we sacrificial beasts have to be salted and preserved from the corruption of the current century.[16]

The distance of Kierkegaard from Goethe is the measure of the divergence of the Sturm und Drang from Hamann. From him his younger contemporaries gained confidence for their own revolt, learned to value the ecstasies and to face the disasters of surrender to subjective conviction. But just as they grappled more realistically with the meaning and implication of this doctrine in the circumstances of actual life, so also their main effort went towards a synthesis of inner and outer powers and reality, instead of remaining content to assert an ' anguish in the world '.

MERCK

Merck was a character totally different from Hamann, and his close association with the Sturm und Drang illustrates the realistic ingredient in the movement. He was nine years older than Goethe and in 1771, when they met, was Paymaster-General of the small state of Hesse-Darmstadt, and general factotum at the court. To all the Stürmer und Dränger, above all to Goethe, he was a shrewd and sympathetic critic. His intelligence and practical ability made him esteemed by scientists like Lichtenberg, in whose work he was keenly interested ; and he was sufficiently detached from the Sturm und Drang to remain throughout the 1770s in friendly collaboration with Nicolai. His practical advice was valued by several of the lesser German princes, and the smallness of his own state involved him in many aspects of the administration. His most important duty was to negotiate the marriage of a ducal daughter to the Tsar-Elect, a task which took him to Berlin and St. Petersburg ; but the pettiness of his usual occupations provoked in him an irritableness that was often savagely expressed, and a cynicism which was often directed at the juvenile raptures of Herder, Goethe, or Lenz. Later in life his restlessness drove him to start several businesses, a printing press and textile factories, but he lacked persistence and, after he had once or twice been rescued from financial distress by Goethe and his aristocratic friends, the hopelessness of his prospects drove him to suicide in 1791.[17]

Goethe used to call him ' Mephistopheles-Merck ', a name he remembers in *Poetry and Truth* : a Mephistopheles to Goethe's Faust, because they were necessary to one another, because Merck was, as Goethe wrote, ' the only man who fully understands what I do and how I do it, and yet sees it differently from me ',[18] because of his criticism and sarcasm, which helped Goethe not to lose the ground from under his feet. A Mephistopheles because of his discontent, his inability to be happy in a simple way, to check his own sardonic humour. Caroline Flachsland, in her letters to Herder, her fiancé, often complains of Merck's sarcasm in a way which recalls Gretchen's dread of Mephistopheles—' One can see that he is untouched by anything '.[19] But Merck was exceedingly loyal to Goethe. When Nicolai was furious at Goethe's skits on him, Merck wrote to him telling him that Goethe was completely without malice ; and when all literary Germany was buzzing with indignation about reports of Goethe's scandalous behaviour at Weimar, Merck consistently and stoutly defended him, refuting the rumours, and insisting ' There's no yardstick for such fellows.'[20] He published *Götz*, defended *Werther* in an amusing skit, and loved the early farces and *Faust*. And when Goethe fell beneath the standards Merck believed he could reach, he sharply criticised him—about *Clavigo* he told Goethe : ' You mustn't write me such trash any more. The others can do that sort of thing.'[21] It was Merck who told Goethe he must break away from the entanglement with Lotte Buff at Wetzlar. Merck's own works consist in the main of occasional articles and reviews, most of them published in Nicolai's and Wieland's periodicals, and they have some interest ; but his greatest importance lies in his personal influence with the Stürmer und Dränger, with whose raptures and revolt he sympathised, but whom he checked, as far as in him lay, when their enthusiasm swept them too far above solid earth.

HERDER

Herder's unhappy temperament gives us perhaps the deepest insight into the psyche of the Sturm und Drang, if one may use such an abstraction : not without justification he has been considered to be the prototype of Goethe's Faust, the supreme imaginative symbol of the movement. Coming from a simple, deeply pietistic home, trained for the Lutheran ministry, and happiest in the intimate exchange of religious experience, he had the same sensitive receptivity, the same capacity for enthusiasm as Hamann, the same moodiness and emotive instability. Like Hamann, too, he entered at the university of Königsberg, largely through the agency of Kant, into the full stream of European literature, and measured himself against the boldest thinkers of his time. But he had a much more forceful intellect than Hamann, and more persistently sought for a synthesis of the intellectual achievements of the time with his intuitive values ; and, in even stronger contrast with Hamann, sought to find a synthesis of theory and practice, of thought and action. He was the only Stürmer und Dränger to construct a general philosophy of life, embracing the scientific, practical and intuitive faculties of man. He did not succeed in reconciling all the conflicting values and trends within his times and his temperament, and his work seems often impulsive, unclear, and wilful ; but in contrast to that of his associates it is systematic and has a logic which careful analysis can reveal. His work on poetry and drama, on language, and on history is at the very source of modern thinking.

Through his religious upbringing Herder acquired the belief in intuitive truth, the longing for the feeling of security that the pietist expresses in his devotional exercises, which colours all his thought. The content of his faith however underwent great transformations, and did not achieve any greater homogeneity than his character. A visit to France in 1769 took him among the Encyclopédistes, and his work was so deeply influenced by such writers as Diderot and Condillac that he was suspected of being in correspondence with them. Several times applying for a chair of theology, his only published work by the age of 30 was literary and philosophical, and even the reverse of theological in any ordinary sense. In the early 1770s he had already adopted a form of Spinozism, which he publicly avowed in the 1780s, and his contemporaries soon ferreted out this heresy. At the same time his sermons dwell on the personal, loving relationship between God and man, and in all his works there appears a confident trust in God and the divinity of man's intuitions. The solemnity and tenderness of the Lutheran hymns vibrate through his whole life. These contradictions puzzled and upset his friends. Hamann was shocked by the secularity of his thought, which led him further and further away from the older man ; while

Merck and Goethe found his occasional outbreaks of parsonic zealotry extremely distasteful. It was however precisely this uneasy combination of bold intellectualism with an unusual capacity for feeling, a rare sensitivity of insight and perception, that made him the discoverer of new values in poetry, thought and life.

From childhood too he retained that trust in the senses which at the end of his life made him so determined an opponent of Kant's dualism.[22] The pietistic religion of his home was an extremely tangible, literal faith which nurtured all the powers of the imagination and senses. As he grew away from this fundamentalism he still demanded a philosophy of man which would justify all his capacities, including the senses, that would give all his faculties more intense life and vibration. Thus he delighted in the sensuous imagery of the Bible, of Shakespeare, of folksong ; he admired early civilisations because he believed that in them the intellectual, sensory, and practical sides of man were not separated, and he condemned his own society because thinkers were cut off from practical life and the enjoyment of the senses, because they were locked up in their studies. Thus he was attracted by, and deeply indebted to the empirical and sensualist philosophers, Locke, Hartley, Diderot, and the rest. Yet he never won through to a clear observation of nature ; he had neither the objectivity of the scientist nor the clear vision of the poet. Theory, ideas were much more real to him than things and men ; he remained a man of the study and pulpit. If he liked occasionally to walk or ride in the open country, he would have a Shakespeare, a Young, Homer, or Ossian in his pocket ; he could not enjoy a day's skating like Klopstock or Goethe. If he restored folksong to the rank of poetry, he left it to others to go among the common people and collect their songs. His distaste for the practical duties of his office was profound. He was imaginatively able to conceive the ideal of an all-sided man, could express this ideal in his writings, but was himself far from entering the promised land.

Herder was acutely conscious of the disharmony within him arising from his temperament and upbringing. In the intimate letters to Caroline, his betrothed, between 1770 and 1773, he often refers to his predilection for melancholy, his indulgence in feeling, which he feels hold him back from full participation in life. ' I was born into simple circumstances, obscure but not necessitous, and from childhood I remember nothing but either scenes of sentimentality and emotion or a mental dream which was usually enlivened by plans of ambition.' [23] His temperament drove him continually to magnify, to idealise and distort, to over-sentimentalise his situation and experiences. The theme running through these letters is his effort to check this self-indulgence, to train himself to see life as it is, to prepare himself to take an active part in life, to direct his emotive and imaginative powers towards society. He was liable to idealise Caroline's ' innocence ', but when he calls her his ' Grecian ', his Psyche, as he often does, he is expressing his appreciation of the balance he saw in her character between feeling and social duty, between the inner life and the compulsion of household existence, a balance he needed in a larger sphere. She urged him in this direction too ; and it was to meet her rebukes of his melancholy that he writes that he seeks to combine ' feeling and practice, imagination and activity '. [24]

The Journal of his sea-voyage of 1769, when he travelled from Riga to Nantes, contains highly interesting observations on his temperament and its dangers. His innate trend, he writes, is towards the rhapsodic, the sublime, the lachrymose.

Hence my taste for speculation, for the sombre aspects of philosophy, poetry, tales, and thoughts ! Hence my inclination for the shadow of Antiquity and the remoteness of past centuries ! . . . Hence my calling for the ministry, to which no doubt local prejudices of my youth contributed a great deal, but also no doubt the impressiveness to me of church and altar, of pulpit and clerical eloquence, of the celebration of the services, and the veneration paid to the clergy . . . hence too my half-understandable, half-sombre style. . . . My life is a progress through Gothic vaults, or at least through an avenue full of green shades : the prospect is always venerable and sublime : I set foot in it with a sort of awe. [25]

The frankness of this self-analysis recalls that made by K. P. Moritz in *Anton Reiser*, and, like Moritz, Herder was not content with ' Gothic gloom ', but sought to emerge into the full light of day.

If temperament and home encouraged him in ' grotesque distortions ' of life, his school education fed this taste even more. He has become, he writes, ' an inkpot of learned scribbling '. The abstract instruction of the grammar school has detached him even further from the real world, and stifled his powers of clear observation and objective thinking.

What in my past condition has earned me the fate of seeing shadows, instead of grasping real things through my feeling ? I enjoy little, i.e. too much, excessively and therefore without taste : the sense of touch and the world of delightful sensations—I have not enjoyed them : I see and feel in the distance, I hinder my own enjoyment through untimely presumption, and through weakness and clumsiness in the moment itself. . . . And so, on all sides, determined by an inflated imagination, which wanders from the truth and destroys enjoyment. . . . The same in love, even : it is always Platonic, more in absence than in the present, more in hope and fear than in enjoyment ; more in abstractions, in spiritual ideas, than in realities.[26]

This self-analysis is strongly critical. Its trend is the opposite of that of Warton's *Pleasures of Melancholy*, no doubt because Herder's imagination was infinitely more powerful than that of the Englishman ; even more, because he tried to live according to the dictates of his heart. Herder tried to control his imagination, tried to contemplate and act upon real life without weakening that intensity of feeling which alone in his view gave value to life. He cannot be said to have succeeded in his aim. He entered on his pastoral and administrative duties at Bückeburg and at Weimar with characteristically extravagant hopes of finding a sphere worthy of him, but in both cases found his hopes dashed by a petty and rigid society, and by multifarious duties which he could only feel to be a burden. For many years he alternated between rapturous enthusiasm and melancholy hypochondria, exalted by religious experience, by love or poetry, and lapsing frequently into gloom and despondency. What is man's life, he wrote to his betrothed, but ' a transition from something to something ' ; what are men but ' lightning-flashes in the night '.[27] The harmony he sought he injected into his philosophy, his literary criticism, into his seductive reconstructions of past and distant societies.

And as he grew older, he fell more and more into an uncritical and exalted trust in Providence and Divine Law which fits uneasily upon the more realistic elements of his thought.

The dissonance within him, and between him and the outer world, provoked in him a sardonic bitterness which often wounded his friends. He combined an admiration for the enthusiastic Shaftesbury with delight in Swift, and liked to be called ' the Dean '—he wrote to Merck : ' In your articles you are always Socrates-Addison ; Goethe is usually an arrogant young lord with fearful scrapes and bows ; and when I come along, it's the Irish dean with his whip.' [28] But he lacked Swift's clear discernment of social prejudices and his clarity of expression ; it is true to say, too, that he saw deeper than Swift into the potentialities of human nature and life. Herder's criticism of others never finds the objective form of satire, it is never witty or humorous. He attacked his enemies passionately and sharply, often with ostentatious indignation, often to his own regret ; to be spiritually or practically indebted to anyone was likely to provoke his resentment, and he taunted his own friends in a personal way that they often found humiliating and unjust. His first letters to Lavater, in whom he found a kindred soul, were so sharp as to arouse mixed feelings in this exceptionally kindly and generous man. Lavater wrote about their effect : ' Tears of adoration for God slid out of my eyes, though his letters are all very humiliating for me,' [29] Goethe's account of the ' vicious bite ' in Herder's character is well-known ; Herder could be so bitter and wounding that Goethe hid from him his plans for writing *Götz* and *Faust*.[30] Wieland wrote, soon after Herder had taken up residence in Weimar :

The man is like an electric cloud. In the distance the meteor makes a very fine effect ; but may the devil have such a neighbour hovering over his head. . . . I can't abide it, when a man is so convinced of his own worth ; and worse still, when a strong fellow never stops enjoying making fools and laughing stocks of others, then I'd like to have a dozen pyramids between me and him.[31]

In retrospect, Goethe ascribed this bitterness of Herder's, from which he himself had often to suffer, to a sense of social grievance—' Herder would always poison the best days, for himself as for others, for he could never manage to moderate the discontent which necessarily gripped him in his youth.' [32] Goethe may here have had in mind Herder's later democratic sympathies, which certainly may be ascribed to his early experiences as the child of poor parents in an autocratic militaristic state.   It is true, also, that he was excessively sensitive, and found a compensation for his own vulnerability in wounding others.   Some of his works, notably the *Oldest Document of the Human Race* of 1774, abound in harsh, arrogant, even jeering criticism of his literary opponents.   On several occasions he tried to hide his authorship, so fearful was he himself of criticism.   The jibes he suffered because of his advocacy of folksong made him withdraw many of his claims, and it was with an audible sigh of relief, and a half-apology, that he completed his edition of folksongs in 1779. [33] Sensitive and arrogant together, he was a difficult man to get on with, and was too likely to suspect his friends of malice.   Merck was not merely flattering willing ears when he wrote to Nicolai that it was impossible to keep Herder as a collaborator on the *Allgemeine deutsche Bibliothek.* [34]   The *Oldest Document* caused all his friends acute discomfort.   Merck wrote to Nicolai, who was puzzled and indignant, that the work was dear to him as an expression of Herder's personality, but that it was insufferable for its boasting tone, its conceit, its exhibitionism. ' Herder is like a man who rides through the streets on horseback in his dressing gown, and demands into the bargain that everyone should approve.' [35]

In 1775, when Herder with wife and child stayed with Merck, the latter found him ' incomparably more tolerant and moderate '—' he is still vicious, but it is so wrapped up that he no longer scratches '. [36]   But though Herder's works after his removal to Weimar were much less polemical and violent, he was often sharp in his utterances.   When, on the occasion of the christening of the first child of the ducal family, the Duke made one of his rare appearances in church, Herder preached such a sermon that Goethe is reported to have said : ' After such a sermon there's nothing left for a prince to do but to abdicate.' [37]   Herder was often scathing in his letters and conversation about court life, the fashionable cult for art, about his fellow-clergymen. He never hit it off with Wieland, who was ready to be friends with all men ; and except for a short period in the 1780s was estranged from Goethe throughout the long years of his residence at Weimar.

Despite this temperamental maladjustment, Herder's character cannot be considered to be morbid or pathological ; it shows nothing comparable for instance to the obsessions of the last years of Rousseau. Unhappy as his temperament was, it mirrors a cultural crisis, the conflict within his century ; his failure to reach an inner harmony is essentially the measure of the profundity of his challenge to the ruling ideas and principles of his time ; and, at the same time, it indicates in a very direct fashion the failure of the Sturm und Drang to define how, and in what direction, the world might be changed.

GOETHE

Goethe's childhood, guarded by affluent parents who in their different ways nurtured tenderly and eagerly the boy's swift intelligence and lively fancy, was very different from that of the other Stürmer und Dränger. His early upbringing was of course religious, in a city which was a stronghold of pietism ; but his parents were intelligent and rational in their outlook, their relatives and friends people of substance and authority in the proud imperial city of Frankfurt. His somewhat pedantic father saw to it that this promising son had an excellent education, supervising it himself ; his mother was a sociable and practical woman whose gift of story-telling and humour made her a delightful companion to the children and their friends. Goethe was a somewhat delicate child, thrown much upon the resources of the home and the companionship of his sister, but his imagination was fed also by the theatre of the French occupation forces during the Seven Years War, and by the artists who decorated his father's house. From early on he showed a gift for story-telling, for little plays, and delighted in make-believe. As he grew older the influence of the modish literature of his time is evident in his poems. When he went to the University of Leipzig in 1765, he gave himself up to social and literary pursuits in the Frenchifying rococo manner of this ' little Paris ', had a love-affair with a flirtatious sort of girl, took up painting in an amateurish fashion, and dressed and behaved like a fashionable fop—even a friend called him an ' arrogant dandy '. His self-confidence was already marked, and was to remain with him all his life ; he never suffered from those tortured self-questionings which were characteristic of Hamann, Herder, and Lenz.

A severe illness put an end to his Leipzig period in 1768, and a long convalescence at home helped his true self to emerge. After the social life of Leipzig he was thrown upon his own resources and those of his family. With the pietist friends of his mother and sister he began to pay greater attention to his inner life, and to discuss intuitive perceptions with them, dabbling too in the alchemistic and mystical works current in these circles. In 1770 he went to Strassburg to complete his legal studies, met Herder there, and entered on his Sturm und Drang. Herder opened up to him the world of Shakespeare, the folksong, Ossian, of the *Encyclopédie*, and ridiculing rococo frivolity encouraged him to trust his own imagination and feeling and to let his mind range freely and boldly. He began to harden his body and to discover the delights of walking and riding in all weathers over the countryside—when he returned to Frankfurt he was to be an ardent skater. His childhood's delight in pretence led him to allow himself to play harmless jokes on people, dressing up quaintly and adopting an assumed name, as in the famous first visit to Sesenheim, where he appeared and behaved like a poor, awkward student of theology, a typical, gay childlike expression of his resistance to definition and finality.

Here at Sesenheim he fell in love with Friederike Brion, a country parson's daughter, sweet and unassuming, like him of a rather delicate constitution, and his poems for the first time express his own direct feeling, unspoilt by conventional mannerisms. When he returned to Frankfurt in 1771 he gathered round him a society which he infected with these values, a lively band of young people who ignored staid convention and propriety, and enjoyed themselves in outdoor excursions, in games, and in the feeling of their own potentialities. Wherever he went—to Wetzlar among sober lawyers and officials, to Darmstadt among the rather sentimental court ladies—his personality fascinated. On a visit to a friend at the undistin-

guished University of Giessen he charmed the stodgy professors
with his imaged and intelligent talk.[38] By 1774 Frankfurt had
become a place of pilgrimage for the leading figures of German
intellectual life ; among others, Klopstock, Lavater, Basedow,
the young Duke of Weimar called on him. Merck even said
that Nicolai would succumb to Goethe if only he met him.[39]

His interests were as multifarious as his character was varied.
By training he was a lawyer, but he never took his legal duties
very seriously. He played the cello, and took lessons in painting—his sketches of landscapes, houses, friends, of his own room
are not without charm, and show in particular a careful
attentiveness to visual reality which he found a valuable self-
schooling in years when emotive tensions often distressed him.
He sought out the company of pietists with whom he liked to
discuss spiritual experience ; in Strassburg his daily companions were medical students in whose studies he participated.
He was well read in philosophy and was reckoned a powerful
thinker by his friends, even by professors and experienced
officials. He was educated in the classics, of course, and was
well read in the modern literature of England, France, and
Italy as well as Germany. He liked as much to listen to folk
tales as to participate in philosophic discussion ; he liked meeting men of practical achievement. Interests and moods could
change so swiftly that he puzzled and sometimes vexed his
friends ; Herder, who in this early period felt himself to be
Goethe's mentor, wrote disparagingly of his levity and said he
was ' too much of a sparrow '.[40] Indeed, as Goethe grew
older and his circle of friends and their demands on him
increased, he began to feel the burden of his multifarious
interests. His letters to Auguste zu Stolberg in 1775 show
how intolerable this strain was becoming, and partly explain
his decision to cut his moorings and go to Weimar. The long
letter of September 14 to 19 gives a diary of external distrac-
tions and internal distractedness [41]—' Baleful fate that allows
me no intermediate state. Either gripping hard to one point,
or roving to all points of the compass.' [42] In October he
wrote to Bürger that that last three-quarters of a year had been
' the most distracted, most confused, most complete and full,
the emptiest, strongest and silliest of his life '.[43] Sometimes
he says that he is marked with the brand of Cain.

His capacity for intense feeling took him into regions of experience which had been placed out of bounds by generations of European intellectual leaders. He found the sense of life in ' surrendering himself from moment to moment ', even though this brought torment as well as rapture.[44] He was often obsessed by longings that seemed to have no goal, like his Faust or Werther : ' I am delighted ! I am happy ! I feel it, and yet the whole content of my joy is a surging longing for something I do not possess, for something I do not know.'[45] He could cry out : ' I should like to pray like Moses in the Koran, Lord, enlarge my narrow breast.' [46] His worst torment was the apathetic vacuity which might possess him after the exhilaration of passion and enthusiasm. Just as Werther finds his deepest misfortune in deadness of soul, when even nature finds no response in his heart, so dullness of soul, ' Dumpfheit ', was Goethe's most dreaded experience. He knew that it was a necessary concomitant of rapture. ' I am not always attuned to great feelings, and without them I am as nothing.' [47] Against this threat nothing availed except work and discipline, which he learned as he emerged from his Sturm und Drang ; but to the end of his life he suffered deeply from the desolation of periods of feelinglessness, and in his last great love poem, the *Marienbader Elegie*, though he seeks a consolation in scientific activity, he recognises that it is only a second best.

For the internal pressures which threw him hither and thither he found relief in imagination and poetry, giving his longings form and clarity, bridging in symbols the gulf between his inner life and the obdurate external world. His imagination was as rooted in his experience as were his feelings, and whether in grotesque riotousness or sublime vision fulfilled an essential function in restoring his balance. A young visitor wrote in 1773 :

His expression is serious and sad, but lit at times by a comic, hilarious and satiric whimsicality. He is very eloquent, he overflows with ideas that are very witty. Indeed, as far as I know him, he has an exceptionally visual [' anschauend '] poetic power of feeling himself right into objects, so that everything becomes local and individual in his mind. Everything is immediately transformed in him into a dramatic form.[48]

Kestner wrote : ' He possesses an extraordinarily lively imagination, so that he usually expresses himself in images and metaphors.' Herder put this aptitude in the words : ' Everything
with you is vision,' a criticism Goethe felt to be justified.[49]

This power of intense experience and imaginative expression
fascinated his acquaintances, but at times made them fear for
his reason. Lerse, a boon friend at Strassburg, with whom he
made several excursions over the countryside, tells how at
night, in bed, Goethe would fall into such ecstasies that he
thought he was going crazed.[50] Fritz Jacobi called him ' a
man possessed ',[51] and Lavater is reported to have said that
' he seems to be carried away by a torrent '.[52] Those who
knew him less well, or who lost contact with him, were harsher
in their judgments. A Strassburg professor, who was probably
shocked at his unorthodox views on religion, said he was ' a
bit loose in the upper storey '.[53] Fritz Jacobi wrote, just before
he met Goethe, ' he is and remains an unbridled, unruly
fellow '.[54] Staid friends like his brother-in-law Schlosser, after
some months of separation, could reverse a favourable view
and express alarm at the ' excesses ' reported of him—' Goethe
goes too far for me ', he wrote to Lavater : ' You are right,
he is effeminate ' ; and he warned his correspondent, who had
not yet met Goethe, ' you need a certain strength of soul to
remain Goethe's friend '.[55] Even Jung-Stilling, who had owed
so much to Goethe's support, wrote that ' he is like an enormous
wild bucking bullock, fattening in the pasture '.[56]

Such evidence might persuade one that Goethe was in this
period a highly unstable character ; but it is not the whole
story. At the same time he struck his friends as being a strong,
self-reliant personality. Lavater did not find Goethe difficult or
' effeminate '. Soon after meeting him he wrote : ' He is not
only wise and good-humoured, but also strong.'[57] Jacobi wrote :

> Goethe is the man my heart needed to bear and sustain all the
> loving ardour of my soul. Now at last my character will acquire
> its proper and genuine consistency, for Goethe's outlook has given
> an unassailable certainty to my best ideas and best feelings, hitherto
> so lonely and rejected. The man is independent from top to toe.[58]

—an important testimony from a man who, though of a sensitive and gentle character, was already an able administrator.

Lavater and Jacobi were both older than Goethe, yet they looked up to him as a stronger personality ; he was a prop to them, ' to me, a thousand times the weaker ', as Lavater wrote. [59] Kestner was not only older than Goethe, but also a staid, settled official, yet in his view too Goethe was a strong independent person. ' He is violent in all his emotions, but yet has much power over himself ' ; and he was astonished that Goethe's love for Lotte Buff, Kestner's fiancée, could wreak such havoc in a man ' who is otherwise one of the strongest and most self-reliant of men '. [60] The picture Lenz draws of Goethe in *Pandaemonium Germanicum* (1775) shows him almost as the self-confident, all-conquering ' Olympian ' he later became.

Goethe's life and poetry in the Sturm und Drang period show us in fact a man capable of a bewildering variety of moods, from the rapturous to the agonised, the sublime to the grotesque, the rebellious to the yielding. He had not the security of those who are fortified by the feeling that they have no quarrel with dominant social and moral standards ; but he was not, for that reason, an unstable sentimentalist. He refused to subject the ' glorious feelings ', which in his view gave value to life, to the requirements of the petty world around him ; but through his imagination, his poetry, he was not only able to express them, but also to restore his balance, a balance not of motionless equilibrium, but more that of a soaring fountain. His consciousness of contrary trends is clearly mirrored in the poetic images he created. He projected his own stresses into a series of masterful figures like Götz, Caesar, Prometheus, and Mahomet, just as he did into unstable, emotional men like Weislingen, Werther, and Clavigo. Lotte and Gretchen are the opposites, in their absorption in homely tasks and purposes, of the insatiable and restless Werther and Faust. In Goethe's poems we find pairs of contrary but complementary symbols, the wanderer and the cottage, the mettlesome horse and the restraining horseman. He could write to Kestner, ' Werther must, must be ' ; [61] but at the same time could criticise Werther's character as that of ' a young man who, gifted with a deep and pure power of feeling, and true penetration, loses himself in ecstatic dreams and undermines himself with speculation '. [62] In the same spirit he wrote for the second edition of the novel (1775) the quatrain that closes with the line : ' Be a man and do not follow on my path.' [63]   It was part of the richness of his character, perhaps even part of his strength, that Goethe could not tie himself down, but compensated one extreme of intense experience by another.

It is characteristic of him that he easily became furious at shallowness, pedantry, intellectual arrogance, and that his imagination led him to express this fury in startling, sometimes grotesque, forms.   When Wieland or Nicolai annoyed him with their lack of understanding, their paternalistic and pedantic nagging, he wrote farces in which he imagined them in ridiculous situations ; he ridiculed the sentimentalist Leuchsenring in his farce *Das Jahrmarktsfest zu Plündersweilern*, wove an extravagant fantasy out of the sentimentalities of the Jacobi brothers, burlesqued Herder's excessive nature-cult in *Satyros*. He was fond of giving vent to his vexation in violent and coarse expletives.   The malaise of his relationship with Lili Schönemann in 1775, which brought him into the formal drawing-room society he detested, led him to fancy himself as a bear in a French garden, always grumbling and untidy, but always coming to heel when his mistress calls ; or he could write, in a poem to his beloved, of the ' unbearable faces ' round the card table.[64]   Vexatious experiences of this type were accompanied, throughout this period, by a stream of doggerel in which his fury dissolves in quaint images.

Goethe's pugnacity seems always to have been mixed with laughter over himself.   Knebel, a member of the Weimar court, found him in a characteristic mood—

Goethe lives in a constant inward war and rebellion, since all things have a most violent effect on him.   It is a necessity for his spirit to make enemies with whom he can fight ; and you can be sure he doesn't choose the worst to be his foes.   He spoke to me about all the persons against whom he has taken up arms with a quite particular and feeling respect.   But the lad is pugnacious, he has the spirit of an athlete.   And he is the most peculiar fellow there's ever been, for the other night in Mainz he held forth thus : ' Now I'm on good terms with them all, the Jacobis, Wieland— that doesn't suit me at all.   My soul is so constituted that, just as I have to have something to which I can attribute my ideal of excellence, so I must have something for the ideal of my anger.' [65]

His humour had the same function with regard to his minor vexations as his poetry had for more serious stresses ; it transposed them into an imaginative realm, turned them into gaiety, and dissipated all unfruitful rancour.   Merck was quite justified in telling Nicolai that Goethe's sallies against the Berlin pundit were without malicious intent :

Whatever he may have said or written about you, it's nothing but the caprice of a faun—he hasn't the mind, and neither has he the time, for revengeful intentions which might lead to lampoons and tittle-tattle, for his head is always whirling with new fancies.[66]

Goethe's lucky childhood seems to have passed without distorting his temperament.   There is hardly anything which may be called pathological in his reactions—Freud has written an interesting article on the only incident which suggests a suppression.[67]   Perhaps for this reason he was so affectionate, so easily and unaffectedly sympathetic with others.   He had an immense capacity for love, for men as for women, a love which sometimes was of an intense, overwhelming character as for Friederike Brion, for Lotte Buff, for Max von la Roche or Lili Schönemann, sometimes was ecstatic like that for Lavater or Fritz Jacobi, sometimes was a warm affection for weak and helpless people like Jung-Stilling or Lenz.   Remarkable too is the permanence of his affection for his friends even after the extreme ardour was passed.   His correspondence with Jacobi and Lavater went on warmly and affectionately long after their differences of outlook had declared themselves ; and the letters he exchanged with Kestner, Lotte, and Lotte's little brother, after he had been forced to leave them because of his passion for Lotte, show what a strong and deep affection held him to them for years.   When Kestner and Lotte thought they were travestied in *Werther*, and Jacobi was upset by the ' immorality ' of *Stella*, Goethe defended himself in letters overflowing with gaiety and affection which no one could resist.[68]

Jung-Stilling tells in his autobiography how at their first meeting Goethe championed this awkward country lad against

the sneers of the smarter students, and it was to Goethe that
Jung turned when he was in distress over the illness of his
betrothed.[69] Professor Höpfner called him ' the best, most
good-hearted and lovable man '.[70] He was infinitely gentle
with Lenz, troublesome as the latter was ; though in the end,
at Weimar, where he himself was struggling to adapt himself
to new ways, he had to break his ties with him—his description
of Lenz in *Poetry and Truth* is a rare instance of a personal
injustice. He did not always escape the sentimentality of the
times, and particularly on his first visit to Darmstadt seems to
have conformed to the taste of the court ladies, the Fräuleins
von Roussillon and Ziegler ; but in general his relations with
women and men were characterised by a simple naturalness
and candour entirely lacking in pose and sentimentality. Even
on this visit to Darmstadt, Caroline Flachsland comments on
this : ' We were not sentimental, but very cheerful, and Goethe
and I danced minuets to the piano.'[71] She tells too how
Goethe played with Merck's children. He was often fond of
romping with children, and later, at Weimar, he taught Frau
von Stein's children to walk the tight-rope.[72] His relations
with women were in general easy and candid, and he had a
gift for appreciating them in their peculiar character and surroundings. Betty Jacobi he liked, as he says, because she was
' without the least trace of sentimentality '. It was the little
house-mother that he loved in Lotte Buff, whose susceptibility
to Klopstock's poetry ran along with the unsentimental practicalness with which she looked after her brothers and sisters,
cared for the sick and poor, and nursed the dying. Goethe's
individualism, selfishness as some called it, was always anchored
by his love for others ; his capacity for exaltation was balanced
by his delight in persons whose whole character was realised
in devotion in the small circle of home and friends. These two
poles of his temperament might often seem opposed, and in
Werther and *Faust Part I* Goethe depicts men who end in
catastrophe because they are pulled in these two irreconcilable directions. But in himself they appear more like the two
foci of an ellipse. At times he seems to go to extremes, but
the path he described is never truly erratic.

What was it that made his life and character seem so
purposeful, so assured, to men like Lavater and Lenz ? He

did not fall back on a divine Redeemer, for he rejected firmly the ' fairy-tale ' of Christ ; nor would he sublimate his problems through religious devotion. He took his practical work as a lawyer very lightly, and as long as possible shirked settling down—in fact, he went to Weimar in 1775 largely in order to avoid the irksome responsibilities of practical and social ties. It is not sufficient merely to say that he was a poet, and was content with the calling of a poet. Without being concerned directly with moral or practical purposes, his poetical and artistic work had an ethical content. Through it he sought to develop what powers were within him, to express his inner stresses and the world around him, to ' purify ' himself, as he often puts it. He sought, not to blunt himself in the struggle with life, but to retain ' all the deep feeling of joy and sorrow ' in him.[73] He sought in his works not to teach or preach, but to find a form for his experience of the world, and through this form to grow in range and depth. It was a difficult aim to make clear, and often enough his friends could vex him by suggesting that he ought to define a moral and social purpose.

He expressed his aim most clearly to a correspondent he had not met, Auguste zu Stolberg, of whom he made a spiritual companion and confessor. To her he describes himself :

Ever living in himself, striving, working ; seeking to express the innocent feelings of youth in little poems, the sharp spice of life in all sorts of plays, the figures of his friends, his surroundings, his loved room in chalk on gray paper ; asking neither to right nor left, what people think about what he is doing—because as he works he rises a step higher, because he does not want to leap after an ideal but wants to let his feelings develop into capacities, through struggle and play.[74]

In his mind, as in Herder's and Lenz's, practical achievement stood as the goal for which poetry prepared him by fulfilling and shaping his personality. But the form of practical achievement is unclear, he could not as yet find a mould into which his capacities could be poured. From this same letter, as from many others, we can see how distracting social life was becoming for Goethe. His friends used and abused him, emotively and practically, his love for Lili threw him into a turmoil of social obligations and pleasures. ' Oh, if I didn't write plays now I should go under.' [75]   In a long letter, written in bits and pieces between the 14th and 19th of September to Auguste, he describes the whirl of his daily life, and his longing for serenity. ' Will my heart, in deep and true enjoyment and suffering, at last be able to feel the bliss granted to men, and not continue to be driven on the waves of imagination and over-tense sensuality, up to Heaven and down to Hell.'   And, reviewing at the end of the letter the crazy patchwork of his activities, he concludes :

Yet, dear, when I feel that, in the midst of all this emptiness, a few more skins have been sloughed from my heart, and the tense convulsions of my foolish little constitution relax, my glance over the world is more serene, my relations with men become surer, firmer, more extensive, and yet my innermost self remains for ever and ever devoted to holy love, which bit by bit expels all alien matter through the spirit of purity, which is love itself, and so, in the end, will become as pure as spun gold.—So, I let things go on as they are—And perhaps I deceive myself.—And thank God.[76]

Goethe's purpose was thus highly subjective, difficult to define, and dissociated from normal social or moral values. The narrow round of Frankfurt official and business life could only fret him—in 1781 he wrote to his mother, explaining his decision to leave Frankfurt : ' The disproportion between the narrow and slow-moving bourgeois sphere and the range and swiftness of my nature would have made me crazy.' [77]   Salz-mann, of Strassburg, and Lavater had both thought he might be better suited in the service of a prince.   Now, in the autumn of 1775, Goethe accepted the proposal to become a sort of companion to the young Duke of Weimar, without defined responsibilities, and feeling drawn to the young man and his entourage.

Many considerations contributed to his decision to go to the court of Weimar.[78]   He thus cut through the entanglement with Lili—he had fled from Friederike and Lotte in the same way.   He broke with all social ties in Frankfurt, with his own circle and interests, which had become such a net around him. He removed himself from the looming responsibilities of burgher occupations, from the moral pressures which a settled position would have entailed.   At the court he had something of the position of a nobleman, and was in fact soon to be ennobled ; and this position meant much, it meant he could disregard moral pedantry and burgher scandalmongers, it meant freedom for his own tastes and pursuits. As the favourite of a prince much was allowed him that no burgher in a burgher environment could enjoy.

For a time, it was this freedom which was most important to him. He and the Duke made excursions over the little state, rampaged in Weimar and the country districts, mixed a little state business with a lot of gaiety and pleasure. Weimar society was turned upside down, with festivals and plays and a freer, more spontaneous intercourse. From Weimar Goethe and Wieland encouraged Bürger in his ' popular ' style, as against the more dignified verse of the Klopstockians, and Goethe enlisted all the Weimar court to guarantee financial support for Bürger's translation of the *Iliad*—an unprecedented event in German cultural annals. The Sturm und Drang seemed merely to be transposed to a freer environment, and Lenz and Klinger came to participate in the new splendour ; scandal was busy all over Germany and Klopstock wrote him an indignant protest against his alleged corruption of the young Duke.

For some time Goethe felt it to be a temporary home, and brought to Weimar a considerable scepticism about court life. After a few months he wrote to Merck :

I am now involved in all the court and political squabbles and shall hardly be able to get away. My position here is advantageous enough, and the Duchies of Weimar and Eisenach are after all a stage on which to see how one likes cutting a figure in the world. So I'm not going to be overhasty, and the main conditions of my new form of life will be freedom and contentment, though I'm more than ever in a situation to recognise the muckery of temporal splendour.[79]

But he himself began to change. From the beginning he had been able to fit himself into the requirements of court life, and had respected the outer forms, the class conventions, which he and the Duke could ignore when they were together on their excursions. The change grew greater as he began to take an active interest in the affairs of the little state, in the maintenance of roads, the well-being of the peasants, the mineral resources, even the finances. His attempt at re-opening the mines at Ilmenau led him to the study of mineralogy, and his attitude to nature began to be enriched by the scientific study of the laws of nature ; it did not remain a merely subjective relationship. He began to accept social convention as a condition of the success of his activity. His love for Frau von Stein, a lady of the court, brought him to respect the social propriety which seemed a natural and integral part of her character. Klinger and Lenz found Weimar no new Sturm und Drang, and left in some disgust with Goethe. Goethe's poems begin to be reflective instead of explosive ; *Iphigenie* and *Tasso* are the opposite, in theme and style, of *Götz*, *Faust*, and *Werther*. In *Wilhelm Meisters Theatralische Sendung* there sounds that note of irony towards enthusiastic idealism which is characteristic of the mature Goethe. This complex set of changes began imperceptibly and very soon after his arrival at Weimar ; they mark Goethe's emergence out of the Sturm und Drang.

LENZ

In Lenz the dangers of the Sturm und Drang temperament appear in their sharpest form. He was unable to master the conflict between the inner life and outer reality and his life and works are a record of a torn, tragic personality.

He was the son of a Lutheran pastor in Dorpat, a tiny provincial town in the vast empire of Russia. The German community, directed mainly by pastors and tutors, was cut off from public affairs, and morally sustained by pietism. His father was a stern, deeply religious man, who brought up his children in the consciousness of sin and death. Lenz was delicate and impressionable, and this pietistic upbringing left its stamp on his mind. Destined for the ministry, he was sent to Königsberg to study theology, but was much more attracted to philosophy and literature ; like Herder he heard with appreciation the lectures of Kant and was introduced by Kant to the ideas of Rousseau.

On the eve of his examinations he agreed to accompany two Baltic barons, the brothers von Kleist, to Strassburg, where he arrived in 1771 in time to meet Goethe. The Kleists

had come to join the French army, and he moved about with
them and their regiment in Alsace, receiving board and
lodging in exchange for services as interpreter and companion.   With them he got to know the seamy side of garrison
life, and, a middle-class dependent, was often tortured by their
coarse jokes at his expense.   In 1774 he cut away from them
and settled in Strassburg, maintaining himself as best he
could by giving lessons and by the meagre honoraria from his
writings.   He tried once more to study theology, but without
success, and his only serious occupation was writing.   A
helpless, puckish, affectionate character, he won the sympathy
of Salzmann and Lavater, who like Goethe helped him from
time to time, but who, like his family, became most anxious
about his future.   Harebrained schemes of taking military
service, or gaining a post as an administrator, passed through
his mind, though he was utterly incapable of consecutive
labour and application.   In desperate hope he turned up at
Weimar in 1776, and was for a time delighted with Goethe's
aristocratic friends.   But he committed many social blunders,
and most of the months he spent there as the Duke's guest
were passed in a country retreat.   He began to resent Goethe's
social success, and it was probably a skit on Goethe's relations
with Frau von Stein that led to his summary dismissal from
the Dukedom at the end of the year.   He was given hospitality
by Schlosser, Goethe's brother-in-law, and by several Swiss
friends of Lavater's, but no one knew what to do with him.
After restless and purposeless wandering over Switzerland he
sought refuge with an Alsatian country parson, in a state of
complete nervous collapse.   He was tortured by hallucinations
and a sense of guilt, several times attempted suicide, and
on one occasion tried to raise a girl from the dead in the
manner of Elisha.[80]   His brother fetched him home, where he
recovered.   He went to St. Petersburg and Moscow in search
of a position, but was too absent-minded and scatter-brained
to maintain himself, despite the sympathy he met amongst
the enlightened Russian gentry and intelligentsia.   He died in
misery in 1792 in Moscow.

Moods of despair and enthusiasm, irony and fantasy, satire
and veneration alternately mastered him. driving him to
excess and caricature.   He fell in love easily and helplessly,

II. HAMANN

From Lavater's 'Physiognomische Fragmente'

III.   HERDER, *ca.* 1775
From Lavater's 'Physiognomische Fragmente'

and was unhappy enough never to win love in return. He loved Friederike Brion after Goethe's departure, but without hope. He stumbled into an obsession for Cleophe Fibich, the flirtatious fiancée of the elder Kleist, and served to pass away the time of this rich goldsmith's daughter. He became attached to Goethe's sister Cornelia, a young married woman living in the neighbourhood of Strassburg, but without avowing his feelings. He fell in love with a woman he knew only through her letters to a third person, and tortured himself about her. His *Diary* and *Moral Conversion of a Poet* describe and analyse his relations with Cleophe and Cornelia,[81] and *Der Waldbruder* is the reflection of his obsession for Henriette von Waldner.

He was often acutely aware of this dissonance between his feelings and reality, and yet was convinced that life was unbearable unless he was carried away by emotion : ' the greatest misfortune is lack of capacity for feeling'.[82] He wrote to Lavater : ' So we are heroes twirled by every breath of air. . . . My greatest sufferings are caused by my own heart, and yet, in spite of all, the most unbearable state is when I am free of suffering.'[83] To Sophie von la Roche he wrote that from childhood he had been running his head against a wall.[84] Extremely dependent on others, his friends all feared for him—in Weimar, Goethe wrote, they had to treat him ' like a sick child '. Wieland, on whom Lenz had made sharp and personal attacks, told Merck : ' One cannot like the lad enough. Such a strange mixture of genius and childishness ! Such a delicate mole-like feeling, and such a misty glance ! Altogether, so harmless, so timid, so affectionate.'[85] Harmless to others, but a disaster to himself— ' a riddle to my noblest friends, to myself an example of the judgment of God '.[86] Lenz was sometimes ironically, sometimes desperately aware of the perversity of his imagination. ' Give me more real sorrows so that the imaginary ones don't overwhelm me,' he cried to Lavater.[87] With all this, in letters and essays he insisted that man must take an active part in the world, that ' action is the soul of the world ' ; but he could never even define what form activity should take, and feeling and action remained opposites in his life. Numerous admissions in his letters and essays show how racked he was by the consciousness of his own ineffectualness—he wrote to Merck :

My plays are still without style, patched together in a very wild and negligent manner. I lack the leisure, warm air, and happiness of heart to be a poet ; my heart lies half sunk in mud upon the nettles of my fate and only with a desperate effort can work its way up.[88]

Into several of his works, notably the play *Der Engländer* and the story *Der Waldbruder*, Lenz projects ironically and whimsically this perversity of his character. It is characteristic that of all Shakespeare's plays he should have translated *Love's Labour's Lost*, delighting in its irony and quibbles. But when he wrote about the outer world he showed himself to have the gift of sharp observation. *Der Hofmeister* gives a remarkably clear picture of the situation of a private tutor in a noble home, and *Die Soldaten* is a most penetrating study of a group of officers, on the one hand, and a burgher family on the other. But these, his best works, are spoilt by inequalities and crudities, by the lack of discipline so characteristic of his whole character. He had a keen sense of comedy, of incongruity, but the characters of his plays often turn into caricatures. Goethe's satire is also grotesque, but it is fanciful, gay, good-tempered, and without very serious moral pretensions ; Lenz's is serious, sharp, wounding, and often over-reaches itself.

Although Lenz felt no vocation for the Church, he was fond of theological speculation, and many of his essays—most of them papers read in the Strassburg literary circle—deal with theological and moral themes. His style is, like Herder's, rhapsodic, broken, often difficult to follow. He told Salzmann ' my philosophical reflections must not last more than two or three minutes, otherwise my head aches ',[89] and though we need not take this statement literally, it is true that his essays are disjointed, unsystematic, in a way that Herder's are not. What is really disconcerting is to find that in them he often remains within the framework of the rationalistic theology of the times. Despite statements here and there which link up with the religious views of Lavater, Herder, Goethe himself, Lenz accepts without analysis the normal concepts of perfectibility, happiness, Christian humility, selflessness, sexual purity. Perhaps this confusion was due to the influence of Salzmann, who himself was fond of theological moralising in the fashion of the normal rationalist Christians of the time,[90] but it illustrates not only Lenz's dependence on stronger personalities, but also his failure to weld the various aspects of his experience into a whole.

The obscurity of his future, his successive misadventures in love, increased in Lenz his consciousness of personal failure. He could find a symbol of himself in Tantalus, ' serving as a farce to the Gods '. In *Pandaemonium Germanicum*, where he depicts the victory of true German poetry over imitations from the French, he represents himself pulling faces at the French, and puts into Goethe's mouth the words : ' The good lad, Lenz. Even if he achieves nothing, yet his surmise was great.' Because of his failure, because of the violent conflict within him of imagination and reality, he became morbidly introspective. The self-irony, the self-denigration of his *Diary*— ' the history of a pathological passion ' Kindermann calls it [91] —are related to the pietist sense of sin, but also have something curiously modern about them. In his waywardness he experimented in literary forms which anticipate both realistic and expressionistic drama. But it seems a strange misconception of his character and work to maintain that, because Lenz anticipates some of the later views and forms of the Romantics, he transcends the Sturm und Drang [92]—even were it to be granted that Romanticism itself was a ' transcending ' of the Sturm und Drang, a view that is too uncritically accepted in German literary history. Able to share in the insight of Hamann, Herder, and Goethe, capable of feeling their raptures, Lenz was not able to mature ; he wrote of his other self, the tortured Herz of *Der Waldbruder*, ' he lives and moves in sheer fantasies '. Karamsin, the distinguished Russian man of letters, who frequently met Lenz in Moscow between 1785 and 1788, and who showed more sympathy with his fate than his German friends, wrote on his journey through Germany : ' That deep capacity for feeling, without which Klopstock would not have been Klopstock, nor Shakespeare Shakespeare, was his undoing. In other circumstances Lenz would have been an immortal.' [93]

KLINGER

Compared with the other leading personalities of the Sturm und Drang, Klinger was psychologically uncomplicated. If Lenz corresponds to the Werther type of symbol, the image Klinger made of himself is more like the heroic superman, the Prometheus, the rival of the Gods. He was the son of very poor folk in Frankfurt, and was enabled to study only through the generosity of a patron. He revolted against the dullness of study as against the narrowness of his circumstances, but with an exuberant self-confidence which often appears juvenile. His numerous plays, all written at great speed, are almost all built round a hero of great power and potentiality, but lack both psychological insight and worldly knowledge. Greatness appears more in rhetoric than in deed ; the best of them, *Die Zwillinge*, expresses the rhetorical resentment of a young man who is frustrated by circumstance. His best friends complained about the declamatory and monotonous violence of the language of his plays.[94] His natural longing for activity could find no satisfactory outlet, and he was often rampageous and violent in his speech : Heinse addresses him, in all innocence, as a ' roaring lion '.[95] When Lenz came to Frankfurt in 1776 Klinger and his friend Schleiermacher went out to escort his coach in triumph, dressed in the famous costume of Werther, blue frock-coat and yellow waistcoat. He was one of the liveliest members of the Goethe circle in Frankfurt, and when he visited Goethe in Weimar in 1776 his exuberance caused Goethe great anxiety—' Klinger is a splinter in our flesh.' [96]

Klinger's restlessness did not arise from any dissonance within his character, or any profound feeling of social malaise. He tells his friend Schleiermacher that he is exalted by ' divine and satanic intimations, such as poets, fanatics and idiots have ',[97] and that he is living ' in the inward struggle of energies and activity against the frontiers imposed on men by the Gods ' ; [98] but by 1775 he already considered that he would find satisfaction in a military career. For a time he took a post as theatre-poet in a wandering troupe of actors, but Goethe's friends in Weimar got him a commission in the Austrian army for the abortive campaign of 1778, and his taste for military service, with its hardships and charm, ' this slavery that flatters our ambition ',[99] was confirmed. In 1780 he joined the Russian army, proved an excellent officer, and rose to high rank. In several plays at the end of the 1770's he had derided his own idealisation of the ' Kraftgenie ', and in the numerous prose works he wrote in Russia all that is left of his Sturm und Drang is a Rousseauistic hankering after the simple life and criticism of the corruption of courts.

Klinger's Sturm und Drang is the naïve revolt of youth against the world, exacerbated by his own social position, the pettiness of circumstances, and the example of Herder and Goethe. It is little more than a gesture, a kicking over the traces. In its self-conscious innocence, as when he attacks the corruption of courts or the lasciviousness of Wieland, and in its boisterous coarseness, it shows the unthinking self-assertiveness which is bound to decline as age comes on. The title of one of his plays, *Sturm und Drang*, has now been applied to the whole movement of which he was a part, and serves to remind us that the movement itself is closely associated with the values of youth. But he experienced only the more superficial of the impulses which were overturning established values and were to form the basis of a new outlook and a new poetry.

SCHILLER

In Schiller's personality we find divergences from the type of Hamann, Herder, Goethe, and Lenz which illustrate the peculiarities we shall find in his works. Ten years younger than Goethe, he had no personal contacts with the other Stürmer und Dränger ; in fact, the Sturm und Drang proper was over by the time he began to write. He was the son of a regimental surgeon in Württemberg and was brought up in modest but not straitened circumstances. His mother and father were devout, pious folk, but Schiller was not subjected to the emotional strains of pietism. Like many other boys of his age, he liked to put on his mother's apron and preach to his sisters, but from the time of his earliest works was insensitive to religious exaltation and its problems. From boyhood he attracted the attention of the Duke of Württemberg, with whom he became quite a favourite. At the Duke's suggestion he was educated at the latter's military academy, choosing medicine as his profession. In 1780 he became a regimental surgeon. His school-years, though subject to severe discipline, were not unhappy. Like other boys he liked to imagine the joys of freedom, but he was docile and hardworking.

In the later years at the academy the contours of his character become clear. He began to seek relief for his pent-up emotions by reading Klopstock, Ossian, Goethe, and Shakespeare, and by writing poems and plays of his own ; but in his outer life he respected his duties and his superiors. In his mind the ideal world remained curiously separate from the real environment. Thus he won the respect of other students both for the enthusiasm of his rebellious idealism, and for his firm, moral character.[100] When he was seized by his imagination or by the works of his favourite authors, he was thrown into fits of rapture—he would snort, stamp about the room, or fall into a trance-like state ; but these transports arose from ideal enthusiasms and problems, not from personal relationships, and subsided if they found an outlet in his literary works. As he said to Frau Körner, ' the poet must live in an ideal world . . . must find refuge in the realm of ideals from the wretchedness of reality '.[101] His personal awkwardness and gawkiness, the bleakness of his personal environment, did not set up complex reactions within him, but were swallowed up in the ardour with which he devoted himself to his writing and ideals. Indeed, Schiller's biography lies much more in his works than his private life.

His position as a subordinate officer was wretched enough, under the eye of an omnipresent and omnipotent Duke. He suffered reprimands and detention for attending without leave performances of his first play, *Die Räuber*, in the neighbouring Mannheim, and was instructed by the Duke to write no more. He could not give up his literary work, and slipped out of the town, trying to make a living as theatre-poet. His next play, *Fiesco*, deals with social rebellion ; the following tragedy, *Kabale und Liebe*, depicts the destruction of youthful idealism by corrupt absolutism ; and the last of his early plays, *Don Carlos*, shows the unavailing struggle of political idealism against the selfish interests of State and Church. These plays, separately and together, hold far more direct and violent criticism of contemporary society than any works of the other Stürmer und Dränger ; they are the successors to Lessing's *Emilia Galotti* and *Nathan der Weise* rather than to *Götz von Berlichingen* and *Werther*. Yet, at the same time, though Schiller had great difficulty in making two ends meet, could see little hope for the future, and was dependent on the generosity of friends, in his personal life and expressions there is none of that resentment against life, that self-torture which we find so frequently in Herder or Lenz. He was lacking in their nervous sensitivity. He fought his way through without vacillation and personal rebelliousness, with a disinterested impersonal idealism and confidence that won the respect of many friends.

His lyrical poems are the very opposite of the Sturm und Drang lyric. They express, not his experience, but his reflections about love, music, and so forth. His friends knew, and he told Frau Körner later, that the ' Laura ' to whom he addressed certain poetical raptures was not a girl he loved, but an elderly landlady of his to whom he could conveniently attach his reflections on the power and nature of love.[102] None of his works arise out of emotive tensions, like Goethe's or Lenz's. If he impressed others by his rectitude and moral strength, his disregard for a petty environment, he was also lacking in that charm, appeal, almost femininity which others noticed in Herder, Goethe, and Lenz. His feelings lacked variety, subtlety. If he read his own works aloud, the strident unmodulated over-emphasis of his delivery often put his hearers off.

There is something of the Sturm und Drang in the feelings of exaltation with which Schiller was overwhelmed when in the throes of composition, and the main characters of his three first plays have something in common with the ' Kraftgenie '. They are heroic personalities, seeking to impose themselves on a world they despise. He wrote for the first performance of *Fiesco* a notice which seems to belong completely to the Sturm und Drang :

If, to the misfortune of mankind, it is so common and daily an occurrence that the best seeds of greatness and goodness are buried under the pressure of burgher life ; if petty quibbling and fashion mutilate the bold outlines of nature ; if a thousand ludicrous conventions exercise their inventiveness on the divine image— then a play cannot be without purpose that places before our eyes a mirror of our whole energy, that enkindles anew the dying spark of heroism, that raises us out of the narrow, musty realm of every-day life into a higher sphere.[103]

But Schiller always directs our attention to the conflict of man with his social environment, never to the obscure complexities within man. His plays are richer in dramatic action, but poorer in psychological insight, than those of the other Stürmer und Dränger. Indeed, his conception of man is nearer to that of the earlier moralising sentimentalists of the generation of Richardson than to that of Herder and Goethe. This excessively simple conception of morality, and of the theatre as a vehicle for morality, is expounded by Schiller in his treatise, *The Stage considered as a Moral Institution* (1784). He identifies feeling with goodness, calculation and self-interest with evil. Only in the first play, *Die Räuber*, do the hero's feelings betray him to evil action, and Karl Moor himself recognises his fault and voluntarily atones for his error.

If we consider the central writers of the Sturm und Drang, we find in them a cast of mind which has a definite individuality of its own. All are convinced of the primacy of feeling, of intuition, among human values. Nurtured in pietism, and constantly stimulated by religious experience, this conviction widens and deepens under the influence of all the boldest thought of their times, for they are highly intellectual men who measure themselves against their best contemporaries, despising the security of dogma. Sensitive and imaginative, they greedily seek sustenance for their senses and feeling ; this sustenance they find in the main in poetry, and their poetry and rhapsodical prose arise directly from their emotive experi-ence. They suffer continually under the pressure of practical life, not only in the form of routine work but also in that of social morality. The normal definitions of good and evil are irrelevant to their values, for they seek above all intense life, joy and woe, without which all human relationships are meaningless for them. They are tossed about by their emotions and imagination, are unstable, can see no perspective for the realisation of their ideals, and often feel themselves to be a prey to forces within them which they worship even in their destructive power. The subjective streak which is evident in the melancholy of Young, Gray, and Thomas Warton becomes all their being. Much more like Rousseau, they do not dally with it, but stake their existence on it.

One side of their dilemma, their desire for personal significance within an environment they considered worthless, was in their own time subjected to a most penetrating analysis. K.P. Moritz, in his autobiographical *Anton Reiser*, tells how he, the intelligent child of extremely poor parents, found an outlet for the repressions of a narrow, hostile environment first in pietism, then successively in the ideal of becoming a preacher, a poet, an actor. The discordance between him and society is reflected in his unhappy, inharmonious temperament, his isolation, his melancholy brooding, his raptures over the tragic fate of Goethe's Werther, of Guelfo in Klinger's *Die Zwillinge*, characters in whom he sees himself. But Moritz describes only the more pathological elements in the Sturm und Drang temperament. The chief Stürmer und Dränger were conscious of being endangered, threatened by their own ideals ; and they seek, obscurely and painfully, to find a new moral framework within which their subjective values may be set, to work through to achievement, to a state of personal fulfilment which will allow them to operate upon the world, not merely capitulate to existing society and morals ; they seek to perceive a reality more fundamental and permanent than that recognised by pedestrian common sense, in which the dynamic forces within them will find an outlet.

CHAPTER II

THE STURM UND DRANG AND THE STATE

Der Staat tötet die Freiheit.—LEISEWITZ.

LACKING POLITICAL consolidation and economic development, Germany suffered in the seventeenth and eighteenth
centuries from an almost complete dearth of political thought
and public opinion.[1] The early expansion of Prussia had been
the cradle of Pufendorf's important work, but the growing
despotism of Prussian kings had stifled any further political
thought. Winckelmann turned 'in horror' from this 'despotic land'.[2] Lessing, whose hopes of the Prussian king are
mirrored in *Minna von Barnhelm*, uttered privately the harshest
criticism of this 'most slavish land in Europe'.[3] Justus
Möser attributed the general lack of public conscience in
Germany to the bureaucratic rule and mercenary armies of the
absolute princes.[4] But, though there was no political or social
movement of resistance in Germany, the intellectuals were well
aware of British and French political thought, and read with
admiration of Voltaire's defence of Calas and Sirven ; from the
middle of the century there was more and more outspoken
criticism of the excesses of irresponsible and spendthrift princes,
who were unable to censor or punish authors outside their
state-frontiers. Thus the Göttingen professor, A. L. Schlözer,
and the free-lance administrator, F. C. von Moser, became
renowned and feared for their attacks on princely abuses.[5]
But neither of these men challenged the principle of absolutist
government ; like Lessing, in his *Dialogues for Freemasons*,
they relied on the enlightened monarch to limit luxury spending,
reform the administration, the poor-law and education, to
grant greater freedom of religion. The social interests of the
German Enlightenment remained within these limits.

In contrast to this modest and practical reasonableness,
Klopstock voiced an emotional protest against the subjection
of the citizen to the absolute prince. He it was who first
held up to Germans the ideal of freedom, which led him to
attack the greedy power-politics of the King of Prussia,[6] and

later to support the principles of the French Revolution. But he could not find a substantial meaning for his ideal within Germany, and in the main it took the form of an idealisation of the virtues of the Ancient Germans as described by Tacitus, through which he hoped to infuse in his contemporaries a new national pride. Several of the younger generation carried his enthusiasm to absurd lengths, particularly the Klopstockians associated with Göttingen. Voss, the Stolbergs, Schubart intoxicate themselves with dreams of the bloody overthrow of tyrants, the victory of freedom and virtue, and the establishment of a mighty German empire.[7] Some of the Stürmer und Dränger were touched by this infection. Maler Müller wrote an ode entitled *Song of a Blood-drunk Eagle of Wotan* ; Herder occasionally grieved for the ancient Germanic constitution and a religion which admired heroism.[8] But in general they spoke with repugnance of these ' tirades of fantasy ', ' monstrous hyperboles, noise and battle-cries ', this ' phantom of a fatherland '.[9] Merck wrote sarcastically about ' the blue heaven of freedom and happiness ' that these poets thought they could win by simply running after it ' as after a white butterfly '.[10] Goethe, Herder, and Lenz were deeply concerned to discover native and true principles of art and forms of life, particularly at Strassburg, face to face with France. But, on his journey up the Rhine with the Stolbergs, Goethe could not participate in their frenzies against the French nation ; nor could he share in their ecstasy over the free soil of the Swiss republic.[11]

The only positive theory of society to exert influence on the Stürmer und Dränger was that of Justus Möser, the capable and experienced administrator of the small state of Osnabrück, who was to be a sturdy champion of their poetical work. His reflections arise directly out of the practical concerns of his narrow environment, and for that reason have a concreteness that is absent in other German political writers of the time. In his *Patriotic Fantasies*, published from 1768 onwards in the local Osnabrück paper, Möser discussed almost all the economic, social, and cultural affairs of his small state. In marked contrast to his contemporaries, he shows loving attention to the specific and peculiar character of the mode of life of each class and district, and relates this concretely to material conditions and social tasks. Keenly concerned for technical

improvements, he interested himself in all the social factors
involved. He expressed a strong dislike for large states, for
their bureaucracies and general impersonal laws, where
administrative efficiency is bought at the expense of local and
corporative solidarity ; and he insisted that each state, each
town and village indeed, may have its own specific constitution,
corresponding to its peculiar history and character. He
valued traditional communal ties, and sought to preserve
ancient corporations, estates, and guilds, where these corresponded to a real community of interest and occupation.
Aware of the advantages of factory-production, he sought to
establish new forms of production with as little disturbance as
possible in the social fabric. He considered a prosperous
peasantry to be the basis of a healthy society, and his hostility
to the despotic state and to the social upheaval caused by
capitalism led him to defend feudal privileges, even serfdom.
But these views should be assessed in the light of his antagonism
to the concentration of political power and his defence of the
rights of the common man. ' In despotic states the Lord is
everything, the rest is a mob. The best constitution descends
from the throne in gradual stages, and every stage has its own
degree of honour ; the seventh has the same right to be
preserved as the second.' [12]

The mixture of progressive and reactionary doctrine in
Möser's extremely concrete and realistic writing illustrates
the main political dilemma of the Germany of his time, from
which the Stürmer und Dränger could not escape. After the
French Revolution, his views could be quoted in favour of a
reactionary changelessness. [13] But in his own time, his theory
seemed to be the only one to make sense of the disintegrated
Roman Empire and to open up a perspective of social development within the small state. [14] His support of old corporations
was a defence against the encroachments of princely power,
and his apology for the noble estate, in which he concurred with
F. C. von Moser, was a principle of freedom. Many writers
associated with the Sturm und Drang, including Schubart,
who suffered long years of imprisonment for his advocacy of
liberty, saw in the nobility ' the only counterweight to despotism ', ' the rampart against the autocracy of a single
man '. [15]

The positive elements in the political thought of the Stürmer und Dränger, their predilection for the small state, their delight in early social forms, for example the Biblical patriarchate, belong to Möser's train of thought. In *Götz von Berlichingen* and *Egmont* Goethe celebrates the type of leader and community that Möser admired. In Maler Müller's idyll, *Das Nusskernen*, the magistrate describes just such a state and prince as Möser commended. In theoretical writings, and in many plays, they approve the functional division of social estates, as a principle of social constitution ; only in the sphere of personal relations did the separation of classes appear to them as problematical.

The problem of class-relationships frequently appears in the imaginative literature of the eighteenth century in the symbolic form of the love between a bourgeois and an aristocrat. Despite a great deal of sympathy for a Pamela or Saint-Preux, the Stürmer und Dränger conceive inter-class marriages to be impossible or disastrous. They often show that the reading of sentimental novels turns girls' heads and proves their undoing—Klinger, for instance, in *Das leidende Weib*, and Lenz in several plays. Sophie von la Roche's novel, *Das Fräulein von Sternheim*, won their praise because of the precision with which the authoress delimited the spheres of aristocracy and middle class. Perhaps the most characteristic treatment of the problem is found in Lenz's *Die Soldaten*. In his first play, *Der Hofmeister*, he had shown how a girl of noble family had thrown herself at the head of a bourgeois tutor, partly as the result of her sentimental reading ; but neither of the unfortunates had thought of marriage. In *Die Soldaten* complete disaster overtakes Marie, the jeweller's daughter, because she stakes everything on the hope of marriage with an aristocratic officer. The Gräfin speaks for Lenz when she seeks to persuade Marie of the wrong and folly of looking beyond her class.[16]

But this principle is not accepted without murmurings. In the same play Lenz suggests that the sons of noblemen should be educated in public schools with bourgeois children. When Werther's intimacy with Fräulein von B. is abruptly stopped by social convention, this snobbery is clearly condemned. In Wagner's *Die Kindermörderin*, the aristocratic officer actually does intend to marry the butcher's daughter, in spite of the prejudice of his class, and is thwarted only by a brother-officer's intrigues. Schiller's *Kabale und Liebe* presents the Sturm und Drang view in its problematical ambiguity. His hero, the nobleman Ferdinand von Walter, is determined to marry the bourgeois girl he loves, and in this sense the play is a plea for the rights of natural feeling against convention and social prejudice. But, at the same time, Ferdinand is aware of the enormity of his intention. To Luise's doubts and fears about the future he answers with his plan of fleeing out of society, away from social ties. Even this high-spirited Junker can imagine no place within society for so hybrid a pair. The Sturm und Drang view on mésalliance indicates the beginnings of a crisis in the relations between middle class and aristocracy ; but in the German circumstances of the time they did not believe that the classes could mingle. Later in life, in order to gain greater freedom of scope for themselves or their children, Goethe, Herder, Klinger, and Schiller had to accept ennoblement.

Much as the Stürmer und Dränger owed to Möser, there is another strain running through their work. Different in age and temperament from the Osnabrück administrator, and without social responsibilities, they often responded to the pressure and pettiness of circumstances with passionate protest, condemning the very idea of political organisation. In Rousseau's *Discours sur l'inégalité* they found the expression of their own malaise, and they followed him in the rejection of the modern ' policed state ' and modern civilisation altogether, seeking a compensation in an idealised past and in private and domestic happiness.

Hamann was well suited, by situation and temperament, to give them a lead in this direction. He shared the local patriotism of Königsberg and other cities of the Baltic littoral, and resented the continual infringement of their traditional rights by the Prussian crown. It is likely that his mission to London in 1757 was part of an abortive plan to detach the Baltic provinces from Prussia and establish them as an independent republic.[17] For years he was condemned to the petty occupation and miserable pay of an excise clerk, under French officials introduced by Frederick, and his criticism of

Frederick's mercenary economic policy and the bureaucracy was so sharp that after 1772 his Königsberg publisher refused to print his books.[18]   When his wretched salary was cut, even the petition he addressed to Frederick was provocative in its ironical bombast.[19]   But he did not criticise the monarchy as an institution, nor sympathise with reformers like Schlözer or Moser.   The only social institution he felt to be necessary was the family, and political organisation seemed to him to be hostile or irrelevant to the deepest needs of man ; his indifference to social organisation and efficiency is characteristic of the Stürmer und Dränger.   Merck put the same idea from the point of view of a capable official, in an essay of 1779, *On the Narrow-mindedness of the Germans* : [20]

The spirit of order, that rules in all the internal institutions [of the German states], has brought about a more rapid execution of business, and its result is that everybody behaves more or less like his neighbour, and a whole department presents arms in line and at the same speed, just like a battalion.   But the statistical spirit has ousted the individual.   And since everybody has to be as good as the rest, it's not easy for anyone to do better than the others.   The powers and honesty of each man are so closely con-trolled, and everyone is so subordinate to someone else, that it is hardly worth while to earn confidence which is refused in advance.

This distaste for political organisation appears in a more or less extreme form in the lives and works of all the Stürmer und Dränger.   Herder's bitterness against his homeland, Prussia, remained with him all his life ; his wife wrote of his ' ineradicable aversion for the Prussian state and its constitution '.[21]   And though he hoped much from the small states of Bückeburg and Weimar, he came to feel little but hostility to their government and his administrative duties.   Of Frederick the Great he wrote that his power, efficiency, and tolerance merely disguised ' encroachments on the true personal freedom of men and countries, citizens and peoples '.[22] In *Another Philosophy of History* and *Causes of the Decline of Taste* he ascribes to ' policed government ' the decline of taste and culture.[23]   Goethe wrote in 1770 that he was ' not interested ' in Moser's *Lord and Servant*,[24] and he was as unconcerned for the public affairs of his native city as he was for wider political issues. His enthusiasm for Frederick the Great was due to the latter's personal heroism, and had nothing to do with the Prussian system. When he began to think seriously of a career, he rejected the idea of working in a state : ' The talents and powers I have I need too much for myself . . . And then, before I could learn political subordination ! . . .' [25] His departure for Weimar was primarily an escape from the dull routine of duties in the burgher city, and he never lost the consciousness of the pettiness and servility of courts, the hollowness of aristocratic pretension. As he settled down in Weimar and began to take an active share in the administration, he emerged from his Sturm und Drang ; but his Sturm und Drang was still present as a principle of unrest and dissatisfaction, not so much with political subservience as with the barriers which institutions set up against practical activity. His supreme work, *Faust*, ends with a vision of a social situation in which men have unlimited scope for activity ; but its political structure, and the means by which the old state is abolished, are left in obscurity. [26]

In other Stürmer und Dränger, this antagonism to political constitutions is expressed more crassly, and nowhere more explicitly than in Leisewitz's play, *Julius von Tarent*. That Leisewitz could be sharp in his criticism of despotism we see from his fragmentary *Besuch um Mitternacht* and *Die Pfandung*. [27] But, in his only completed work, social questions play no part. The prince of the little state of Tarento is here described as a true father to his people, a tolerant and wise guide to his two sons. He asks his son, Julius, to renounce the woman he loves in the interests of the state, that is, to act as an enlightened monarch, ' the first servant of his people '. But Julius, for the sake of his love, would renounce all social responsibilities and flee to an idyllic solitude. He cries out :

And must the whole human race, in order to be happy, be locked up in states—where each man is a slave of the others, and no-one is free—where each is riveted to the other end of the chain by which he holds his slave fast ? Only idiots can dispute whether society poisons mankind—both sides admit that the state murders freedom.—(Act 2, Scene 5.)

The freedom that Julius seeks is not freedom within the law, but freedom from law. The hero of Klinger's *Die Zwillinge*, too, revolts not against an evil society or an oppressive authority, but against the whole natural order, which has ordained that he is a second child and therefore not heir to his father's authority. Lenz's *Der neue Menoza*, which was professedly a satire of contemporary European civilisation (though in fact a very poor caricature of it), does not so much suggest reforms as oppose to it an (equally feeble) ideal of unsophisticated man. The theme of escape from society into the remote countryside occurs frequently in the works of the Sturm und Drang, in *Werther*, *Julius von Tarent*, in Klinger's *Das leidende Weib*, in Schiller's *Die Räuber* and *Kabale und Liebe*.

Side by side with this type of hero, who flees from social action, there runs in the works of the Sturm und Drang another type, the great man of action. In Goethe's works we constantly find an alternation of the two, Götz and Werther, Prometheus and Ganymed ; he thought of writing works on Mahomet and Julius Caesar, men who imposed their will on the world. The types appear again in Klinger's plays as the great warrior, like Simsone Grisaldo or Otto, and the frustrated man of feeling like Guelfo in *Die Zwillinge*. But these great heroes are, almost without exception, admired irrespective of the political content of their behaviour. Lenz was deeply affected by Shakespeare's Brutus, but what moved him most was the mastery with which Shakespeare conjures up the tense uncertainty of the fateful night before the assassination of Caesar.[28] Herder wrote a little play on Brutus, but its theme is the powerlessness of man to rule his own fate.[29] Goethe wrote the character of Brutus for Lavater's *Physiognomy*, and discovered in his lineaments the ' mighty and pure spirit ' of a man of action, one who can be and bear no master : ' Here is the Gordian knot that no earthly lord can untie.' But his admiration for Caesar, ' the essence of all human grandeur ', was even greater.[30] Such a lack of political partisanship puzzled the good Swiss republican, Bodmer. For him Caesar was a traitor, and it was painful to him to find, as he tells us, that Goethe considered Brutus and Cassius to be the villains of the piece, merely because they killed Caesar from behind. ' It is strange that a German who bears [political] subjection with extreme insensitiveness has such an ideal of

E

intrepidity.' [31]   We may say that it was precisely the lack of any political resistance to princely power in Germany, it was the stagnation of political life, that led the minds of the Stürmer und Dränger to idealise action and heroism irrespective of its political content.

In 1775 the American War of Independence broke out, at the height of the Sturm und Drang, and its impact was felt in Germany in a very direct manner, since 30,000 Germans were sold by several German princes to England as mercenaries. Klopstock and some of his disciples like F. L. Stolberg praised the cause of the colonists.   Schubart wrote odes in their defence, like his *Freiheitslied eines Kolonisten*, and praised them in his *Deutsche Chronik*.   The Stürmer und Dränger looked askance at this emotional exuberance, which seemed to have so little actuality in Germany ; but less justifiably they failed, in strong contrast to their French contemporaries, to detect anything significant in this struggle, just as they had allowed the Partition of Poland of 1772 to pass without significant comment.   Herder's feelings may be guessed from a passing reference to the Prussian ' wolf ' which had seized Poland ; and bitter comments he wrote in 1797 on the slavish readiness of Germans to be sold for the profit of their princes : [32] but, like the other Stürmer und Dränger, he wrote very little about the issue of the American conflict.   Lenz, who prided himself on his military knowledge, told a friend of his, the Hanoverian Lindau, who had volunteered for service against the Americans, ' Tell the colonists that they are fools, fighting for a freedom that does not lie in the nature of the English constitution and that is only an abuse that has crept in.' [33]   Lenz himself wanted to follow Lindau's example.   Klinger did everything he could to get a commission in some detachment leaving to fight the colonists, being completely indifferent to the meaning of the war—just as he did not care whether he served under the Prussian, Austrian, or Russian crown.   The war figures in many of their literary works, and always as a means by which young men can let off steam, can escape from the oppressions of their personal life.   Two characters of Lenz, both of whom are self-portraits, Herz in his *Waldbruder*, and Constantin in *Henriette von Waldeck*, join a Hessian regiment to win ' fortune and honour ' in fighting against the colonists.

Werther tries to enlist. Klinger's young men in his play, *Sturm und Drang*, actually go to the battle front in America. In a parallel case, while the hero of Stolberg's *Die Insel* refers to the subjugation of Corsica as ' a stain on our century ', Fernando in Goethe's *Stella* tells his friends how he escaped from the dilemma of love by fighting against the freedom of the ' noble Corsicans '—the phrase indicates his consciousness of the cynicism of his behaviour. These young men did not take sides ; the war was looked on purely subjectively, as a means for action, for heroism maybe. ' Where war is, there am I,' wrote Klinger ; and, in the mouth of the hero of his *Sturm und Drang* : ' War is the only happiness I know.' [34]

When the Stürmer und Dränger looked for positive principles of social organisation, they found them only in the past or in moribund and threatened institutions of their own times. The bitterness of their criticism of the contemporary state is here replaced by nostalgic wistfulness, or a feeling of tragedy. Herder's *Another Philosophy of History* is the only extensive discourse on social principle, and it is an extremely emotional, wilful, a most Rousseauistic work. To the modern state, English, French, or Prussian, with its greed for conquest and wealth, its disregard for the welfare of its subjects or of other peoples, he opposes the patriarchal society of the Bible, the ' organic ' communities of early civilisations, in which organisation and authority grow naturally out of the occupations and functions of their members. Here, he repeats, men are not separated by the division of labour, the thinkers not divorced from labour nor the rulers from the ruled. Society is an extended family ; men are held together not by fear or greed, but by cooperation, natural affection, common belief. The individual is a whole man. In the Athenian democracy he finds the highest form of natural society, because it developed organically out of the simple human relationships of Homeric times, because it preserved the public character of speech, art, and government, and because in it philosophy, education, and art ' were directed to the life of the republic, the activity of the citizen '. [35] Here he descried the vigour and substantiality of early society, which are attentuated and destroyed by wealth, power, and modern political organisation.

When Herder considers what should be done in his own

time to create a true community, he can only call, without much confidence, for the strengthening of those ties by which men are bound together in a true community of interest. Like Möser, therefore, he seeks to preserve traditional corporations, the traditional divisions of the social estates. The small state seems to him, as it did to Rousseau as well as Möser, to be the best framework for a closely knit social fabric. But his experience made him lose any active faith that he might have had.[36] In the main work of his maturity, the *Ideas on the Philosophy of History*, he again attacks modern society with the utmost violence, and cannot do more than insist that the family, and the extended family of the patriarchate, is the only natural genetic community.

Such ideas do not add up to a political philosophy. In some respects they are frankly reactionary, in some they are a-political. But there is an important element of humanism in them, of significance for later political thought. The criticism of modern society is subjective and irresponsible, the description of early society often unrealistic and illusory—one can understand why the later Herder could both welcome the principles of the French Revolution and be utterly confused and dismayed by its course. But he was asking a fundamental question : what social organisation can be found or invented that will promote personal well-being, activity, goodness, beauty, and happiness. Politics is seen as a question of social culture. His attitude seemed juvenile and impertinent to his sober contemporaries, but since that time it has broadened out into a major issue of political thought.

Of the others, Goethe was most clearly aware of this question, though his answer was given in the form of historical tragedy. Götz von Berlichingen is the head of just such a natural community as Herder admired, who stakes his all against the lust for power of a neighbouring prince. The play is a lament for the inevitable destruction of the independent spirit and communal feeling. Egmont too is the leader of a ' natural ' social group, the people of the Netherlands, and opposes to Alba's idea of orderly centralised government the value of traditional institutions and mutual trust between ruler and ruled. The dramatic conflict is not only, perhaps not primarily, political. Egmont is a symbol of liberty essentially in his reluctance to limit himself by politic calculation, in his desire to follow his own generous personal impulses, and thus is contrasted not only with Alba, but also with William of Orange, who sees the necessity of subordinating his actions to political expediency. The play, completed in Weimar, has a wider political range than any purely Sturm und Drang work, and shows a deeper understanding of the problems of government ; but the antagonism between the ' sleepwalking ' popular hero, Egmont, and political reality belongs truly to the Sturm und Drang.

In many respects Schiller's political attitude was different from that of the earlier Stürmer und Dränger.   In early comments, and in *Kabale und Liebe*, he shows marked sympathy with the American colonists in their struggle against England.   *Die Räuber* is based on an ideal of political freedom which is strikingly opposed to that of *Götz* or *Julius von Tarent*.   His hero wishes, it is true, to live quietly in his native halls, but, disinherited through the intrigues of his younger brother, Karl Moor is swept away by political idealism.   His robber-band is a society of equality and fraternity, and through it he seeks to reform the world, to fight against the powerful, wealthy, and corrupt, and succour the poor.   Only at the end does he discover that the means he adopts result in anarchy and injury to the whole of society, and so the ' majesty of the laws ' is upheld.   But the reader cannot view him as a villain.   Karl Moor is not a figure of horror ; though his intentions cannot be realised, we still sympathise with the idealism of his purpose. So clear a political purpose, so precise an onslaught on the contemporary state, belong more to the Lessing tradition than to the Sturm und Drang proper.

Ferdinand, the hero of *Kabale und Liebe*, is in many ways closer to the Sturm und Drang, particularly to Julius von Tarent.   He is a nobleman, the son of the all-powerful chief minister at a small court, but is ready to give up all in order to retire to some distant spot with the bourgeois girl he loves and whom social convention forbids him to marry.   But, though Ferdinand is far from any thought of political action, he is indignant at the vice of the court ; his virtuous idealism makes it seem all the blacker.   Stirred by his example the English mistress of the Duke revolts against the heartless exploitation of the people, and returns to her own free country.

Through the Duke's lackey we hear precise charges against the Duke which remind one of Lessing's *Emilia Galotti* and give the play a political point sharper than that of any contemporary play—sharper because our anger is stirred not against society in general but against a particular form of corrupt government.

Schiller's deep concern for political affairs is expressed in both his other early plays. *Fiesco* is a study of a republican revolution which turns into its opposite, a more sober, historical representation of the tragic contradiction between intentions and deeds which had already been the theme of *Die Räuber*. In *Don Carlos*, first conceived as a ' domestic tragedy at a court ', the theme of the liberation of the Netherlands from Spain, and in particular the advocacy of religious tolerance, fill the body of the drama and give a heightened significance to the personal tensions between the prince and his father. Though the main purpose of Marquis Posa, the advocate of freedom, is to influence the absolute ruler, underneath there pulses the preparation of national revolt against the foreign overlord. The contrast between this play and *Egmont*, between Posa himself and Goethe's ' sleep-walking ' hero (as Schiller called him in his review of the play), indicates to what an extent, in Schiller's mind, political ideals took the place of the longing for personal, unhampered activity which is characteristic of the Sturm und Drang proper. Posa is a political hero who knows how to subordinate, even sacrifice, his personality to his political purpose.

In Heinse we find a peculiar modification of Sturm und Drang political thought, which varies from the common pattern still more than Schiller's. He constructed, in his late novel *Ardinghello* (1787), a society in which the sensual and hedonistic egoism of Helvétius was combined with youthful resentment against the privileges of wealth and power. His hero forms the nucleus of a society based on piracy, in which complete freedom is allowed its members to follow their own desires, and in which property (including women) is communally shared. The work presents a curious and uneasy combination of that admiration for the amoral individualism of ' Renaissance man ', which focused during the nineteenth century the resistance against democratic or socialist trends, with an abstract communism similar to the theories of Mably or Morelly. But while both these trends indicate possible developments from the Sturm und Drang attitude to the state, they both diverge markedly from Sturm und Drang formulations. Heinse's egoistic sensualism is opposed to the Sturm und Drang longing for organic, emotive social ties and stimuli ; and his dissociation of property from personality was the opposite of the Sturm und Drang desire to root personality in real life and things, the desire to overcome the abstractness and impersonality of modern social life. Such speculations as Heinse's do not suggest any very firm grip on political or social principle, and it is not surprising to find that he was an ardent admirer of Frederick the Great, even to the point of championing his cause in the War of the Bavarian Succession. Just as self-assertion was the highest characteristic of the individual man, so war and conquest were for him the proof of an estimable state ; the social structure of the state is judged only by the military power it develops.[37]

CHAPTER III

THE STURM UND DRANG AND
THE SOCIAL CLASSES

Aus dem besondersten einzelnen Bedürfnis stieg jede Bildung
herauf und kehret dahin zurück—lauter Erfahrung, Tat,
Anwendung des Lebens, in dem bestimmtesten Kreise.—
HERDER.

THE NOBILITY

OF BURGHER stock, sharing in the traditional defensive pride of
the cities, the Stürmer und Dränger give plenty of evidence
of hostility towards the nobility. Herder and Lenz, in particular, suffered much direct humiliation in the service of
princes and noblemen. Goethe, in Darmstadt or Wetzlar, had
plenty of opportunity of observing the court aristocracy. He
spoke for them all when he exploded, in a review in the
Frankfurter Gelehrte Anzeigen, against an author who described
the manners of the nobility as typically German—the national
characteristics are to be found, he writes, in the bourgeois
family, the farm, the workshop, the study.[1] When Brander,
in the *Urfaust*, takes Faust and Mephistopheles for noblemen,
he whispers : 'They are noblemen incognito, they've got
something discontented and malicious in their faces.' Werther
is publicly slighted when he seeks friendly intimacy with a
young noblewoman, and suffers with intense irritation the
self-importance of his aristocratic superiors.

There is criticism of the manners of the aristocracy in the
Sturm und Drang, but no criticism of the estate as such. In
Der Hofmeister, Lenz gives a vivid picture of the sufferings of
a bourgeois tutor in an aristocratic family. The parents indulge
their feelings for their children without any respect for the
tutor or education, they treat him like a servant, and humiliate
him with intent. The mother is a vain coquette, the father a
blustering tyrant ; to cap it all, they swindle the tutor out of
his salary. But, contrasted with them, the father's brother,
the Geheimrat, is a wise and tolerant man with enlightened
ideas. Lenz does not therefore criticise the nobility as such,

56

but only foolish habits which should be corrected. Similarly, he attributes the vices of the aristocratic officers in *Die Soldaten* to their enforced celibacy, and proposes a fantastic remedy. In both plays his criticism of the middle class is as sharp as that of the nobility.

The Stürmer und Dränger distinguished between different types of noblemen, and their most scathing words were reserved for the court-aristocracy, with its parasitic idleness, its formalism, its imitative Frenchified culture, its concern for precedence, its lasciviousness and foppery. Merck warned Lenz, when the latter was on the way to Weimar, not to get submerged in the affairs of ' the great world, where man loses all his individuality '.[2] More sharply and crudely he approved Goethe's resistance to court life : ' For it's better to go whoring with dogs and cats than with the populace of a princely capital, which is stained and beshitten with lackeys and courtiers, and where the best thing you can do is to build high walls so that you can't see the good-for-nothings.'[3] In *Götz von Berlichingen* the courtiers of the Prince-Bishop of Bamberg are treacherous, fawning, corrupt, and lascivious, servile and ruthless by turn ; so also in Lenz's *Der neue Menoza*, in Klinger's *Simsone Grisaldo* and *Das leidende Weib*. It is noticeable, however, that such descriptions are almost stereotyped caricatures of the corrupt court of Lessing's *Emilia Galotti*. The practical business of a court appears scarcely at all ; these young men knew precious little about courts, as Goethe himself admitted at this time. Schiller's *Kabale und Liebe* contains a much more precise picture of a court—wasteful, vicious, foppish, and oppressive—though here again the dominant note is an emotional repudiation of the whole form of court life, rather than a realistic analysis of its faults.

But there are good noblemen amongst this aristocracy, men who seek energetic action and take their duties seriously. Some are admired simply because of their generous impulses, which distinguish them from the petty and calculating type —Simsone Grisaldo is Klinger's hero because he is a warrior, a lover, out of his element in the intrigues of a court. Egmont belongs to the same breed, distinguished by his martial valour, his sympathy for the common folk, his love of a simple burgher girl, and by his candour and self-confidence. Such noblemen are at odds with their environment and often cannot maintain themselves ; in *Das leidende Weib* the honest noblemen retire in the end to their own estates, as Galotti and Appiani would do in Lessing's play. The ideal of the country gentleman appears here and there, though the German countryside was not rich in Sir Roger de Coverleys ; the country hobbledehoy was commoner.⁴ Culture was much more bound up with courts and cities in Germany than it was in France or England. But in his *Geschichte des Herrn Oheim* Merck, the sharpest critic of court society, draws an attractive picture of a nobleman who withdraws from the court and devotes himself to his estate. Here he learns arts more difficult than literary style and court conventions—pruning and grafting his trees, loading hay and binding straw, ploughing, sowing, threshing ; here he finds a true community, in which religion has its natural function, expressing a form of life and linking the living with the dead ; here he is never alone : ' where there is earth, there men collect round me, and I see more and more clearly with every day, they are flesh of my flesh and bone of my bone '.⁵

Equally the Stürmer und Dränger admire noblemen who devote themselves to public service in order to reform the administration. F. C. von Moser was an example of this type, and Goethe himself at Weimar sought to introduce simpler manners, to lessen court extravagance, and to develop the natural assets of the state. Klinger's hero in *Geschichte eines Teutschen der neuesten Zeit*, written after he had taken Russian service, tries to persuade the court nobility to renounce some of their meaningless privileges and pretensions, and persuades the prince to reform the system of taxation in favour of the productive agriculturists. In general, however, the intrigues of courtiers and bureaucrats and the irresponsibility of princes make such efforts abortive.

Nearly all the heroic characters created by the Sturm und Drang writers belong to the aristocracy. Those who do not, like Werther, are as much in revolt against bourgeois existence as against the nobility, and Faust, significantly enough, adopts the style and dress of a nobleman in order to free himself from the confines of his narrow life. Usually these heroes belong to the past or to foreign nations, for it was difficult to ascribe heroic independence and strength to the contemporary German nobility. Goethe's Egmont, Klinger's Otto, Grisaldo, and Guelfo, Leisewitz's Julius von Tarent, Lenz's Englishman are all members of the nobility. Goethe tells us in his autobiography that his *Götz* had put him high in favour with the German nobility.[6] But even in plays of a directly contemporary character, such as Klinger's *Das leidende Weib* or Schiller's *Die Räuber* and *Kabale und Liebe*, the heroic, challenging characters come from the nobility. We never find in their works an idealised middle-class hero challenging the corrupt world of the aristocracy, as is frequently the case in English and French literature of the eighteenth century ; their bourgeois heroes aim at little more than a defence of the innocence of the bourgeois or private world. So crass an identification of virtue with the middle class and vice with the nobility as Lenz allows himself in *Die beiden Alten* is rare, and was probably due to the direct and temporary influence of Sebastian Mercier's social aesthetic. His *Der neue Menoza* offers the more typical contrast between the upright virtue of a Prince Tandi and a Herr von Biederling and the corruption of courtiers and hypocrisy of bourgeois place-seekers.

The attitude of the Stürmer und Dränger to the nobility is therefore ambiguous ; it reflects indeed a social situation in which the social function of the aristocracy was declining, but in which the middle class had not as yet any confidence in its own power to replace it. The dilemma is present even in the old age of Goethe, who clung to his hope in a reformed aristocracy, which would justify its privileges by work—but with what doubts in its will to do so ! Herder at the end of his life wrote of Swift words that seem a personal confession : ' What depressed the Dean most was the upper classes. He considered them incorrigible, and he had so clung to them, had relied on them so much ! '[7]

THE TOWNSFOLK

In the burgher sphere, the stagnation of German economic life had hardened the distinctions between the various groups. Differing in occupation, privileges, and manners, there was little mixing between patricians, merchants, professional men, artisans, and shopkeepers ; beneath all these were the day-labourers ; apart from them all lived the Jews in their ghettoes.[8] Marriage between the upper and lower groups was almost as rare as that between noble and bourgeois. Though, as we shall see, the social sympathies of the Stürmer und Dränger were wider than those of their predecessors, they accepted the social hierarchy within the bourgeoisie without protest. They felt it to be most incongruous that Sophie von la Roche's daughter should on marriage live among barrels of cheese ;[9] Goethe felt himself out of place among the banker and merchant friends of the Schönemann household.[10]

The social importance of the great merchants of France and England had won for them an exalted place in literature. Hamann, Herder, and Goethe knew merchants in Königsberg and Frankfurt, but such men could not compare in enterprise or social prestige with their counterparts in London or Paris. Lessing, in order to write a tragedy which centres in a bourgeois household, had to choose an English merchant to give the work the necessary elevation. The German merchants in Goethe's works have no aura of greatness. The correspondent of Werther, the Wilhelm of *Die Geschwister*, are sympathetic characters, but we are left in no doubt about their pedestrian minds. Wilhelm Meister abandons money-making without regret, and leaves his affairs in the hands of Werner, the man of routine.

Much more prominent in the works of the Stürmer und Dränger are the lower burgher strata, butchers, jewellers and drapers, music-teachers. This social group enters into German literature with the Sturm und Drang under the dual aspect of admiration and criticism. Möser and Herder praised the class of practical men, their more natural manners, their unvarnished speech, and their simple wisdom, and Goethe's delight in the language of Luther and Hans Sachs shows the same predilection ; but the uncouth behaviour and general ' philistinism ' of shopkeepers and artisans repelled them as well. So the descriptions of such families show sympathy for their sturdy independence but also ridicule of their limitations.

The family of the jeweller Wesener, in Lenz's *Die Soldaten*, was recognised at the time as highly realistic. Marie, the younger daughter, is a frivolous girl who wants the pleasures that aristocratic officers can offer her. Her mother and sister grow spiteful towards her. Her father, who loves her dearly, at first tries to put an end to her affair with an officer by forbidding him to give her presents and take her to dances ; work and her playmates will keep her well and happy, he says. When the girl gives her parents the slip and goes to a ball, Wesener shouts at her and sends her supperless to bed. But Marie plays on his affection and wins him over, and he himself begins to believe she may become a ' lady '. When the unscrupulous officer runs away to escape his creditors, Wesener pays his debts, hoping to persuade the young man's parents to force him to return and marry his daughter. They do not, of course, and Marie too runs away. Wesener sacrifices his business in the search for her ; he finds her in the prostitute who accosts him in another town. Lenz very skilfully shows the tensions in the bourgeois family, the mixture of severity and indulgence, of puritanism and social ambition in the father, of natural desire and frivolity in the daughter ; her ' good ' sister is spiteful and unattractive.

The family of the butcher Humbrecht, in Wagner's *Kindermörderin*, is of the same type, though the traits are coarsened. The theme of the play is the seduction of the daughter, Evchen, by an officer, after a ball to which her mother has taken her in deceitful defiance of the father's command. The mother is a foolish indulgent woman, easily flattered by the officer, and the direct cause of her daughter's downfall—the type of woman we find again in Goethe's Marthe and Schiller's Frau Miller. The father is a violent puritanical man, who loves Evchen but expresses his love in tyrannical prohibitions. He forbids all intercourse with the officers, a class he despises, and when he hears that a maid has misbehaved with a sergeant he drives her with coarse threats of bodily violence from the house, swearing that if his daughter did any such thing he would drive her out of the house too. His wife and daughter are terrified of him, and this fear contributes largely to Evchen's downfall. The butcher's brother, a schoolmaster, tries to mediate, but in vain. Wagner well brings out the character of this class of tradesmen, whose rigid virtues turn a girl's innocent fault into a disaster.

Schiller's Miller in *Kabale und Liebe* has the same good qualities as Humbrecht. He too detests the Junker class and knows that no good can come from his daughter's association with Ferdinand von Walter. He has the same rugged independence and defies the all-powerful Präsident. His foolish easy-going wife is of the same brand as Frau Humbrecht. But, though the tragic outcome of this play is determined above all by the omnipotence of the nobility, Miller is by no means represented as the hero of an oppressed class. The limitations and timidity of his outlook are stressed, as are those of his daughter, who cannot rise to the boldness of the nobleman Ferdinand ; and in a painful scene at the end he momentarily forgets the threatening disaster when the Junker gives him a purse of gold which will, so Miller thinks, solve his problems. It is characteristic that the sentimental climax of the play is the final reconciliation between the dying Ferdinand and his remorseful father, while Miller, the burgher, is left, broken down, in the background.

The attitude of the Stürmer und Dränger to the *petite bourgeoisie* is then a mixture of sympathy and criticism, and the criticism of the coarse narrowmindedness of this class rather outweighs the admiration of their moral independence. In *Egmont* Goethe even stresses the lack of ' civil courage ' in the artisans ; when Egmont is arrested their spirit utterly fails. The problem is exhaustively analysed in C. P. Moritz's autobiography. He was the son of extremely poor parents, whose oppressed state was relieved only by pietism. Among cobblers and other artisans he finds excellent characters, and when circumstances force him to be bound apprentice to a hatmaker, he finds an unexpected, inexplicable delight in the hard and painful work.[11] But these simple virtues and joys cannot satisfy a spirit that craves a richer personal and intellectual life. Only through a professional calling can he escape from the social humiliations and spiritual distortions of the artisan class.

For one type within the lower bourgeoisie the Stürmer und Dränger showed exceptional sympathy—for the young daughters. Most of the domestic plays and novels of the earlier part of the century had culminated in marriage, and in the works of Frau Gottsched, Gellert, and such, there was a well-defined type of young woman, usually of the upper middle class, sensible and affectionate, and conscious of duty and virtue.[12] The heroines of the Sturm und Drang are predominantly from a lower social stratum. Some of them, like Evchen Humbrecht and Luise Miller, link on to the older tradition through their devotion to duty and their parents, but even these characters strike a new note, since they cannot so easily accommodate feeling and virtue, love and duty, as their predecessors. Their emotive and moral vigour distinguishes them from the passivity of Miss Sara Sampson and Emilia Galotti. Goethe and Lenz, however, penetrate much deeper ; the poignancy of their lower-class heroines arises from the very fact that their charm lies in their unsophisticated and unreflecting simplicity, and that their natural affectionateness brings them into irreconcilable conflict with morality.

The Marie Wesener of Lenz's *Die Soldaten*, frivolously flirtatious as she is, has all the charm of a self-willed, simple girl, wanting nice things and gaiety, unsure of herself, capricious to others, hurting those of whom she is fond. Even the affectation of her letters is touching. There is something poetic in her flirtatiousness, her hankering for more elegant forms of life. By turns she defies, deceives, and wheedles her father, and in the end causes him untold distress ; yet she has an affectionate disposition and loves him. Lenz makes her charm all the clearer by contrasting to her her spiteful, self-righteous, obedient sister. To her aristocratic admirers he opposes her bourgeois lover, Stolzius, a draper, who is loyalty and honesty itself, and even becomes an officer's batman in order to watch over her welfare—and ultimately takes a dire revenge on her seducer, Desportes. But Stolzius is an awkward, graceless fellow, a man we can at best pity. Are Marie's charms, her whims, her capacity for affection, to be buried in the back-parlour of his shop ? Lenz is not suggesting that Marie is right in running after the officers. The ' official ' moral of his play is expressed by Gräfin La Roche, who explains to Marie how necessary it is for her to marry in her class. But in fact he brings out the whole questionableness of this principle ; prudent it may be, but how insecurely related to happiness and nature.

In the Sturm und Drang works of Goethe we find that the typical Aufklärung pre-occupation with virtue and obedience is ignored. Characteristically, the relations of Gretchen, Lotte, or Klärchen with their parents are not prominent or decisive ; we are concerned with their own inner stirrings and energy. Klärchen turns from her bourgeois lover half in contempt, half in pity, and surrenders completely to her love for Count Egmont, in defiance of what may come ; the energy she reveals comes not from virtuous ideals, like that of Luise Miller, but from her love. The substance of Lotte's character arises not from ideals, nor from obedience to parents—her father plays no part in the story, her mother is dead—but from her character as house-mother, her active care for the home and family, for the neighbours. Her engagement to Albert is not the outcome of prudence, but the expression of her whole home-making character. She does not do her tasks out of duty, but out of natural inclination, and Werther, who detests men of principle and duty, falls in love with her because of this, when he sees her giving her brothers and sisters their supper. Her affection for Werther borders on the tragic not because it is the opposite of duty and prudence, as with Luise Miller, but because it shakes the security, serenity, wholeness of her character.

This new order of values is most profoundly revealed in Gretchen. Her father is dead, and her mother does not appear in the play. The tension between this simple, uneducated girl and her mother is not that between feeling and virtue ; it is the natural, inevitable tension which occurs when a girl must break from the parental home and make one of her own. Faust loves Gretchen from the moment when, entering her room, he builds out of these simple circumstances a picture of the family life in which her ' inborn angel ' has unfolded ; her daily duties have made the substance and loveliness of her nature. And Gretchen, in her own account of her domestic tasks, reveals both her unquestioning devotion to them, and her natural resistance to her mother's authority. Her love for Faust matures all these small resistances, and she gives herself to him, simply and irrevocably. Faust appears to her as a ' noble Junker ', but the difference between them, which in the time of passion fuses in so moving a unity, appears to her as one of temperament and intellect, not one of class. She is not torn by moral scruples and is even unaware, until it is too late, that there can be a conflict between what she feels to be good, and what is commonly accepted as good. She therefore does not question the validity of conventional ethics, and is only puzzled and wretched when her friend Lieschen, at the well, brings home to her the normal attitude to such 'carryings-on' as hers. Her tragedy is, that her love is good, and yet social morality is unquestionable ; that her deepest instinct makes her act against herself, makes her the instrument of the death of her mother, her brother, and her child. Here Goethe has shaped a problem which cannot be solved on the plane of moralising ; it shatters Gretchen's mind.

The same type of girl appears in Lenz's poem, *Die Liebe auf dem Lande*, which was originally based on his unrequited affection for Friederike Brion. She is the daughter of a country parson, whose little domestic duties and pleasures have been transfigured by her love for a man who once came and stole her heart. She is wooed by the loud-mouthed successor to her father, marries him at her father's command, and tends him faithfully, finding in service the deserved mortification for the first love she can never forget.

Goethe and Lenz do not idealise or sentimentalise these girls. They give its full inherent spiritual value to the practical realism of such girls in their limited sphere, which through love becomes touchingly and delicately beautiful. When Faust hears Gretchen's description of her home duties, he wants to idealise them and her—' You must have felt the purest joy '— but she checks him, and stresses the wearisomeness of her tasks ; her happiness is very mixed but, she concludes, 'you enjoy your sleep and you enjoy your food '.[13] With fine insight Goethe shows how Werther is puzzled by Lotte's apparent heartlessness :

A girl friend came to visit Lotte, and I went into the next room. . . . I heard them talking softly, they gossiped about unimportant matters, the news of the town : this girl was married, the other ill, very ill. She's got a dry cough, her bones are jutting right out of her face, she's always fainting, I wouldn't give a penny for her life, one of them says. So-and-so is also in a bad way, said Lotte. Yes, he's all swollen, said the other. And my lively imagination set me at the bedside of these poor folk, I saw how reluctantly they turned their backs on life—and my young women

F

were talking about it just as one would talk about a stranger dying.[14]

The beauty in this earth-bound practicalness was discovered by the Stürmer und Dränger. Their own invasion of this confined sphere they felt to be fraught with disaster, for their restless individualism would shatter the limits which created the charm of their Gretchens and Maries.

It is, however, wrong to believe that their ideal of woman was limited to the unsophisticated, unlettered girl and Hausfrau. There runs through their work, it is true, a polemic against cultured women. Möser repeatedly attacks the cultural pretensions of the bourgeoise, and opposes to the ideal of elegance his own—in the words of a widower : 'I want an upright Christian wife, with a good heart and sound commonsense, easy and homely, lively and yet retiring, an assiduous and busy housekeeper, a clean and sensible cook, and a careful gardener. And I no longer find any such.'[15] In book after book the Stürmer und Dränger mock at the sentimental reading, the stilted manners, the French fashions of women who thought that thus they were more imposing, more soulful, more intellectual. This is the theme of the practical, cheerful mother in Goethe's *Erwin und Elmire*, as she reproves her daughter for her ' refinement '.[16]

This criticism of the fashionable feminine ideal did not, however, mean that woman must be confined to the home and was incapable of intellectual companionship. The women friends of the Stürmer und Dränger shared all their interests. Caroline Herder was a good mother and housekeeper, but she shared her husband's intellectual interests and helped him a great deal in his work, often preparing his manuscripts for the press. Lotte Buff knew her Klopstock and liked talking on equal terms with her philosophical fiancé and their friends. Such women as Fräulein von Klettenberg or Johanna Fahlmer were on the same intellectual level as their young men friends ; so was Klinger's sister Agnes and his friend Albertine Grün. Lenz discussed *Tom Jones* with Friederike Brion, and had the greatest enthusiasm for Sophie von la Roche, a lady of some social standing and considerable intellectual parts. In the lives and works of the Stürmer und Dränger, women enjoy a

much higher spiritual status than in earlier German generations. They were no more concerned than the Aufklärer for
a change in the legal status of women ; but they replaced the
earlier male arrogance and patronage towards women by a
grateful appreciation of woman's capacity for feeling and
devotion, for practical household and family tasks, and for
intellectual companionship. The frank and easy intimacy
they established with women friends was a new stage in the
relationship of burgher man and woman, carrying further the
Aufklärung efforts (initiated by Gottsched) to give greater
intellectual opportunities to women. The great change in the
status of women that has since occurred owes much to the
Sturm und Drang.

The significance of the predilection for the practical woman
can better be grasped when we take into account the harshness
with which the Stürmer und Dränger treated, in their works,
the professional classes—officials, lawyers, professors, doctors,
and parsons. The productive class of tradesmen had, in spite
of its limitations and crudity, a common sense, independence,
and naturalness that could be admired by men who sought
unrestrained expression of their energies. But the professional
people, concerned mainly with theoretical issues and locked in
stiff formalism, appeared as a caricature of true humanity.
The Stürmer und Dränger themselves belonged to this group,
and the bitterness and distortions they allowed themselves in
their description of it mirror their resentment at the social fate
threatening them.

Many of Möser's essays ascribe the weaknesses of German
society and culture to the extravagant pursuit of learning.
' Learning has weakened and perverted all human pleasures.' [17]
The decline of German literature and language since the
Middle Ages he ascribes to the dominance of men educated in
Latin ; the German conception of knowledge is reading and
writing, his ideal is the professor, ' while the Englishman goes
to sea in order to collect experiences '.[18] Nicolai and Mendelssohn could sympathise with Möser's attack on scholasticism,
but they replaced it with a dogmatic and metaphysical rationalism which was almost as remote from personal experience.
Herder's attack on abstract learning is much more absolute
and sums up the Sturm und Drang attitude : in his essay on

Ossian, praising the clear and vigorous language of savages, he writes that it is not distorted

by shadowy concepts, semi-ideas, and symbolic letter-reason : still less by artifice, slavish expectations, timidly slinking diplomacy, and confusing premeditation. Savages, blissfully ignorant of all this mental enfeeblement, are either silent, or speak when they are deeply affected with a spontaneous firmness, certainty, and beauty which our learned Europeans have always had to admire and can never reach. Our pedants, who go gleaning beforehand and have to learn everything by heart, in order to stammer it out methodically ; our schoolmasters, sextons, half-educated ; apothecaries and all those who play the scholar, whose only booty is that in the end they speak vaguely and unclearly and as if in the last confusion of death, like Shakespeare's Launcelots, constables and grave-diggers—these learned gentry, what are they compared with the savages ? Do not look among such, if you want to find in our time traces of this firmness ;—if I have truly defined eloquence, then unspoilt children, young women, people of natural commonsense, educated more by activity than by speculation, are the only and best orators of our time.[19]

All Herder's theoretical work, on religion as on poetry, is an onslaught on men who think ideas and speculation are more true and real than feeling and ' sensuous certainty '. His bitterness is paralleled by the caricature and burlesque which so often appears in the others. On his journey with Lavater and Basedow, Goethe laughed at their preoccupation with religious speculation and gaily dug into the good food which their argufying made them forget.[20] He burlesqued a theologian who had subjected the evangelists to rationalist criticism by describing how the great scholar is horrified by a visit of the evangelists with their symbolic animals and in their traditional costume, so unsuited to modern proprieties.[21] In the same way he poked fun at a hypocritical priest in *Pater Brey*, a farce in Hans Sachs' manner. Wagner, in *Faust*, is the typical pedant, the ' slinking dullard ', who believes that all truth is to be found in books, and that wisdom is the result of learning. The doctor in *Werther* is shocked at Werther's romping with the children, and considers they should be bridled and disciplined, not spoiled. In the early part of the book Werther enjoys a visit to a country parsonage and sits with the old parson under the ancient chestnuts of his garden. But the successor to the living has them cut down, because his wife is so preoccupied with theology that she cannot abide the trouble they cause.

Just imagine, the falling leaves of the chestnuts make her court-yard untidy and musty, the trees take the light, and when the nuts are ripe the boys throw stones at them, and that gets on her nerves and disturbs her in her deep cogitations.[22]

Lenz, in *Der neue Menoza*, shows a hypocritical pietist in the person of Magister Beza, a pious ascetic by profession, who opposes any worldly philosophy, but who is ready to twist Holy Scripture and his conscience in order to curry favour with a noble lord. The father of the tutor in *Der Hofmeister* is a cringing, servile parson, ready to accept any humiliation in order to win preferment. The parson in *Die Liebe auf dem Lande* is a ranting, obtuse vulgarian. Schoolmasters and the half-educated frequently come on to the scene. In Maler Müller's *Fausts Leben*, Magister Knellius is a conceited rule-of-thumb literary critic, who pursues Faust with venomous malice. In Müller's idylls the schoolmaster, devoid of generosity of heart, talks an involved, pompous German and tries to substitute a ' higher ' taste for the peasants' natural delight in their own songs. The wits of the day are frequently pilloried, often in most inappropriate settings, as for instance in Klinger's *Das leidende Weib*. Much later, Goethe was to insert in *Faust* a satire of contemporary critics and wits which has no function in the play. Whenever the administrative bureaucracy appears in the works of the Sturm und Drang it is shown to be a nest of intrigue and chicane, oppressive to the poor and servile to the rich, the breeding place of legal tricks which the simple folk cannot understand. Such are the officials who force the chief character of Merck's *Herr Oheim der Jüngere* to leave agriculture and himself find a snug living as a bureaucrat. The secretary of the Amtmann in Merck's *Eine Landhochzeit*, though he is a peasant's son, is only interested in putting the screw on the peasants, and emphasises in costume and manners his superiority to the common folk. Wurm in *Kabale und Liebe* is the chicaneer turned villain.

The Stürmer und Dränger detest the professional classes

because of their arrogance, their dogmatism, their pretension
to be superior to practical men. Active men concerned with
social amelioration win their warm approval, whether they
are of noble or bourgeois stock, though they do not appear
prominently in their works ; the sturdy Amtmann in Merck's
Landhochzeit or in *Werther* is only faintly sketched. But they
have affection also for village parsons and schoolmasters if they
fit into the village community, though their affection is combined with amusement at the necessarily narrow character such
a life engenders. Goethe quite took to Friederike Brion's
friendly and communicative father, whose preoccupation with
detail was a little trying to the young visitor.[23] He wrote his
little pamphlet on religion in the character of just such a
benevolent village parson. The village schoolmaster of *Der
Hofmeister* is a pleasant, contented old fellow who at first sight
seems to belong to the eighteenth-century idyllic tradition.
He explains to the tutor the happiness of his lot, the secure
round of duties, his little pleasures of a pipe and a bottle of
wine, the routine by which he overcomes his small temptations.
But underneath there is something Dickensian in the portrait,
something cramped, ugly, sub-human. Love is not only ruled
out of his life, but is condemned as something immoral ; he
may have built a contented, useful life, but he is wearisomely
verbose and has all a schoolman's pride in Latin tags ; and
the contortedness of his character appears clearly when he
approves the tutor's self-castration.

The Sturm und Drang criticism of the professional classes
reminds one of Nietzsche's, a hundred years later.[24] But they
have nothing of Nietzsche's fierce amoralism and nihilism,
nothing of his contempt and fear of the common man. In
the figures of the parsons and professors and officials whom
they satirise and caricature they were attacking not only one-
sidedness, limitation, as they did when they satirised the philis-
tine tradesmen, but also that one-sidedness which worshipped
dogmas or abstractions as the only reality, which derided and
condemned the joy which comes from simple practical life,
from sense and feeling, and which moreover claimed all moral
authority for itself.

THE ' VOLK '

With noblemen and townsfolk the Stürmer und Dränger stood in personal contact and intellectual exchange ; they were separated from the poorest journeymen, carters, messengers, day-labourers, and above all from the peasants, by a great gulf of manners and education. Yet it is this class which they most admire, and to which they refer when they speak of the ' Volk ', a class which, absorbed in practical work, was free of the intellectual and moral tensions from which civilised society suffered. A happy and prosperous society, so Möser believed, must be based on a numerous class of peasant pro-prietors ; Herder saw in the labour and community of the peasantry the only modern parallel to the Biblical patriarchate and the Homeric heroic age. Here sturdy individualism and communal ties, realism and religion were reconciled.

There is nothing mystical or romantic in their predilection for the peasantry. The peasantry does not appear in their works as the incorporation of the national spirit, and it is not turned into a symbol of feudal resistance to principles of constitutional reform. Such an interpretation of the ' Volk ' belongs to the German Romantics, following on the impact of the French Revolution.[25] Highly conscious of being sensitive intellectuals, the Stürmer und Dränger do not con-template the possibility of ' merging ' with the Volk, of living as peasants, as H. von Kleist later thought to do. If like Rousseau they go to live in the country, or imagine their heroes doing so, they do so, like Rousseau, not to enter a peasant life or community but in order to pursue their private purposes in an environment free of the pressures and vexations of civilised obligations. Wordsworth's retreat to Somerset or the Lakes is not unlike their ideal, though his sympathy for the poor has an element of charitable zeal which is in general absent from their work. They knew little about, and paid little attention to, the laws and customs of the village community by which labour and morality were governed, and see it as a society of individualists, held together by the seasonal routine, a simple religion, and communal festivals.

The Sturm und Drang conception of the peasant has of course nothing to do with the rococo tradition, in which shepherds and shepherdesses are given the characteristics of courtiers. German porcelain shows how strong this tradition was in the eighteenth century in the upper classes, and its literary expression in the so-called Anacreontic style was harshly ridiculed by Herder and the rest.   Strangely enough, the Hermit of this convention crops up several times in Sturm und Drang works, as a more or less serious example of a natural way of life. [26] More characteristic of the bourgeois attitude to the labouring classes was the attempt, by such writers as Gellert and Gleim, to create a 'popular' literature appropriate to their occupations and suited to their intelligence.   Gleim's *Songs for the Common People* are characteristic of a condescending attitude towards the simple-minded, and have a clear moral purpose.   He wrote too several jocular romances, gentle parodies of the folk-ballad, which illustrate both his feeling of superiority to the common people, and his desire to improve its taste.   Examples of such humorous ballads can be found in Bürger and Goethe.

Closely associated with this attempt to provide 'improved' poetry for the lower classes went a bourgeois idealisation of the peasantry, and the idylls of the Swiss Gessner won immense popularity in France and England.   Here the peasant appears in his family, in the fields, as the ideal of bourgeois morality, a good father and son, Christian, obedient, contented.   A real philosophical Swiss peasant of this type, Kleinjoggeli, won wide fame, and Lavater took Goethe to visit him and admire. Contemporaries of the Stürmer und Dränger like Claudius, Schubart, Hölty wrote many poems in praise of the joy of agricultural labour and the moral contentment it brings. Thomson's *Seasons* was widely read, with its pleasant scenes of the year's tasks safely and successfully done.   This bourgeois idealisation of peasant life was taken further in Germany than in England, where even before Crabbe the hardships and disasters of village life were appreciated.   Hölty's adaptation of Gray's *Elegy* dwells on the thought that 'greater mental gifts' are buried in the village churchyard than in marble vaults, but it does not reproduce the lines on 'some village Hampden' and 'the tyrant of his fields'. [27]

The Stürmer und Dränger rejected the idealisation of the peasant ; Gessner's world is seductive, writes Herder to Caroline, but without strength and truth. [28]   They did not wish to see in the peasantry the idealised virtues of the middle class, but valued in it what was opposed to the self-made image of the moral bourgeois. Their picture of the peasantry is largely determined by their own philosophy, but it contains many new, more realistic elements.

Though they were not primarily concerned with the political or social position of the peasants, they were not blind to their exploitation by callous lords. In early life Herder welcomed the liberation of the serfs which a Livonian baron had carried out.[29] Merck, while he was in Russia, wrote a memorandum showing the social and moral advantages of the abolition of serfdom and asserting that work gives the right to ownership.[30] Later, like Herder, he was to welcome the liberation of the serfs through the French Revolution.[31] In West Germany, where all the Stürmer und Dränger lived in the 1770's, there was relatively little serfdom, but Merck frequently refers in his short sketches to the chicanery and unprincipled taxation from which the peasants suffered, particularly in *Herr Oheim der Jüngere*. In *Götz von Berlichingen* this sympathy is transferred to the peasants of the sixteenth century, though when the peasants take power into their own hands they lose Götz's support and Goethe's sympathy. Leisewitz, in his short scene, *Die Pfandung*, shows a peasant cursing his prince, whose taxes have caused him to sell up his home. There is flaming indignation over the sufferings of the poor in Schiller's *Die Räuber*. But the concern of the Stürmer und Dränger for the political status and social welfare of the peasantry does not go beyond Aufklärung views, though more violently expressed. What is specific to them is their sympathy for the mode of life, the temperament and culture of the peasantry.

Goethe's *Werther* expresses most adequately, perhaps, the Sturm und Drang feeling for the peasantry. Werther is a sensitive, emotional intellectual who is, and feels himself to be, worlds apart from the peasants, as far as he is from Homer or Ossian ; but in their mode of life he cherishes something of inestimable value. With his Homer in his hand he sees them carrying out the primeval human tasks, ploughing, drawing water from the well, bringing up the family. The schoolmaster's daughter tells him simply and frankly of her husband's journey to get his legacy, she scolds and praises her children

with the same directness.   But the village life is not all May-
time and hope.   Autumn comes, and with it the bleak side
of peasant life emerges.   The woman's husband returns ill
and without the legacy, one of the children dies.   In the
definitive version, shaped in the 1780s, Goethe strengthened
the contrast by introducing the figure of a labourer who
serves his mistress and loves her with the quiet pertinacity with
which Jacob wooed Rachel.   In the latter part of the book
Werther hears that he has been rejected because of his poverty
and in surly resentment has murdered his rival.   The dark
side of peasant life may be considered as the appropriate background for Werther's own hopelessness ; but it is nevertheless
a salutary correction to the usual idealised picture of country
life.

In *Eine Landhochzeit* and *Geschichte des Herrn Oheims* Merck
gives an attractive picture of the earthy occupations of the
countryside and the blunt honest simplicity of those who are
content with them.   Like Goethe, he himself could not accept
the Christian religion or any dogmatic articles of faith, but
he had no criticism of the simple piety of the peasants, in his
view the completely adequate expression of their dependence
on the weather.

Since these folk make the daily experience that their knowledge
and foresight is of no use unless sun and rain favour them, they
see everything as a grace, for it can so easily be withdrawn from
them.   They are therefore the only people who still speak with
conviction of the blessing of God, and who believe that they
receive everything directly from his hands.[32]

Faust too, in a scene written in Goethe's maturity, respects
the common people's religion, so embedded in their form of
life :

> They celebrate the Resurrection of the Lord,
> For they themselves are risen again.[33]

It was of course a common attitude amongst rationalists
and sceptics to deprecate any weakening of the faith of the
lower classes.   Hume and Voltaire and Lessing [34] could all
agree that if artisans and peasants lost their traditional fear

of Church and God they would turn like wild beasts on earthly authorities. The Stürmer und Dränger shared this view. Lenz's village schoolmaster says :

Take from the rabble its superstitions, and they will free their minds like you rationalists and will knock you on the head. Deprive the peasant of his devil, and he will become a devil to his lord and prove to you that there are real devils.[35]

But they also, more profoundly, see that the religion of the peasants rises from their form of life, and, respecting this form of life, they also respect the piety which is its natural philosophy.

Lenz several times contrasts the artless simplicity of the peasant class with the formalism and tortured temperament of nobles and townsmen. In the last act of *Der Hofmeister* a peasant girl enters like a fresh breeze, breaking the tutor's despair with her artless wiles, telling him with unembarrassed candour of her preference for a soldier or a clergyman, dispelling his and the schoolmaster's doubts with her direct persistence. In *Die Kleinen* there is a polemical and systematic contrast of the simple countryfolk to ' society '. The chief character, a young nobleman looking for patronage, meets a girl carrying home the potatoes she has just lifted. He tries to sympathise with the trouble she has in digging them and carrying them, but she cannot understand what he is talking about. He tries to flirt with an attractive chambermaid, but she pertly holds him off, though she is ready to defy her master for the sake of her true love, a journeyman. And when he sees peasants playing cards in the inn, he cries out :

What an expression in their faces ! How dull, weak, and distorted are the features of most of our townsfolk ! All more refined faces make me sick. The small stakes for which they are playing only serve to give a relish to their pleasure. How weightily they play their trumps and yet so imperturbably, with the true ardour of self-certainty ! Trump ! Trump !—Lads, you'll damage your fingers—I should like to kiss them ! Woe on anyone who would infect these innocent hearts with passions ! Woe on the dramatists who would bring the dissonance of alien, unnatural feelings into these classes ! . . . It is the very hardness of their fibre, their very apathy, that makes these people happy. You more delicate, idle folk, keep your passions for yourselves and do not refine them ! Your culture is poison for them ! [36]

Lenz does not pretend that the peasants are ideal, that they have all the virtues ; he likes their blunt simplicity and shrewdness in itself. He puts his view quite clearly in *Der Waldbruder*, a work which is largely autobiographical and reflects his isolation in those awkward months in Weimar. Herz has retired to a hermitage in the neighbourhood of a village, and he writes to a friend :

When I go down to the village and review the narrow circle of ideas in which these children of Adam so completely exist, their simple and never-changing monotonous tasks, and the security and certainty of their joys, my heart grows so constricted, and I could curse my fate, that I was not born a peasant. They often look wonderingly at me, when I slink so homelessly among them and cannot enter into their fun or their serious affairs, so that in the end I get ashamed and try to fit into their ways, and then they exercise their wit with masterly skill, as they think, on my clumsiness. But this does not give me offence, for they are mostly in the right. . . . But, if I am to choose, the mockery of an honest countryman is a blessing compared with the jeering of the empty dandies and coquettes of the towns.

In his next letter Herz mentions that ' a rascal of a peasant ' has stolen his last money—' but what was the money good for anyhow ? ' [37] Lenz makes no bones about it—the peasants are narrow-minded, coarse, sly, but they can be admired and envied because their qualities are concrete and real, because their lives, characters, and views are one.

The idyll, with its idealising tendency, was not a genre entirely suitable to the Sturm und Drang conception of the peasantry, and Maler Müller's idylls do not fully reach the insight of Goethe's and Lenz's descriptions. Yet they are a notable advance towards realism, when we compare them with Gessner's. His peasants are engaged in real country tasks, grouped together for shearing the sheep or for kernelling nuts. They have worries about taxes, law-suits, their children. They speak in a natural idiom, with some dialect expressions, not in the elevated prose of Gessner. They like old folksongs about the Nut Brown Maid or the Pfalzgraf Friedrich. But there are contradictions in his work. His most admired character is the rich peasant Walter, whose crony is the schoolmaster ; and though the latter is ridiculed for his cultural and stylistic pretensions, Walter gives a most elegant and sentimental rendering in prose of a ballad in *Die Schafschur*, and the songs his daughter sings, particularly that on ' The Throne of Love ', are of a modern, abstract, sentimental type. Even the labourer Veitel, whose broad dialect makes a humorous effect, sings a somewhat sentimentalised lovesong. It is incongruous too to find this circle of peasants discussing infanticide, and to hear a long and eloquent defence of the crime of an unmarried mother from the peasant Walter.[38]

In one work the life of the peasantry is evoked with superlative deftness and truth, the autobiography of Heinrich Jung, *Heinrich Stillings Jugend*. The Strassburg circle was enchanted by Jung's tales of his village childhood, and encouraged him to write it down—Goethe himself saw it through the press. The first three parts, published in 1777-8, give a description of village life paralleled in the eighteenth century only by the Swiss, Ulrich Bräker's, *Der arme Mann im Toggenburg*. The story is free of polemical intention, and sets out merely to show how Jung made his way.

Jung's grandfather was a peasant and charcoal-burner, and his father, forced by physical disability to become a tailor, lived with the old folks. We see in the autobiography the simple household and the round-the-year tasks, the hard-working and cheerful men and women, the confined life of his father, who shares with his mother, the daughter of a deprived sectarian clergyman, the ecstasies and miseries of pietism. Without intending it, almost without being conscious of it, the healthy cheerfulness of the outdoor workers is contrasted to the moodiness of the parents of the boy, whose father is often sour and harsh towards the child, whose simplest pleasures are condemned as sinful. Equally naïvely Jung does not hide his own desire to get out of the village, to become something better, first a schoolmaster then a doctor. All the peasants have a natural respect for the learned, for the despotic parson, for the uncle who has become a land-surveyor : indeed the later parts of the autobiography are unpleasant in their social and spiritual arrogance. But in the early parts this ambition appears as a naïve and natural desire to gain a living, and it does not prevent Jung from remembering gratefully the labour and community of the peasant home, the charcoal-burning, thatching, the sowing and reaping and milking, the songs they sang, the simple piety, the respect for the parson and the independence of his grandfather. Scenes of peasant brutality are recounted with the same simplicity as those of evening peace, when work is finished and the evening hymn sung. Jung, as a poor village schoolmaster, had to suffer much from the conservatism and arrogance of the village elders, and he was not likely to idealise people on whom his livelihood depended. So also the parson is both tyrant and patron.[39]

It is one of the secrets of the charm of Jung's *Youth* that he was sublimely unconscious of any contradiction between his delight in peasant life and his own desire to rise above it. In Herder's views and their development the ' Problematik ' in the Sturm und Drang attitude to the peasantry is uncovered. His childhood had not left him with happy memories and he was a man who never found it easy to get on with others, least of all with simple folk. Though he occasionally longed to be a country parson, his sermons do not lead us to believe that he would have made much of a success of it. He did justify his advocacy of a simple biblical religion on the grounds that preachers are concerned ' with the common people, the greatest, more sensual part of mankind, not with brooding thinkers '.[40] But his sermons do not read as if they would appeal to simple people, nor do they reflect a simple naïve faith ; their form, like that of all his religious writings, is so complex that it is clear that they could have meaning only for the more intellectual and imaginative of his hearers. Yet Herder, more than any other man, was responsible for a new esteem for the culture of the common people. He was brought to them not through direct personal contact, but through his love for the ballads collected by Percy. Reversing the usual contempt for the clumsiness and coarseness of folk poetry, he praised the songs of primitive peoples precisely because they arose from an unlearned, practical society—' from direct experience, from direct enthusiasm of the senses and imagination '.[41] In his own time only the common folk, he writes in the Ossian essay, still enjoy and preserve true song, compared to which the Bardic odes of Gray and Mason are cold and artificial. Even Klopstock's odes depict only ' fine nuances ' of feeling, as compared with the ' whole duties, deeds and forms of the heart ' found in folksong. True poetry is ' woven out of real objects ' and is therefore near to the common people, endowed with ' more senses and imagination than the studied scholar '.

After quoting *Sweet William's Ghost*, Herder goes on to direct the attention of his contemporaries to German folksongs.

I know, in more than one province, folksongs, provincial songs, peasant songs, which are not inferior to many of the Scottish romances in liveliness and rhythm, in naivety and strength of diction. But who is there to collect them ? to bother about them ? to bother about songs of the common people ? on streets and lanes and fish-markets ? in the unlearned rounds of the country folk ?

He suggests that if a search were made, perhaps half as many might be found as in Percy's *Reliques* ; and bit by bit he set about making a collection.

Percy's delight in old songs had been accompanied by an antiquarian interest in the manners and customs of his fore-fathers. Herder shows little antiquarian interest, in the narrow sense of the term. He is much more enthusiastic over their aesthetic qualities, but at the same time much more polemical, than Percy. He sees folksongs as historical docu-ments interpreting national cultures in the widest sense. But he uses them as evidence of the superiority of early society and simple folk over sophisticated civilisation, and at the same time as examples of true poetry upon which a new definition of the nature of poetry may be built. From the inception of his plan for publishing a selection of folksongs, with which he was occupied from 1771, these three themes are evident, sometimes combined, sometimes in contradiction to one another.

In unpublished essays of 1773 he defends the value of folk-songs on historical grounds : his collection is to be ' a living, practical grammar approached from the most instructive and pleasing side ! a new study for linguistic experts, historians, philanthropists and philosophers '. These ' national pieces ' illustrate the ' national soul ' of the peoples. At the same

time they are to serve a cultural purpose, for they will show
Germans the way to rescue ' the remnants of living national
temperament' now almost submerged under learned imitation.[42]   And, carried away by his desire to restore German
poetry, Herder does not confine himself to folksong.   Even in
the Ossian essay he quotes Shakespeare's *Come away Death*,
under the impression, gained from Orsino's description, that
it is a folksong ; and his translations of songs from Shakespeare's plays formed the nucleus of his collection of folksongs.
In spite, however, of his confusion of purpose and lack of
discrimination, his championship of folksong was clearly
recognised to mean a revolt against the culture of the educated
and a defence of that of the common people.

His plan was supported by a few friends, like Goethe,
Bürger, Gleim, and the publisher Boie, but the literary leaders
of Germany greeted it with hostility and scepticism.   The idea
that the poetry of the ' rabble' could surpass that of the
cultured was treated with disdain.   Schlözer sneered at Herder.
Ramler, one of the stars among the formalist poets, wrote
that no true poet would demean himself by writing for the
obtuse and vulgar mob, and defended with hurt dignity good
taste and regular form.[43]   But the zealous leader of the
opposition was Nicolai, who enlisted his friends in the task
of searching for folksongs in order to prove how vulgar and
tasteless they were.   In 1777–8 he published his two-volumed
collection, *Eyn Feyner Kleyner Almanach* . . ., with much dialect
and an outrageous orthography.   In the preface he wrote
that these songs were suitable enough for the simple people,
but of course without aesthetic value : and shrewdly enough
he told Herder and Bürger that if they really wanted to revive
folksong they had better become artisans.   Though Herder
called it ' a dish of filth ', the collection is not without value,
and was the first collection of genuine folksongs to be published
in Germany.   From Lessing Herder received no encouragement at all.   After he had written to ask Lessing if he had
come across folksongs in the library at Wolfenbüttel, the latter
answered that he knew of nothing that could be called songs ;
he could find only moralising rhymes and the verses attached
to engravings and woodcuts.[44]

Till 1777 Herder maintained his point of view.   In this year he published in Boie's *Deutsches Museum* an essay, *On the Similarity of Medieval English and German Poetry*, in which much of the matter of earlier drafts was incorporated. He defends the legendary and superstitious element in folksong on the ground that the greatness of English poetry, of Spenser and Shakespeare, is due to its being rooted in traditional beliefs and forms. His admiration of the ' Volk ' that ' operates with a whole, undivided and unformed soul ' is qualified by his admission that one has to exercise tolerance towards the naïve expressions and beliefs of the people—they are the ' body of the nation ', not the spirit ; but he attacks that snobbery which would completely disregard them. Popular culture is not ' the dregs of fairy-tales, superstitions, songs, crude speech ', it is the foundation of all great national poetry, and without the ' Volk ' there would be ' no public, no nation, no language and poetry which is ours and lives and works in us '. He emphasises once again that folksong is ' the impression of the nation's heart, a living grammar, the best dictionary and natural history of the people '.[45]

But, with his usual touchiness, Herder began to beat a retreat even before his collection of folksongs appeared. He had to be urged on by his friends, and the selection he made was affected by his desire to give as little opportunity for jeering as possible. He wrote to Gleim : ' One of my main concerns in the First Part [of the Collection] must be, to give Nicolai and Consorts nothing to jeer at, and so I must go gently, especially with the German [songs].'[46] The preface to the First Part is in fact merely an anthology of remarks of other writers in praise of folksong, and in the postscript he expressly states that he does not wish to see the folksong imitated today, or the more regular, sophisticated poetry replaced. In *On the Similarity* . . . he had praised Bürger's modern ballads, but now he repudiates them. The introduction to the Second Part of 1779 is in many ways a direct recantation. He distinguishes here the two meanings of the word ' Volk '. All great poetry has a ' folk ' origin, he asserts, and the greatness of Homer, Pindar, Dante, and Shakespeare lies in the very fact that they are ' folk-singers ', that their material and form are ' fairy-tale, legend, living folk-history '. This assertion, important as it was, was only a half-truth, for Herder does not discuss those elements in their work which distinguish it from the Border ballads or the German folksongs he printed ; the confusion is evident when he includes Pindar, Aeschylus, and Sophocles among the folk-singers. But he clarifies his view when he discusses the medieval German Minnesänger, whose poems were then being appreciated and imitated by poets like Hölty and Voss. He was conscious of their knightly origin, of the courtly nature of their poetry, and in their defence he makes serious concessions to the view of Nicolai and Ramler.

They were and were not folk-singers, as you may take it. To be a folk-singer it is not necessary to belong to the rabble or to sing for the rabble ; just as it is no dishonour to the noblest poetry to sound in the mouth of the common folk. The ' Volk ' is not the rabble on the streets, the rabble never sings and composes, it shouts and mutilates.

This was a capitulation. The common people of his own day, to whom Herder had earlier attributed the excellence of primitive communities, is now denied culture and creativeness. The First Part of his collection contained a few German folksongs ; the Second Part has none at all, and in their place we find formal poets of the seventeenth century like Opitz and Dach, and acceptable writers of his own day, Claudius, Goethe, Herder himself. He repeats what Lessing had written to him : Germany is weak in folksongs which can be read today, but rich in rhymed proverbs and suchlike. ' Song proper is either lost, or it is a bad and thankless task to be a German Percy, if one does not want to serve up filth and weeds.' With sarcasm indicative of his lack of self-confidence he excuses the irregularity of the Border ballads he had translated in the First Part, which had abused ' the classical sanctity of our language and our lyrical majesty '. But, he goes on, since he has been charged as making a principle of ' the lack of all correctness ', he has included in the collection ' poems which are not folksongs and as far as I know never will become folksongs '. Such folksongs as are included must be considered ' not as poetry, but as the raw material of poetry '—the ' wild flowers ' of German folksong cannot bear transplanting into a book.

This introduction concludes with an analysis of the musical quality of lyrical poetry which has become famous ; but in this passage Herder deals not with folksong but with the lyric in general. In his final postscript he bids farewell to folksong with an audible sigh of relief : ' There is a time to speak of folksongs, and a time to speak no more of them. I have come to the latter, and I have heard enough for years of the so desecrated name of folksong.' [47]

Herder did not lose his delight in folksong, but he never again defended the culture of the common folk. His interest in the collection itself was sustained chiefly by his search for examples of the temperament of early, in the main foreign, cultures, ' a living voice of the peoples ',[48] and it was in accordance with his own taste that the second, posthumous edition, prepared by his friend J. G. Müller in 1807, was entitled *Stimmen der Völker in Liedern*, ' Voices of the Nations in Songs '.

His development was paralleled by Bürger's, whose naïve enthusiasm for folksong had led him to write several imitations, one of which, *Lenore*, won international fame. In a rhapsody of 1776, the *Effusion on Folk Poetry*, Bürger asserted that nature, fancy, and feeling were the element of poetry, and he called on the learned to abandon their arts and return to nature, to mother earth, to the poetry of the common people, with its imaginativeness and its natural language. Folk-poetry is ' naturally poetic ', ' true outpourings of indigenous nature '. He has often heard its ' magic tone ' among artisans and peasants. Higher lyrics may be all very well for Gods, but not for ' the race of earthly men '. Folk-poetry is at the source of Homer, Ossian, Ariosto, Spenser ; German poetry must again become popular, and thus regain ' that living breath that sweeps over the hearts and minds of men '. More confidently than Herder, Bürger asserts that there are many songs of true poetic worth to be picked from the lips of ' peasants, shepherds, huntsmen, miners, artisans, tinkers, flax-porters, carriers, etc.'.[49]

In his own poems Bürger adopted themes and a style which were ' popular ' in the simplest sense, sensational and humorous themes, rollicking rhythms, a simple, often coarse vocabulary. He justified himself in the preface to his poems of 1778. ' I have reached my goal . . . if my poems appeal to the majority of all classes. . . . All descriptive poetry can and must be popular, for that is the seal of its perfection.' To make the common people the test of perfection, this was degrading the concept of 'Volk' indeed, and Herder could not follow Bürger here ; even Bürger himself shows his uneasiness by adding that by 'Volk' he does not mean only the 'rabble'.[50] But later, Bürger too retreats under the ridicule of the critics. In 1789 he writes that his popularity is scarcely due to the crude onomatopoeia of his diction or his occasional coarse expressions, nor to his use of popular fairy-tale, but to the clarity, order, and harmony of his thoughts and images, the truth and natural simplicity of the emotions ! He is still proud of being called a Folk Poet, but by 'Volk' he does not mean any particular class : 'The concept "Volk" sums up only those characteristics in which more or less all, or at least the most estimable classes, agree.' All he would ask is that poetry, which must be written by the learned, should be composed 'not for scholars as such, but for the people'.[51] In a last, posthumously published essay, he denies that folk-song forms a special type of poetry.[52]

This recoil from the belief in the common people and its cultural creativeness is not an isolated event in the Sturm und Drang, nor has it a merely aesthetic significance. It illustrates with particular vividness the whole position of these young men in the society of their times. Beating against the partitions of society, they were incapable of defining any method for altering the social structure, since the preconditions of social change did not exist. The social problem turned therefore in their minds into a cultural one, they sought in society for those moral and aesthetic values which best corresponded to their needs ; and at the same time they tended to idealise, to find a way out of their dilemma by exaggerating the moral qualities of certain classes. But they were not content with an ideal compensation, and sooner or later accepted the reality of life, sometimes with humour, sometimes bitterly, sometimes with a deep sense of the tragedy of their position.

Their ideal wavered between opposite extremes, between the symbol of the independent, self-confident nobleman, who would challenge a despicable world, and that of the practical men and women of the lower classes, of the peasantry, whose ideas and morals have the substantiality of their existence, absorbed in the essential, primordial tasks of mankind. But the nobleman of their dreams did not exist in their contemporary actuality ; even more, though they could admire the great figures of the past, the heroes of Shakespeare, they could not imagine what sort of activity such a hero should pursue in their own times. And the *petite bourgeoisie* and peasantry could not provide the scope they needed for high achievement and feeling. Their nearest symbols are therefore men like themselves, nobles or bourgeois, who are distinguished not by greatness of action, but by ardour of intuition and feeling and desire. The greatest of their works show the catastrophe of such a temperament brought up against the powers of this world. Werther and Faust reveal the essence of their problem—intellectuals who ardently desire significant activity, but who discover only the deeps of emotion ; whose whole passion is fastened on a world of the smallest scope within which they know they can never find fulfilment.

The realism with which the Stürmer und Dränger reproduced the inner and outer world turns at times to caricature, at times to idealisation. Even in comparison with Rousseau or Blake or Wordsworth they fall into excesses, into a subjectivity beyond theirs, provoked by a social and cultural life far more static and rigid than that of France or England. But they did not run away from reality, they did not deceive themselves —or not for long—with idealistic solutions and compensations, as did Klopstock or the theologians or rationalists. In depicting their social situation in terms of conflict and tragedy, in their robust appreciation of the ' Volk ', they expressed for the first time the modern revolt against class society, against a social organisation in which each social group is locked in a culture of its own, narrowed, falsified, enfeebled by its own limits ; in so doing, they smashed the dams of a stream of thought which, flowing in political or cultural channels, has since their time brought new life to social being. Their

Germany was no place for the political formulation of new concepts of society, but for that very reason it sharpened their hunger for new moral and aesthetic values.   To these we must now turn.

CHAPTER IV

RELIGION

Nein, ich schreie—Vater ! Retter !
Dieses Herz will ausgefüllt,
Will gesättigt sein ; zerschmetter
Lieber sonst dein Ebenbild.—LENZ.

THERE ARE several important reasons for beginning an exposition of the philosophical and literary ideas of the Stürmer und Dränger by analysing the character of their religious beliefs and their attitude to religion. Religion as they understood it is not a mere code of belief in a supernatural reality, a mere discipline or rule of behaviour, but the expression of a total relationship between man and the universe, man and his fellows, and between the different faculties of man ; it embraces theory and practice. At the same time, it was for that generation the emotive and intellectual cradle of their childhood, in which their surmise of life took shape. A source of emotive experience and an interpretation of the universe, it condensed all the vague ideas and feelings of youth, stimulated and gave a heightened meaning to their consciousness of their growing powers. It is no accident that Hamann's whole work was primarily religious, that Herder and Lavater were clergymen, Lenz a candidate for the ministry, Jung-Stilling a prominent pietist ; Goethe, a Protestant like the others, was one might say brought up like them on the Bible. The development of the Sturm und Drang may be considered as a development from this early religious consciousness of their childhood, a development in the true sense since, while it remained a substantial element of their being, they shed its cultic and theological form as they grew to maturity.

By the time that Herder visited France in 1769, the campaign of the *philosophes* against religion had reached its height. In Germany the struggle for reason and tolerance was confined to Protestant lands ; and, faced with the local power of the orthodox clergy, had from Christian Wolff to Lessing taken a

87

rather abstract theological form—a very large number of the
leading German writers were in fact theologically trained.[1]
Along with it went the revolt of pietistic fundamentalists
against dogmatic orthodoxy and clerical authority. The
Sturm und Drang owed much to both movements, but found
both insufficient. The emotive communings of the pietists
became intolerable because of their intellectual and moral
narrowness, because, as Goethe wrote in *Poetry and Truth*, their
religious principles failed to fertilise ' social morality '.[2] The
abstract God of the deists had no function in personal experience. Even the most rationalistic of the Stürmer und Dränger,
Merck, could write thus of the Aufklärung :

> Now we have got the freedom of believing in public nothing
> but what can be rationally demonstrated. They have deprived
> religion of all its sensuous elements, that is, of all its relish. They
> have carved it up into its parts and reduced it to a skeleton without
> colour and light . . . and now it's put in a jar and nobody wants
> to taste it.

He adds a typical eighteenth-century comment :

> It's lucky that this deterioration has affected only the smaller
> part of society, which belongs not to the productive class but to
> the consumers, so it won't make any plough or wheel stop working.[3]

If a common religious attitude is to be found among the
Stürmer und Dränger, it cannot, clearly enough, be found in
dogmatic belief or religious practices. Hamann was a puzzle
to ecclesiastics, even to his fellow-pietists ; Herder was the
chief Lutheran clergyman in his little state, and at the same
time suspected by his own cloth of the worst heresies. Lavater
was of the Reformed persuasion. Lenz had the greatest difficulty in keeping to theological studies, Goethe and Merck were
ready to avow themselves non-Christians ; Schiller was nearer
Lessing's rationalism than the rest of them. They were linked
not by formulations or religious observance, but by a common
awareness of feelings within them whose origin lay beyond
their knowledge and which they could not control ; feelings
of intense exaltation which dwarfed all other values and to
which they felt they must surrender. Such exhilaration might

arise from personal relations, from nature or from art ; but they recognised religious feeling to be its prototype or analogy, and they called it ' divine ', ' holy ', ' sacred '. This highly subjective interpretation of religion, ranging from the near-fundamentalism of Hamann to Goethe's or Merck's hostility to Christianity, could be condemned as heresy or Spinozism by the orthodox clergy and could cause plenty of tension among the Stürmer und Dränger themselves, but it held them together in mutual sympathy and a consciousness of a common purpose.

This new conception is already evident in Klopstock's poetry. His *Messias* only hints at a new interpretation, sufficient to cause much controversy amongst theologians, in England as in Germany, but still within the accepted religious terms, since here his exaltation is centred directly on the figure of Christ. But in his odes all his deepest feelings, love, enthusiasm for virtue or nature, are put on the level of religious experience. The poetic language he invented is full of religious metaphor, both spiritualising all secular experience, and providing, as Korff has put it, a ' new and modern ' language of religious experience.[4] Klopstock was incapable of building his frag-mentary poetic intuitions into a new conception of religion. He remained an orthodox Lutheran, and his essay on religious poetry, in which he defines it as a special branch of poetry dealing with religious subjects, shows that he was not conscious of a new meaning in his own work.[5] It was for the Stürmer und Dränger to develop the implications of his poetic idiom in terms of a religious philosophy.

Hamann's whole life was devoted to this task, and though his thought was eccentric, angular, and much more confined in the hothouse of pietistic religious experience than that of the others, it forms their starting-point. Brought up in a rigidly pietistic home, he was comforted by the Bible during his spiritual collapse in London, finding in it the record of his own raptures and distress : ' In the history of the Jewish people I recognised my own backslidings, I read the story of my own life.'[6] From that time he read the Old and New Testaments as symbolical accounts of the life of the soul and sought to identify himself imaginatively with them. His works are starred with Scriptural references which show to what a degree he found a personal meaning in all corners of the Bible.

But Hamann did not, like the normal pietist, distinguish between the sacred and the secular sphere, between a religious and a neutral or sinful world. In the whole of nature and of history he found analogies of spiritual experience.

> All natural phenomena are dreams, visions, riddles, which have their interpretation, their secret meaning. The books of nature and of history are nothing but cyphers, hidden signs, which need the key that expounds Holy Scripture and is the intention of its inspiration.[7]

Such an attitude interpreted the common pietistic practice of ruminating over the symbolical interpretations of nature as found in alchemistic and mystical writers like Paracelsus or Jacob Boehme ; but in Hamann's best period it expresses too his delight in and justification of any intense natural experience, which he could link up with a divine significance. The world seemed to him a living web of meanings, instead of an objective, impersonal structure. In all its parts God may be apprehended. The purpose of life is not moral or intellectual improvement, but a continual kindling of the individual soul through the power of the ' hieroglyphs ' of God. Self-love becomes the primary principle of life—not the calculating self-love of a Frederick the Great, nor the practical and sensual egoism of a Mandeville or Helvétius, but the self-love which finds truth and purpose in rapturous religious experience.

Just as Hamann widened the scope of religious experience to include the whole of the secular world of nature and history, so he included all the faculties of man as channels for the perception of the Divine. He was a man of keen sensitivity, responding ardently to nature and poetry, easily stirred by people and events, emotionally very unstable and subject to strong sexual impulses. Man's consciousness of the Divine, he felt, comes through his feelings and sense, his imagination ; abstractions are anti-Christ, for religion must set the whole personality vibrating. Thus he welcomed the thought of Bacon or Helvétius in so far as they stressed the dependence of ideas on experience, but he gave the meaning of experience a characteristic twist. ' Nature works upon us through senses and passions. . . . Every impression of nature upon man is not only a memorial, but also a pledge of the basic truth :

Who is the Lord.' That is, God can present himself to us earthly men only through the senses, in the form of symbols ; our whole effort must be directed towards full activity of senses and emotions, which reveal the Divine. The stronger the impulse, the more fully it reveals the Divine—thus he frequently uses images of sexual life as examples and symbols of the Divine force. The abstractions of reason, of theology, are not nearer to the truth of God, but further away, since they weaken or destroy the exhilaration of direct irrational contact with God. 'The natural use of the senses must be purified from the unnatural use of abstractions.' [8]

From his first work, *Socratic Memorabilia*, Hamann stressed his indebtedness to the English empiricists and sceptics, to whom he likewise gave a peculiar interpretation. Bacon or Locke were welcome allies, since they insisted on the empirical source of ideas and thus helped him to justify his trust in instinct, feeling, and sense. Hume, whose *Dialogues concerning Natural Religion* he translated, was of even greater help to him, for he used Hume's criticism of the validity of reason in order to justify the simplest, most subjective type of belief.

Cannot you learn at last, you philosophers, that there is no physical link between cause and effect, means and ends, but a spiritual and ideal one, to wit, that of vulgar belief [' Köhlerglaube '], as the greatest earthly historian [Hume] of his motherland and of natural religion has pronounced.[9]

He defends the crudest superstitions as being more true than rational deductions, for the basis of existence is belief. ' Our own existence and the existence of all things outside us must be believed, and can be proved in no other way.'[10] Other thinkers had used the same sort of argument to defend faith. But with Hamann the argument justifies the most subjective, personal faith, the most arbitrary and self-willed belief— ' People of genius ', he wrote to a friend, ' have always been permitted to be ignorant and transgressors of the law.' [11]

This irrational religious philosophy of Hamann is therefore totally distinct from traditional religion. He does not base it on a dualism of soul and body, but, glorying in nature and the flesh as the ' Word ' of God, insists that the sensual world is in every respect a symbol of God, and that the senses and

feelings are religious organs. This religion can be expressed
not in rational exposition or dogma, but through the reproduction in sensuous metaphors and emotive ejaculations of the
apprehension of the Divine. The more intense the sensuous
imagination, the stronger the consciousness of God. Thus he
was a thorn in the flesh not only of orthodox theologians and
rationalists, but even of his own pietistic fellows, who were
shocked at the earthiness of his religious raptures, at his coarseness, his frequent use of sexual metaphors. What was one to
think of a pietist who put the head of a satyr on the title-page
of one of his books, and liked to be called ' Pan ' ?

Hamann's religion has a double significance. He gives a
religious stamp to all aspects of experience, and therefore
justifies feelings, instinctive urges, and sense-perceptions as the
highest human qualities ; the individual in his totality becomes
the vessel and focus of the Divine. His two works, *Golgotha
and Scheblimini* and *Metacritique on the Purism of Reason*, both of
1784, contain shrewd and characteristic criticism of Mendelssohn and Kant, the one for divorcing religion from personal
experience (Revelation), the other for divorcing reason from
experience. But at the same time he always tends to reduce
experience in the last resort to Revelation, and to cut short
all argument by an appeal to convictions which come from a
transcendental sphere. The world is a symbol of the Word,
Logos, and in this Word, sometimes understood as the Biblical
tradition, sometimes as a purely subjective conviction, all problems are resolved. ' I stick to the Letter, to what is visible
and material, as to the finger of a clock :—but behind the
clock face there is the art of the maker, wheels and springs,
which need an apocalypse.' [12]

These twin aspects of Hamann's thought have since then
diverged. It is the latter that appealed to Kierkegaard, the
doctrine that beneath the existential world, where man is
not at home, there is another, the true one. This doctrine
too is most prominent in Hamann's later development, and
in the last years of his life he turned entirely to speculations
on the Logos, the Last Judgment, the Apocalypse, seeking in
cabbalistic brooding what he thought to be the true nature
of life. But it was the first aspect that was of greatest significance to the Sturm und Drang, his justification of all experience,

all inward activity, as good, as divine ; it links on to their interpretation of Spinozism and like the latter partakes as much of materialism as it does of spiritualism.

The characteristic weakness of Hamann's religion is its passivity. It is a religion entirely of surrender to instinctive responses, and lacks any active side ; it transparently betrays his unwillingness or incapacity to face up to the tasks of active and practical life. It is similarly conspicuously lacking in intellectual discipline. His thoughts are fragmentary, loosely connected or even wilfully disconnected, and often he allows the thread of argument to be broken by a rapturous metaphor or obscure reference, by a noisy ejaculation or by religious fargon, as if his mind were too weak to maintain a steady course. His friends often did not understand him, and his enemies dismissed his work as ' chaotic obscurity '.[13] His failings were, however, the inverted expression of his significance, as Goethe shrewdly and sympathetically writes in his autobiography. Here, after pointing out Hamann's hostility to the separation of man's faculties, and the impossibility of preserving the unity of experience in literary expression, he goes on :

Since Hamann sought to speak in the unity in which he felt, imagined and thought, and since he demanded the same of others, he was at loggerheads with his own style and with everything that others wrote. In order to achieve the impossible he stretches out his hand to all the elements : the deepest mysteries, where nature and spirit meet in the secret places, luminous lightnings of reason, which flash out from such contacts, meaningful images which dwell in these regions, telling quotations from sacred and profane authors, and all sorts of humorous interpolations, all this forms the wondrous totality of his writings. . . . When one opens them, their equivocal twilight always appeals to us, though one has to give up the hope of understanding them in the usual sense of the term.[14]

This obscurity of Hamann's writings, their ' sibylline ' style, their scintillating half-light, gave them an added attraction to the young Stürmer und Dränger, reluctant as they were to imprison their intense feeling of the unlimited potentialities of experience in firm and final forms.

Herder was, and considered himself to be, Hamann's pupil

and ally ; their correspondence shows how attentive he was to the older man's criticisms. But, though Herder too was moody and sensitive, he was a much more sturdy character than Hamann, more disciplined, less subject to outbreaks of intellectual waywardness. His religious development was not without its ups and downs, but he became less and less inclined towards passive spiritual receptivity and mystical ruminations. To the end of his life there remained in Herder's thought undigested elements from his religious upbringing and his profession ; but his thought is distinguished by a constant effort to find a comprehensive definition of a common source of scientific thought and subjective intuition, of practical and spiritual life, as we find it in his *Dialogues on God* of 1787 and the *Letters for the Furtherance of Humanity* of 1793–7.

Herder never doubted his calling for the Church and was a preacher with heart and soul. But he had a distaste not only for his administrative duties, but also for liturgy and ceremonial, for dogma, for theology.[15] His sermons deal often, of course, with practical morals, but dwell above all on the feeling of a bountiful God. ' My sermons have nothing but the name in common with other sermons,' he told his betrothed ; and again, ' My sermons are as little clerical as my person, they are human sentiments of a full heart.'[16] His early publications were all on secular topics, classical and modern literature, language, scholarship, history ; when in his reviews for the *Frankfurter Gelehrte Anzeigen* he dealt with theological matters, he provoked Nicolai to a joke about his ' very secular theological articles '.[17] In 1773 he had the misfortune to see his writing publicly branded as unfitting a member of the cloth. He had sharply criticised the inadequacies of Schlözer's *Universal History*, and the latter retaliated in a volume of 200 pages.[18] He asserted that Herder was the instrument of an insidious clique, that he wrote in an unmannerly style completely unfitting a scholar and a clergyman, that he had insulted the whole university of Göttingen and his prince, and he denounced him to his own flock as a vain, malicious, irresponsible braggart : ' what sort of behaviour is this for a clergyman ? '

Schlözer was one of the most influential professors at Göttingen—and it was here that Herder hoped for a chair !

These circumstances must be borne in mind when considering Herder's first expressly religious works, the *Oldest Document of the Human Race* and *To Preachers : Provincial Letters*, both of 1774. Both were written with an eye to a theological appointment ; Caroline states indeed in her *Reminiscences* that the latter was written with the direct intention of strengthening his application.[19] The appointment did not go through, and Herder realised that it was because ' his orthodoxy was in question '.[20] His religious works themselves can hardly have improved his chances. In his first year at Weimar he complained that he was suspected of being ' an atheist, a free thinker, a Socinian, an enthusiast ' [21]—and one must admit there were grounds for confusion about his views. Goethe had a real struggle to get him appointed at Weimar against the wishes of the local clergy.[22]

The most important statement of Herder's religious views in the Sturm und Drang period is contained in his *Oldest Document of the Human Race*. It has been called ' the dominating work of Herder's Bückeburg period ', i.e. of the years between 1770 and 1776 ; [23] and Herder, in a letter to Hamann, recommended it to his old teacher in some such terms.[24] But it is inadvisable to accept Herder's statement at its face value. He had recently quarrelled with Hamann, who was distressed over the secularity of the *Origin of Language*, in which Herder had brushed aside, with a good deal of acerbity, the belief that language had been given to man by God, as told in Genesis. He had broken with Nicolai in 1773, and thus had a double reason for making it up with Hamann. In the first years at Bückeburg he had been strongly under the influence of French thought, and ruefully told Hamann how narrowly he had escaped being a wit ; [25] with his marriage in 1773 he had settled down, in a calmer temper, to his parochial duties, and the *Oldest Document* reflects the extreme of his rebound from intellectualism. But even while he was writing it he was preparing his treatise on epistemology, a work as secular in character as his *Origin of Language*.[26] Unger goes too far, however, in calling the *Oldest Document* ' only an episode ' in the development of Herder's thought.[27] The *Oldest Document*, along with the contemporary *Another Philosophy of History*, represents a crisis in Herder's thought where, as Korff has well said, on the point

of leaving traditional religious paths, Herder sees the ancient
faith illumined by 'a wondrous light'.[28]

Herder's approach to the Bible had hitherto followed in the
wake of Lowth,[29] that is, he had rescued it from the attacks
of scientists and rationalists by emphasising its poetical qualities.
But what had poetry to do with truth? Nicolai had put
this question to him in a letter discussing the intellectual
inadequacy of the emotional response to religion in Klopstock's poetry.[30] Were the results of the emotive, intuitive
response to the world incompatible with those of science and
reason?

Herder begins his work on the Biblical story of the Creation
by a frank acknowledgment of the contrast between it and the
conclusions of modern science. He throws no doubt on the
truth of the discoveries of Descartes, Galileo, Newton, and
Euler. On the contrary he pours scorn on the attempts of the
Church and of theologians to suppress scientific investigation and its conclusions. His attack is directed against two
attitudes : that represented by Voltaire, who had condemned
Genesis as ridiculous because of its own contradictoriness,
e.g. because light is there supposed to exist before the sun was
created ; and that represented by a German theologian,
Michaelis, who had sought to demonstrate that the Biblical
account could be squared with the results of modern science.
Perhaps the recent controversy over Buffon was in Herder's
mind, for the latter, when challenged by the Sorbonne, had
asserted that his account of the history of the earth's crust was
anticipated by Genesis, the 'days' of Creation symbolising
epochs of nature ; many theologians, like Needham, had found
in Buffon's type of argument a means to reconcile revelation
and science.

Herder's studies in the poetry and language of primitive
peoples made him aware of the absurdity of this approach ;
more importantly still, in his view, such an interpretation of
the Bible took away from it all its specific meaning and character. He defends Genesis, not as a clumsy anticipation of
modern knowledge, but in its own historical character.

Science, he affirms, describes the world in terms of our
modern consciousness ; its results are truth as known to the
modern mind. Genesis is the product of a primitive pastoral

LENZ
After a drawing by H. Pfenninger

LAVATER
From Lavater's ' Physiognomische Fragmente '

IV

V.   KLINGER, 1775
A drawing by Goethe

people, and describes the Creation in terms of their experience. Moses had to manage without physics and metaphysics ; why should not physics and metaphysics manage without Moses ? Why expect the one or the other to present the whole truth ? It is spiritual presumption to believe that man can know truth as it really is, truth in its inmost being. The truth we can arrive at is ' nothing but a collection and structure of human concepts, assembled from outside, within our sphere of life, according to the nature of our organs '.[31] All modes of perception and thought lead to truth, but all differ according to the different social and human constitution in changing times and places. Criticism of the one truth by another is ridiculous ; each is justified in relation to the men and society who shape it.

This argument is an interesting combination of Hume's scepticism with Montesquieu's historical relativism. Herder had already applied the same method in his defence of Shakespeare as the poet of ' Nordic man ' and of Elizabethan times, in contrast to the Greeks. But just as his essay on Shakespeare culminated in an unqualified preference for Shakespeare, so his argument for the validity of both the Mosaic and the Newtonian cosmology turns rapidly into an enthusiastic exposition of the superiority of the Genesis account.

The main part of the work is devoted to his interpretation of the story of the Creation in terms of the simple sense-experience which in his view inspired it. He sees it as a description of the dawn. The primitive shepherds of ancient Israel saw this miracle daily, and it was for them the supreme symbol of God's creative power ; through it they were daily filled with the grateful consciousness of the divine force. This is not a ' true ' description of the origin of the universe or of God, for both appear in a form determined by the limited experience and nature of the early Hebrews ; but it is fuller, truer, than the modern metaphysical, rationalist conception of God, because God is a living reality for these shepherds, vibrating throughout their whole being, not an abstract construct of their minds. And for modern man, too, this symbol of God is truer, more significant and satisfactory than the Newtonian abstraction, since it sums up the totality of the creative force and appeals with intense power to man's imagination and feeling. This conception of God expresses, in fact, the energy of Leibniz's monads, the forces of nature, that is, the deepest insight of modern science, better than the abstract God of physicists and theologians.

For our philosopher, God is a metaphysical Something ! an exalted Somebody, and this feeling is so sublime that he can say and think nothing about him : the Deist-religion scorns the simple who have to make a Something, an image, a symbol of the God to whom they pray, in whom they trust, who has created them and who preserves them every moment through his might—— But if there must be image, symbol, if sensual, reverent humanity (call it superstitious, if you will, as these gentlemen insist) has need of such : what in the whole world of beings is a more beautiful, splendid, all-gladdening image of the revelation of God than— Light ! . . . What earlier, simpler symbol of Good and Evil than Light and Darkness.[32]

The truth of Genesis is therefore both particular and universal.   Herder had already asserted that the unique power and beauty of early poetry, of folksong, Homer, and Shakespeare, was due to its source in the vigorous, active, sensuous life of communities not yet split by the division of labour, where men's relations to one another and to nature were not yet muddied by speculation and calculation.[33]   The truth of Genesis, like its poetical power, arises likewise from the vigorous character of early patriarchal society and the essential, elemental nature of its tasks, which engage the whole man ; for this reason the account in Genesis gives a wonderfully apt image of the relations of God with his creation.   In this sense Genesis is ' the oldest document of the human race '.   It has the essential characteristic of truth in that it impresses itself on our whole being, and not merely on the mind.   It arises from ' perception, evidence, sign, experience ' and truth lies ' in the total, unfragmented, deep feeling of things '.[34]

In the later parts of the book Herder seeks to interpret the religious wisdom of the ancient civilisations of the Near East as splinters of this original truth, but he loses his way in daring hypotheses and speculations.   The central thesis of the *Oldest Document* is taken up in two other works of the same year. *Another Philosophy of History* [35] will claim our attention in another context (Chapter VII), and here we need only take note of its religious implications. The object of the work was to attack those writers who exalted modern times as the climax and purpose of all past history, and who asserted that God's purpose could be comprehended as the growth of reason, law, and order. In the early part of the book Herder shows how the succession of the Hebrew, Egyptian, Phoenician, Greek, and Roman cultures is not a simple progress ; each culture has specific qualities which are absent in the others. He shows how these qualities develop according to the material circumstances and occupations of these peoples, insists that it was God's method to work through such natural means, and thus lays the basis for a scientific study of history as the interaction of man and circumstance. This part of the book is developed in his major work on the philosophy of history, the *Ideas*.

But in the main part of *Another Philosophy of History*, the very possibility of a scientific approach to history is denied. It is a sweeping attack on modern society in all its aspects, and particularly on the modern state. Herder does not attempt to discover a principle of social development, but insists ove rand over again that the outcome has been disastrous for personal life. Man is ' an ant on the wheel of fate ' and cannot possibly find a rational meaning to modern history. A meaning may be surmised only if we consider the world in terms of God, not of man, only if we look for a standpoint outside the human race, outside this world.[36] Herder's words often take on a prophetic, fanatical note, especially where he avoids the issues raised by his contemporaries ; his call to religious adoration in place of scientific study seems a *salto mortale*, resulting from violent tensions and untamed moods ; or rather, a leap in the dark, without confidence or serenity.

The little work *To Preachers: Provincial Letters*, which is couched in far less extravagant language than the two greater works of 1774, clarifies certain of the fundamental principles of the *Oldest Document*—though one cannot say it has any of the subtle irony and penetration of Pascal's work, the title of which Herder borrowed. Herder here advises preachers to avoid turning their sermons into philosophical or moral disquisitions ; even more to avoid turning religion into a buttress of the State. Religion must be living experience, it must engage the whole personality.

' The education of children grows out of experience and history ; the former opens eyes and senses, the latter ears and thoughts : therefore let religious instruction do both.' [37]   The Bible is the supreme means ' to nourish most deeply the soul, and for ever ; to enlarge it gradually, but in all its powers : the imagination begins to acquire brightness and clarity ; judgment, still a closed, fragrant bud, begins to break forth ; natural bents gradually emerge like shoots from the seed of the tender plant ; the essence of man develops its powers as it does its limbs.—And behold, the great vehicle of education, the history of religion . . . not intended as a primer of sugary moral examples, but for the whole development of human powers through the revelation of God.' [38] The preacher ' strengthens the whole man ; the sentient and credulous obscure forces, resting on authority, and yet so living and active, on which everything in life depends, as well as our small capacity for clear understanding.' [39]

There is no special organ of religion in man, there is no division into ' higher ' and ' lower ' faculties ; [40] religion consists in, and promotes, the full development of all sides of man.

Finally, the whole of religion is, essentially and fundamentally, fact ! history ! Built on the witness of the senses and not merely of the higher mental powers ; upon faith, that embraces all powers. Directed, according to its purpose and content, to the common people, the largest, more sensual portion of mankind, and not to brooding thinkers, in order to transform their being and language and guide them with all their instincts.[41]

In these works of Herder, then, we find the same double-edged conception of religion as in Hamann.   On the one hand they are a call to a simple faith, to simple immersion in the Bible ; but on the other hand they find the justification of this faith in the intensification of all-sided experience.   Faith is not a matter only for the soul, the organ of the divinity, not a means to a sentimental or moralising religiosity, such as was advocated by writers like Matthias Claudius ; it is the expression, and the means to, an enhanced vigour of senses and feeling in combination with mind, to full development of all human capacities.

The *Oldest Document* caused a considerable stir in intellectual circles in Germany, and not least because of its tone.   If the content was heretical, the tone was parsonic in the worst sense, arrogant, fanatical, and obscure. The work is full of intolerant and unjust criticism of contemporary theologians, to some of whom, such as Michaelis, Herder owed a considerable debt, and the few passages of imaginative insight are almost lost in a welter of presumptuous hypotheses and tortured ejaculations. Nicolai and such could dismiss it as the work of a fanatical zealot. Hamann and Lavater admired it intensely, not least for the support it gave to a fundamentalist reading of the Bible. More interesting is the reaction of those Stürmer und Dränger who were not attracted to the specifically Christian aspects of the work, Merck and Goethe.

Merck's opinion was given in a letter to Nicolai, and it reflects to some extent the opinions of the addressee ; but the distaste Merck felt is undoubtedly genuine :

Herder is like a man who rides through the streets on horseback in his dressing gown, and demands into the bargain that everybody should approve, and approve his reasons too. The arrogance of the headings, the beggarly pretentiousness of the quotations, and then the whole wayward style must revolt everybody. These trumpetings over a rubbishy hypothesis . . . were and are extremely unnecessary.

But, though Merck calls it ' the most revolting book ever written ', even to Nicolai he adds : ' Yet it is dear and estimable to me as the imprint of Herder's mind.' [42]

What Merck liked about the book was more fully expressed by Goethe. When visiting Jung-Stilling Goethe fell in with a company of pietists who criticised Herder's work, but he defended it warmly. What he said can be guessed from a letter he wrote at about the same time :

The *Oldest Document* is such a mystic whole, flashing so many meanings, a living, revolving world throwing out such a profusion of twining branches, that neither can a foreshortened sketch reproduce the effect of its giant form, nor can a faithful silhouette of its separate parts strike a melodiously sympathetic note in the soul. He has descended into the depths of his feelings, has stirred up there all the lofty holy power of simple nature, and now leads them up into the wide world with Orphean song, sometimes dark like early dawn, sometimes flashing like sheet lightning, here and there decked with the smiles of morning.[43]

As contrasted to Merck, Goethe here shows his appreciation of the allusive, wayward style ; but like Merck he values it above all not as an interpretation of Genesis but of Herder's own impulsive, imaginative personality, of the ' holy power of simple nature '.

Goethe made his attitude clear in a letter of the following year, on receiving two smaller religious works from Herder :

> I've got your books and refreshed myself with them. God knows, that is a world known through feeling ! A vitalised rubbish heap ! And so, Thanks ! Thanks !—I had to mark all the pages with pencil to indicate the argument and yet—— If only the whole doctrine of Christ were not such a mucky affair that sends me crazy, limited, needy man that I am, I should also like the theme. God or devil so treated is dear to me, for he is my brother. —And so in all your being I do not feel the shell and veil out of which pop your Castors or Harlequins, but the never-changing brother, man, God, worm and clown.—Your way of sweeping— and not just to sieve gold out of your sweepings, but to palingenesise them into a living plant—always makes me go down on the knees of my heart.[44]

Goethe was nearer than he knew to a true interpretation of Herder's religion ; its meaning lay not in the religious formulation or content, but in the assertion of the creative urges of man.

In spite of Herder's genuine love of Old and New Testament, of his veneration for his Church and his office as clergyman, it is very questionable whether his religion can be called Christian. In *Another Philosophy of History*, though he writes most tenderly of the Hebrew patriarchs, he shows an equal veneration for the spiritual achievements of the ancient Egyptians and Greeks— indeed for any community whose spiritual values grow out of an undivided totality of activity, feeling, and direct experience. At this time and later he expressed somewhat violently his regret that primitive Germanic society and religion had been disrupted by Charlemagne and the introduction of Christianity : a religion which divided thinkers and priests from the rest of the active community, and which taught men to be pious, passive, slaves. ' Was not Arminius good enough to be a God for you ? '[45] In the *Ideas on the Philosophy of History* he comes near to defining Christianity as the religion appropriate to a particular stage of cultural development, an interpretation fully developed by the young Hegel.

During the 1770s Herder did not find a satisfactory formulation of his outlook on religion. He wavers between a secular intellectual and an exalted religious approach to problems. Even in his religious writings, where he insists on the reliability of religious intuition and on the need for an inward, intuitive source of value and activity, he recognises the changing form such intuition takes in history and therefore its relativity. Close to pietism in his surrender to a purely emotive, immediate religious feeling, he was at all times remote from it in his refusal to accept the belief that the content of such feeling, any particular dogma, was generally and absolutely valid. For many years he sought to define his position clearly—an extremely difficult task, for as a clergyman he was actually engaged in preaching a particular religion and carrying out the offices of a particular cult. It was no doubt his fear of unpleasant consequences that made him refuse to allow his correspondence with Lessing to be published. But the great controversy over Spinoza in the 1780s brought him to clarity.

F. H. Jacobi was responsible for its beginning. Shortly after Lessing's death in 1781 Jacobi let it be known that in a conversation Lessing had admitted to him that he was a Spinozist. Mendelssohn, Lessing's old friend and a leading deist, refuted Jacobi's assertions, and Jacobi began to write a book which was a refutation of Spinozism and a defence of the idea of intuitive religious feeling and a personal God. He visited Weimar in 1784 and discussed the whole problem with Goethe and Herder. These two, at that time working in closest harmony in their separate fields of natural science and philosophy of history, both declared themselves for Spinoza. Herder's letters contain an express avowal. He calls Lessing a ' co-believer ' of his, and while criticising Spinoza's mode of argument asserts that he is the only philosopher who has given systematic form to his own fundamental beliefs.

The Spinozist philosophy is the only one which is at one with itself. . . . The basic error, dear Jacobi, in your system, and that of all anti-Spinozists, is that God is an abstract concept, a O ; but for Spinoza he is the most real, most active unity, that

speaks to itself, ' I am that I am, and shall be in all the transformations of my appearance what I shall be.' What you mean,
you dear people, with your ' existence outside the world ', I do
not understand ; if God does not exist in the world, everywhere
in the world, and everywhere unmeasured, whole and indivisible,
then he exists nowhere.   There is no space outside the world ; space
comes into being as a world comes into being for us, as the abstraction of a phenomenon.   Just as little can a limited personality
be applied to the Infinite Being, since personality comes into
existence with us only through limitation.   This fantasy must be
dropped in the concept of God, he is the highest, most living,
most active One ; not in all things, as if the latter were something
outside him, but through all things, which appear as sensuous
expressions for sensual creatures.

And again, later in the year :

God is, it is true, outside you and works in and through all
creatures (I do not recognise an extra-mundane God).   But what
is a God, if he is not in you and you do not feel and taste his Being
in an infinitely inward fashion, and if he does not enjoy himself
in you as an organ among his thousand million organs ?   You
want a God in a human form, as a friend who thinks of you.   But
consider : if so, he must think of you in a human, i.e. a limited,
way, and if he is your partisan, then he must be the partisan of
others.   Say then, why do you need him in human form ?   He
speaks to you, he works upon you through all noble human forms.
. . .   You therefore enjoy God only and always according to your
inner self ; and so he is the source and root of the most spiritual
eternal life in you, unchanging and indestructible. . . .   If you
make this innermost, highest, all-embracing concept into an empty
name, it is you who are the Atheus, not Spinoza ; according to
him he is the Being of Beings, Jehovah.   I must confess, this
philosophy makes me very happy.[46]

Herder had felt drawn to Spinoza for many years.   In 1775
he had recommended his friend Gleim to read him,[47] and
had planned for some time a work on Spinoza, Shaftesbury,
and Leibniz.   There are references to Spinoza in *On Knowledge
and Perception,* which he had started in 1774 and published in
1778, and many traces of pantheism in his *Ideas.*   In 1787 he
summed up his religious attitude in the work *Dialogues on God,*
a work he re-published in 1800 and considered his final state-

ment on religion. He said he had begun this work twelve years before.[48]

The *Dialogues on God* cannot be considered as belonging to his Sturm und Drang. But, in showing his development out of the Sturm und Drang, it brings to light some of the fundamental features of the earlier period. The differences are marked. The emotional pessimism of *Another Philosophy of History* has changed to a serene acceptance of the world. Agitation over an inscrutable fate in whose hands men are helpless has changed to reverent awe before the divine necessity which controls all things. The thunderous, ostentatious exaltation of the *Oldest Document* has been replaced by joyous contemplation. The workings of the divinity are now seen, not merely in the sacred texts of the Bible, but in the whole of creation. God is not to be apprehended in inner visions, but through the loving study of his creation. But though science now takes the place of imaginative experience as the chief means to know God, there is much of the Sturm und Drang in this mature philosophy of Herder. As ever, he is opposed to an abstract conception of God, a God deduced by metaphysical reasoning, a God outside the world. God can only be considered to be real in so far as he is an active force in the world and in us, as he is evident to sense and feeling. God's purposes cannot be known, they cannot be interpreted in terms of human judgments and intentions. The resolute and serene affirmation of the universe as divine, which pervades this work, arises not from argumentation about God, but from a deep feeling of the goodness of life, an affirmation which has the same subjective source as the alternating rapture and despair of his earlier works. At all times Herder's religion arises from this vital love of life, it expresses his consciousness of inexhaustible sources of delight in life, welling up first through love and poetry, and later extending to the study of history and nature ; to the end of his life he opposed all metaphysics and mysticism.[49]

As with most Shaftesburian Spinozists, Herder's religious attitude has not cleared itself of the preconceptions of orthodox religion or of deism.[50] The God of this pantheistic universe always threatens to take in his imagination the form of a good and wise father, which provokes the traditional Christian feelings of gratefulness, love, and awe. Further, he shares the optimism of the deists, which had caused him to defend Shaftesbury against the charge of atheism as early as 1770.

> An atheist who preaches nothing so much as order, harmony and highest wisdom in the structure of the world, the first to bring optimism home to the heart . . . such an atheist, with his World-Spirit (to me the most sublime name for God), is more to me than ten philosophical botchers.[51]

But such optimistic enthusiasm, deriving from the contemplation of the universe as a whole, tends to blur the individual reality of things, and to encourage self-delusion. It is only too often that one finds Herder, therefore, asserting with unsubstantiated conviction the goodness and divinity of the world, and soaring beyond experience and reason.

The contradictions within Herder's religious thought are even more evident if his works of exegesis and edification are contrasted with his more general, philosophical writings. In the former he is writing or speaking directly to believers, not to the broader circle of his intellectual contemporaries, and the terms he uses remain within the sphere of Christian doctrine : in them he often seems close to Hamann. This is partly true of the *Provincial Letters*, themselves addressed ' to preachers ', in which he asserts that all history of man, all natural history, is in essence the revelation of God, and has meaning ' only from the standpoint of Revelation '.[52] In his commentary on St. John's Gospel it is not easy to see whether he interprets ' In the beginning was the Word ' symbolically or literally. To some extent he interprets ' the Word ', like Goethe's Faust, as the archetypal act of will, ' the first shaping of what is to come, energy and deed ' ; to some extent he takes the Word as the direct message of God.[53] Later in the same work, polemising against the rationalists who tried to find a natural, semi-scientific explanation for the miracles of Christ, he insists on the literal truth of miracles, on the presence of ' God's angels and forces ', which true faith perceives.[54] It is lost labour to try to reconcile these differences. Herder was impulsive and often inconsequent ; he was deeply attached to his childhood's religion and his profession, though his thought in many ways did not fit in with them ; he was influenced by the particular purpose of a work, the circle he was addressing. But we can have no doubt as to the relative importance of his various works ; those into which he threw the greatest energy, which he believed to be the completest statement of his views, are not the more orthodox works of exegesis and edification, but the *Oldest Document, Another Philosophy of History*, the *Ideas*, and the *Dialogues on God*. And the dominant character of his religious thought is its secular and dynamic humanism : the rejection of traditional Christian dualism, the conception of God as a symbol of the oneness and goodness of the universe, as the seal of Herder's belief in the goodness of all those powers in man which link his life with nature.

Goethe's religious feeling was the least spiritualistic, the most humanistic in the Sturm und Drang group. The atmosphere of his youth was not tensely charged with pietism, as was the case with Hamann, Herder, and Lenz, and he experienced neither the religious tortures, nor the ecstasies, that were their lot. His tolerant and somewhat rationalist religious upbringing led him to slip easily, at Leipzig, into the attitude of a freethinker. But even here, his need to feel that his existence was rooted personally in the universe brought him into friendly relationship with a devoutly religious older man, Langer. On returning to Frankfurt he found his mother and sister were members of a pietist community, and during his illness he too took part in their meetings. He shared their religious exercises, their hymns and discussions of the state of their souls, their search for a feeling of identity with a loving Christ ; and for a time, though he confessed himself ' no Christian ', he did not give up hope of becoming one. He wrote to Langer that the latter's urgings were bearing fruit, ' love and tolerance towards religion, a friendly feeling towards the Gospel, a holier veneration for the Word '. But he was conscious, and so were his pietist friends, of big obstacles from his worldly interests, ' his ardent head, his wit, and his endeavour and fairly justified hope of becoming an author '. ' The Brothers look on me as a man who has a good will and some feeling, but is too dissipated by his attachment to the world—and they are not mistaken.' [55]

This religion seemed warm, substantial, meaningful, compared with the ' unevangelical chatter of our modern pulpits '. But Goethe's love of life, and his lively intellect, could not be satisfied by it for long. When the pietists met in his mother's house, the meeting turned into something ' like a party ', with wine and sausage and rolls, a piano and two flutes, and gay lights. But always ' weakness in faith '.[56] In November 1769 Goethe's letter to Langer is full of his revived artistic interests, and about his pietist mentors he writes with curt disdain that they are ' in their old state of inanition and stupidity without the least sign of ever emerging out of it '.[57] When he first arrived at Strassburg, he took up with the pietist community there, but soon broke with them—he wrote to his mother's pietist friend, the Fräulein von Klettenberg, that he could not bear the narrowness and boredom of their company.[58] Indeed, he came to be known at Strassburg as a Voltairean, a ' crazy scorner of religion '.[59]

But this judgment was not just. During the whole of his Sturm und Drang Goethe retained a deep sympathy for believing souls, for men and women like Jung-Stilling, Lavater, Fräulein von Klettenberg ; but at the same time he considered the content of religious belief to be quite arbitrary and ranked himself among the unbelievers.   To Herder and Merck he wrote quite openly, calling Christianity a ' mucky affair '.[60] Kestner's jottings on his character in 1772 give a reliable impression of Goethe's views at that time :

He is not what is called orthodox, but not out of pride or caprice in order to make himself important. He speaks of certain main issues to few people, and does not like disturbing others in their quiet convictions. He hates scepticism, strives for truth and for clarity on certain main issues, and thinks he is clear on the most important : but so far as I have observed he is not as yet. He does not go to church, nor to communion, and he rarely prays. For, he says, I am not liar enough for that. . . . He reveres the Christian religion, but not in the form our theologians give it.[61]

Religious faith was for Goethe essentially the expression of the goodness of life, delight in life with all its vexations and tensions. He understood that it can and must take different forms with different peoples, with different individuals, but that these forms have no more than a personal or local validity. His doctoral dissertation in its first form sought to show that Christianity was the product of Christ's successors, not of Christ himself, and was only a specific and temporary clothing of its true spirit. From the beginning he had a particular distaste for the doctrine of sin and contrition, for the tone of 'fear and trembling ',[62] for all religion that directs men away from life. On Good Friday, 1773, he wrote to Johanna Fahlmer of the lovely spring they were having, expressing the hope that she would be more edified by the 'holy life' than the 'holy grave '.[63] Faith for him was trust in life, love of life. He defined his youthful attitude very accurately in *Poetry and Truth* :

In religious faith, I used to say, the important thing is *that* one should believe ; *what* one believes is of no concern. Faith is a great feeling of security for the present and the future, and this security arises out of our confidence in a grandiose, all-mighty, and inscrutable Being. Everything depends on the steadfastness of this confidence ; but the manner in which we think of this Being depends on our other capacities, yes even on our circumstances, and is of absolutely no concern.[64]

When the wife of his friend Fritz Jacobi asked him about the religious education of her children, he wrote : ' Whether they believe in Christ, or Götz, or Hamlet, it's all one, but see that they do believe in something. If you don't believe in something you despair about yourself.' [65]

From this point of view he felt a deep sympathy for his religious friends. Fräulein von Klettenberg ' stood to Christ as to a beloved ', Lavater ' as to a friend ',[66] and Goethe respected in their faith the sublimated expression of their capacity for love and friendship. Of the fundamentalist Jung-Stilling he writes :

The element of his energy was an indestructible faith in God and in His power of sending aid. . . . The trend of his mind attracted me, and I did not interfere with his belief in miracles, which stood him in such good stead.[67]

Lavater wrote of Goethe :

He is the most crushing Hercules of all presumptuousness. Yet no one is more just in his verbal judgment of others—no one more tolerant than he. I have seen him with Basedow and

Hasenkamp [a rigid pietist]—among Herrnhuters and mystics, menfolk and womenfolk . . . and always the same noble, penetrating, tolerant man.[68]

Like his Faust he would hold his own beliefs, and leave others undisturbed in theirs : ' I wouldn't rob anyone of their feeling and church.' [69]

It was thus without artifice that Goethe could write two little religious pamphlets in the manner of a clergyman.   Both show the influence of Rousseau's *Savoyan Vicar*.   In the *Letter of the pastor at *** to the new pastor at ****, an old clergyman exhorts a newcomer to tolerance.   Luther, he says, did not intend to establish a church and orthodoxy, but ' gave the heart its freedom again, made it more capable of love '. Religion consists of ' inexpressible emotions ', and to insist that men must feel what they may be incapable of, or that their feelings are damnable unless they are formulated in an orthodox way, is ' tyrannical nonsense '.[70]   In *Two important hitherto unexamined Biblical Questions* Goethe tries to distinguish between the universal and particular in the Mosaic law.   ' The only useful religion must be simple and warm ', the only true religion must rise ' from the deepest, holiest feeling '.   ' If the eternal Spirit throws a glance of his wisdom, a spark of his love into one of his chosen, let him step forth and stammer his feeling.' [71]

This was Goethe in his mild vein.   But narrowness and intolerance could make him boil over with fury or ridicule. The pietists at Jung-Stilling's, when Goethe visited him in 1774, provoked him with their narrow-minded strictures on Klopstock and Herder.

> Goethe could not keep his seat.   He danced round the table, pulled faces, and showed in every way, in his usual fashion, what a royal pleasure the company gave him . . .   They [the pietists] thought, God bless us, the man can't be in his right wits.[72]

When he heard of the suicide of his acquaintance Jerusalem, the son of a well-known clergyman, he wrote to Kestner in a violent rage :

> The unhappy man.   But those devils, those abominable men who enjoy nothing but the chaff of vanity and who delight in

idols and preach idolatry, and dam up healthy nature, and over-strain and pervert man's powers, they bear the guilt for this misfortune, our misfortune, may the devil take them, their brother. If that cursed parson his father isn't responsible, God forgive me for wishing he breaks his neck like Eli.[73]

Goethe's home circumstances, and his resilience and self-confidence, were such that personally he did not suffer more than vexation from the orthodox who wanted to change or convert him. And this vexation found a vent in his farces, outbursts which he did not take too seriously but which tell us a good deal about his feelings. *Pater Brey* is a skit in the manner of Hans Sachs, but this hypocritical priest has an eighteenth-century smirk on his sixteenth-century face : [74]

Er meynt, die Welt könnt nicht bestehen
Wenn er nicht thät drauf herumhergehen
Bildt sich ein wunderliche Streich
Von seinem himmlisch geistgen Reich
Meynt, er wolle die Welt verbessern
Ihre Glückseeligkeit vergrössern
Und lebt ein jedes doch fort an
So übel und so gut es kann.
Er denkt, er trägt die Welt aufm Rücken
Fäng' er uns nur einweil die Mücken !
Aber da ist nichts recht und gut
Als was Herr Pater selber thut.
Thät gerne eine Stadt abbrennen
Weil er sie nicht hat bauen können
Findts verflucht, dass ohn' ihn zu fragen
Die Sonne sich auf und ab kann wagen. . . .

He thinks the world would be undone
If he didn't strut about thereon,
Ponders with no end of pride
The heavenly realm he has inside.
Thinks he'll make the world progress
And multiply its happiness,
Yet all go on from day to day
As well or badly as they may.
He thinks his back holds the world up—
If only he'd drive the flies from our soup !

But nothing's right and nothing goes
Saving what the Parson does.
He'd be glad to burn the houses down
Just because he didn't build the town.
He swears at the sun, since without his leave
It rises at morn and sets at eve. . . .

With the same hilarity Goethe made fun of Wieland's milk-
and-water religion, which ' condemns any truth, greatness,
goodness, or beauty outside itself'.[75] And, at the opposite
extreme, he poked fun at the mystic mumbo-jumbo by which
a satyr seduces the people from their normal, sensible creed
and life : a satire of the unbalanced enthusiasm of Herder.[76]

It was clearly more than Goethe's tolerant sympathy with
religious folk that attached Lavater or Jung-Stilling to him,
and made them overlook such irreverent outbursts. In his
capacity for feeling, his love of persons and of nature, they
found something akin to their own attitudes ; and while they
felt that Christ was the source of their raptures, Goethe, too,
often expressed this self-surrender to emotion in religious
terms. The intense vibrations of his being brought him the
consciousness of being subject to something greater than himself, of being part of the great process of being, of nature.
This experience he recognised to be analogous to the religious
feeling of his pietist friends, and he frequently uses religious
symbols to express it. But the divinity of which he speaks is
not any particular one, not Christ, not a God outside or above
the world, but a God whose reality exists only within nature
and within the ' inexpressible feelings ' of the human heart.
Thus Werther, surrendering himself to the creativeness of
spring, feels in the sprouting grasses and the myriad insects
' the presence of the Almighty, the breath of the All-Loving ' ;
he feels his soul to be ' the mirror of the infinite God '.[77] Even
though destruction belongs to this God, as much as creation,
Werther worships him. But characteristically, in his distress
he rejects the advice of his friend to find a refuge from his
anguish in the ' consolations ' of religion. Using terms from
the passion of Christ he cries :

Is it not the fate of man to suffer his fill, to drink the cup ? . . .
Why should I pretend it tastes sweet ? . . . Is it not the voice

of the oppressed creature, insufficient to itself, irresistibly hurled into the depths, groaning from the abyss of its vainly struggling powers : My God, my God, why hast Thou forsaken me.[78]

It is possible, indeed, to discover an analogy between Werther and Christ ; the title might be rendered *The Passion of Werther* as aptly as *The Sorrows*.

In the two lyrics, *Prometheus* and *Ganymed*, the religious and irreligious implications of this attitude are made manifest, as they are in *Faust*. Prometheus is the symbol of the rebel, continuing on his way in blasphemous spite of the Gods, subject only to ' fate and time '. Ganymed yields to Zeus, is caught up rapturously in the embrace of God, the summation of all the mighty ' holy ' yearnings awakened in him by the spring, the flowers, the morning wind, the nightingale.[79] The *Prometheus* lyric was printed by Jacobi as a text in his discussion of Pantheism ; but *Ganymed* might have been quoted equally well.

In Faust the rebellious and yielding aspects are brought into tragic juxtaposition. He has freed himself from theology, religion : ' fearing neither hell nor devil ' he seeks the ' living forces of nature ', the ' living nature ' in which God created man. The love that Gretchen awakens in him is the revelation of God, and the channel to God ; when she anxiously questions her lover about his tenets, he answers in words which sum up Goethe's own belief : [80]

> Wer darf ihn nennen ?
> Und wer bekennen :
> Ich glaub ihn !
> Wer empfinden ?
> Und sich unterwinden
> Zu sagen : ich glaub ihn nicht !
> Der Allumfasser,
> Der Allerhalter
> Fasst und erhält er nicht
> Dich, mich, sich selbst !
> Wölbt sich der Himmel nicht dadroben ?
> Liegt die Erde nicht hierunten fest ?
> Und steigen hüben und drüben
> Ewige Sterne nicht herauf !
> Schau ich nicht Aug in Auge dir
> Und drängt nicht alles

I

Nach Haupt und Herzen dir
Und webt in ewigem Geheimniss
Unsichtbaar Sichtbaar neben dir !
Erfüll davon dein Herz, so gros es ist,
Und wenn du ganz in dem Gefühle seelig bist,
Nenn das dann wie du willst,
Nenn's Glük ! Herz ! Liebe ! Gott !
Ich habe keinen Nahmen
Dafür. Gefühl ist alles,
Nahme Schall und Rauch,
Umnebelnd Himmels Glut.

Who can give Him a name
And who proclaim
I believe in Him ?
Who can feel,
And steel his will
To say : I don't believe in Him ?
He who embraces all,
He who sustains all,
Does He not embrace and sustain
You, me, Himself !
Are not the heavens arched overhead ?
Does not the earth lie firm below ?
And the eternal stars
Do they not rise with friendly glance ?
Do I not gaze into your eyes,
And do you not feel a flood
Surging into heart and head ?
Are not all things seen and unseen
Woven beside you in eternal mystery ?
Fill your heart with this feeling, great as it is,
And when you find full bliss in it,
Give it whatever name you please,
Call it rapture ! heart ! love ! God !
I have no name for it.
Feeling is all ;
Name is noise and smoke
Obscuring the glow of Heaven.

The context of this passionate declaration is of the greatest significance. Faust's belief is contrasted to Gretchen's simple faith and observance, which is anchored in her way of life. His outburst immediately precedes her seduction. That is,

Faust's faith is not only in conflict with the Christian religion as it actually exists, but also with the morality it upholds. His God is only a projection of his ardent feeling, and justifies his surrender to his passion.

But Goethe's religion is never purely subjectivist. The deep and permanent sympathy he felt for Spinoza's doctrine indicates how closely he felt his inner life was bound with the reality of the universe. The rebellion of his Prometheus against the Gods is sustained by his veneration for the mighty universal forces, ' time and fate ' ; Werther's subjectivism links him with the ' divine ' forces of nature. So Goethe's highly personal religious feeling is sustained, like Faust's, by a blissful consciousness of being one with the universal process ; his joy in life arises not merely from an intense feeling of individual life, but also from consciousness of being a part, an instrument of a whole. It was this veneration for the whole process of ' living nature ' that gave a religious character to so many of his utterances, and brought him near to devoutly religious folk —just as it made him so dangerous an enemy to religion.

His attitude did not change essentially as he matured, though he stressed in later life the laws of the universe rather than the subjective response of the individual. The veneration expressed in the ode, *Grenzen der Menschheit*, seems the very opposite of Prometheus' revolt, and the tone and temper of the two poems form a striking contrast ; yet the Gods whom Goethe here adores with childlike devotion are not very different from the ' time and fate ' that Prometheus recognises as his masters—they are remote, impersonal symbols of a permanence which is beyond human reach. The moral ideal expressed in *Das Göttliche* is the opposite of that of Faust or Werther : ' Let man be noble, helpful and good.' But the ' theology ' of this ode is only a new variation on an old theme. Man's Gods have no independent existence ; they are images he makes in the likeness of his own best qualities :

> Und wir verehren
> Die Unsterblichen,
> Als wären sie Menschen,
> Täten im Grossen,
> Was der Beste im Kleinen
> Tut oder möchte.

> And we revere
> The Immortals,
> As if they were men,
> And did in the large
> What the best in the small
> Does or would wish to do.

The same thought makes Faust tolerant of the people's celebration of Easter :

> Sie feiern die Auferstehung des Herrn,
> Denn sie sind selber auferstanden.

> They celebrate the resurrection of the Lord,
> For they themselves are risen again.

Some of Goethe's friends were not only repelled by his growing coldness at Weimar, but shocked by his growing paganism.   F. L. Stolberg, with whom he had gone on the gay journey to Switzerland in 1775, was in the following year appalled at Goethe's refusal to accept revealed religion, at his ' obdurate defiance '.[81]   Fritz Jacobi, his bosom friend in 1774, who learned from Goethe ' to hearken only to the voice of my own heart ', now expressed the greatest alarm at his lack of religion and morality : ' Goethe is without God, without a friend, without virtue.' [82]   But this was an unjust outbreak of personal vexation, and Jacobi later entered into appreciative, if distant, relations with his old friend.   This is not the place to discuss Goethe's later attitude to religion. He remained a thorn in the flesh of the orthodox and religious moralists and a butt of their attacks ; when he used religious terms he gave them a new and clearly symbolical meaning which removed them from their normal Christian context. But he could still appreciate the subjective meaning of faith, as he shows in the *Confessions of a Beautiful Soul*, as the effluence and image of a particular type of personality, though with no wider validity.[83]   Even *Iphigenie*, which has been called a Christian interpretation of the Greek Gods, has this characteristic ambiguity ; for Iphigenie does not hesitate to modify the cult and interpretation of the Gods at the behest of her own heart, and obdurately abandons her duties to Diana and her moral obligations to the barbarians for the sake of family and home. Lavater hit the nail on the head when he said that Goethe was ' the warmest friend and the most dangerous enemy of religion and virtue '.[84]

It was the undogmatic, subjective interpretation of religion that brought Lavater into the orbit of the Sturm und Drang. He was a clergyman almost exclusively concerned with religious affairs, and it was only in the short period of his intimacy with Goethe and his friendly correspondence with Herder that he came into touch with secular thought and *belles lettres*. Indeed, much in his work was repugnant to them. His first important work, *Opinions on Eternity*, had provoked Goethe's rather tart criticism, because it consisted of reasonings about life after death and did not express the full heart of a feeling man.[85] Lavater never lost this speculative bent, which led him into strange regions of thought. He was fascinated by *Revelations*, and never gave up hope of disentangling its true meaning. He believed literally that faith could move mountains, and was always seeking for proof of the power of the spirit. He tried to collect data to prove once for all the efficacy of prayer, though his own experience provided him only with the rather meagre example of being rescued by divine intervention from a storm on the Zürich lake. He eagerly sought out any person reputed to have powers of second sight or miraculous healing, and was apt rashly to commit himself to their support in his voluminous writings. He was one of those who believed in Cagliostro and welcomed his powers as evidence of the reality of spiritual forces, and he was one of the most ardent disciples of Mesmer, even giving his own wife hypnotic treatment on Mesmer's prescription. At the end of his life he was persuaded that St. John was still among the living, and searched for him in Germany.

He was impulsive and rash in his beliefs, ready to believe whole-heartedly and obstinately in what he considered to be divine messages. At one time a conviction came to him that he was called to convert the Berlin Jew, Mendelssohn, and in the simplicity of his heart he wrote an open letter to Mendelssohn calling on him to declare himself for Christianity—and he was sadly disappointed when the latter firmly and courteously explained that Lavater's arguments were not convincing.

He was perpetually forcing himself on people, engaging them in correspondence on religious issues, asking them to collaborate with him in proving his tenets. The authorities of the Reformed Church, to which he belonged, made complaints about him, for his orthodoxy was often in question. Rationalist theologians polemised against his irrational and often inconsequent beliefs.[86] Pietists, who were often drawn to him, found his versatility disturbing and his 'worldliness' un-Christian.[87]

With all this, he was a man much loved, and the centre of a spiritual community which extended beyond the frontiers of his native Switzerland. There was no malice or pedantic dogmatism in his obsessions ; even those he pestered, like Mendelssohn, retained a high esteem for his personality. Rash in adopting a belief, he was extraordinarily candid and confiding in his polemics, and ready to admit his faults and tactlessness. As a clergyman he was devoted to his flock, and famous for the help he could give others in spiritual distress. The centre of his religion was love of Christ, which expressed itself in love and honour of man, and this love spreads through his works and was the chief source of his great influence. One of his chief 'heresies' was, characteristically enough, his assertion that the wicked were not eternally damned, and he was distinguished from most pietist and orthodox clergymen in his trust in the goodness of man and nature, his cheerful good nature, his unassuming enjoyment of simple pleasures.

Lavater responded in his usual impulsive way to the generous spirit of Goethe's and Herder's early religious writings, and to *Götz von Berlichingen*, and they too were attracted by the candour and warmth of his spirit. They fortified him in his practice of a religion based on intuition, inner persuasion, 'the immediate feeling of Christ', as he interpreted it ; a religion which built not on dogma or argument, but on 'sensuous experience', and which discovered God in man and nature.[88] His work on physiognomy, which engrossed his attention during the Sturm und Drang years and to which Herder, Lenz, and particularly Goethe contributed, was the practical expression of this religion. It is introduced by several quotations from Herder's *Oldest Document*, rapturous assertions of the divinity of man, the image and ' hieroglyph ' of God. This human divinity resides not merely in the soul, but is evident to the senses : ' Whoever wishes to know man must know his physical appearance, that which strikes the senses.' [89] All man's potentialities are good : ' As certainly as man has corporeal powers and an instinct to work and create, to use his powers, as certainly is it good and useful that he should use his bodily powers.' [90] The most reliable knowledge about man comes from experience, and in the portraits of great men we can detect the expression of their inner powers, the working of God, the Divine itself. Lavater defined his own purpose as ' to arouse the feeling of the dignity of man, joy over mankind, the perception of God in man, the opening of a new, inexhaustible source of human gladness '.[91]

The humanism in these principles linked Lavater closely with the Stürmer und Dränger ; but there is always, in him, a marked determination to stress the superhuman, unearthly source and meaning of the best powers in man.

Religion is the need for higher invisible things and a faith in them ; religion is always sense, feeling, genius for the invisible, the higher, the superhuman, supermundane ; religion is always faith ! Even when it is superstition or [sectarian] enthusiasm, superstitious or true faith in non-existent beings, in invisible forces which do not operate upon us, a diseased religion, religion without reason, the belief of enthusiasts in delusions instead of true experience in the invisible world, even if it is religion without experience.[92]

This defence of intuitions which are completely detached from sense-experience and practical activity indicates the latent opposition between Lavater and the Stürmer und Dränger. The essence of his faith was belief in Christ, belief in a spiritual force more real than the natural world. He was thus deeply shocked and grieved at the naturistic, Spinozist conception of God in Herder's *Ideas* and *Dialogues on God*. But the difference between them was always there, and Herder always preserved a certain scepticism about Lavater. One can contrast Herder's expositions of the New Testament, in which he seeks the human, secular meaning of images and parables through his insight into Oriental circumstances and mentality, with Lavater's cabbalistic and supermundane pre-occupation with *Revelations*.[93] The story of Lavater's relations with Goethe shows the unfolding of these differences, and throws light on the peculiar nature of Goethe's attitude to religion.

Lavater was first attracted to Goethe through the publication of the latter's two pamphlets of 1773. Their correspondence began when Goethe sent Lavater a copy of *Götz von Berlichingen*, and it continued without a serious break till 1784. Their friendship was strengthened and refreshed by personal meetings in Frankfurt and Zürich in 1774, 1775, and 1779, and by a joint excursion to Ems. Each loved the other's generosity and candour, each entered into the other's circle of friends, they were held together by their practical charity and collaborated in helping others. But from the beginning Lavater never ceased urging Goethe to avow belief in Christ, which seemed to him the only source of his values and activity. ' You must become a Christian ' ; [94] ' One must be either an atheist or a Christian.' [95] He tried to get Goethe to draw an ideal head of Christ for his collection of physiognomies.

Frankly, but sympathetically, Goethe tried to make his position clear. ' I am no Christian '—' if you want a Messiah, hold fast to him who has promised you the living water '.[96] And, in a most characteristic letter to Lavater's friend Pfenninger, who had tried to argue Goethe into belief :

Thanks, dear brother, for your warm concern over the salvation of your brother. Believe me, the time will come when we shall understand one another. Beloved, you speak to me as to an unbeliever who wants to comprehend, who wants to have proofs, who has not experienced. And it is the very opposite in my heart. . . .

Am I not more resigned as regards rational comprehension and proofs than you ? Have I not experienced exactly what you have ?—I am perhaps a fool that I do not do you the pleasure of expressing myself in your words and, by a simple experimental psychology of my inner self, demonstrate to you that I am a man, and therefore cannot feel anything different from other men, so that our differences are mere quibbles which result from the fact that I feel things in other combinations and, in expressing their relativity, have to name them differently.

Which ever was and ever will remain the source of all con-
troversies.

And you always want to lay hold of me with proofs and witness ?
To what end ?   Do I need proof that I exist ?   Proof that I feel ?
—The only proofs I esteem, love, adore are those that show me
how thousands before me have felt exactly what strengthens and
confirms me.

And so the word of man is God's word to me, whether parsons
or whores have laid it up and rolled it into a canon or strewn
it about in fragments.   And moved in my soul I fall on my
brother's neck, Moses !   Prophet !   Evangelist !   Apostle, Spinoza
or Machiavelli.[97]

Such letters did not make Lavater give up hope.   When he
was with Goethe he would check Goethe's livelier outbursts
with a good-humoured clap on the back and a broad Swiss
' Bisch guet '.[98]   In his letters of the next few years, which
were mainly connected with their common physiognomical
studies, he returned to the attack over and over again—
fortunately, owing to his correspondence with Wieland, he was
kept from the common prejudice on Goethe's behaviour at
Weimar.   He asked Goethe's advice on the reputed wonder-
workers in whose powers he so dearly wished to believe ; he
asked for Goethe's opinion on his own speculations about
the Apocalypse.   Goethe's answers became more decided as
time passed.   Expostulating over the barrenness of Lavater's
concern with *Revelations* he wrote :

I am a very earthy man, the parables of the unrighteous steward,
the prodigal son, the sower, the pearl, the mite, etc., are more
divine for me (if there is anything divine in them) than the seven
bishops, candlesticks, horns, seals stars and tribulations.   I think
I speak in truth, but in the truth of the five senses.[99]

When he received the second volume of Lavater's *Miscellaneous
Writings* in 1781, he wrote to tell him how much he liked his
published letters, for here his personality came to light.   In
no other work can he so fully accept Lavater's Christ, for here
he can see the ' crystal vessel ' into which Lavater must pour
his feeling or be wretched.   ' It is splendid that an image has
come down to us from olden times into which you can transfer
your all, in whom, mirroring yourself, you can adore yourself.'

Goethe meant this sincerely, not ironically, for he had love and respect for Lavater's personality.   But he continues :

I cannot help calling it unjust, and sheer robbery, which does not fit the goodness of your cause, that you pluck out all the lovely feathers of the thousandfold birds under the sky, as if they had usurped them, in order to deck out your bird of paradise with them—this is what must necessarily annoy us and seem intolerable.

You must bear with those of us, he continues, who are content with human wisdom ; ' allow me to call physical well-being what you call an angel.' [100]

Again, after receiving Lavater's work on Pilate :

Since I am no anti-Christian, no un-Christian, but a decided non-Christian, your *Pilate* has made a distasteful impression on me. . . . I even began to parody it, but I hold you too dear to amuse myself in this way for more than an hour.   So, let me hear your human voice so that from this side we may remain on good terms.[101]

Dryly and decisively : ' In our Father's dispensary are many prescriptions.' [102]   In protest against Lavater's ineradicable craving to be taken in by men like Cagliostro, Goethe gave him the round answer that Lavater's belief in miracles was ' blasphemy against the great God and his revelation in nature '.[103]   Irritated by Lavater's persistence he wrote that he was as ready as anyone to believe in a world outside the visible, but it must be refined and purified of ' the stupidity and squalor of human excrements ' which these charlatans display. ' Enough, I return from these supernatural contacts not a whit wiser and not a whit better, and that would be the only condition under which I could have any respect for these unknown friends.' [104]

These last words give the clue to Goethe's whole attitude to religion.   He could call himself, in his maturity, ' resolutely pagan ', yet he was not intolerant of religious belief in others, and himself often used religious terms to express his outlook. He did not, in fact, consider that metaphysical statements were statements about reality ; they had a symbolical validity, and their value arose from their function in the individual. He could employ religious terms, use Christian myths in his poetical works, and approve them in others, as symbols of, and a means to, human activity and aspirations ; they were valuable in so far as they fertilised and enriched man, made him capable of a fuller life. ' Only what is fruitful is true,' he was to write.[105] Such an attitude was ' decidedly non-Christian ', it was bound to lead to the estrangement from Lavater. But it was not such as to make him forfeit Lavater's love and respect, and even after a last chill meeting in Weimar in 1788 Lavater was to write a most appreciative and moving sketch of his character in its complex unity and confident strength.[106] They avoided one another from that time, though Lavater's new craze, his search for St. John, put him in the pillory of Goethe's *Xenien*.

Of the other Stürmer und Dränger only Lenz busied himself much with religious problems, and it is exceedingly difficult to sum up the attitude of this wayward, irresolute, easily influenced man. He swayed between the influence of his pietist upbringing, of rationalist Christians like Salzmann, and of Herder and Lavater, and it is difficult to say which element is the dominant. In some of his works he tries to interpret Christian dogmas in the manner of rationalist theologians like Spalding, whom he much admired.[107] So, in the *First Principle of Morality*, he defines the purpose of religion as the encouragement of our ' instinct ' for perfection ; Christ came to strengthen ' our constant effort to make one another happy '.[108] In the *Opinions of a Layman* he interprets the ' intentions ' of God in revealing such truths as the Fall and the Mosaic law,[109] and in other works suggests rational explanations of the meaning of Christian dogmas (*On the Tree of Knowledge of Good and Evil*).[110] At the beginning of the latter work he shows that he shares the normal pietist view on the sinfulness of sex, and can turn out commonplaces like ' Moral freedom consists in the strength with which we withstand natural instinct.' [111] At the end of his life he wrote a play on Catharine of Siena which Kindermann sees as a forerunner of the Romantic plays of religious ecstasy.[112] It is, however, much more a study of religion as a refuge from sexual love, for Catharine's devotion is the result of a disappointment in love ;

and her self-flagellation is a means to drive her desire for her lover from her mind.[113] He thought too of writing a play on the theme of Abelard. Then again the pietistic longing for death appears here and there in Lenz, in an early poem, in *The Englishman*, in *Catharina von Siena*—for death as a voluptuous experience.

But interwoven with these traditional elements is another theme, close to Herder's religious feeling, and more organically connected with the personal experience of Lenz. Concupiscence, he wrote, led our first parents to fall, but concupiscence is also the path to good. ' God willed that man should be active, not merely passive.' Man is to feel the harmony of the world, but also to be ' free, a little creator '.[114] In the *Opinions of a Layman* of 1775 he attacks the identification of religion with morals. He points out that moral ideals change with time and circumstance ; and in any case a moral ideal means a static objective which is contrary to the whole purpose of existence. Such an objective implies that ' the whole caravan of our knowledge, experience, observations and deductions ' is to arrive at a ' resting point '.—

But is such a resting point possible ? is it necessary and useful, is there any pretext for advising it, recommending it, or even pardoning it in a finite being? A finite being, whose whole existence is striving, whose striving never slackens, however much he may try to suppress it, until this heavenly flame is put out that makes him strive, that through endeavour makes his whole body, his whole machine sensitive, capable of enjoying the happiness he strives after, and that sinks back into its earlier insensitiveness, its earlier indolence, if this striving slackens. . . . Cursed be rest and consigned for ever to the inventory of blind matter ; but we, who feel spirit in our veins, only rest when we collect new forces for a still higher flight, when we seem to sink in order then to soar far beyond the horizon of ordinary mortals.

It is not necessary to ponder anxiously the morality of an action or the feelings that accompany it ; the important thing is to do, to strive—Lenz here assumes in his rhapsodic way that there will be no conflict between our inner urge and goodness. This is the essence of religion for him, the principle of inner movement and creation.

It always seems to me that the central intention of Christ's doctrine is in the one word that John the Baptist cried, pointing to Christ : Μετανοεῖτε, μετα, μετα ! ! and I do not know how men came to translate that by ' Repent ye ', why not, ' Lift up your spirit ', which of course presupposes repentance, turning from sin ; but μετα ! μετα ! beyond all your earlier opinions of perfection and happiness, beyond your *non plus ultra*, beyond your ideal itself, and incessantly beyond, as long as you can go on and on.

Religious faith is the spirit which drives us onward, without respect to a destination.

Faith gives wings to all our powers, kindles them, sets them aflame. . . . Faith is a secure confidence in what one hopes . . . it is not at all supernatural, it is quite, quite natural, *tout à fait* pure, pure nature, that faith alone can make us happy in the world.

And if we trust nature, we shall have and trust faith, ' and proceed on our way, which the heathen can follow as well as the Christian, if he has a sufficient motive to remain true to his nature : therefore we truly do not always need to see the city and goal in order to be reassured that we shall arrive '. A difficult and apparently dangerous principle to follow in practice, Lenz admits ; but if we surrender ourselves confidently, who knows what wings we shall grow, what tree will grow from this mustard seed ? [115]

In this, his most mature theological essay, Lenz interprets religion in the same subjective way as Herder and Goethe ; its reality and value lie in liberating all the inner capacities of man. But, just as he was less able than they were to rid himself of pietistic and rationalistic modes of thought, so he gives a spiritualistic twist to their naturalism, in his suggestion that out of the dark instincts of man, with all their complexity of good and evil, something new, a spiritual soul, will emerge in some unknown future. This belief is expressed in his psychological essay, *On the Nature of our Mind*, with almost tragic intensity.

He begins this little paper by a reflection on the material determinants of mind, reflecting the opinions of a La Mettrie or Helvétius.

The more I investigate myself and reflect on myself, the more reasons I find to doubt that I am really an independent being, despite the burning desire within me to be so. I don't know, but the thought of being a product of nature, to have to thank nature and the confluence of fortuitous causes for everything, to have to depend utterly on her influence and to contemplate my dissolution with complete acquiescence in her higher decisions : this has something frightening, something annihilating, about it—I do not know how the philosophers can be so unmoved at the thought.

And yet it is true !—But my grieving, anguished feeling over it is equally true. I appeal to the whole human race, is it not the first of all human feelings, that makes itself felt in swaddling clothes and the cradle—to be independent ?

What then, I only a plaything of circumstances ?   I——?   I go over my life and find this dismal truth confirmed a hundred times. But how does it come about that, when I recount all the vicissitudes of my fate, I summon up all my intelligence to subordinate them as far as I can to myself, to my cleverness, to my activity ; and then, whence comes the anxiety that I feel at the same time, the scruples that suggest you have not contributed so much yourself as you imagine—and then the labour I take to overcome these scruples, to forget a hundred petty incidents, in order to deceive myself with the proud thought : *you* did that, *you* were the cause of that, not nature or the impact of alien forces. This pride of mine—what is it ? where are its roots ?

Might it not be a hint of the nature of the human soul, that the soul is a substance, though not born independent, but with a movement, an instinct within, to work its way up to independence ; to separate itself out, as it were, from this great mass of intertwined creation and to establish itself as a being existing for itself ; a being that again unites with creation only so far as its independence will tolerate. Might not the greatness of this instinct be the measure of the greatness of the spirit ?   Might not this feeling, about which people declaim so much, this pride, be the unique seed of our soul, which is engaged in the process of becoming, and which strives to rise above the surrounding world and to create out of itself a God that rules above it ? . . .

So, I would say, the soul creates itself and therewith its future state. . . .   So all our independence, our whole existence is based on the number, the scope, the truth of our feelings and experiences, and on the strength with which we face up to them, think about them or, what is the same, are conscious of them.[116]

This conception of ' emergent evolution ', with its emphasis on the self-creation of soul, links Lenz up with the later German ' Nature philosophers ', with Schelling above all. That is, it is a characteristic attempt to reconcile modern science with traditional religious concepts, the intellectual apprehension of law with the feeling of freedom. Herder and Goethe, much stronger personalities than Lenz, were to move in a different direction and to stress, in their different ways, the permanent interdependence of soul and matter, the ' divinity ' of the law to which man in all his parts remains subject. Yet neither of them ever got quite free of thoughts analogous to those Lenz expresses. Herder several times gave expression to the belief that man was an intermediary creature between animals and higher spiritual beings, which might be brought into some sort of existence through the spiritual growth of man.[117] Goethe too, in a characteristically cautious fashion, sometimes hankered after a similar possibility. His comments in *Poetry and Truth* on d'Holbach's *Système de la nature* echo in a subtle and sophisticated way Lenz's outburst.

We were ready to admit that we could not escape the necessities of days and nights, of the seasons, climatic influences, of physical and animal conditions ; yet we felt something within us that appeared as perfect freedom of choice, and then again something that tried to hold the balance with this freedom. We could not give up the hope of becoming more and more rational, of making ourselves more and more independent of external things, yes even of ourselves. The word freedom sounds so sweet that one could not do without it, even if it were to denote an error.[118]

Goethe does not here make assertions about the independent reality of a spiritual part of man ; he wisely speaks only of the urge and desire to believe in it. But the desire is still so important to him that he does not utterly abandon the belief.

But, in the young Lenz, such soaring speculations were only rare moods. What distinguishes him from the Romantics and unites him with Goethe and Herder was his willingness, his urge to ' face up to feelings and experiences ' ; and his true character appears in his self-surrender to feelings which he felt to be the whole meaning of life, and yet to which he helplessly, pathetically succumbed. It was this apprehension

of the need, and the consuming power, of feeling that enabled
him to write the only haunting religious lyric of the Sturm
und Drang. It was first entitled *My First Hymn* ; and then
changed to *Eduard Allwills Only Hymn*, when he recognised in
the central figure of Jacobi's novel the reflection of his own
longings and stresses.   The poem was written in 1775 or 1776,
at the very crisis of Lenz's life. [119]

Wie die Lebensflamme brennt !
Gott du hast sie angezündet,
Ach und deine Liebe gönnt
Mir das Glück, das sie empfindet.

Aber brenn' ich ewig nur,
Gott du siehst den Wunsch der Seele !
Brenn' ich ewig, ewig nur,
Dass ich andre wärm', mich quäle ?

Ach wo brennt sie, himmlisch schön,
Die mir wird in meinem Leben
Was das Glück sey, zu verstehn,
Was du seyst zu kosten geben !

Bisz dahin ist all mein Thun
Ein Geweb von Peinigungen,
All mein Glück ein taubes Ruhn,
Meine Lust, mein Dank erzwungen.

Du erkennst mein Innerstes,
Dieses Herzens heftig Schlagen,
Ich ersticke seine Klagen,
Aber Gott, du kennest es.

Es ist wahr, ich schmeckte schon
Augenblicke voll Entzücken,
Aber Gott !—in Augenblicken
Steht denn da dein ganzer Lohn ?

Funken waren das von Freuden,
Vögel die verkündten Land,
Wenn die Seele ihrer Leiden
Höh und Tief nicht mehr verstand.

Aber gäb es keine Flammen
Und betrög uns denn dein Wort,
Sucht uns gleich der klugen Amme
Einzuschläfern fort und fort?

Nein ich schreye—Vater! Retter!
Dieses Herz will ausgefüllt,
Will gesättigt seyn, zerschmetter
Lieber sonst dein Ebenbild!

Soll ich ewig harren, streben,
Hoffen und vertraun in Wind?
Nein ich lass dich nicht, mein Leben,
Du beseelig'st denn dein Kind!

*   *   *

How the flame of life doth burn!
God, it kindled at thy will.
And thy love grants me in turn
All the joy it may instil.

But to burn for evermore?
God, thou seest my soul's desire!
Must I burn and nothing more,
Warming others, self on fire?

Ah where burn, in what a land,
Flames of heaven that may impart
Knowledge of what joy is and
How to taste thee as thou art!

Till then all that I fulfil
Is a web of agony,
All my joy is deaf and still,
Thanks and pleasure wrung from me.

Thou my inmost self dost know,
In my breast the heavy beat,
I suppress its swelling woe,
But, O God, thou knowest it.

Once I tasted, it is true,
Moments full of sheerest bliss.
But in moments, God, so few,
Thy reward should lie in this?

K

Sparks they were of high delight,
Birds that told the fall of land,
When its sorrows' depth and height
Passed what mind could understand.

Will they never burst to flame?
Can it be thy Word should lie,
Seeking like a nurse to tame
With a cunning lullaby?

No, I cry—O Saviour! Father!
My heart's yearning must be stayed,
Must be sated; if not, rather
Smash the image thou hast made!

Must I strain then to the last,
Hope and trust in wind and wild?
No, my Life, I'll hold thee fast
Till thou bless with joy thy child.

One can understand that, on reading this poem in 1783, Knebel jotted down in his diary : ' Read *Allwills Hymn* yesterday with deep emotion. The effect is not at all comforting.' [120] It is indeed a deeply moving expression of the tortured ardour of Lenz's character, and must have recalled to Knebel the catastrophe of Lenz's life. If the poem is considered only as a personal document, even its artistic weaknesses are deeply characteristic and express his powerlessness to master himself. But the poem is more than a personal document. It expresses starkly and throbbingly the ardent yearning of the Sturm und Drang, the ' burning fire shut up in their bones ' which sought to become pure flame, which was their glory and their torment ; a longing which they felt to be a longing to adore God, and which in its unchecked intensity, its clamorousness, turns or threatens to turn to utter blasphemy.

In their religious attitude the Stürmer und Dränger link up with the most subjective belief of their times, the belief that God is known only through personal experience. But, at the other end of the scale, they link up with the Spinozistic doctrine which, while sanctifying the world, makes the Divine co-extensive with nature. They show little or no concern for the essential principles of Christianity : the divinity and resurrection of Christ, conviction of sin, hope for salvation. They are indifferent to dogma, doctrine, cult. They define the soul in a totally un-Christian fashion, for it is for them a vital centre, a nucleus of energy and impregnated with sensuous experience. They attribute a religious significance to all-shattering and rapturous experience. In the name of this type of experiénce they reject too the ' mournful atheistic half-night ' of the materialist d'Holbach, as Goethe calls it. Not that they were fundamentally at odds with the view that the universe was but ' matter eternally in motion '. In his discussion of their reaction to d'Holbach's *Système de la nature* Goethe wrote : ' We could even have put up with this if the author had really built up the world before our eyes out of his matter in motion.' But, instead of telling them about ' physics and chemistry, astronomy and geology, natural history and anatomy ', d'Holbach had ' transformed what is higher than nature, or what appears in nature as a higher nature, into material, ponderous nature, moving it is true but without direction and shape'. They were presented with a ghostly, ' corpse-like ' analysis, instead of ' the gaily decked world '. And very characteristically Goethe tells how this book cured them of all metaphysics, and turned them ' to living knowledge, experience, activity and poetry '.[121] It was not the materialism of d'Holbach that repelled them, but his abstractness ; not his sensualism, but his lack of appeal to and understanding of the sentient, emotive, imaginative core of the individual man.

Though nagged at by the orthodox, they were not concerned with the reform of Church or dogma. They were ready to allow each man to construct his own peculiar faith and system, as his own inner experience demanded. For themselves they discarded all theology, since it transferred the meaning of life from actual existence to a realm in which only spiritual or intellectual ideas were recognised, thus divesting life of its substance. Rejecting the deistic God and the teleological conception of life, they asserted a consonance between the inner determinants of being, those which issue from the individual personality, and the energies of nature. Here, in the creative soul, throbbing in response to all creation, with its craving for intense experience and full life, was the nucleus of being and of value.   Religion was not a separate realm from which man acquired value and direction, it was the justification of their intuitions and instinctive urge, the principle by which they claimed the right to extend the frontiers of being, to unfold their capacities to the full.   In their religion the Stürmer und Dränger worship not God but man ; they do not define God's claims on man, but man's claims on God and nature.   As such they belong to the great process of humanism ; and the specific contribution of the Sturm und Drang is its emphasis on man's need to give rein to his senses and feelings, on his need to feel himself intensely alive, to feel within himself those forces that sustain nature and other men.   They used religious terms for this consciousness because they felt these forces were greater than themselves, driving and shaping them ; they used them with all the more emphasis because the rationalistic humanism of their times ignored the claims of the individual to a truly personal existence, and considered the individual only as a means to an end, only as an instrument. The chief significance of the religious outlook of the Sturm und Drang was, however, not a contradiction of humanism, but a necessary widening of it to embrace the subjective, spontaneous forces of man, which drive him on, through rapturous and bitter experience, to unknown shores.

CHAPTER V

THE CREATIVE PERSONALITY

Das tiefe, unersetzliche Gefühl des Daseins.—HERDER.

THE GREAT extension of human achievement and knowledge in the seventeenth and eighteenth centuries was the fruit of the marriage of human dynamism and energy with science, the growing comprehension and mastery of the laws of nature. The supreme effort of consciousness was, naturally enough, the discovery and formulation of laws governing all branches of human experience. Whether these laws were formulated as the operation of phenomenal nature or of metaphysical Reason, not only was the idea of God depersonalised, but man's substance and individuality tended to be broken up into a web of abstract laws. In the abstract Wolffian metaphysics this divorce between man's actuality, his will and energy, and law appears at its crassest, and was properly satirised in *Candide* ; but equally the materialism of La Mettrie and Helvétius, though it accepted, as the basic reality, material influences and sensual existence, conceived of law as an impersonal, all-determining external power. Much of the satire of the eighteenth century expresses a consciousness of the contradiction between this notion of law and the actual behaviour and powers of man. Swift and Voltaire show the contradictions between men and their own ideal of themselves, between the disorder in human affairs and the idea of an ordered society and universe. Fielding and the writers of picaresque novels rejoice in the crude vigour of men. Among the philosophers, Hume shook the prevailing confidence in an understood, law-governed universe. Rousseau went much further and refused to respect law which seemed to deprive personal life of meaning and delight.

The Sturm und Drang was to fashion out of these diverse trends an outlook, the main principle of which was the supreme value of dynamic feeling and direct experience. This achievement bears all the marks of the restricted social life in Germany, and of youthful turbulence ; but, despite these limitations, it asserts the dynamic creativeness of man and nature and in so doing prepared the way for a deeper understanding of the interaction of man and nature and for a truer conception of law.

Only Herder attempted anything approaching a systematic exposition of the Sturm und Drang conception of man and his purpose. But this conception is not episodic and incidental in the experience of the Stürmer und Dränger. It is expressed in all parts of their work, in their behaviour, in their letters, in their critical and philosophical treatises, above all in their poetical works. Obscurely but determinedly they refuse to see man as the instrument of external forces or as chained to external purposes, be they religious, metaphysical, physical, or social ; they refuse to exalt one side of man, his soul or reason or sense, át the expense of others ; they destroy the image man made of himself as an abstract intelligence, or a sentimental idealist, or a sensual egoist in the Mandeville or Helvétius sense. Man exists, in their view, to be himself most intensely, to develop all his powers to the full. All limitation is bad. This is what Goethe, reflecting over his youth, detected as the importance of Hamann : ' The principle to which all Hamann's utterances can be reduced is : All that a man undertakes, whether it be by deed or word or anything else, must spring from his whole united powers ; all separation is to be rejected.' And, speaking from experience, he adds, ' A splendid maxim ! But hard to follow.' [1] Thus defined, it is a completely subjective goal, and collisions with the external social world were bound to be many and shattering.

In its very definition of human capacities, this attitude was the contrary of that of the rationalists. The metaphysician Mendelssohn could sympathise with Herder's formulation in 1769 : ' The development of the forces of our soul is the purpose of our existence on earth,' [2] and Kant could summarise the purpose of history, in similar terms, as the development of all the innate capacities of man.[3] But Mendelssohn understood these ' forces of the soul ' as intellectual powers which achieved their full development in apprehending a metaphysical root and purpose of being ; and Kant defined them, in conscious opposition to Herder, as man's rational faculties, which enable him to detect, through the complexity of existence, an ultimate social and moral goal which justifies human existence. For Herder, however, these forces are all the complex powers within him, sense, thought, feeling, activity, striving for expression and satisfaction. They were present, he felt, in his love for Caroline, in his delight in nature and poetry, in his admiration of primitive society ; they justified him in his savage and unreasonable repudiation of modern society, a society whose greatest and unforgiveable sin was in his view precisely that it mutilated man. He wrote to Caroline : ' Everyone's actions should arise utterly from himself, according to his innermost character, he should be true to himself : that is the whole of morality.' [4] And in a poem he wrote for Caroline : [5]

> I am not here to think ! but to be ! to feel !
> To live ! to rejoice !

Herder spurned the usual objectives of virtue or contentment. Happiness is not a constant state to be reached, but arises continually afresh from the violent vibrations of our being. Thus all experiences and moods are good, if only they are intense. When Caroline expressed her concern over his moods of gloom and urged him to care for his health, he wrote : ' When I prefer loneliness, when I am depressed and confused, when I am in a pensive, sombre mood—then that's good too, my dear.' [6]

This principle became in Herder's hands a lever to turn all contemporary theory upside down. With it he discovered a new approach to history. It was customary at his time to judge all past periods of human history in the light of the ' policed ' government, the morality, and prevailing standards of polite behaviour of his times. In his first essay on history, however, *Another Philosophy of History* of 1774, he utterly rejected his own times because they had weakened ' desire, instinct, activity '.[7] He exalted patriarchal society, and praised even the anarchical violence of the Middle Ages, because he considered that in these times men were more fully alive, more responsive to natural and spontaneous feeling, than his contemporaries : what would modern times be without the vigour and independent feeling of the feudal period ? [8] So he comes to his most important historical insight, which he was to develop through the whole of his later *Ideas on the Philosophy of History of Mankind* : there is no absolute or fixed ideal of virtues or happiness ; man is born with indefinable potentialities, which find a different fulfilment at different times and in different circumstances—' each nation has its centre of happiness in itself, as a sphere its centre of gravity '.[9]

It is characteristic of Herder that, in this period of his life, the passionateness of his beliefs blinded him to some of their implications. In the first version of his *Essay on Human Knowledge and Perception*, written in the same year as Goethe's *Prometheus* and *Werther*, Herder expresses a trust in the compatibility of his subjective values with moral goodness and activity which is infinitely more naïve than Goethe's apprehension of the problem. The theme of this essay in epistemology is the characteristic one that there is no knowledge without feeling and action, that mind, feeling, and will are ultimately one. It is man's mission, in Herder's view, to develop all these sides of his being. Feelings may be conflicting and obscure, but they are ultimately the only guide to truth : ' Whatever does not recommend itself as good through our feeling, considered in its highest and purest scope, is rejected by the soul ; it lies in the nature of a sentient being that it frees itself from error.' [10] Feeling may err, but it can only be corrected by feeling. Only the man of deep feeling can come to deep knowledge, and there can be no conflict with morality for such a man. ' Altogether, reason and virtue are not abstractions sucked out of thin air ; they are born in struggle and assert themselves among passions and instincts in royal power and order, which itself can and must become the strongest, purest passion.' [11] Though Herder seems to qualify his belief in feeling : ' All strength without reason and goodness is either adventurousness, sublime folly, or monstrosity,' [12] he sees ' reason ' and ' virtue ' as themselves natural or instinctive in origin, and recognises their validity only when they are the outcome of true feeling. The inner and outer world must be in harmony—thus he can write ' We live in a world we ourselves create.' [13]

This first version of Herder's epistemological treatise raises the fundamental issues of the Sturm und Drang belief in personality. The purpose of man is to develop all his capacities, and the driving force, and test, of this process is his consciousness of vital existence—' the deep, irreplaceable feeling of being alive ', as Herder later defined it.[14] He believes that there is no real conflict between knowledge and feeling, and that the stronger the desire for experience, the deeper will be the truth discovered. Equally, there is for him no ultimate conflict between morality and subjective desire. The provisos he expresses, which become much more prominent in the later versions of this treatise, are drowned in the flood of his enthusiasm. Clearly enough Herder's intoxication with the idea of full personal development, which finds its most naïve form in the cult of the ' genius ' or ' superman ', the ' Kraftgenie ', blurs his perception of the practical and moral consequences of this doctrine.

There is a comparable obscurity in Lavater's enthusiastic advocacy of the ideal of personality. In his first work, *Opinions on Eternity*, Lavater was concerned with rational-religious speculations on the form of man's perfection in the next world, which Goethe tartly criticised because of their ' meaninglessness for the heart '.[15] His interest in physiognomics arose in the first place from his belief that the spirit determines the body, and that the laws of this spiritual power can be scientifically defined ; at the same time he was moved by a pastoral concern for comforting and converting his flock, and hoped, by deciphering the outer form of head and face, to find a sure way to the soul. But under the influence of Goethe and Herder his intention and methods changed. Instead of measuring human physiognomy against the accepted conception of virtue, he and his collaborators began to seek for the individual character in the personalities they discussed. Much to the vexation and bewilderment of rationalists and scientists like Nicolai and Lichtenberg, who thought physiognomics, as an alleged science, would claim to establish a method for the interpretation of facial features, and much to the dissatisfaction of his pietist friends, who found these pursuits far too worldly, Lavater contented himself with the exposition of what was unique and individual in each of his subjects. His *Physiognomical Fragments* are not the materials of a science, but commentaries, often rhapsodic in form, on the inherent individuality of man ; and, like Herder, he turned this type of

observation into an ethics of individualism. ' Be what you are
and become what you can.' [16] Like Herder too he called
this process of self-realisation a divine calling, and, seeing in it
a parallel to God's creative purpose in the world, he refused
to consider that there may be a conflict between the unhampered self-expression of man and the demands of society.
The creative genius is a little God and the highest example of
man :

> Where there is activity, energy, deed, thought, feeling, which
> may not be learned or taught by men, there is genius ! . . . Genius
> is not learned, not acquired, not to be learned, not to be acquired,
> it is our unique property, inimitable, divine, it is inspired. Genius
> flashes, genius creates ; it does not arrange, it creates !

And he continues his rhapsody :

> Gods in human form ! Creators ! Destroyers ! Revealers of
> the mysteries of God and men ! Interpreters of nature ! Speakers
> of unspeakable things ! Prophets ! Priests ! [17]

These two clergymen, Herder and Lavater, carried away
by their naïve trust in God, fell into a temporary belief that
self-surrender and self-realisation must harmonise with the
intentions of God and therefore with the claims of morality.
Herder never lost his sympathy for Shaftesbury's view that
human nature, like external nature, is in itself divine and
virtuous. The other Stürmer und Dränger were far more
aware of the problematical character of their longing for deep
feeling and self-expression. Yielding to the need to give rein
to the infinite longings within them, they were aware of a
double difficulty : how to reconcile this never-satisfied urge
with action, with achievement, which alone makes real
personality and which necessarily imposes self-limitation ; and
how to justify the inevitable conflict between unrestrained
subjectivism and the outer social and moral world. Most of
the heroes of their imaginative works are emotive supermen,
men who are urged blindly on to surpass themselves ; but
they are nearly always caught in the contradictions of their
purpose, succumb to their own overwhelming longing, destroy
what they worship, or fail before the powers of the real world.

No one grasped so clearly as Goethe all the implications of this new moral outlook. Far from presenting us with ideal men and achievement, his early works focus attention on the dilemma in which he found himself. The simplest form of it is presented by the sturdy man of action, Götz von Berlichingen, who builds his life on his strong arm and his inner feeling of rectitude, but is maimed and broken by stronger social forces. This loyal subject of the Emperor is forced by the times into lawless actions, into an alliance with the rebellious peasantry, and overwhelmed by the superior force and cunning of a powerful neighbour. There is no longer room in the world for the ' freedom ' he has lived by, and he dies broken-hearted. Weislingen, Götz's former comrade-in-arms, and now his enemy, reveals contradictions within the heart itself. He is tossed about by his feelings and ambition, destroys his own happiness, and dies crying : ' We men do not guide ourselves. Evil spirits are given power over us to exercise their evil caprice to our destruction.' The heart is no sure guide. The man of feeling and the man of action are at the mercy of forces which break them.

In his succeeding works, these symbols become richer through mutual impregnation. Götz and Weislingen are held together only by youthful memories, they are in actual fact totally different, incompatible characters. But the figures in which in the following years Goethe symbolised achievement show that he is seeking for the inner springs of action which relate the man of action to the man of feeling. In his poem *Mahomet* he interprets the great hero as a mighty river rushing to its creator, the ocean ; [18] and in his fragment, *Prometheus*, the great rebel who opposes the Gods feels his own creative power as an imperative inner calling which he cannot resist. [19] Here, creativeness, achievement, is matched (or determined) by the strength of his desire for the realisation of his inner powers ; his outer efficacy is the measure of his inner intensity.

> Hast du's nicht alles selbst vollendet
> Heilig glühend Herz ?

> Hast thou not achieved all thyself
> Holy glowing heart ?

Thus the Ganymed of the contemporary poem,[20] who yields in ecstasy to Zeus and feels himself merging in the whole of creation, is not the unrelated opposite of Prometheus, but Prometheus in his subjective aspect. Goethe has indicated this most subtly in the dramatic fragment, *Prometheus*, when Prometheus' brother reproaches him :

> Du stehst allein.
> Dein Eigensinn verkennt die Wonne
> Wenn die Götter, du,
> Die deinigen und Welt und Himmel all
> Sich all ein innig ganzes fühlen.

> Thou standest alone.
> Thine obstinacy knows not the joy
> When the Gods, and thou,
> Thy creatures, world and Heaven and all
> All inwardly feel themselves a whole.

Prometheus can cry, bitterly and scornfully, ' I know all that ' ; but in the reverent passage in which he explains to Pandora the life that rises from the self-loss of love, he himself affirms the subjective sources of activity :

> Wenn aus dem innerst tiefsten Grunde
> Du ganz erschüttert alles fühlst
> Was Freud und Schmerzen iemals dir ergossen,
> Im Sturm dein Herz erschwillt,
> In Tränen sich erleichtern will und seine Glut vermehrt
> Und alles klingt an dir und bebt und zittert,
> Und all die Sinne dir vergehn
> Und du dir zu vergehen scheinst
> Und sinckst und alles um dich Her
> Versinckt in Nacht, und du in inner eigenem Gefühle
> Umfassest eine Welt,
> Dann stirbt der Mensch. . . .

> Wenn alles, Begier und Freud und Schmerz
> Im stürmenden Genuss sich aufgelöst,
> Dann sich erquickt in Wonne Schlafft,
> Dann lebst du auf, aufs iüngste wieder auf,
> Aufs neue zu fürchten zu hoffen und zu begehren.

When in the innermost, deepest depths
Shaken and shattered thou feelest all
That joy and pains ever poured on thee,
And in that storm thy heart swells up
Would soothe itself with tears but glows still more,
And all within thee rings and reels and trembles,
And all thy senses quail,
And thou seemst to pass away
And sink, and all around thee
Sinks into night, and in thine innermost feeling
Thou claspest a world,
Then man dies. . . .

When all, desire and joy and pain,
Dissolves in the storm of delight,
And then refreshed sleeps in joy,
Then thou revivest, new and young again,
Again to fear, to hope and to desire.

This self, that loses itself in love in order to grow, is the same self that rejoices in independence and creation ; yet the play is truly fragmentary, for how can Prometheus' harsh rejection of the claims of worship be reconciled with the longing to dissolve in intense experience ?

In his poems and fragments Goethe expresses the rapturous feeling of the liberation of personality, in the *Mayfest* the joy in the feeling of oneness with nature and his beloved, in *Wandrer* the deep satisfaction in the creative process of nature which builds as it destroys, in the poem *Prometheus* joy in the rebellious independence of man. In his major works of this period, *The Sorrows of Werther* and *Urfaust*, he wrestles, however, with the total implications of his attitude.

The tragedy of Werther, as of Faust, arises from the polarity within his own longings. He is a young man who rejects everything that does not heighten his feeling of existence. The routine of his profession, the class distinctions which hamper personal intercourse, provoke his contempt or despair ; in contrast, the prolific creativeness of nature, its infinite boundlessness, causes all his being to vibrate. Lying in the lush grass he loses himself in the feeling of oneness with the universe, but finds himself too as part of reality, nature, God.

Yet he recognises the threat to his individuality in these feelings : ' I succumb to the excess of glory in these pheno-mena.' [21] The occupations of men seem petty to him, and his own inner life infinite ; yet he is conscious that he lives in a dream.

When I observe the confines in which the active and intellectual forces of man are imprisoned, when I see how all activity amounts to nothing but the satisfaction of wants which in their turn have no purpose but to prolong our poor existence ; and then, that all our comforting assurance over certain points of enquiry is only a dreamy resignation, by which one paints the walls within which one sits imprisoned with coloured figures and bright perspectives. All this makes me dumb. I turn in on myself, and find a world ! More in surmise and obscure desire, than in clear shape and living force. And then everything floats before my senses, and I smile on, dreaming, into the world. [22]

The catastrophe which engulfs Werther because of his sur-render to his longing for deeper and more significant experi-ence threatens from the beginning. He is inevitably brought into collision with practical necessities, with social obligations, to which he cannot accommodate himself.

But there is another, equally significant source of tension within Werther. For all his distaste for society, Werther loves the simple folk. In the village of Wahlheim he finds himself at home, here he meets people and sees scenes which give him an unexplained contentment. The children waiting for their mother, her return and simple speech, have for Werther all the meaning that Wordsworth found in certain scenes he recalls in the *Prelude*. [23]

I tell you, when my senses are bursting, all the tumult is soothed at the sight of such a creature that in happy serenity paces out the narrow circle of its being, manages from one day to the next, and, seeing the leaves fall, only thinks that winter is coming. [24]

This delight in concrete self-fulfilment finds its fullest in-tensity in Werther's love for Lotte. It is a love for his opposite. Like the peasants in their narrow round, Lotte is completely and happily absorbed in her household duties, in her care for her brothers and sisters and her neighbours. She does not do her work out of a sense of duty—her capacity for feeling is indicated by her appreciation of Klopstock, her affection for Werther, even more by her serene happiness. But her feeling takes concrete forms, and her care for others is unsentimental —at times, in Werther's view, even heartlessly practical.[25] Werther, driven on to undermine her peace, risks breaking up what he holds most dear, her wholeness, her trust in the world and herself; their embrace cannot be a beginning, it is an end, for Werther and Lotte are two poles of being.

The *Faust* tragedy moves in like manner round a twin focus. Smashing the confines of the study, of religion and morality, Faust violently seeks experience, the source for him of true knowledge as of all values. Happiness is indifferent : all he longs for is to feel himself alive : [26]

> All Erden weh und all ihr Glück zu tragen,
> Mit Stürmen mich herum zu schlagen
> Und in des Schiffbruchs Knirschen nicht zu zagen.

> To bear the joy of earth, to bear its pain,
> To battle with the wind and storm
> And in the crash of shipwreck not to squirm.

His ' superhuman ' longing drives him to seek the communion of the spirit world, until the Earth Spirit harshly rejects him ; he must find the fulfilment of his violent feeling in the real, limited, human world. And to his astonishment, this miracle occurs. Fleeing from the ' prison ' of his study, he finds bliss in the ' prison ' of Gretchen's room : [27]

> In dieser Armuth welche Fülle !
> In diesem Kercker welche Seeligkeit !

> What plenty in this poverty !
> And in this prison cell, what bliss !

From the very first moment of the dawn of his love he is torn by the contradictoriness within his feeling : ' Poor Faust, I know you no more.' His feeling can ripen and acquire substance only in this precise form ; indeed, it is Gretchen's

complete and loving absorption in homely duties that crystal-
lises his passion ; yet all the time his passion threatens to
burst the frail vessel of reality, and to smash, as it eventually
does, Gretchen herself.

This conflict provides the dramatic tension of almost every
scene. Mephistopheles finds it easy to dub it hypocrisy, and
thus to try to undermine Faust's whole trust in life and feeling.
Will Faust not, he asks sneeringly but appositely, be swearing
eternal love and faith to Gretchen, and will it ' come from the
heart ' ? And Faust can only answer with a violent outburst
which cannot hide his own feeling of insecurity : [28]

> Lass das, es wird. Wenn ich empfinde
> Und dem Gefühl und dem Gewühl
> Vergebens Nahmen such und keine Nahmen finde,
> Und in der Welt mit allen Sinnen schweife
> Und alle höchsten Worte greife,
> Und diese Glut von der ich brenne
> Unendlich, ewig, ewig nenne,
> Ist das ein teuflisch Lügenspiel ?

> Stop that ! It will. When in the grip of feeling,
> In nameless turmoil and fever,
> All my senses, reeling,
> Range over the earth's extent,
> And I snatch the highest words men invent,
> And call this fire in which I'm caught
> Eternal, eternal, infinite—
> Is this a devil's lying sport ?

And in the next scene where Faust declares his love to Gretchen,
his consciousness of the double, contradictory meaning of
' infinite ' or ' eternal ' love breaks through as he calls on her
to surrender to love : [29]

> Sich hinzugeben ganz und eine Wonne
> Zu fühlen die ewig sein muss !
> Ewig !—Ihr Ende würde Verzweiflung seyn.

> Utterly to give oneself, and feel
> A joy that must be eternal !
> Eternal !—Its end would be despair.

Its end *is* despair, its very intensity breaks its being ; and in the following scene, where Gretchen sits at the spinning wheel, we see how the ripening of her love, her natural fruition, is disrupting her own limited character and preparing her own collapse.

There are works of Goethe of this period in which he suggests that surrender to feeling need not lead to disaster—in *Stella* Ferdinand, wavering between two women, sets up at the end a *ménage à trois*. As in the case of Weislingen, and of Clavigo, his restlessness amounts to little more than a moody inconstancy. But in his greatest works Goethe persuades us that, in breaking the bounds of society and morality, his heroes discover a deeper meaning in life, a fullness and richness unknown to those who observe external codes. This highest intensity of being is the extreme of individualism, but at the same time its dissolution, its self-loss in feeling, in nature, in God. It longs for self-fulfilment and cannot attain it, even destroying it, where it finds it in others, through its own ardour. It is directed both into the infinite, the limitless, and into a precise reality, into the finite. Goethe stands above all the other Stürmer und Dränger since he grasped fully this contradictoriness in the new aspiration and, creating the symbols of each polar trend, refused to force a reconciliation. His works affirm the new longing for life, but set it out in its bleak problematicalness.

In the others the new longing for vital experience finds a more one-sided expression. Such hangers-on as Goethe's Wetzlar acquaintance Goue can for instance depict a Götz expressing understanding and sympathy for a Werther—a strange misunderstanding of their polarity.[30] In some of Klinger's works, as in *Simsone Grisaldo* and *Sturm und Drang*, the hero can find fulfilment for his longing for overwhelming passion and great deeds ; Grisaldo's king even begs him : ' Teach me to live.' This unripeness is evident in Klinger's own rampageous conduct.

I live like all true sons of Prometheus in the inward war of energies and activity with the bounds which men have imposed on demi-gods for their own comfort, for otherwise they would be crushed for ever. Brother ! man's job is double : creation and destruction ; and whoever is incapable of accomplishing both to the full satisfaction of his feeling (however high it may swell), he lives like me.[31]

Klinger's best play, however, *Die Zwillinge*, shows a man driven by a longing for greatness, which in the frustration of his position turns to envy and malice, to a pathological passion which leads him to murder his elder brother and invite his own death. Recognised by the young Moritz as a powerful expression of the frustration of his generation, it is a study of Sturm und Drang longing grown malignant and paralysing. Lenz's Robert Hot, in *Der Engländer*, is a young man consumed by a passion which overpowers him and brings him to his death. In all such characters, determined by their own one-sidedness or a misfortune of situation, the tragedy of excessive vitality is not fully grasped. Guelfo is destroyed by the fortuitous circumstance of being a second son ; Hot has scarcely seen the woman he loves and is a pathetic victim of an overheated imagination.

The same criticism may be made of Maler Müller's Faust, who is brought to make a pact with the devil, and thus abjure the real world, through the intrigues of men who envy him his independence and ability. These intrigues make his inner compulsions seem less urgent ; but even so, the conflict within him is only that between a longing to surpass the normal bounds of man, and the claims of ' justice and law '. Müller shows no inkling of the irreconcilable inner conflict into which Goethe's Faust is thrown. The rhapsodic *Dedication* of the work is a highly characteristic document :

Faust was in my childhood always one of my favourite heroes because I recognised him straight away as a great fellow ; a fellow who had felt all his strength, felt the bridle that fortune and fate had put on him, and that he wanted to break ; who seeks ways and means, and has daring enough, to break down everything that comes in his way and tries to hinder him. . . . Soaring as high as is possible—to be fully, what one feels one might be—it lies in our very nature.—And that resentment against fate and a world which presses us down and bends our noble self-reliant nature, our active will, through its conventions.

Passive, indifferent creatures are, he continues, monsters issued prematurely from the womb of nature.

If self-interest and self-love are the machine which keeps the pulse of the world going, what wonder then if the strong and great fellow asserts his rights, even if his courage drives him beyond the world in search of a being that fully suffices to him ?— There are moments in life—who is not aware of them, has not experienced them a thousand times ?—when the heart leaps beyond itself, when the best, the most splendid fellow, in spite of justice and laws, craves absolutely to surpass himself.[32]

The expression is crude, and Müller fails, in his play, to make evident the impulsive force which he here describes ; his Faust seems merely a turbulent, dissatisfied fellow. But he is here trying to put into words that inner and ' divine ' unrest which all the Stürmer und Dränger shared, and which caused them to question all the conventional morality of their times. It was above all a feeling of inner creativeness, comparable with the creativeness of nature, or the palingenesis which Herder detected in the course of human history ; its supreme symbol they found in Genesis in the story of the Creation. They treasured all situations and relations which called forth in them this feeling of creativeness ; those moments in which, as Lenz said,

we feel so intoxicated with the feeling of being alive that we embrace the whole of the world in one glance, traverse it with one stride.[33]

Friendship and love called forth this transforming, transcending power in them :

Let us, friends, press close together and idealise ourselves to our heart's content ; that sends sparks flying through soul and heart ! We electrify one another to activity, and as a result to happiness ! That is inspiration, the wondrous creative power to set souls alive, like the electric spark, perhaps, in blood and sun.[34]

Art and poetry give rise to this expansion of being, just as they are its result. On his third visit to Strassburg, Goethe wrote, reflecting on the inspiration he drew from the Minster :

As before every great thought of creation, there awakes in the soul all the creative power that is within it. In poetry it stammers in exuberance, in scrawling lines it hurls [' wühlt '] on to the paper adoration to the Creator, eternal life, all-embracing, inextinguishable feeling of what is and was and is to come.[35]

The ejaculatory and enthusiastic style of his paper on Shakespeare, of Herder's essays on Ossian and Shakespeare, of Lenz's review of *Götz von Berlichingen*, bears witness to this creative response to poetry.

Expansion of the personality, the renewal and growth of self, was for them a necessary purpose. But what was to be created ? Were they only to feel this potentiality within them, but, like Werther, never be able to realise it ? Their frequent use of the word ' activity ' indicates how aware they were that energy consists not merely in a feeling, but in outward operation upon the world ; in their own lives they were continually concerned to seek to define a sphere and mode of activity which would realise their vital potentialities. In so far as the Stürmer und Dränger ignore this problem, in their lives or works, they lay themselves open to the charge of juvenility. But in so far as they show themselves aware of it, even though they do not do more than demonstrate the tragic alienation of their poetic heroes from worthy activity, they contribute to the most important of moral problems, the relation between inner power and values and outer forms.

Lenz's review of Goethe's *Götz von Berlichingen* sums up in most poignant terms this dilemma of the Sturm und Drang. He begins with a sarcastic statement of the accepted belief that our lives are determined by forces outside us, and then cries :

But can that be called being alive ? can it be called feeling your existence, the spark of God ? Ah, the attraction of life must lie in something better : for to be a plaything of others is a dismal, oppressive thought, an eternal slavery, an artificial, rational, but for that very reason all the more wretched brutishness. What do we learn from this ? . . . This we learn : that action, action, is the soul of the world, not enjoyment, not sentimentality, not ratiocination, and only so do we become images of God, who incessantly acts and incessantly rejoices over his works. This we learn : that the active force within us is our spirit, our highest portion, which alone gives our body with all its sensory properties and feelings a true life, and true consistency, and true value, and without which all our enjoyment, all our feelings, all our knowledge are merely passive, merely a postponed death. This we learn : that this our active energy may not rest, may not cease to operate, to stir, to rage, before it has created freedom about us, room for activity : good God, room for activity, and even if it be a chaos that you have created, waste and void, but freedom would dwell therein, and then, like Thee, we could brood over it till something emerged—— Bliss ! Bliss ! a godlike feeling, that !

But Lenz's elation is checked. Where can he find this ' room for action ', what sort of action can be imagined ? He goes on : for the moment ' we are only supers on the great stage of the world '. ' Since at present our hands and feet are bound,' the best we can do is to prepare ourselves for the time when we have a rôle in the world itself, by absorbing into our minds the character of Götz, a man ' always busy, active, warming and beneficent as the sun, and like the sun a consuming flame when anyone gets too close to him '.[36]

The dilemma was a real one. In the petty, stagnant circumstances of Germany there seemed no outlet for the man who, driven by strong feeling, would impress his personality on the surrounding world. Even Schiller's Karl Moor, who follows a clear line of political action under the impulse of his enthusiasm for freedom and justice, finds his achievement so much the contrary of his intentions that he renounces not only action but life itself. Thus there is often a strong element of escapism in the Sturm und Drang idea of greatness. Heinse illustrates the extreme of this trend. The hero of his *Ardinghello* is a ruthless and amoral egoist for whom a fantastic world is created, the ' blessed isles ' of which Heinse writes so frequently in his letters, where all normal human and social relations are dissolved. For Heinse the symbol of the wanderer is not associated, as with Goethe, with any idea of home and construction : ' Man, the infinite creature, is created according to my system to wander from zone to zone, and to take possession with his soul of all that is good and lovely ; and that is his true and only wealth.' [37] Such a conception, obviously related to the Sturm und Drang, is in fact an aberration from the path of the Stürmer und Dränger, for it ignores their effort to come to grips with reality.

We have already examined how intractable their problem was when reduced to political or social terms. The personal or moral solution proposed by their sharpest critics among the rationalists only emphasises the impossibility for them of reconciling their longing for intense personal life with society. Lichtenberg, whose diaries are so full of contemptuous references to the ' Frankfurters ', lived quietly and impersonally for his science, and could find a really significant social life only in England, in London, and near the court. Nicolai's point of view is put, in a nutshell, in his refutation of Goethe's *Werther*.

His dissatisfaction with this book took the quaint form of a sequel or corrected version that he composed. [38] He picks up the story just before Werther's suicide, easing the problem by making Lotte the betrothed, not the wife, of Albert. In Nicolai's version, Albert is so moved by Werther's and Lotte's attachment to one another that he renounces his engagement, and they marry. But now troubles come thick and fast. The duties of married life force Werther to lose some of his fire and reluctantly to settle down to work ; Lotte, dejected and disappointed, begins to hanker after another young and sentimental fellow. The marriage almost breaks up. Albert intervenes once again as a true friend, brings the young pair to their senses, and reconciles them with their lot. Werther finds increasing pleasure in working for his home, Lotte becomes happy with a numerous family. In course of time they become prosperous, have a nice house in the country, and can enjoy nature and domestic affection without feeling any collision with social obligation.

In view of some of the wilder behaviour and writings of the Stürmer und Dränger, one can perhaps understand Merck's approval of this work. [39] He wrote to Nicolai that the *Joys of Young Werther* was an ' effective anti-toxin to all the chatter of these immature and feeble souls, who always have action and decision on their tongues, and yet are utterly taken aback by the least obstacle on their snail's path '.⁴⁰ But Nicolai's counter-blast is a complete travesty of *Werther*. He dismally fails to understand Lotte, who is loved by Werther precisely because her personality finds such full realisation in home, friends, neighbours ; he utterly fails to see that Goethe was not writing a moral piece, holding up Werther as an example to be followed, but was expressing the tragic incompatibility between so rich an inner life and the practical life for which it hungers and cannot fit itself. With complete sincerity Goethe could write to an acquaintance, describing his book, that Werther is a young man ' who loses himself in ecstatic dreams and undermines himself with speculation '.⁴¹ He found a worthy answer to Nicolai's impudence in an angry little poem in which Nicolai arrives at Werther's grave, relieves himself there, admires his excrement, and departs saying, ' if only Werther had been able to relieve himself like me he would never have died '.⁴²

In actual fact, a solution to the Werther-problem had already been proposed before *Werther* was written. Rousseau's *La nouvelle Héloise* is its prototype, and though the relations between Saint-Preux and Julie are hindered primarily by the incompatibility of class, their characters are akin to those of Werther and Lotte. Rousseau complained that his readers sympathised with the misfortunes of his characters, rather than with the solution he worked out with all his earnest moral passion. The most important part of the book was, he said, the Fourth Book, in which Julie and Wolmar build ' un bonheur social et humanitaire '.⁴³ But even Rousseau could not make Saint-Preux's acquiescence seem anything but outward and precarious, and he succeeded in reconciling love and duty only by focussing our attention on Julie. Goethe threw the spotlight on to the man ; and for Werther there were no voyages, no English lords to help, not even to enable him temporarily to forget his sufferings.

Persons more sympathetic than Nicolai to the Sturm und Drang feared the implications of its individualism. F. H. Jacobi shared rapturous exchanges with Goethe, and was swept away by *Werther* ; but, alarmed by the bigamous ending to *Stella*, he began to draw back. He put his own view in two epistolary novels, *Eduard Allwills Papiere* and *Freundschaft und*

Liebe, the former of which bears directly on Goethe.[44] Into a family circle, sustained by sentimental affection, steps All-will, a man of impulse and imagination, who surrenders to his feelings and encourages others to do the same, who believes that it is man's obligation to develop all his capacities and that only restraint is evil. In himself innocent and good, he spells disaster for those who trust him, particularly for young women ; his cult of nature destroys the most sacred bonds of nature, and in disregarding the proprieties he undermines the whole of morality. Jacobi's criticism is pertinent, and not so very different from what might have been Goethe's. But he hastens to the conclusion that such men as Allwill should tame themselves, enter the bosom of the family, entertain only moral sentiments, and settle down to work ; that is, he wishes to ignore the deep problems that preoccupied the Stürmer und Dränger and stifle the questions they raised.

Werther appeared to such men as childish, and they sug-gested in effect that he should put his childishness away. The Aufklärung valued in children only what they approved in the adult. In Lessing's *Miss Sara Sampson* a child is introduced, as in many contemporary sentimental novels and plays, as a symbol and focus of virtuous sentiment and domesticity. In the works of the Sturm und Drang children often appear, but in their own right, and embodying in their uninhibited natural-ness that wilful independence that is the early form of per-sonality as the Stürmer sought it. Lotte's brothers and sisters in *Werther* are attractive because they are real romping children, pestering Lotte when they are hungry, snotty-nosed, by turns refractory and obedient, fond of sweets and presents, of fairy-tales. The peasant children whom Werther admires as they wait so quietly for their mother to return from town have broken a pot the day before quarrelling over a tit-bit. One day, when the doctor finds Werther romping with Lotte's children and spoiling them, as he says, Werther breaks out against his contemporaries, who treat children as their ' sub-jects ' and try simply to break their will. This obstinacy of theirs, he cries, is the seed of future firmness of character ; their exuberance will allow them to surmount, later on, the dangers of the world. He loves them because they are ' so unspoilt, so whole '. So also he respects the imaginative world of children. When he kisses a little girl at the well, she begins to scream because she believes she will now get an ugly beard, but Lotte calms her by telling her to wash her face quickly and all will be well. How vexed Werther is when an acquaintance remonstrates against this indulgence in superstition ! [45]

Scattered in many of the early writings of Herder are comparable views about childhood. Like Lessing in his *Education of the Human Race*, Herder equated the early history of man with childhood, but the meaning of this concept is strikingly different in the two authors. Lessing is concerned only with the means by which the child is weaned from error and trained, through dogma and guidance, to a rational, i.e. moral, way of life. The problem is infinitely more complex for Herder. The child is for him not merely an intelligence but a whole bundle of potentialities ; childhood, whether in the individual or in the social group, has for him its own value, its own right, even though it has to develop into something different, into maturity, which again has its own characteristics.

For Herder there is no general man, no universally valid type of education. Both are moulded by society, which has different needs and characteristics at different periods. But he finds education in its true, deepest sense in early society, before schools and academies came to have a vested interest in intellectuality, when education meant the development of sense, feeling, and activity to prepare the child for a full and active life ; when therefore education was not a matter of books and mere intellectual training, but of ' deed, custom, example, and a thousandfold influence '.[46] In the *Journal of my Voyage* of 1769 Herder defines the characteristics of youth as inquisitiveness, imagination, feeling, and friendship, and he suggests that it is the task of education to stir these potentialities to a more intense life. Borrowing largely from Locke and Rousseau, he sketches a plan of education which would relegate the more theoretical, abstract studies to the latest stages of education, and stresses above all the need for employing and developing the senses, the imagination, and the practical experience of the child—through natural history, practical scientific experiments, geography. Education should not be the imposition of adult thoughts on the child, but 'the awakening of ideas that sleep in us'.[47]

It is rather lost labour to enter on a discussion of Herder's ideas of a system of education. Like Goethe and the others, he had neither the experience nor the patience to carry out a reform of education like Pestalozzi or Basedow. What is more, these young men found it repugnant to divide up subjects in a way which suggested a separation of the faculties of the personality ; their most important insight was precisely the complex unity of the personality of the child, the preciousness of his total powers, the need not to lose sight of this totality and all the influences that develop it. As Herder said in the Shakespeare essay, as an analogy of the development of mankind as a whole, 'the education of a child cannot and does not take place through reason, but through perceptions, impressions, the divinity of example and custom'.[48] Goethe took to the educational reformer Basedow because, as he says, he liked his plan of making teaching lively and natural, but he disliked his curriculum because the subjects, as Basedow defined them, did not in his view correspond to the associations of actual experience.[49] All the Stürmer und Dränger rebelled against the separation of man's faculties into different compartments of different worth. Their most important contribution to educational thought was their insistence on that part of education which takes place outside the curriculum, in the rough and tumble of school life, as Lenz stresses in *Der Hofmeister*, in the associations and activities which arise from and prompt their inherent vital energy. Herder's *Another Philosophy of History* is not only a polemic against modern society, but against all education of the modern type ; Götz contrasts his own vigorous childhood, in which he simply picked up in play what was necessary to his life, with the book-learning of his tender little son, which fits him only for a monastery. Heinse spoke for once very much for the others when he wrote in his notebook : 'The art of education is nothing but a farce. Geniuses must educate themselves, none has so far been educated.'[50] To bring out what is best in the child, his creative energy, the best thing is to leave him as far as possible untouched by school and discipline.

Later in life, when their Sturm und Drang was over, Herder

and Goethe were to make amends for their earlier distaste for systematic education. The educational responsibilities which fell to Herder's lot as superintendent clergyman were to be among his most agreeable duties, and the ideas Goethe expressed in *Wilhelm Meisters Wanderjahre* have a considerable importance in the history of German education. But as Stürmer und Dränger they failed to make use of the inheritance of the Enlightenment. Without any of the profundity of the French or English Enlightenment, the German Aufklärer were more successful than their foreign teachers in spreading their ideas widely, and in no respect more than in education. Their leading ideas came in the main from Locke and Rousseau ; and in the treatises and experimental schools of Basedow, Campe, and von Rochow, sturdily supported by Nicolai's *Allgemeine Deutsche Bibliothek* and by most of the leading rationalists, a revolution in educational method took place. Education became more practical, linked with experience instead of being mere memorising, physical exercises were introduced. The teaching of religion became less dogmatic and sectarian, and efforts were made to separate school from the Church. Few of the experimental schools that were founded lasted for long, but the movement that began at this time was a groundwork for advances in the early part of the following century that made German primary and secondary education far and away the best in the world.[51] Though the Stürmer und Dränger felt some sympathy for reforms of this type, their hostility to organisation and discipline made them incapable of taking part in any educational experiment.

Their infertility with regard to education illustrates their general failure to define any way in which torrential vitality might be canalised into fruitful activity. There is indeed, in most of them, a marked tendency to idealise turbulence. Goethe found an appropriate symbol of the rough and ready ' Kraftkerl ' in his Götz, a medieval knight, ' a self-helper in wild anarchical times '. But to transpose such an ideal to modern times was inept. Klinger, Lenz, Maler Müller all at times show the rough and coarse behaviour of students as something admirable.[52] This rebellion against conventional polite forms is tasteless and juvenile, as if the little lads with whom Werther played had grown old but not up. It is

noteworthy that in the first version of *Auerbachs Keller*, for all
the laughing satire of the drunkards, Faust himself carries
out and enjoys playing the prank on them ; it was a later
Goethe who wisely left him standing on one side, in disgusted
and embarrassed boredom. In the scene ' Dismal Day ' there
are references to crude practical jokes which Mephistopheles
—and presumably Faust—had once enjoyed playing on un-
suspecting passers-by, and we can assume that Goethe's first
conception of Faust's unrest had not yet freed itself from these
coarse remnants of the popular puppet play. Compared
with this, the wild pranks of Karl Moor and his student friends,
which we hear about at the beginning of *Die Räuber*, are much
better assimilated into the character of the ' Kraftkerl '. They
are described as the expression of student exuberance which
Karl now wishes to put behind him ; and they give a necessary temperamental background to his later social ideals and
action, which are the sublimated, more mature form of his
zest for life. Those of his companions who are unable to rise
to his idealism do not remain harmless, rampageous students,
but develop into ruffians and criminals.

On the whole, however, the vulgarisation of spontaneity
and naturalness is only a temporary aberration in the works
of the Stürmer und Dränger, as it was in their lives. Just as
they occasionally liked to use coarse expletives, so in their
works they enjoyed a boisterous revenge on propriety and
sentimentality. Herder, somewhat older than the others and
a clergyman, never fell into vulgarity. Lenz described the
coarse practical jokes of the officers in *Die Soldaten* as an unfortunate result of garrison life. Goethe's exuberance always
took an imaginative or humorous form and found its main
literary expression in the gay farces and doggerel he wrote
for the private amusement of the Frankfurt circle and Merck.

In these farces Goethe frequently makes fun of the conventional obliviousness to the physical aspect of sex ; the
Stürmer und Dränger refused to pretend that sexual functions
do not exist. They delighted in the picaresque novel, in the
earthy realism of Cervantes or Fielding or Sterne, who took
particular pleasure in showing sexual relations shorn of their
idealisation. They were not for nothing admirers of Voltaire's and Diderot's novels. Some extravagances occur in

their works. Hamann seems almost morbidly fond of using sexual metaphors to describe spiritual experiences. In Heinse free sexual intercourse, arising from passing infatuation, is a characteristic of his heroic man of power, whose ' superiority ' is supposed to be evident in his freedom from the bonds of love as well as of marriage. In his earlier works, like *Laidion*, his eroticism appears in an even lascivious form, a more ardent expression of the playful and intellectualistic eroticism of Wieland's novels and comic epics. Klinger's Simsone Grisaldo, like the hero of *Ardinghello*, proves his ' greatness ' by his capacity for physical love.

On the whole, the Stürmer und Dränger were without prudery with regard to sexual relationships, but they rejected decisively unimpassioned eroticism. Their often heated indignation with Wieland was not due to a conventional horror at the mention of physical sexual relations, but to his dissociation of sex from love ; Goethe, on his first acquaintance with Heinse, regretted his ' lewdness '.[53] They treated the sexual act with the reverence due to its importance as the culminating point of love, and because of this found extreme distaste in real or imaginary indulgence in it as an end in itself. There is therefore little sexual sensuality in their works except when they have a satirical purpose, like that of Lenz when he describes the licentiousness of celibate officers.

No other modern writer has Goethe's power to describe the outer and inner reality of sexual union ; of that moment that Prometheus describes to Pandora : [54]

> Da ist der Augenblick der alles erfüllt,
> Alles was wir gesehnt, geträumt, gehofft,
> Gefürchtet meine Beste.

> That is the moment that fulfils all,
> All that we longed for, dreamed, and hoped,
> And feared, my dearest.

A moment which is the fruition of love, and which, all-consuming, leads to new life, new love. The scene in *Faust* where Faust asks Gretchen to receive him at night, a version of a seduction which has a thousand crude or sentimental parallels, is incomparably tender in spite of its directness, in spite of the

preparedness of Faust, who has come with the sleeping draught
ready : [55]

> Ach kann ich nie
> Ein Stündgen ruhig dir am Busen hängen
> Und Brust an Brust und Seel an Seele drängen?

> Ah can I never
> Hang on your bosom one short hour
> Pressing breast on breast and soul on soul?

Body and soul here appear identified, the sexual act becomes
beautiful because of the spiritual longing of which it is the
expression and culmination. The most drastic expression of
bodily yearning thus appears most spiritual : Goethe learned
from the Bible, from the Song of Solomon that he translated,
the spiritual power of drastic physical expression. Just as
Joseph's ' bowels yearned for Benjamin ', so Mignon, in *Nur
wer die Sehnsucht kennt*, sings ' My bowels are burning '. Gretchen, in the original version of the spinning song, cries : [56]

> Mein Schoos ! Gott ! drängt
> Sich nach ihm hin.

> My womb, ah God !
> Yearns for him.

Because such love is highly personal, directed towards a
particular individual, all physical longing is impregnated with
spirit, has the energy of the total personality. The German
word for yearning, ' Sehnsucht ', has itself, and particularly
in Goethe's usage, an incandescent physical quality about it.
Contrast with this the sensual, de-personalised sex of which
Mephistopheles speaks to the student, with its technique of
seduction. Sex for Goethe was never something to be manipu-
lated and played with as an instrument ; he could speak of it
so openly because it was for him a function of man's whole
being in its highest exaltation, because it was the self-surrender
and renewal of his whole personality. His whole life was
accompanied by an unparalleled series of vibrant, reverent
poems in which sexual union is celebrated—in the *Römische*

Elegien, Die Braut von Korinth, and *Der Gott und die Bajadere,* symbolically in the figure of Helen in *Faust Part 2,* and in all forms and variations in the *West-Oestliche Divan,* above all the deep reverberations of *Selige Sehnsucht.*

It is common enough to find in Sturm und Drang works criticism of forced sexual continence. The monk in *Götz von Berlichingen* set the tone, when he said to Götz :

' Ah Sir, what are the burdens of your life compared with the miseries of an estate which curses the best instincts through which we grow and thrive, out of a misunderstood urge to move closer to God ? ' [57]

Conventual life appears always as a half-life, or rather a half-death ; Julius von Tarent feels himself entirely justified in snatching his beloved from the convent. Doubly painful is therefore the ending of Läuffer's trials in *Der Hofmeister.* Unable to bear the torment of sex, Läuffer castrates himself —one of Lenz's baroque contortions, made more absurd and revolting by the tutor's subsequent marriage with a peasant girl ; but painful too as a final commentary on the catastrophic effect of his social position. Somewhat similarly his Catharina von Siena tames her sexual desire by self-flagellation. But Lenz's attitude to sex was abnormal. Just as his characters often succumb to a rootless imaginary love, so he himself seems to have been tortured by sexual promptings which he could not bring into a natural relationship with his own feelings. Thus he inclined to condemn sex as sinful, and his *Diary* is a record of his efforts to mortify the flesh. [58] The same morbidity and inability to grasp the spiritual function of sex is evident in his obsession with the idea of controlling the sexual excesses of officers by creating public ' nurseries ' of women for them —a project he proposed in all seriousness to lay before the princes of his age. Lenz's parodies, *Menalk and Mopsus* and *Eloge du feu M. Wieland,* are quite unworthy scurrilous distortions of Wieland's eroticism. [59]

If we disregard the more juvenile and erratic forms that the Sturm und Drang longing for full development of all their faculties took, it remains an assertion of human claims on life which is a permanent inspiration—just as Goethe's *Faust* remains a supreme symbol of spiritual endeavour. In their works they found no means of reconciling this longing with reality—yet they were concerned, not just with the poetic presentation of this problem, but also with its solution. Lenz, falling more and more a victim to his own fruitless emotions, himself lost all contact with reality and fell a victim to hallucinations ; and when he recovered he could only seek to come to terms to life by renouncing his past insights. Klinger, inclined more than the others to a vulgarisation of the ' Kraftkerl ', turned abruptly over and showed, in his *Die Falschen Spieler*, the shallowness of a character who believes that revolt against home, against decency and honesty, is a sign of inner greatness. Goethe's development was more subtle and arduous.

In the first years at Weimar he was charged by Lenz and Klinger, whose irresponsibility when visiting him caused him much vexation, with betrayal of his old self. He was, so Lenz indicated in *Der Waldbruder* and other works of this period, subtly accommodating himself to court convention.[60] On the other hand, he was charged by the more remote educated public with introducing outrageous behaviour and morals into court circles, and in particular with leading the young Duke astray. Klopstock wrote him an indignant letter on this subject, which Goethe answered tartly.[61] There was some justification for these contradictory complaints, but none took into account the slow process of change which Goethe was undergoing, and the severity of his problem : how to reconcile his longing for full development and intense feeling with the claims of the outer world.

This development took place more easily in his outward behaviour than in his inner being. He began to take an active part in the administration of the little state, and for this purpose had to fall in with the ways of the court and the bureaucracy ; his practical administrative work set him, as he later told Kanzler von Müller, to study nature scientifically, and led to his growing pre-occupation with science, that is, with the laws of nature which man has to submit to if he is to master nature.[62] His love for the court lady, Frau von Stein, a married woman who accepted naturally and without question the obligations of marriage and court life, helped him to conform to proprieties. His lyrics of the early Weimar period,

An den Mond or *Ueber allen Gipfeln*, celebrate the joys of reflection, peace, friendly intimacy, in contrast to the violent emotions of his earlier period. In the early '80s comes that series of odes in which he recognises the bounds of human life, and seeks to formulate the conditions under which men may attain to firm personality and achievement (*Das Göttliche, Grenzen der Menschheit*). But the lyrics represent only moments of balance and reconciliation. How arduous, and how incomplete, his inner struggle was we can see best from the three great works of this first Weimar period, none of which was completed by the time he ran away to Italy.

Iphigenie deals, in a sense, with the restoration to moral health of the rash, violent Orestes. Through the pure and selfless love and candour of Iphigenie, Orestes abjures his old instinctive and catastrophic behaviour. Such a conversion from Sturm und Drang, as we may call it, is a distillation of the influence of Frau von Stein upon Goethe, and depends for its persuasiveness on the extent to which we identify ourselves imaginatively with the process of self-purification in Iphigenie herself. This is in fact the main theme of the play. We see in her a woman who discovers the necessity for ' counsel, moderation, wisdom and patience ' not primarily through moral reflection, but through the peculiar, womanly instinct within her, and chiefly through the intensity of her unwavering love for her family. In one way, therefore, Iphigenie links up with the Sturm und Drang, for she too (and more markedly in the early prose version of the play) is an instinctive creature, who follows her inner feeling even though it brings her into tense, almost tragic conflict with the prevailing conception of the Gods and with what might be considered her moral obligations to the barbarians in Tauris. But, in direct opposition to the instinct of the Sturm und Drang heroes, her instinct combines service and love, service to the family which she loves. It is a sketch of the ideal, an indication of Goethe's aspiration ; but what if ' purity of heart ' and instinct do not harmonise with service ?

Torquato Tasso seems to take up this very question. Here again a woman character, the Prinzessin Leonore, combines natural desire with social obligation and observance. But the poet Tasso cannot learn her balance, much as he desires

M

to do so. His temperament, his imagination, lead him into conflict with the court which tends him so carefully, even to shatter its harmony. Rescued on the brink of despair by the court's chief man of business, he reaches a precarious balance which can scarcely be more than temporary.

In the third of these early Weimar products, *Wilhelm Meisters Lehrjahre*, or rather, in that part of the novel which Goethe completed before the Italian journey, we actually find a new version of the old conflict. Wilhelm is not a Sturm und Drang ' Kraftkerl ', he is not consumed by ardent longing and desire for great deeds ; but he is at variance with the dull routine of middle-class business, and following his bent for the theatre, drifts into a wandering troupe of players. In the first plan of the novel he is to find fulfilment in the production of Shakespeare's *Hamlet*. The indefinable longings of the Sturm und Drang appear in rarefied, spiritualised form in Mignon ; the bitter feeling of alienation from reality is expressed by the Harper : but in a setting of mystery that makes each of them an exceptional, peculiar case, not representatives of mankind. The work expresses Goethe's feeling of unease in the world, yet it is no longer a rebellious, rapturous assertion of inner values but an elegiac, often ironical acceptance of the lack of beauty and worth in the social world.

Later, in the completed *Lehrjahre* of 1795-6, Goethe was to direct his hero into the real world, but now in a completely different sense from the Sturm und Drang. Under the influence of a group of noblemen and noblewomen Wilhelm learns the necessity of self-limitation, of concentration on a particular practical faculty and profession, and through this he contributes to social welfare and at the same time to the clarification and rounding of his personality. The concept of self-limitation becomes dominant in Goethe's moral thought, and with this the acceptance of limitations which the world imposes. His classical period is determined by this acceptance of objective reality and his search for worthy human achievement within existing social conditions. To the world of classical antiquity he looked back with veneration as a time when men could reach all-sided self-development ; but ' now is the time of one-sidedness '. In his essay on Winckelmann, 1804-5, he wrote :

Man can achieve a great deal through the purposeful use of separate powers, he can achieve extraordinary things through the combination of several powers ; but he can achieve something unique, something completely unexpected, when all qualities are equally united within him. This last was the happy lot of the Ancients, particularly of the Greeks in their best period ; fate obliges us moderns to choose between the first two possibilities.

That something in Goethe rebelled against this self-limitation is clear. Even in his middle period he could recapture the spirit of Faust and complete *Part 1* ; and the Faust of *Part 2*, which was mostly written in the last six years of his life, the man ' who desires the impossible ', is still a symbol of unrestrained and unlimited human striving.[63] In his poems, particularly the *West-Oestliche Divan*, the expression of man's power to surpass himself, to break the shell of his being, often reminds one of the Sturm und Drang Goethe, though now it takes a more symbolical form. But, in general, he passed from the Sturm und Drang in recognising and seeking laws of being which imposed self-restraint in the interests of practical achievement.

A similar change occurred in Herder, but it was less a change of personality than of idea, and was therefore expressed more quickly and violently. We can watch the process in the three versions of his *Essay on Human Knowledge and Perception*, particularly in the passages on genius, in which Herder sought to define his conception of full personality. Some passages of the first version of 1774 have already been quoted as examples of Herder's views in the full tide of the Sturm und Drang. When he comes to consider the genius, he accepts Helvétius' distinction of two types,[64] but for one, the ' esprit ', the philosopher or man of science, he shows little regard. The characteristics of the true genius, he states, are depth and intensity of experience ; he is urged on inwardly to action, and greatness of achievement follows from this inner quality—' if he comes to activity, he produces a powerful effect, since his action comes from the depths of his soul '. Herder admits that it is rare to find all sides of man developed equally intensely, and that one-sided geniuses are monstrosities, but he disagrees with Helvétius' view that genius is necessarily opposed to reason and virtue ; the true genius has in him all the seeds of virtue and wisdom, which are not abstractions but arise from deep passions and instinct.[65]

Such true geniuses, Herder continues, are to be found in the early stages of society, before the division of labour ; such geniuses ' were everything, poets, philosophers, surveyors, legislators, musicians, warriors '. Feeling was not divorced from knowledge, nor science from practical activity : ' complete truth is always and only deed '. But, with the development of society, human activity and faculties have been split up, and so we find ' half-thinkers and half-feelers ; moralists who are not doers, epic poets who are not heroes, orators who are not administrators, aesthetic legislators who are not artists '. Theory is divorced from practice. Therefore, Herder concludes, the task of the modern genius is to stride over the limits of this one-sidedness, to unite theory and practice, knowing and feeling.[66]

In the second version of this treatise, 1775, though Herder still keeps his motto, ' Est Deus in nobis ', he begins to doubt the reliability of intuition. The characteristic of man he defines as ' expansion almost without retreat, love almost without hatred and restriction, activity almost without rest and exhaustion '—the ' almost ' indicates a significant cooling of his earlier optimism. Herder again asserts that true morality must be rooted in deep feeling, and is not a matter of calculation and reasoning, and he again attacks the morality which arises from weakness of feeling, from lack of energy, and which weaves a ' spider's web ' of speculation round men's instinctive vigour. But he emphasises more than in the earlier version the danger of passion and energy if they are not tempered and guided by reason and goodness, and praises simple, practical men, who do not fall into the errors of either the genius or the abstract moralist. The common practical man unites theory and practice in his normal existence, and thus fulfils the destiny of man : ' Perhaps speculation and the flood of false emotion have both been put upon us as a punishment ' ! [67]

In the third section of this version Herder's change of emphasis almost amounts to a recantation. He dwells for many pages on the balance of capacities in such men as Bacon, Locke, Rabelais, Swift ; their balance is the true sign of genius ; genius resides in ' inner apperception ', and its children are marked by serene reflection, by quiet mastery. Men who are torn by their passions, like ' hounds of Hell ', are pseudo-geniuses, monsters. They are consumed by a desire to reach a one-sided extreme—

hence that eternal uneasiness, misanthropy, zealotry, envy and thirst for revenge in their hearts . . . the gnawing hunger for knowledge and superpower . . . If this is genius, who would not cross himself against it ? Its first instruments, the rulers and leaders of the human race, were cast out by nature as if they had trespassed on a forbidden sanctuary. Prometheus, the first genius, who stole fire from heaven, is gnawed by the vulture ; the poet who drove the chariot of the sun between earth and sky is hurled from his car ; and the bold geniuses with the hundred hands, who stormed heaven, lie beneath Etna.[68]

In the final version of the treatise, published in 1778, the trend of the innovations in the 1775 version is fully confirmed. The Sturm und Drang cult and conception of the genius is again presented as an infertile reaction against the dominance of abstract theorising, in its violence perverting nature and instinct into monstrous passion.[69] Again he asserts the justice of the punishment of Prometheus, this dearest symbol of the Sturm und Drang. Condemning the rule of abstract, inactive moralising, he sees the Sturm und Drang revolt largely as its direct counterpart, not as its corrective ; as a cult of feeling, not of achievement and activity. He writes bitterly of ' the petty giants with their high chests, strong passion and energy ', with their slogans of ' inspiration, creative power, originality, primordial force that unfolds from itself and soars up to heaven '. How soon does their ' exuberance, impertinence, daring, and excess end in wretched weakness and exhaustion ' ! [70]

There is more in Herder's criticism than a mere change of taste, due to his repugnance for some of the extravagances of the Stürmer und Dränger. In the 1775 version he touches for a moment on the nature of freedom, and shows his irritation with those who ignore the reality of necessity and law : ' We can never become free, i.e. lawless, blindly arbitrary.' [71] In the final version this theme is emphasised, and may be considered his fundamental refutation of the Sturm und Drang (it was to be developed at length in his later work, *Gott*).

> It is easy to chatter about freedom. . . . The first seed of freedom is, to feel that one is not free and by what bonds one is tied. The strongest, freest men feel this most deeply, and strive to advance ; crazy slaves, born for prison, jeer at it and, full of exalted dreams, stick fast in the mud.

And most appropriately Herder refers as authorities to Luther and Spinoza.[72]

Herder was not as yet able to develop these ideas fully, and perhaps he never gained full clarity on them. The relation between freedom and necessity still has a taste of Lutheran dogmatism about it, so that the word ' freedom ' indicates a metaphysical relationship of man to God which is rather an avoidance of the practical-moral issue than its solution—' Where the spirit of the Lord is, there is freedom.' [73] But the reference to Spinoza is a clear pointer to the way in which Herder's thought was to go. What is of importance is that Herder is expressing here his new awareness of the illusoriness of the Sturm und Drang conception of subjective freedom ; freedom cannot be, he sees, a mere rejection of law ; such ' freedom ' results merely in subjection to un-recognised forces, and it does not lead to mastery. Mastery can result only from the understanding of the laws which govern the universe and man. At this point is born Herder's conception of ' Humanität ', his ideal of man as ' lord and servant of nature ' ; [74] the ' perfection of his innate capaci-ties ',[75] the fulfilment of man's desire for feeling and for activity, must be conditioned by natural and social circumstances. He never, however, loses his idealistic tendency, because he is sustained by the optimism of his religious confidence that if man is attuned to nature he can only work for good and there will be no conflict within him, or between him and his fellows.

The dilemma of the Sturm und Drang is thus mastered by Herder in a way similar to Goethe's in *Iphigenie*. Both recog-nise that self-realisation and harmony within the self depend on the discovery of a way to fruitful activity ; and that fruitful activity depends on the recognition of law, of necessity. Both believe at this stage that the intuition, if freed of fortuitous accretions and allied with knowledge, can be a sure guide : Goethe through the example of Frau von Stein, Herder through his religion. Goethe's realism did not allow him to rest content with this idealisation of man ; it was Herder's misfortune that his trust in a loving God often led him to simplify problems and bring an argument to an abrupt stop. Herder's criticism of the Sturm und Drang in his treatise asserts the inadequacy of the new longing for fullness of experience. It was a self-criticism, as well as an attack on his contemporaries. But it was, like much of Herder's criticism, over-fierce and violent, and in some respects a misrepresentation. We can sympathise with his anger at his disciples' distortion of some of his own ideas, at the stridency of the Göttingen group, the extravagance of Klinger's behaviour, Lenz's ineffectualness, Goethe's much-criticised ' immoralism '. There are, in the essay, signs of his concern over works and ideas which seemed to suggest a religion of immoralism—' they adore a monster as an angel of light, which they give the most divine names and yet describe as a devil ' : [76] the ' mysticism of lawlessness and quietism of immorality ' that Fr. Jacobi censured. [77] But he fails to do justice to the severity of the problem that the Stürmer und Dränger raised. At their most naïve they do, it is true, suggest that the immoderate feeling of inward power is identical with greatness of soul and greatness of achievement. But even in crude pastiches like Klinger's *Otto*, the hero of which calls himself ' a reptile with a giant soul ', they are aware of a bitter contrast between the illusion and the reality of greatness. And in their greater works, all, and particularly Goethe, were aware of the dissonance between their exalted intimations, their feeling of the creative potentialities within man, and the outer world of society and morality, which is both the cause of the etiolation of man, and at the same time the only means for self-realisation. Their work is sometimes, indeed, obstreperous and strident, but permeated with a tragic consciousness of their incapacity to reconcile the two poles of being.

In this, the Stürmer und Dränger formulate a general problem which, first brought to light by Rousseau, has fructified moral and social thought since their time. They assert that the boundaries of being, as confirmed by practice and by dogmatic thought, are not sacrosanct ; the restless urge within them to break and enlarge these boundaries must not be denied, it is the principle of life itself, and without it life is not worth living. They reject a merely emotional, subjective, or theoretical solution, attempting—though vainly— to conceive a mode of action which would correspond to the potentialities they felt within them. This challenge is a permanent challenge to the fixities of society and morality, and it was rightly, in this wider sense, considered to be immoral and revolutionary by their contemporaries in England as well as Germany.[78]

The emergence of Goethe, Herder, and Klinger from the Sturm und Drang meant their readiness to adapt themselves to the specific conditions of their times. Goethe's development, though it brought a radical change in his attitude as in his art, was the most productive because it embodied in its later forms so much of the insight of the Sturm und Drang. His Sturm und Drang works show, as Lukács has pointed out, a deeper insight into the contradictions within personal and social life than those of his fellows.[79] In Lenz the problem appears usually, as in Klinger's *Die Zwillinge*, as a psychological one, the incapacity of characters subject to feeling to get on terms with reality, to conquer hallucinations and ' imaginary sufferings '. In Müller or Wagner it appears as the result of a particular fault in society or other men, which might be remedied. Goethe grasped the total dilemma of his times, the unease of man in a society whose limitations are not partial or arbitrary but can never give scope for man's potentialities. When, in middle age, he began to think of the Second Part of *Faust*, he did not try, in accordance with much gratuitous advice, to reconcile Faust to his ' small-world ' environment, but transposed him to a new social sphere ; not settling the problem, but taking it on to a higher level. So in his life, too, while finding a *modus vivendi* and a temporary balance in his own time, he continually shows his awareness of the polarity of life which is ever striking a balance only to discover ever new sources of conflict. At the level of the Sturm und Drang, this dynamism of the life-process was conceived, no doubt, too youthfully, too subjectively to be an adequate philosophy of life ; subjective interpretations of the Sturm und Drang spirit since that time have led in a different social setting to dangerous aberrations which have played a disruptive part in German history—in Nietzsche, Spengler, in some of the currents of Nazism. But it has also sustained a productive unrest which, combining self-criticism with criticism of established forms of living and thinking, has stimulated a great movement for transforming society according to the potentialities of the individual, according to his capacity for full life as a sentient-intellectual-active being.

CHAPTER VI

THOUGHT AND REALITY

Ueberhaupt ist in der Natur nichts geschieden.—HERDER.

IN SEEKING, as a supreme obligation and highest value, the development of the total capacities of man, the Stürmer und Dränger came into conflict not only with conventional religion and morality. Both their trust in inward intimations, and their response to sense-perceptions, brought them face to face with perhaps the central issue for the philosophers of their times, the problem of the nature of mind and matter and the relationship between the two. Their ardour of feeling, and their youthfulness, did not make them always, nor all of them, willing to think out these complex and subtle questions. Lenz for instance was incapable of doing more than express explosively his conviction of the creativeness of the soul as against the determinations of the external world, and postulate the emergence of spirit as an independent entity.[1] Goethe did not enter the arena of argument on these points, except in the figure of Faust. But both Hamann and Herder recognised that the problem demanded their attention, and the latter made several attempts to solve it—his thought on epistemology, from his early Sturm und Drang to the controversy with Kant in the last decade of his life, shows a remarkable consistency of approach. Whatever the occasion of his writings, we find him always opposing any form of philosophical dualism and seeking to formulate one single source of nature and man. His work in this field is therefore deeply characteristic of the Sturm und Drang.

LANGUAGE AND CONSCIOUSNESS

Herder's first writing on the nature of mind gained a prize offered by the Berlin Academy of Sciences for a dissertation on the origin of language. The subject was one which focussed the attention of contemporary philosophers as the most tangible form in which the relationship of mind to matter could be discussed, and it involved Herder in the welcome task of clarifying his attitude to the three dominant types of interpretation : the theological, which asserted that language was given ready-made to man by God, as is told in Genesis ; the idealistic, which claimed that language was the product of the human mind ; the materialistic, which considered language as developing from sense experience. Between these three interpretations Herder was to weave his way to a theory which has been called ' the first rude foundation of the science of comparative philology and of the deeper science of the ultimate nature and origin of language '.[2]

The older tradition of considering language as a divine gift found adherents throughout the century. In England James Beattie maintained this opinion ; in Germany J. P. Süssmilch upheld it in a work on the divine origin of language, published in 1766. In general, however, this view was derisively rejected, as being irreconcilable with the new knowledge about the nature of primitive language and the historical growth of language ; and in any case as involving an anthropomorphic conception of God which most of the philosophers abandoned. Even where men were not disposed to throw doubt on Genesis and began their speculations on the origin of language with its ' rebirth ' at the Tower of Babel, their method, as in the case of Vico, opened the way to a purely secular approach to the theory of language. The most significant argument was therefore that between idealists and empiricists.

It is defined in Locke's analysis of words, in which the characteristic ambiguity of his philosophy appears. Even abstract words, he says, are based originally on experience, on ' sensible ideas ' ; but then again, ' general and universal ' words ' belong not to the real existence of things, but are the inventions and creatures of the understanding '. Equally ambiguously he states that language, communication by means of words, comes into being ' by use or consent '.[3] A similar ambiguity is present in Leibniz's observations. On the one hand he insists that language cannot, as Locke had suggested, be deduced from the physiological structure of the speech-organs, and cannot be merely the instrument and bond of society, but that ' something invisible ', spiritual, is at its source. On the other hand, he also notes the dependence of language on human

experience and needs, and in the first place on the imitation
of animal sounds : in particular he pointed out the value of
etymology to the historian.[4]

Most later writers on language followed one or other of these
two approaches. Rationalists or idealists like Maupertuis and
Moses Mendelssohn asserted that language is a creation of
mind, established as a more or less arbitrary system of communication, a theory analogical to the contractual theory of
the origin of society. At its simplest this school held that men
were always endowed with reason, and at some moment in
history decided to create language.[5] On the other hand, the
empiricist, or better the sensualist, school considered that
language was born out of human experience, that it consisted
in the first place of involuntary and emotive ejaculations, perhaps imitated from the utterances of animals, and that human
reason has developed out of this first crude language a complex
instrument for the expression of ideas. With minor variations
this theory was expounded by many of the writers connected
with the *Encyclopédie*, by the Scottish philosophers of Adam
Smith's school, and in Germany by the historian Gatterer.[6]
It is an important aspect of the new approach to history and
poetry which will be discussed later in this book. Here we
are concerned only with the implications of this theory as
regards the relationship of mind and the environment.

Herder's delight in primitive poetry had brought him early
to appreciate the historical growth of language. In the *Fragmente* of 1768 he had energetically protested against the thesis
that language had sprung in all its perfection from a divine
birth, as Süssmilch had maintained.[7]

In short, the whole hypothesis of the divine origin of language
is contrary to the analogy of all human inventions, contrary to the
history of all world events, and to all philosophy of language. It
presupposes a language fully developed by thought into an ideal
of perfection, and clothes this child of its caprice, that is clearly a
later product and the work of whole centuries, with the beams of
Olympus, to cover its nakedness and shame.

Süssmilch, says Herder, lacks the philosophical spirit to explain
language as ' a development of reason and a product of the
spiritual forces of man '.[8] When therefore the Academy of

Sciences set the origin of language as the subject for its prize dissertation, Herder eagerly took the chance of developing his own ideas.

In his treatise, *On the Origin of Language*, Herder summarily dismisses the thesis of Süssmilch and his like. Skilfully using the data provided by travellers on the speech of primitive and early societies, he shows how untenable is the opinion that God presented Adam with a perfected linguistic instrument. At the same time he refutes the thesis on general grounds. It detracts from the dignity of God and man, since it anthropomorphises God and, in refusing man, the highest of God's creatures, the power of creating language, ' destroys all the activity of the human soul '. But Süssmilch was small game. The important and original part of Herder's argument arises out of his discussion and refutation of the modern philosophy of language, that of Diderot, Rousseau, and particularly of Condillac.

Human language was originally, according to Condillac, spontaneous passional utterance, like the language of animals. He noted that all primitive language is associated with movement and gesture, with dance and rhythm, just as early writing is hieroglyphic. But man is distinct from animals in possessing mind, reflection, the power of regulating the operations of the soul. With the passage of time the relations between passional cries and the needs they signify are understood, the usage of these signs becomes more conscious, and with this development the operations of the mind become more complex ; so language develops.[9] With remarkable acuteness, and a good deal of bluster, Herder opposes this theory. He does not doubt that language has ejaculatory and onomatopoeic elements in it, akin to the cries of beasts and birds ; but these, he says, are not the ' roots ', but only the ' sap ', of human language. Man is not an animal with reason superimposed. And he proceeds to formulate his own theory of the origin of language, that is, of the source of consciousness.

Animals, he begins, differ from men in existing within a very narrow realm. The narrower the range of their ' wants and labours ', the stronger are their instincts, and the less therefore they need language. The so-called language of animals is only ' an obscure, sensuous understanding between them over their lot, in the orbit of their activity '. Man has no such uniform and narrow scope. His instincts and senses are therefore weak. The function of the instincts in animals is fulfilled in man by his reason, which is not a separate attribute of man, but ' the mode of organisation of all his powers '. Man is not just an animal endowed with reason. He has a totally different physiological organisation, a different and infinitely wider sphere of activity, and reason (Herder uses Condillac's term, reflection, ' Besonnenheit ') is a necessary natural product and function of human nature. Human language was therefore never animal language, just as men never had ' the claws of the griffin '. Language is the natural expression of man : not the mere result of a peculiar conformation of mouth and throat, not a mere ejaculatory cry, not an imitation of the cries of birds and beasts, not a social convention ; but the necessary concomitant of human reflection and communication. ' Language is a natural organ of the understanding, a sense of the human soul, just as the instinct of the bee builds its cell.' Language and reason are the distinguishing characteristics of man, as instinctive behaviour is characteristic of animals. Thus man can fashion words which are not signs of a mere instinctive or passional relationship to objects, but reflect the complex relationship of a more complex creature with the whole world in which he moves and works. Reason and language are twin aspects of man's real nature ; ' there is no reason without language, no language without reason '. Reason, no more than God, invented language ; reason and language develop necessarily from the nature of man.[10]

Herder therefore rejects both the Cartesian-rationalist conception of the mind as something separate and autonomous, and Rousseau's ' phantom ' notion of natural man. Man is at all times both rational and ' natural '. Language is the expression both of reason and of experience. It may be based, in certain respects, on the sense of hearing, but Herder points out that it only becomes true language when all sense-impressions are reduced to linguistic terms, transformed into sound. The senses do not exist in separate compartments of man, they permeate one another, and consciousness is the outcome of their combination. The attempts of Buffon, Condillac, Bonnet, or Diderot to isolate and analyse particular senses reduce man to an unreal abstraction, for his characteristic is the interlocking and interpenetration of all the senses. ' We are one thinking sensorium commune ' : ' The sense for language has become our sense of mediating and combining ; we are creatures of language.' Language interprets our total relationship, as thinking-sensual-active beings, with the world. Thus Herder can come to the important suggestion that the original words were verbs. All his predecessors, emphasising the contemplative, rationalist side of man, and perhaps influenced by Genesis, thought that nouns, the naming of things or of sense-impressions, were the original stock of language ; Herder's interpretation of consciousness as the function of interpenetrating senses enabled him to hold that language in the first place expressed through verbs the active relationship of man with his environment.[11]

In the latter part of the treatise Herder discusses the growth of language. His own preference for the language of early societies becomes clear, for in its marked rhythms and visual imagery he finds that unity of sense and idea which in his opinion is the true and essential characteristic of language and man. He follows up Leibniz's suggestions on the significance of language for the historian, and asserts that the development of language is a natural consequence of man's social nature. He refrains, however, from the violent attack on modern language and culture which appears in other works of these years, largely, no doubt, as he himself said to Hamann, because he wished to keep within the scope of the question as understood by the Academy of Sciences.[12]

It has been stated that Herder's treatment of his subject directs attention away from the actual problem of the origin of language and towards the comparative study of its history since the earliest times.[13] The influence of the work in this respect was certainly great. But it would be wrong to believe that Herder merely pushes the problem of the origin of language out of sight. Without the modern conceptions of biological and social evolution, Herder's idea of the origin of language was of course faulty and wanting. But his approach to the problem of consciousness, and his conception of the function of language with regard to the human constitution, for the first time clears the way for a scientific study of the problem of origins. Though his expression is often confused and confusing, and though he, as always, falls into teleological modes of expression, he frees language and reason from the attribution of a metaphysical ('angelic', as Leibniz put it) origin, and likewise refuses to consider it as a mere mechanical reflection of the environment. Both language and reason are for him the product of the activity of men in their total relation to their environment, of men impregnated with their environment and of the environment impregnated with human activity and perceived through the human senses. The work is a characteristic product of the Sturm und Drang. Striking out a line of his own between idealists and mechanical materialists, Herder rejects all dualistic philosophy, and seeks to define one single source of experience and thought, reflecting in his philosophy the unity of experience which he himself felt.

It is not surprising that the position he took up was not always clear, and was precarious too. Its instability is evident from his correspondence with Hamann which followed the publication of the work. The latter had looked forward to finding in Herder's treatise a refutation of the 'philosophical' approach, and he was bitterly disappointed in it. He put his own views in several reviews and articles of 1772. He was as much opposed as Herder to the idea that language was invented by men ; and equally he ridiculed the notion that men had been taught language by the beasts, that the origin of man was, as La Mettrie and d'Holbach indicated, in 'marsh and slime'. But his dissatisfaction with rationalists and materialists only turned him back to the conception of a divine origin of language. Our experience teaches us, he writes, that language is learned by instruction ; therefore the first language must have been taught men by God. God is not merely 'a potter of plastic forms', but 'a father of fiery spirits and breathing forces'. Hamann would solve the whole problem in his customary sibylline fashion by a play upon the meaning of the 'Word' of God. In the Garden of Eden

every phenomenon was a word—the sign, symbol, and pledge of a new, secret, inexpressible but all the more intimate union, communication, and community of divine energies and ideas. Everything that man heard, or saw with his eyes, or touched with his

VI.   LOTTE BUFF, 1772

VII.   CAROLINE FLACHSLAND
From Lavater's ' Physiognomische Fragmente '

hands, was in the beginning a living Word ; for God was the Word. With this Word in his mouth and in his heart, the origin of language was as natural, as near and easy, as a game.

Always, when Hamann writes on the origin of language, he identifies ' word ' with the religious term ' Logos ' and quits the field of scientific study.

Herder had therefore gone wrong, writes Hamann, in his approach to the problem. He had followed along the track of the philosophers of the ' ungodly ' century, of Buffon, La Mettrie, Rousseau, Condillac, Diderot. He had got himself into a maze, for he first of all proved that man is no animal, and then had shown that he is an animal. That is, ' because animals cannot invent language, and God must not, this apocalyptic being, man, who is no animal and yet is one, must have invented it '. And Hamann allows himself a somewhat jeering parody of Herder's arguments and style.[14]

Herder was puzzled, wounded, but also stung in his conscience by this criticism of his oldest and closest friend. He wrote to Nicolai, who expressed complete bewilderment as to Hamann's real meaning, that Hamann was only saying the same as he himself ; but he was writing ' prosaically ' what Hamann ' was prophesying with his sensuous intuition '.[15] But that he recognised the difference in their interpretations is clear from his letter to Hamann. He answers Hamann's dig about his own obscurity with a *tu quoque*, but goes on to excuse the secular argumentation of his work by the need of writing for the Academy of Sciences in terms it would accept. And he promises to make up for it in a new work, the *Oldest Document of the Human Race*—a promise he kept. His letter is very much in the Hamannesque style, sibylline, exalted, full of biblical phrases, and it concludes : ' You are right, dear Hamann, all learning is of the devil, like the lusts of the flesh.' [16] It interprets his fear of his own thought, for Hamann was right—Herder's theory of the origin of language did in fact treat man as a member of the animal kingdom, though a peculiar genus, and did eliminate God as a direct agent in the creation of language and reason. What is more, the work represents the main trend of Herder's thought. If in the *Oldest Document* he oscillates violently towards the Hamannesque view

N

of religion, this work itself does not take him off his path of essentially secular thought.[17]

In several of his later works Herder writes on the origin of language, and not always consistently. Sometimes he seems to sway towards the belief in a divine origin ; but his final view fully bears out the opinions expressed in *On the Origin of Language*. He furthered the translation of the first part of Monboddo's work *Of the Origin and Nature of Language*, with which he expressed full agreement ; and it was Monboddo's thesis that language and reason have a common source, that they are neither a gift of God nor of nature, but ' of our own acquisition, and the fruit of industry, like any art and science '.[18] What Herder gladly accepted from Monboddo as a correction of his own earlier theory was the Scotsman's emphasis on the social origins of language. While he had always recognised that the development of language after its first creation was dependent on social activity and communication, he had spoken of the origin of language only in terms of the individual face to face with nature. All his historical work led him beyond this notion to the conclusion that the genus man was not only, from the first, endowed with language and reason, but also was a social entity, and that man's linguistic endowment, all the ' noblest qualities of man ', were ' acquired ' through the nature of man's ' organisation and mode of life '.[19]

MIND AND MATTER

Herder's *On the Origin of Language* was his first serious raid into philosophical territory. Two years after its publication he joined issue with his contemporaries on the main battle-ground of eighteenth-century philosophy and began his most important epistemological work, *On Knowledge and Perception in the Human Soul*—again written for the Berlin Academy of Sciences, though this time Herder did not win the prize medal. Here he sets himself against all the leading philosophers of his time. His approach is distinctive, in that he starts from the fundamental Sturm und Drang consciousness of the inter-penetration in all experience of all the faculties of man. A review of 1772 gives his guiding principles. He attacks the ' philosophical spirit ' of the century, whether it appears in rationalistic or materialistic guise, because it is a ' gaunt ghost ', because it reduces life to speculation. ' Speculation unravels the iron bond of nature, instinct, and nerves, into strings, threads of flax.' The whole fault of a Hume is that he ' plays with things, instead of using them ', that he ' stands still and observes man from afar, instead of running to him and embracing him '. The dynamic of the Sturm und Drang is evident in such a mode of criticism, the desire to marry knowledge with action ; equally characteristic of the Sturm und Drang, and of this early stage of Herder's thought, is his conclusion that religion, faith, answers this need, for it indicates that here he is equating feeling, the impulse to activity, with activity itself.[20] He was to go deeper than this.

Favourably as Hamann and Herder responded to Locke's theory that ideas originate in sense-impressions, they rejected his conception of the mind as a *tabula rasa* ; likewise they expressed the greatest abhorrence for Helvétius' view that the only faculties of the mind are its capacity for receiving impressions ('sensibilité physique ') and memory.[21] Wherever such writers demonstrated or asserted the sensuous quality of ideas, as in Locke's theory of association, or Diderot's analysis of the conceptual world of the deaf and dumb and the blind, Herder showed the keenest and most positive interest, just as he himself tried to deduce a theory of plastic art from touch, the sense to which he thought the art corresponds.[22] But all the Stürmer und Dränger were convinced, too, that the mind, the ' soul ', is active and influences our apprehension of the physical world—for instance in the simplest sense, as when time or place are transformed and given a particular significance by our state of mind.[23] Herder's use of the term ' soul ' is characteristic. By it he does not mean the Christian soul, the immaterial organ of faith. Nor does he, as might often seem to be the case, mean the mind, the conceptual organ. It is for him the source of images as well as ideas, vibrating with feeling and impregnated with material symbols : a conception very close to that of Leibniz's monad.

The importance for Herder's thought of the philosophy of Leibniz can scarcely be over-estimated, and particularly of his *Nouveaux essais sur l'entendement* which were published for the first time in 1765. In place of Locke's *tabula rasa*, Leibniz represents the mind as a chamber with a screen for the reception of images ; but this screen has all sorts of folds and creases, and a sort of tension from which arises a vibration of its own.[24] Matter and mind possess self-activity. Leibniz even asks the question, ' Can matter think ? ' answering that since all matter is ultimately composed of ' immaterial real substances ', it is not dead stuff, and therefore can develop any qualities.[25]   These ideas deeply influenced Herder, as they did Diderot and d'Holbach.   He decisively rejected, however, other concepts of Leibniz, the innate ideas, the rigid distinction between matter and perception and its corollary, ' pre-established harmony ', together with the whole method of metaphysical deduction.

The early eighteenth-century conceptions of God, matter, and mind reflect in many ways the contemporary achievements in the mathematical and physical sciences.   In the opposition of God and the universe, matter and mind, an external force is distinguished from hard, material bodies as in the science of mechanics.   But during the eighteenth century the biological sciences begin to take shape, and the study of the mechanics of living organisms introduces new concepts into the theory of nature as a whole.   The idea of natural law is extended to the whole universe, embracing living as well as ' dead ' matter, and it is not fortuitous that alchemistic and mystical thought often mixes with scientific thought and experiment, for example in Stahl or Swedenborg, and indeed in the young Goethe.   The problem of the origin of species leads to the theories of pre-formationism or palingenesis, which assume an original germ ; the structural similarity between species, so emphasised by Buffon, leads to the theory of transformationism.   Both these ideas are present in Goethe's later notion of the ' primal type ' ; and Bonnet's theory of palingenesis recurs frequently in the thought of Lavater and Herder.[26]

Even more significant was the change in the concept of matter.   Chemists like Boerhave were relating the energy within the elements to that within vital processes.[27]   Haller, the physiologist, had discovered the energy within living tissue. Robinet and La Mettrie, both medical men, considered that the concept of the soul may be discarded, since the vital principle in man is no different from that in animals or plants.

Diderot and d'Holbach, both deeply interested in science, came to their conception of ' self-moving matter ', even, in Diderot's case, to the idea of biological evolution. Diderot decisively ascribed these new philosophical theories to the advances in the biological sciences.[28]

To these developments we should add the discovery of static electricity and the fixation of an electric charge, as exemplified in the construction of the Leyden Jar (1746). Here again were revealed the energies hidden in apparently inanimate matter.

Great changes in the theory of matter were taking place, then, at the time when the Stürmer und Dränger were growing to maturity. Their response to these changes accounts in some degree for their alienation from Kant. In his early work, Kant had indulged in metaphysical speculations, but with the *Dreams of a Visionary* of 1766 began his great critical investigation of the frontiers of understanding. Questions like the influence of the soul on the body, or the nature of free will and reality, are, he writes, beyond the limits of experience and the scope of reason. Important as was his work in disentangling science from metaphysics, it was combated by Herder because in his view it separated what, in nature and experience, is not separated, and put arbitrary limits to investigation. To some extent the difference between them may be ascribed to Kant's lack of appreciation of the revolution of concepts caused by the biological sciences, for these were making possible a new approach to problems which, in the earlier state of science, seemed intractable.

None of the Stürmer und Dränger had any systematic scientific training, and none contributed anything, in the Sturm und Drang period, to natural science itself. Goethe, among his multifarious pursuits in Strassburg, attended courses in natural science and read books on chemistry and electricity.[29] Herder was widely read in contemporary science. Periodicals like the *Allgemeine deutsche Bibliothek* and the *Teutsche Merkur* regularly carried notices of recent scientific publications. But these young men lacked any significant contact with scientists and travellers, and used their scientific knowledge only as material for their philosophy.

With most of them it is evident only incidentally, in terms

and images that they use, rather than in any systematic form,
and it often merges with the alchemistic conceptions of pietistic
circles. So the idea of palingenesis, which we find in Hamann,
Goethe, and above all in Herder, is partly theological and
alchemistic in origin, partly a product of contemporary biological science. It was only later, in the *Ideas on the Philosophy
of History*, that Herder tried to formulate it as a natural law
of social development ; it is perhaps the source of his and
Goethe's concept of metamorphosis, and of Goethe's later
morphological work. The early Faust of Goethe is an al-
chemist and magician, who seeks to escape from abstract and
formal ideas to direct magical communication with the spirits ;
though already here, in his rejection by the Earth Spirit, we
see the Sturm und Drang consciousness that knowledge cannot
be obtained by any magical short cut, but only through
experience. But all of the Stürmer und Dränger delight in
images from contemporary science which interpret the moving,
creative principle of being. They are fond of the term ' elasticity ' ; Herder and Bürger both use the phrase ' elasticity of
the spirit '.[30] Most of all they delight in electrical images, in
this period when Franklin and Priestley were carrying out
their experiments in electricity, and when Merck's acquaintance Lichtenberg was measuring the electric charge in the
atmosphere. Wieland calls Herder ' an electric cloud ',[31]
Lenz speaks of the ' spark of God ', probably a reference to the
charge of the Leyden jar.[32] Goethe wrote to a girl friend :
' Happiness of the soul and heroism are as communicable as
electricity, and you have as much of them as the electric
machine contains sparks of fire.' [33] Herder uses such symbols
over and over again. ' We electrify ourselves to activity . . .
that is the wondrous creative power to set souls alive, like the
electric spark, perhaps, in blood and sun.' [34] Genius speaks
to genius, he writes, as an electric spark sends out its energy ;
he even speaks of Prometheus fetching the ' electric spark '
from Heaven.[35] In such terms as these, ' irritation ', ' energy ',
' elasticity ', ' electricity ', the Stürmer und Dränger link up
the dynamic principle of matter with the creativeness of spirit.
Herder's *On Knowledge and Perception in the Human Soul* is the
systematic exposition of this relationship, an attempt to define
the dynamic nature of being.

The first version of 1774 defines all the essentials of his approach. He rejects the conventional distinction of mind, sense, and will. We have no knowledge unaccompanied by feeling and judgment ; we have no feeling unaccompanied by knowledge. Mind and body, spirit and matter, cannot be separated. Mind is neither a *tabula rasa*, a mere screen for the registration of impressions, nor a complex of innate ideas. In the operations of the mind we detect the deepest influence of the body : we think ' according to the modulation of the circulation of the blood ', according to ' the rhythm of breathing '. Body is ' the expressed image of the soul ' ; knowledge is ' the clear outcome of all the states of feeling of the soul '.[36] All personal experience proves this, and fortifies him in rejecting the theses of Locke and Leibniz.

Upon this direct experience Herder builds his theory of the nature of mind and matter. The mind cannot be an immaterial abstract substance. ' In it there glow forces, living sparks ' ; it seeks ' to transform everything into its own being '. Body and soul are not two unrelated spheres, but both can be broken up into an infinity of substances, just as the Milky Way has been resolved by observation into innumerable systems of stars. Both are an aggregate of ' obscurely perceptive forces ' ; the body is the ' realm ' of the soul, and out of its energies the soul forms its being. The analysis of the body tells us more about the soul than all abstract speculation—' psychological physiology is the most important part of philosophy '. Thus every soul has its own individuality, according to its body (this was the period of Lavater's physiognomical researches) ; and conversely, the nature and character of the sensations experienced are influenced by the ' inner force ' of the soul. The world, matter, is not an unchangeable datum, it is moving, and is shaped by us : ' we live in a world that we shape ourselves '.[37] Thus knowledge, sensation, and activity form one changing whole.

In the final version of 1778 the arrangement of the treatise is improved, and more arguments adduced from modern science. There is nothing static in nature, he writes : gravity, elasticity, magnetism, the electric current, all are expressions of the energy of nature and analogues of the energies within the human soul.[38] He then expounds Haller's theory of irritation to refute all pure

idealism and mechanical materialism. ' Raise Haller's physiological work to the level of psychology—then you can say
something about thinking and perception.' [39] In man, the
nerves correspond to the fibres of plants, they are the organs
of sensation, without which the soul cannot exist. The senses
and nerves detect the waves of light and sound, scents and
stimuli of all kinds, and on their perceptions the activity of
the soul is based, without them no knowledge is possible. The
nerves are ' delicate silver threads, by which the Creator binds
together the inner and outer world, heart and head, thought
and will, senses and all our limbs '.

But the reaction of the soul is greater than the ' irritation '
of sense-perception, indicating an indwelling energy. The soul
has no special locus, such as Descartes' pineal gland, but is the
combination of all the nerves, collecting and unifying within
the imagination all experience. And similarly, *vice versa*, ' our
whole body is filled with soul '. [40]

So Herder asks the question : ' Is the soul then material ?
or have we so many immaterial souls ? ' And he answers :
' I do not know what material and immaterial is, but do not
think that nature has put iron boards between them, since
nowhere in nature do I see iron boards, and would expect
them least of all where nature has most intimately united them '
—i.e. in the human soul. [41] At the source of all phenomena
are energies [' Kräfte '], which cannot be called either material
or immaterial : energies which the natural scientists have discovered, energies evident in our daily experience, observable
in autobiographies and the works of poets. ' Nothing in nature
is separate, everything influences and combines with everything
else in imperceptible transitions.' [42]

It is evident that Herder's treatise does not fit into the
tradition of epistemological writings. It has none of the logic
and discipline of Locke or Berkeley or Leibniz or Hume, it
extends far beyond the scope of psychological analysis, he calls
on poets for confirmation of his thesis, and he allows himself
outbursts of religious enthusiasm to emphasise his feeling that
this structure of nature is good. But the contrast with normal
epistemology is deliberate. He bases his conclusions on the
full experience of man, and for that reason strives to embrace
the total reactions and interactions of all human faculties which

make up the process of thinking, feeling, and action ; and in so doing he wishes to lead men, not to thought or to science, but to experience, to full joy in life. Thus he not only refutes conceptions like Locke's *tabula rasa*, Leibniz' innate ideas and pre-established harmony, and Helvétius' passive perceptivity, but also rejects their whole method of philosophising, which is based on the assumption that the operations of mind or sense can be separated from one another. For him, mind, body, and will have all the same source, their inter-actions are continual, all are dynamic, growing. Every development of life, every response, is the product of some contact between them ; and out of this contact something new grows, something disproportionate, like the plant from the seed, the child from the womb. Life is not a mechanical sum, but a dialectical process ; the mind is the summation of sensual experience, but the sum is greater than its parts. In combining impressions it creates something new, something higher, it establishes a new realm ' of invisible beings and forces, in which the creator-spirit is one and all '.[43] ' What I am, I have become. I have grown like a tree : the seed was there ; but air, earth and all the elements, which I did not establish round me, had to make their contribution to shape the seed, the fruit, the tree.' [44]

In his *Dialogues on God* of 1787 Herder develops much the same ideas, though with a stronger emphasis on law, on the beneficent necessity which binds the universe and which is present in the laws of reason as in those of nature. The work is a defence and interpretation of Spinoza, and nature, experience, and all natural processes are considered to be divine. But Herder attacks Spinoza's geometric conception of extension, which he replaces by the idea of energy. Mind and matter originate from the same ' energies ', the laws of whose behaviour can be discovered in psychology, in the natural and historical sciences. He opposes all metaphysical speculation, all assumptions that there can be an investigable realm beyond nature, or that the intentions of God can be discussed as if he were a person outside his creation. Science is needed, not teleology. Metaphysics should become an ' after-physics ', a further development, over a wider range, of the methods and conclusions of physics and natural history ; it should establish how things happen, not with what intention. The scientist who, modestly pursuing a simple goal, ' seems to forget the intentions of God ', does in fact find ' all of God in every object and at every point of Creation '.   The primary reality is being, ' Dasein ' ;   and the nature of being is dynamic, changing, not static.   Death and evil are not negations of being, but parts of this dynamic process, which must express itself in struggle and conflict.[45]

Herder's conception of matter and of the relationship of mind and matter is elusive.   Does he materialise the soul or spiritualise matter ?   The same question may be put of the doctrine of Hartley, who had founded his psychology on nervous response, and to whom Herder owed a debt.   In 1773 he praised Hartley's work and called him a ' phenomenon ',[46] and Hamann reproved Herder's ' predilection for certain physiological concepts, with which you are more in love than I am '.[47]   His theory of ' energies ' is strikingly similar to that of Priestley's, just as their religious attitudes are related.[48]   On one side Herder seems to anticipate the modern electronic theory of matter, and the view of dialectical materialism on the relationship of mind and matter ;   but also, and almost despite himself, he tends to identify his ' energies ' with unsubstantial, spiritual elements, like modern vitalists and idealists. Thus he is a precursor of Carlyle, who inherited from the German idealists this dynamic conception of nature, but asserts it in an entirely spiritual form ;   [49]   but also of Marx, who in his dialectical materialism fused the ' passive ' side of the older materialism with the ' active ' side of idealism, as he states the problem in the *Theses on Feuerbach*.[50]   The same double pull of Herder's thought is evident in his greatest work, the *Ideas on the Philosophy of Mankind*.   His approach to the origins of man is predominantly materialistic, and yet, like Bonnet, he would see man as a link between earthly forms and a spiritual existence he may some day attain.   With some justification Kant could criticise the first part of the *Ideas* both because of the boldness of the materialistic arguments, and because Herder conceived of the world as ' an invisible realm of active and independent forces '.[51]

The main significance of Herder's epistemology is his resolute determination to justify the fullness of experience, his opposition to all transcendentalism, dualism, and mechanism, all separation of the soul into higher and lower powers. We have seen how Hamann and he justify the senses as agencies of God, and the world of experience as a symbol of God. In this spirit both fought against Kant's *Critique of Pure Reason*. Hamann's unpublished essay, *Metacritique on the Purism of Reason*, which Herder read, contains the fundamental criticism that reason cannot exist without experience and language, without sensuous existence. Herder developed this view, even borrowing the title *Metakritik*, in his prolonged contest with Kant. ' Whoever does not trust his senses is a fool and must necessarily become an empty speculator ' ; and again : ' We are not intended to breathe ether . . . but the healthy fragrance of the earth.'[52]

The other Stürmer und Dränger did not interest themselves in the theory of knowledge. Lenz's wry comment is paralleled in most of them ; why should we curse this body of ours, he asks, this *amicus certus in re incerta*, ' for what a weathercock is our soul ! ' [53] They were far more concerned with the problem of human powers, of the relationship between man and his environment, a much more practical form of the same question. Lavater's physiognomical studies attracted Goethe's cooperation because in physiognomy he saw expressed both the unity of soul and body, and that of man and his environment. He wrote in an essay for Lavater's work :

Man's environment does not only act upon him, he again reacts upon his environment, and as he lets himself be modified, so again he modifies the world around him. Nature forms man, he transforms himself, and this transformation too is natural.[54]

This principle is in fact that of all Herder's thought, though the expression has a clarity and sureness that Herder rarely attains. Goethe does not analyse man as a knowing or sentient being, but sees him above all as an active entity within a larger whole ; it is in activity that the unity of all being is truly evident.

In *Faust* this is the central theme, though it does not become explicit till Part 1 was filled out in Goethe's middle age ; it may be maintained, however, that in completing Part 1 Goethe was successful in recapturing the spirit of the *Urfaust*. Faust begins as a magician, rejecting the separate, abstract disciplines of the Middle Ages because they do not lead him to the knowledge of the ' inner forces of nature '.   His attempt to identify himself with the Earth Spirit fails, for it is a purely mental effort.   But in his interpretation of the first words of St. John's Gospel, with Mephistopheles in his chamber, he gets an inkling of the solution to his problem.   He rejects ' In the Beginning was the Word,' for words represent ideas, and truth cannot originate in the brain.   He rejects, after a moment's hesitation, ' In the Beginning was Sense '—the interpretation of the materialists of his time—with the most pertinent criticism : ' Is it Sense that works and creates ? '   For the sensualist, man is a passive recipient.   So he falls on the translation : ' In the Beginning was Energy,' the theory of Herder.   But warned by an undefined feeling that this is not sufficient, that ' energy ' is too vague and gives him no clue as to what he is to do, he finally writes : ' In the Beginning was the Deed.' [55]   So the beginning of Faust's true knowledge of the world is the ' deed ', his decision to leave his study and enter the world, ' to hurl himself into the torrent of time, into the rolling of events '.[56] Through his love for Gretchen he begins to ' share the lot of mankind ' and to feel his identity with nature, and in the scene *Forest and Cave* speaks gratefully of the deep knowledge this identification has brought.   And his understanding and personality grow throughout Part 2, as his activity widens in range and depth.   In activity, sense and feeling are fused with thought.

One source of the dramatic tension of the play is Mephistopheles' failure to understand Faust's insistent urge towards activity.   He sees his choice as one between spirit and matter, and gleefully points out to the student the alternatives.[57]   On philosophy :

> Wer will was lebigs erkennen und beschreiben,
> Muss erst den Geist herauser treiben,
> Dann hat er die Theil in seiner Hand,
> Fehlt leider nur das geistlich Band.

> If you would know what lives, and describe it,
> First you must expel the spirit,
> Then you've got the parts in your hand,
> All that's missing is the spiritual band.

The senses, on the other hand, are the means to pleasure :

> Grau, theurer Freund, ist alle Theorie
> Und grün des Lebens goldner Baum.

> All theory is gray, dear friend,
> Green is the golden tree of life.

But Mephistopheles thus fails to understand the very essence of Faust's purpose, which is the combination of thought and sense, of theory and practice, through incessant striving. Like Herder Goethe trusts the senses, but with an important modification. Herder simply defended them against Kant's mistrust ; Goethe insists that they can be trusted if they are tested and developed through activity, through practice, through science. ' Man is sufficiently equipped for all true earthly needs, if he trusts his senses and develops them in such a fashion that they remain worthy of trust.' [58] Such observations belong to Goethe's maturity ; but like his later scientific work they are consistent clarifications of the intimations of his Sturm und Drang.

Schiller's philosophical essays follow a line which diverges markedly from that of Herder and Goethe. Particularly from the time of his Kantian studies he adopted Kant's philosophical dualism and categorical imperative, which are directly opposed to their mode of thought ; at best he approaches the Sturm und Drang in his rather unsuccessful attempt to reconcile the moral imperative with natural inclination. But his earliest essay, the dissertation he defended on leaving the academy in 1780, shows important points of contact with the Sturm und Drang. Its theme, *The Connexion between the Animal and Spiritual Nature of Man*, is ' the remarkable contribution of the body to the activity of the soul ', a mean between Stoic and Epicurean doctrine. Without instincts and senses, he writes, the soul would remain lethargic, undeveloped, and he fortifies his statements by his medical knowledge and quotations from historians and poets. The work has however, none of the boldness and brilliance of Herder and Goethe, and the bearing of his thesis is much limited by his acceptance of the postulates of the independent existence of the soul and of its future life after the death of the body.[59] Most of all, it lacks the fire and urgency of the work of the earlier Stürmer und Dränger.

When one compares Herder's writings on the nature of consciousness, and the corresponding statements of the other Stürmer und Dränger, with epistemological works of their English and French predecessors, it is precisely this fire and urgency which distinguishes them. Because of it their work is often ill-composed, their argumentation is often dislocated and obscured by emotive statements and undigested assertions, to such an extent that their views do not find a place in any normal history of epistemology. But it is this same ardour that gives it its importance. Herder is not 'playing' with theories. His thought is a desperate struggle to come to grips with his whole mode of life, to formulate his spiritual and sensuous delight in existence. He tries to combine in one unity his emotive and instinctive convictions with his intellectual activities ; or rather, the latter are for him merely the clarification and generalisation of the former. While Hume could assert the incompatibility of the customs of practical thought and behaviour with the results of philosophy, while Diderot and d'Holbach could combine materialism with a belief in the natural virtue of man, Herder sought a philosophy which would interpret the whole of his immediate experience. His philosophy, and the attitude of the other Stürmer und Dränger, bears the marks of the limitations of the life in which they were placed. It has none of the scope it might have had if their lives had been passed in the capitals of great nations, in the midst of discussions of great political and social issues, if they had been thrown into the society of statesmen, administrators, financiers, scientists, such as could be found in the Literary Club in London or at d'Holbach's house in Paris. It lacked too the discipline of method which such societies imposed on their members. Because of this isolation and provincialism the thought of the Sturm und Drang has inevitably a subjective and somewhat capricious character. But, also because of it, it was free of conventional assumptions, it was not a social pastime, it was relevant to their whole needs and purposes. Herder's philosophical theory is thus a true reflection of the Sturm und Drang principle of full, pulsating existence, and a most significant criticism of the inadequacies of the eighteenth-

century mode of thought. It foreshadows the later philosophies which attempt to define reality as essentially active,
energetic, which seek a single source of nature and man, which
recognise the interpenetration of subject and object, mind
and matter—of the dialectical idealism of Hegel and the
dialectical materialism of Marx.

MOTHER NATURE

In their whole theory of the nature of mind the Stürmer und
Dränger assert the essential unity of man and nature. But,
though Herder in particular calls on the testimony of science to
substantiate this view, their conviction arose much more from
direct personal experience than from the results and method
of scientific investigation. Their conception of nature is therefore not primarily that of the scientist ; nature is for them a
living organism of which they are part, whose energy thrills
throughout their own being, with which they are connected
directly through all their emotions and instincts. Nature is
the mother from whom they are sprung, the nurse on whom
they depend for sustenance. In organic nature, the nature of
woods and fields, they find not only an analogy of the universe
and of themselves, but also a perpetual source of refreshment,
a channel to immediate communication with the ' living
forces ' of reality. Their general theory of nature does not rest
at an intellectual conviction, as with Spinoza or d'Holbach,
but like Shaftesbury's embraces, or even is based on, a spontaneous feeling of affinity with nature, in the sense of the
countryside, the seasons.

Throughout the eighteenth century there was a growing
appreciation of the countryside and rural manners. Addison's
view, that ' we find the works of Nature still more pleasant
the more they resemble those of art ',[60] is extremely understandable in an age when travel was difficult, roads boggy,
and winter a misery except within four well-built walls. But
the pleasanter aspects of country life could be celebrated :
the successful accomplishment of the seasonal tasks in Thomson, the virtues of simple Alpine life in Haller's *Die Alpen*, the
harvest wagons of Gainsborough, the serenity of the countryside that the English water-colourists evoke, the gaiety of

country sports. All these, like the poems of Collins or Akenside, show a conscious appreciation of the countryside, sustained by a sometimes polemical emphasis on the virtues it promotes among country folk, seen from a distance by the landed gentleman or contemplative townsman. The work of Capability Brown and other English landscape artists, the growing taste for the English garden in France, illustrate this combination of pleasure in nature with the decorum of an upper-class mode of life.[61] Gray's and the Wartons' delight in crags and ruins has the same secure background of conventional composure.

The novelty of Rousseau's *La nouvelle Héloise* lay not merely in the descriptions of a wild and lovely landscape, but also in the meaning of this landscape for St.-Preux. It does not appear primarily as a setting for rural virtues, but exists for the lonely heart, who finds ecstasy, terror, and solace in mountains and lakes, and seeks in intimate communion with nature a refuge and restoration from the pains of social life. A mysterious unity between nature and the individual is discovered, as contrasted with the disharmony and ' unnaturalness ' of social relations. The moods of nature are a symbol and a solace for the rapture and distress of St.-Preux—as, in a more rhetorical fashion, the Scottish mountains and mist are for the calamities of Ossian. Nature is here not merely sympathetically observed, it merges with and moulds the individual man. The psychological dangers in this surrender to nature were ultimately held in check in Rousseau's novel, and in Julie's garden wild nature is successfully reconciled with order and art, but in the first part of his novel he defined a relationship between the homeless individual and untamed nature which appealed with tremendous force to following generations, caught in social and political conflict which perplexed and tortured them. Among the Stürmer und Dränger, who were the first Germans to feel distress and doubt over modern society, this new conception of nature came to its full expression.

At the same time as Rousseau, Klopstock was discovering a new source of delight in nature. Like Rousseau, he was fond of physical exercise in natural surroundings, of long walks, swimming, skating, and he wrote poems expressing his delight in movement. Many of his poems celebrate nature, the thunderstorm, the rose. As a rule, however, he gave these experiences a religious or moral reference and twist ; his poem on the Zürich lake leads to thoughts of innocence and love, his *Frühlingsfeier* turns the thunderstorm into a messenger and symbol of God. The frank delight in nature and physical exercise of the young Klopstock shocked many of his pietist friends, so sceptical of earthly pleasures ; yet he himself seems nearly always to have felt the need to justify it in religious or moral terms. In the following period, the delight in nature was to liberate itself to a large extent from these direct religious and moral props, but was rarely to abandon them altogether, even though the religion was to become more mystical or naturistic.

It was from Klopstock that the Stürmer und Dränger learned to love physical exercise, a taste which went along with all the new insight that Goethe acquired at Strassburg from Herder. At Strassburg Goethe learned to skate, and to enjoy walking and riding over the countryside in all weathers. Herder's letters to Caroline tell how he often would find relief in lonely excursions, usually forced on him by the duties of his office. Herder's relationship with nature was never, however, deeply satisfying to him. A description of a natural scene, such as he gives in a letter to Caroline of 2 October 1771, is extremely rare with him. His 'inflated imagination', he wrote, prevented him from seeing and enjoying nature. On his voyage through the Baltic the life on board ship, surrounded by waters or skirting the Norse shores, was a means for him to understand the character of primitive societies, to think of the great deeds told in the Eddas, in *Ossian*. The storm that wrecked his ship becomes significant to him as he reads *Fingal*.[62] When he went into the country at Bückeburg it was with Shakespeare or Homer in his pocket. He tells Caroline of the countryside at Pyrmont in terms which interpret primarily his enthusiasm for this 'most German' region 'where Hermann fought and Varus was defeated' ; the heavy sulphurous atmosphere makes him feel how 'humiliating' it is to be so affected by the elements.[63] Nature is a means for him to pursue his own thoughts, to dream, undistracted by social duties.[64]

With the others, too, nature often enough has only this

negative function of giving their imagination free rein. There
may be a fine view, noble trees, nightingales singing, and
flowers opening, but these win significance only because they
give the opportunity for reflection or imagination. Maler
Müller's delight in travelling expresses this point of view :

So we would always press forward, in the storm, along water-
side and forest, now beyond paths and hedges, following the flight
of heated imagination which soars intoxicated towards a prouder,
more hopeful future. Then one thinks one is winging more swiftly
into time.—And now and again, what does not come into one's
mind ! First love, first friendship, one's first, dearest notions,
one's first feeling of delight in nature—then all the splendour of
the past is reflected back through the soul—and mates with the
hopes of the future ; their children are ecstatic dreams, which for
a time cradle heart and soul in voluptuous slumber.[65]

Lenz's ruminations as he wandered over the countryside can
rarely have been of this ecstatic character. He often found
an outlet for the unease and friction within himself by setting
out alone, particularly in the critical period in Weimar,
Switzerland, and Alsace just before his breakdown, but these
journeys seem to have increased the tension within him. At
Weimar he was half banished into the country, and his attitude
was peevish, rather than anything else—he wrote to Frau von
Stein that he was ' resigné à la campagne '.[66] His long tour
through the Swiss mountains, through the Oberland to the
St. Gotthard, and then back through Glarus, has something
desperate about it, for he was by this time deeply anxious
about his future. In his letters hardly a trace of enthusiasm
is evident ; at best we can guess something of the feelings that
the mountains must have stirred in him by a rare phrase such
as : ' a setting for angels, and the people mostly devils, but
also sometimes angels '.[67] His last tortured wandering over the
Alsatian hills, in snow and ice, has left no mark in his letters
or works ; by this time half-crazed, his journeyings were
mainly a bitter and purposeless flight from himself. But even
in his best days, his love of nature was closely associated with
his incapacity for balance and happiness in society. In
1772 he told Salzmann how his unhappiness drives him into
nature :

Now I hang on nature's breasts with double fervour, even though she may bind her forehead with sunbeams or cold mists, her motherly countenance always smiles on me. . . . Indeed I find in the countryside round Landau [Alsace] new beauties every day, and the coldest North-Easter cannot frighten me away from her. . . . Mountains that bear the sky, valleys at their feet full of villages which seem to sleep there, like Jacob at the foot of his ladder.[68]

Yet this feeling for nature never crystallised into pure and intense experience. None of Lenz's poems is inspired by nature or shows any deep emotion over natural scenes ; even in the lyrics which sprang from his love for Friederike Brion, if he refers to nature, it is in the generalised terms of anacreontic poetry. In plays and novels he often dwells on the charm of simple village people, but rarely on their natural surroundings. It is clear that he was not blind to the beauty of the country, and here and there he touches on the pale and austere charms of winter. His hermit in *Der Waldbruder* writes :

I would never have imagined that the climate could be so mild in winter. The region in which I have built my hut is incidentally very picturesque. Mountains piled grotesquely on one another, whose black plumes seem to push against the weight of the lowering clouds, deep beneath me a broad valley, where the houses of a poor but happy village lie scattered along the banks of a bright stream. . . . Yesterday I went for a walk in a meadow, when the sun was making a St. Martin's summer in the midst of winter. . . . The pale green of the meadows, that seemed to struggle with hoar-frost and snow, the brown, withered bushes, what a refreshing sight for me ! [69]

Descriptions as precise as this occur very rarely in the works of the Stürmer und Dränger, with the exception of *Werther*. But Lenz's hermit cannot free himself from his obsessions and enjoy his surroundings for long. The novel soon takes us into the entanglement of a perverse love which tortures him and obliterates nature from his consciousness.

The peculiar characteristic of Goethe's delight in nature is that it is not an escape, not a mere stimulus for dreams, not a symbol of truth or virtue ; it is the completion of his being, arising from his vital energies and flowing back to strengthen them.   From the beginning to the end of his life it is the expression and source of restoration, of joy.   In some doggerel he sent to Merck, which tells of the rude health that he enjoys because he is busy, he writes : [70]

> Sieh so ist Natur ein Buch Lebendig
> Unverstanden doch nicht unverständlich
> Denn dein Herz hat viel und gros Begehr
> Was wohl in der Welt für Freude wär,
> Allen Sonnenschein u. alle Bäume
> Alles Meergestad u. alle Träume
> In dein Herz zusammeln mit einander
> Wie die Welt durchwühlend Bäncks Solander. . . .

> Lo, Nature's a book, living and full,
> Ununderstood, yet not ununderstandable,
> For your heart has much and high desire
> To find what joys on earth there are,
> All the sunshine, trees and streams,
> All the sea-coasts, all the dreams,
> To store them up within your heart
> Like Banks Solander ploughing o'er the earth. . . .

In Banks' and Solander's journey to Iceland and the Shetlands he finds a symbol of his own joyous discovery of nature.[71] But he did not approach nature primarily as an observer.   In his Sturm und Drang period there are indeed very few actual descriptions of particular scenes.   He felt nature as part of his being, as a prolongation of himself, of the surging longing and energy within him, not as something distinct, to be contemplated.   Neither, for the same reason, does he philosophise about the harmony he felt between himself and nature ;   he states it, as a basic experience of his being.   All aspects of nature are meaningful for him.   In *Mayfest* (later called *Mailied*) the joy in spring merges with joy in love ;   without transitions his celebration of the creativeness of nature slips over into a celebration of love and of the joyous poetic wellspring in himself : [72]

> Wie herrlich leuchtet
> Mir die Natur !
> Wie glänzt die Sonne !
> Wie lacht die Flur !

Es dringen Blüten
Aus iedem Zweig,
Und tausend Stimmen
Aus dem Gesträuch,

Und Freud und Wonne
Aus ieder Brust.
O Erd o Sonne
O Glück o Lust!

O Lieb' o Liebe,
So golden schön,
Wie Morgenwolken
Auf ienen Höhn;

Du seegnest herrlich
Das frische Feld,
Im Blütendampfe
Die volle Welt.

O Mädchen Mädchen
Wie lieb' ich dich!
Wie blinkt dein Auge!
Wie liebst du mich!

So liebt die Lerche
Gesang und Luft,
Und Morgenblumen
Den Himmels Duft,

Wie ich dich liebe
Mit warmen Blut,
Die du mir Jugend
Und Freud und Muth

Zu neuen Liedern
Und Tänzen giebst!
Sey ewig glücklich
Wie du mich liebst!

*   *   *

How lustrous sparkles
Nature to me!
How gleams the sunlight!
How laughs the lea!

From all the branches
The blossoms push,
And thousand voices
From every bush,

And joy and rapture
From every breast.
O earth o sunlight
O joy o zest

O love o love,
So golden bright,
Like morning clouds
On yonder height ;

Thy blessing dowers
The dewy field,
In mists of flowers
The boundless world.

O maiden, maiden,
How I love thee !
Thine eyes how sparkling !
How thou lovst me !

So loves the lark
To sing and soar,
And morning flowers
To breathe the air,

As I love thee
With pulsing blood,
Who givst me youth
And joyous mood

To make new songs
And dances new !
Be ever happy
As thou lovst me !

Spring, love, poetry, all have one source. The 'thou' of stanza five is significantly ambiguous, applying both to love and nature.

But Goethe is no fair-weather poet. He loved to battle through rain and wind, rejoicing in the elements. In *Wandrers Sturmlied* he gaily revels in rain and mud : [73]

> Wen du nicht verlässest Genius,
> Wird der Regen Wolcke
> Wird dem Schlossensturm
> Entgegensingen wie die
> Lerche du dadroben,
> Wen du nicht verlässest Genius.

> Him thou ne'er forsakest, Genius,
> Greets the rain cloud
> Greets the sleet-storm
> With a song as does the
> Skylark thou up yonder,
> Him thou ne'er forsakest, Genius.

The nature that Goethe loved and needed was that which corresponded to his own wide-ranging feeling, the nature on which man depends for his elemental needs, which he may guide for his necessary purposes, but not the nature he consciously arranges for his pleasure. In *Lilis Parck* he mocks at the neat lawns and walks in which he, an unkempt bear, is so out of place.[74] Nor does he seek out beautiful, picturesque scenes. He feels identity with trees and grass and fruits, with the whole process of nature. Nature is a mother, at whose breasts he sucks—an image he often used. ' With deep breaths I suck, Nature, from you, a painful pleasure ' [75] or

> Ich saug an meiner Nabelschnur
> Nun Nahrung aus der Welt.
> Und herrlich rings ist die Natur
> Die mich am Busen hält.[76]

> And at my navel-string I suck
> New nurture from the world.
> And nature round about is lush
> Upon whose breast I'm held.

Nature thus gives him a feeling of confidence, restores him to himself ; it is not a particular sphere of existence, but existence itself. Over and over again he seeks renewal in nature in order to return back strengthened to men. On his visit to Switzerland in 1775 he was struggling with the complexities of his relationship with Lili Schönemann, and in the poems he wrote on this journey we see how nature comforted him, though without providing him with an answer to his problem. The poem just quoted describes how his serenity on the Zürich lake is interrupted by the thought of Lili :

> Aug mein Aug was sinckst du nieder
> Goldne Träume kommt ihr wieder
> Weg du Traum so Gold du bist
> Hier auch Lieb und Leben ist.

> Eye my eye why sink in yearning ?
> Golden dreams, are you returning ?
> Dreams, away with your golden spell
> Here are love and life as well.

And he again dwells, with new delight and deeper composure, on the sunshine and fruit mirrored in the lake. Nature is here no alternative to love, and no Providence ; it rescues him from dreams and enables him to face reality. This spiritual sustenance has no moral or practical content ; it is ' physical well-being ', which rises from the depths.

The grateful consciousness of identity with nature is the foundation of Goethe's conception of nature. It is therefore no confusion of meaning when he uses the word nature to denote humanity, when he cries ' Nature ! Nature ! nothing so completely Nature as Shakespeare's characters.' [77] Art becomes great, in his opinion at this time, when it recaptures those principles of being which he recognises in the great process of nature. In the Strassburg Minster he felt a principle of construction comparable to that of an organic body. In the poem *Wandrer* a traveller finds a peasant family dwelling and working on the site of an antique temple, and he apostrophises the spirit of nature that builds and destroys, creating in a myriad forms existence and enjoyment, and remaining ever the same.[78]

Natur, du ewig Keimende,
Schaffst jeden zum Genuss des Lebens.
Deine Kinder all
Hast mütterlich mit einem
Erbtheil ausgestattet
Einer Hütte.
Hoch baut die Schwalb am Architrav
Unfühlend welchen Zierraht
Sie verklebt.
Die Raup umspinnt den goldnen Zweig
Zum Winterhaus für ihre Brut.
Und du flickst zwischen der Vergangenheit
Erhabne Trümmer
Für dein Bedürfnis
Eine Hütt o Mensch !
Geniessest über Gräbern !

Nature, eternally sprouting,
Thou shapest each one to joy in life.
Like a mother thou
Hast endowed thy children
Each with his portion,
A home.
The swallow builds high on the architrave
Not feeling the beauty
It plasters over.
The caterpillar meshes the golden twig
As a winter home for its brood.
And you, O man, for your need
Among the past's
Sublime ruins
Patch up a cottage !
You thrive upon the graves !

Goethe sometimes identifies his overwhelming rapture in nature with religious feeling. Jove's cupbearer, in the poem *Ganymed*, sums up the glory of spring, of flowers and nightingale, as God, ' the all-friendly father '.[79] But this idea of God has none of its usual religious content ; the term is simply the most comprehensive affirmation of existence, whether it appear in human terms as good or disastrous. Submission to the glory of nature may evoke the highest rapture and consciousness of vital existence, but it means too acceptance of the process of decay and dissolution.

In *The Sorrows of Young Werther* Goethe shows what tensions this conception of nature involves with the social and religious idea of good, how endangered is the heart that, surrendering to nature, makes nature a refuge and not a means to health. Werther's catastrophe arises from his inability to find invigoration in nature, as Goethe himself could. Nature is for Werther the antithesis of society, and stimulates in him feelings which make him ever more incapable of transforming the energy of his inner longings into action in the outer world. His joy in the spring, his feeling of oneness with grass and insects, and through it with the great process of nature, with God, gives meaning to life. But from the beginning he recognises that there is something dangerous in this submission to the splendours of nature. And soon he sees that ' the source of man's happiness is that of his misery as well '. This great force of creation is a force of destruction and death ; all that comes to be must pass away.

My heart is undermined by the consuming power that lies hid in the all of nature, which has formed nothing that does not destroy its neighbour and itself. And so I totter in anguish ! Sky and earth and all the weaving forces around me ! I see nothing but an eternally devouring, eternally ruminating monster.[80]

The same surrender which makes him rejoice in the infinite creativeness and love of nature and God in the first part of the novel urges him to self-destruction in the second part, when he sees the floods pouring into the valley and feels impelled to throw himself into the torrent.

A feeling of horror overcame me, and then again a longing ! Ah ! I stood with outstretched arms over against the abyss, and breathed down ! down ! and lost myself in the joy of hurling all my torments, all my sufferings, down there, to be carried away like the waves.[81]

The worst torment for him is when he finds himself feelingless towards nature. As he describes how untouched he is by the beauty of an autumn day, he cries :

I suffer much, for I have lost what was the only joy of my life, the holy, reviving force, with which I created worlds around me.[82]

This force wells up again as he finds a symbol for his unhappiness in the desolation of winter, the ' withered heath ' and barren hills of Ossian ; like Lenz's hermit he feels a voluptuous melancholy, a sort of fulfilment, which makes his suicide not merely an escape, but also a reconciliation. *The Sorrows of Young Werther* is too often taken as an autobiographical confession. It is clear that Goethe here describes the logic of an attitude some of the elements of which he felt within himself ; but Werther differs from Goethe not only in his lack of will, but also in his attitude to nature. Goethe could surrender to nature, feel its divinity, but rise refreshed from such experiences to face the problems of living. He liked to observe and sketch, while Werther's transports make him lay his paints on one side. He not only loved nature, but tested and hardened himself against wind and weather.

For most of Goethe's friends nature was a guarantee of virtue. Fritz Jacobi wrote him a long letter about an excursion he made into the countryside, ' clothing himself in the splendour of God ', and for Jacobi this sort of experience naturally merged with the pure joys of family life.[83] Even more strongly F. L. Stolberg emphasised the virtuousness of true feeling for nature. In his Klopstockian ode, *Nature*, he asserts that the man who does not love ' divine ' nature cannot love friends, children, his wife ; he is incapable of enthusiasm, of gratitude, of freedom and patriotism.[84] Goethe never makes such claims. Nature for him was as moral or amoral as the creative force within him ; her divinity lay in this creativeness. So, in lines he ' stammered out ' and sent to Merck and Lavater he expresses the unity of his own artistic urge with the formative process of nature : [85]

> O dass die innre Schöpfungskrafft
> Durch meinen Sinn erschölle
> Dass eine Bildung voller Safft
> Aus meinen Fingern quölle !

> Ich zittre nur ich stottre nur
> Ich kann es doch nicht lassen
> Ich fühl ich kenne dich Natur
> Und so muss ich dich fassen.

Wenn ich bedenck wie manches Jahr
Sich schon mein Sinn erschliesset,
Wie er wo dürre Haide war
Nun Freudenquell geniesset

Da ahnd ich ganz Natur nach dir
Dich frey und lieb zu fühlen
Ein lustger Springbrunn wirst du mir
Aus tausend Röhren spielen

Wirst alle meine Kräffte mir
In meinem Sinn erheitern
Und dieses enge Daseyn hier
Zur Ewigkeit erweitern.*

The poem was written to accompany sketches Goethe made
for Lavater's physiognomical studies, and was published by
Lavater at the end of the first volume of his *Physiognomical
Fragments*. It is a true interpretation of Goethe's conception
of their work. They were not finding principles of moral
behaviour, but studying the creative power of nature in
forming outstanding personalities ; and this study awakened
his creative powers too to follow the spirit of nature, and in
this joyous activity to become part of nature. Such devotion
to nature does not need to find an extraneous justification,
moral or religious ; nor is it passive self-surrender. Through
his art Goethe combined intellectual observation, sensuous
and emotional joy, with activity, and thus established that
unity of being which Herder sought to define in *On Knowledge
and Perception*.

* I have failed to invent a verse-rendering which reproduces the
spontaneity and inward pressure of these verses. The following prose
version gives little of its energy and glow :

' O that the inner creative force might resound through my sense, that
an organism full of sap might gush from my fingers. I tremble, I stutter,
yet I cannot leave off ; I feel I know thee, Nature, and so I must lay hold
on thee. When I consider how many a year my mind has been unlocked,
how it now enjoys a living source of joy where formerly was withered
heath, then, Nature, I divine thee entire, and feel thee free and dear ;
thou becomst a cheerful fountain to me, playing through a thousand
spouts. Thou wilt joyously revive all the energies within my mind, and
enlarge this narrow existence to an eternity.'

It is for these energies of nature, this ' living nature ', that Faust calls, for the forces of the universe which correspond to the ' vital stirrings ' within him. They are revealed to him in the symbol of the macrocosm, and are personified in the Earth Spirit.[86]

> In Lebensfluten, im Thatensturm
> Wall ich auf und ab,
> Webe hin und her !
> Geburt und Grab,
> Ein ewges Meer
> Ein wechselnd Weben,
> Ein glühend Leben !
> So schaff ich am sausenden Webstuhl der Zeit
> Und würcke der Gottheit lebendiges Kleid.

> In the floods of life, the storm of deeds,
> I surge up and down,
> Weave to and fro.
> Birth and the grave
> An eternal sea
> A changing pattern
> A glowing life !
> At the whirring loom of time I weave
> The living garment of the deity.

And deeply significant of Goethe's thought, Faust cannot identify himself with this spirit of life and death except through actual experience. The theme was not fully developed until the first part of *Faust* was completed. In the *Easter Excursion* we see Faust's deep joy in the spring, but a joy which turns to torment because he is conscious of being cut off from nature, because the ' two souls ' are still warring within his breast. In *Forest and Cave* he expresses the feeling of intimate contact with nature which his love for Gretchen has at last brought, the knowledge, love, and enjoyment of nature. Mephistopheles can jeer at his retirement into caves and dripping woods, and Faust knows his happiness here does not solve any of his problems, does not help him to renounce Gretchen or find a way out. Nature is not moral and has no moral effect ; but it restores his soul. He cannot argue with Mephistopheles, but only cry out : [87]

Verstehst du, was für neue Lebenskraft
Mir dieser Wandel in der Öde schafft?

Can you not see what new and living springs
This sojourn in the wilderness brings?

Throughout *Faust* nature has this function of restoring health. Battling through the storms over the Brocken Faust recovers the zest in life that he was losing. At every crisis of Part 2 he is spiritually restored, directed to fresh effort, though not morally ' improved ', by the forces of nature. We see in this process an echo of the effect of Goethe's excursion to Switzerland in 1775, and that mid-winter ride through the Harz mountains in 1777, for which he gave thanks in his poem *Harzreise im Winter*.

In the wholeness and intensity of his feeling for nature Goethe establishes a new conception of nature and man's relationship with nature. He interprets nature, without attributing teleological or moral purposes to it, as the total process to which men belong, in which man stands as an active being and to which he has direct ties as to a mother. His scientific work in botany and anatomy in particular was to be sustained both by his immediate delight in the appearances of nature, and by his instinctive feeling of the common principle uniting all living forms which he asserts at the beginning of his work *Morphologie* of 1807. In his Sturm und Drang period his study of nature did not go much further than his careful, realistic sketches of landscapes ; his poetry is not descriptive in any precise sense, and in the main is woven round symbols of the pulsating, fruitful life of nature. The poetry of his maturity shows in this respect a marked development, in attitude and in style. He stands further apart from nature, and his profound awareness of the influence of nature upon him does not hide from him their separateness. Through all the harmonies of *An den Mond* runs the consciousness of the intermingling distinctness of the two streams of nature and his inner being, and this consciousness makes of him a much subtler observer of the outward appearances of nature. Nothing in his early work compares with the sensuous richness of his evocation of nature in *Der Fischer* or *Erlkönig*, not to speak

of the descriptions of *Hermann und Dorothea*. The feeling of
identity with nature becomes intellectually consolidated by an
attitude of attentive and loving observation, such as we find
in his scientific work.

This development is evident in Goethe's different responses
to Switzerland on the two journeys in 1775 and 1779. As he
returned from the first he celebrated the feeling of artistic
creativeness that stirred in him as he gazed at the ' everlasting
snow-mountains ', the ' cloud-rocks and desolate valleys ', the
serene lake of Zürich and the mighty fall of the Rhine at
Schaffhausen.[88] In this nature, ' begotten ' not ' patched
together ', he feels the same mighty spirit as in himself. In
the poem *On the Lake*, he expresses the peace and joy that he
' sucks through his navel-string ' from his mother, nature.[89]
But on his second visit he expresses his consciousness of the
distance which separates ' the conceited lord of the world '
from the virginal peaks ' which the spirit of the sky preserves
in inaccessible regions, for itself alone, in eternal purity before
our eyes '. He reflects on the process which has established
them there in their simple grandeur : ' the thought of so
mighty a motion gives a feeling of eternal firmness '. He
ponders over the laws rather than the principle of creativeness,
and contrasts their splendour with the agitation of men. On
this journey was written the poem, *Song of the Spirits over the
Waters*, in which he compares the spirit of man to the rushing
waters of the Alpine stream, ' ever changing ', in implicit
contrast to the permanency of the universe.[90]

> Seele des Menschen,
> Wie gleichst du dem Wasser !
> Schicksal des Menschen,
> Wie gleichst du dem Wind !

> Soul of man,
> How like to the water !
> Fate of man,
> How like to the wind !

In his maturity he seeks and needs nature, but he is far from
the confident and trustful presumption of his early period.

In his Sturm und Drang Goethe did not write systematically

about his conception of nature. But there is an essay of 1781, written by a young Swiss visitor to Weimar, Tobler, under Goethe's inspiration, which he himself said later in life fully expresses his point of view at that time. This series of aphorisms, entitled *Nature*, arose at the time when he was just entering on his scientific researches, but it is impregnated with the spirit of his Sturm und Drang.[91]

Nature ! We are surrounded and embraced by her—powerless to extricate ourselves from her, and powerless to enter more deeply into her. She takes us, unasked and unwarned, into the round of her dance and carries us away with her, till we are tired and fall from her arms.

She creates ever new forms ; what is, was never before ; what was, will never come again : all is new and yet ever the old.

We live within her and yet are alien to her. She speaks with us without ceasing and does not betray to us her secret. We work constantly upon her and yet have no power over her.

She seems to have made individuality her supreme purpose and she cares nothing for individuals. She ever builds and ever destroys, and her workshop is inaccessible.

She lives in sheer children ; and the mother, where is she ? She is the only artist : out of the simplest material to the greatest contrasts ; without any appearance of effort to the greatest perfection ; to the most exact precision, which she always mildly drapes over with a veil. Each of her works has a being of its own, each of her phenomena has its own isolated concept, and yet it all adds up to one.

She acts a play ; whether she herself sees it we do not know, and yet she acts it for us who stand in a corner.

There is an eternal life, growth and movement in her, and yet she never advances. She transforms herself eternally and stands still not for a moment. She has no idea of permanence, and has put her curse on immobility. She is firm : her pace is steady, her exceptions rare, her laws unchanging.

She has thought, and constantly meditates ; not like humans, but like nature. She has reserved to herself her own all-embracing mind, which no one can detect.

Men are all in her and she in them all. She plays a friendly game with them and is glad the more they win off her. She plays so secretly with many that she finishes the game before they notice it.

What is most unnatural is also nature, even the crudest obtuseness has something of her genius. If you do not see her everywhere, you nowhere see her aright.

She loves herself and clings to herself with innumerable eyes and hearts. She has divided herself up in order to enjoy herself. She perpetually gives birth to new enjoyers, insatiable in her desire to impart herself.

She rejoices in illusion. Those who destroy illusion in themselves or others find that she punishes like the harshest tyrant. Those who trustingly approach her she presses like children to her heart.

Her children are innumerable. She is niggardly to no one in all respects, but she has favourites on whom she lavishes much and to whom she sacrifices much. She has taken greatness under her especial protection.

She squirts her creatures up out of nothingness and does not tell them whence they come and whither they go. They have only to run ; she knows the path.

She has few motive forces, but never worn out, ever active, ever manifold.

Her show is ever new because she is always creating new spectators. Life is her fairest invention, and death is the masterstroke by which she has much life.

She wraps man in darkness and spurs him continually to the light. She makes him dependent on the earth, lethargic and heavy, and is continually shaking him up.

She gives wants because she loves movement. A miracle, that she achieves all this movement with such slender means ! Every want is a benefit ; quickly satisfied, quickly growing again. If she gives another, it is a new source of delight : but she soon comes to a new balance.

Every moment she sets out on the longest race, and every moment she is at the goal.

She is futility itself, but not for us, for whom she has made herself of the highest importance.

She lets every child fiddle with her, every fool deliver judgment on her, thousands pass over her obtusely, seeing nothing ; she finds joy in all and derives profit from all.

We obey her laws even when we resist them ; we work with her, even when we want to work against her.

Everything she gives becomes a blessing ; for she makes it indispensable. She lingers so that we may long for her ; she hastens so that we may not be sated with her.

She has no language or speech, but she creates tongues and hearts, through which she feels and speaks.

P

Her crown is love : only through love does one approach her. She has isolated all beings in order to draw them together. By a few draughts from the cup of love she compensates us for a life full of travail.

She is all. She rewards herself and punishes herself, gladdens and torments herself. She is rough and gentle, sweet and terrible, powerless and overwhelming. Everything is always there, in her. She knows neither past nor future. The present is her eternity. She is kind. I praise her with all her works. She is wise and still. You cannot tear any explanation from her, you cannot force from her any gift that she does not voluntarily give. She is cunning, but with a good purpose, and the best thing is not to pay attention to her wiles.

She is whole, and yet ever uncompleted. As she is now going on, she can go on for ever.

She appears to everyone in a peculiar form. She hides herself in a thousand names and terms and is ever the same.

She has brought me in, she will lead me out. My trust is in her. I submit to her governance, she will not hate the work of her hands. I did not speak of her ; no, she has spoken all, what is true and what is false. Hers is the guilt, hers is the merit.

In his later comment on these aphorisms, Goethe pointed out that these earlier views of his do not include the recognition of the ' two great springs of all nature, the concepts of polarity and intensification '.[92] That is, the essay does not formulate the actual development and process of nature and man, but defines nature from an intuitive, perceptive, sympathetic point of view, rather than from that of the active member of society, the statesman, the scientist, engaged in a process of transformation and self-transformation akin to the evolutionary movement of nature—a movement which, as Goethe grew older, appeared to him more and more as an irreversible process in time. In this respect the conceptions of this essay are characteristic of the Sturm und Drang.

Nature is seen as an all-embracing and self-sufficient process. All anthromorphic interpretations are abandoned ; this ' all ', of which man is a part, is not only inscrutable to man, but has no meaning in a human sense—in the word ' futility ' [' Eitelkeit '], Goethe recalls the ' vanity ' of the Ecclesiast. Man, who owes his existence as well as his destruction to nature, cannot ask for any deeper fulfilment than acquiescence and participation in the natural process. Similar views on the self-sufficiency of nature and her infinite variety had been expressed by Diderot and d'Holbach, and Buffon had anticipated Goethe in his ordering of mankind as a ' point in time ' in the infinity of nature, and in his artistic joy in the variety and vital creativeness of all existence.[93] Goethe fails at this stage to grasp the significance of experimentation, of human operation upon nature, which Diderot had understood ; he does not understand the importance of Buffon's systematic classification of the orders of phenomena ; nor does he try to formulate explicitly the moral and philosophical implications of his doctrine, as d'Holbach sought to do. On the contrary he rebels, as we see from his later observations on d'Holbach, against the latter's reduction of the variety and joy of experience to general principles, which he found disagreeably ' spectral '. But his conception of the universe is as ' naturalistic ' as theirs. More strongly and starkly than they he expresses the profound joy he felt as a total personality in being part of a mighty process which embraces all phenomena.

Goethe's essay stands at the beginning of his turn towards science ; but it does not primarily arise from or contribute to science. It formulates his personal relationship to nature in entirely secular terms, and transfers to secular nature all the worship and submission which traditionally had been the prerogative of God. The stylistic echoes of Biblical phraseology are not fortuitous ; the essay is his Magnificat, his Twenty-Third Psalm. ' I praise nature with all her works. She has brought me in and she will lead me out. My trust is in her.' To nature he owes his individuality, and he will not kick against the pricks because death and disintegration are the conditions of life.[94]

The essay is pantheistic ; but Goethe is concerned not with systematic theory but with the expression of his feeling, his experience, with praise. He does not set the question, is nature material or immaterial, like d'Holbach or Herder. Indeed, in asserting that all is nature, including thought and illusion, he even attributes mind to nature. But this ' thought ' of nature is defined as being something totally different from human thought, ' no one can detect it ', ' she does not betray her secret ' ; he is not proclaiming an idealistic principle, but

stating that nature embraces all spirit as all matter.   Similarly,
though he seems to personify nature, he steers clear of anything
approaching the notion of an intelligible God or Providence,
even in the subtle form we find in Herder or Kant.   Her purposes are not definable in human terms.   She is good, but her
' good ' has nothing to do with human values.   This comprehensive interpretation of nature resolves what are apparent
contradictions in Goethe's poetry.   He can write ' How sweet
and good is nature, who holds me to her breast ' ; [95] and again :

> Denn unfühlend
> Ist die Natur :
> Es leuchtet die Sonne
> Über Bös' und Gute,
> Und dem Verbrecher
> Glänzen, wie dem Besten,
> Der Mond und die Sterne.[96]

> For feelingless
> Is nature :
> The sunlight falls
> On evil and good,
> And moon and stars
> Light the criminal
> As they shine for the best.

But though this poem shows the typical effort of his maturity
to define the specific values of human behaviour (' Let man
be noble, helpful and good '), the conception of an amoral
nature belongs to all Goethe's periods.   At all times he calls
this amoral nature good, because it is all existence, all reality.
' The concept of existence and perfection is one and the same.' [97]

The conceptions of the *Nature* essay have much in common
with Spinoza.   In Herder's mind they merged with his studies
of Spinoza to form the basis of his mature work on history,
the *Ideas*, and his mature philosophy of religion, as found in
the *Dialogues on God*.   Largely through Herder, Goethe took up
in the early 1780s a closer study of Spinoza, whose *Ethics* he
read with Frau von Stein.   The disconnected comments he
dictated to Frau von Stein indicate how much his reading
confirmed him in his earlier obscure feeling of sympathy with

the pantheist. The concepts of existence and perfection are identical, he tells his friend ; we cannot conceive infinity or perfect existence, and can only think it in so far as we can imagine that there is something beyond our power of comprehension—we understand and enjoy a thing only in so far as we think and feel it according to our own nature and mode of being ; we are parts of being, yet so far distinct from the whole that we ' take part ' in it rather than are parts of it.

At the same time, the form and some of the ideas of the *Nature* essay were certainly influenced by Shaftesbury's hymn to nature in the *Moralists*. The mathematical reasoning of Spinoza finds an aesthetic form in Shaftesbury, it becomes a rhapsody to ' divine nature ', the ' common mother ', to her creativeness, harmony, and love, the variety and ever-changingness of her phenomena.

In a suggestive little essay Dilthey has pointed out significant connections and contrasts between Goethe's *Nature* and Spinoza and Shaftesbury.[98] As contrasted with Spinoza, Goethe is scarcely at all concerned with the metaphysical concepts of ' perfection ' and ' infinity ' ; he lays all his emphasis on nature as life, as infinite individuality. He told Jacobi, who sent him in 1785 his book on Spinoza, that he was most reluctant to speak about ' a divine being ' and not made for metaphysical discussion. What he most treasured in Spinoza is that ' he does not prove the existence of God, but shows existence as God ' ; but he himself recognised the divine being in ' rebus singularibus ', while ' individual things seem to dissolve before Spinoza's eyes '.[99] Goethe's attitude is not contemplative but aesthetic, and his joy in nature arises from spontaneous feeling, from an emotive compulsion. Thus his aim is not intellectual understanding of the whole, but direct contact with nature in all her parts, through feeling, activity, and science. In contrast with Shaftesbury, on the other hand, Goethe does not identify nature with morality. Neither Herder nor Schiller could avoid succumbing to the enthusiastic eloquence of Shaftesbury's optimism, and both often accept his definition of human nature as naturally virtuous, and of the natural process in general as perfect and harmonious in a human sense.[100] But Goethe's conception of nature has nothing to do with this sort of wishful thinking. Shaftesbury was intoxicated with the orderliness of the universe as established by Newton ; Goethe's universe was a pullulating biological organism. Though Shaftesbury enjoyed the woods and country views, his *Moralist* wins enthusiasm from the thought of the virtuous life of simple country folk ; and he expresses a definite preference for organic and firm form as contrasted with the wildness of ' shifting sands ' and clouds. The natural feelings Shaftesbury celebrates are essentially social and virtuous. But the nature that Goethe loved revealed herself often in violent storm, the force within her was something different from the harmonious spirit Shaftesbury detected. So the inner promptings that Goethe knew were not necessarily conducive to social virtue, and often played havoc with social requirements.

Shaftesbury's *Moralists*, which begins with a celebration of nature as a whole, is accommodated at the end to more conventional religious thought. He postulates like any Deist a universal mind which governs the universe, and subordinates nature and instinct to higher, innate ideas of beauty and goodness. There is scarcely anything of this in Goethe's *Nature*, where it is stated ' no one can detect the all-embracing mind ' of nature. But in one respect the similarity is very close. Shaftesbury's idealism leads him to assert that each individual organism, each tree, has a spirit of its own—or rather, as he says, each spirit has its tree. In the *Nature* essay we read ' each of nature's phenomena has its own isolated concept '. This conception is an immature form of Goethe's later theory of the ' primal type ', of which he considered all species to be a modification ; through it he is linked with neo-Platonism. But it is important that Goethe later was to deny, to Schiller, that this conception was of ideal origin—he insisted that it was a ' perception ' [' Anschauung ']. It can be called Goethe's interpretation of the scientific theory of pre-formationism. It did not have the function of leading his mind towards metaphysical speculation, ' nature philosophy ', but freed it for the observation of the actual forms of nature.

What links Goethe with Shaftesbury is their common conception of an all-embracing nature, their affirmation that this whole is good, their distaste for speculation on the relations of mind and matter, their aesthetic approach to nature, and their liberation of being and experience from restraints based on theoretical judgments.

There is no opposition for Goethe between ' inner ' natural forces and outward appearance. The alchemistic approach, which appealed to him for a little while in his youth, and which appears again at the beginning of *Faust*, is abandoned along with all teleological attributions. Nature is not a symbol of something else, she is all in all, is herself. ' Do not seek anything behind phenomena ; they themselves are the theory.' [101] So, from the beginning of his great poetry in the Strassburg period, he expressed his consciousness of the identity of natural processes and personal feeling, without making either the symbol of something else. Love or death did not make him think of supersensual realities, as they always did Schiller or Herder who, however hard they tried, could not relinquish longings for the assurance of supernatural sanctions. Nor did natural scenes have any mystical meaning, as they do in Wordsworth who, of all the Romantics, approaches closest to the Goethean conception of nature. Nature was for Goethe meaningful in herself, the process of being ; he fulfilled himself in submitting to her promptings. The secularity of Goethe's interpretation of nature is complete ; he has shorn nature of all the moral, religious, and metaphysical attributes with which his times usually trimmed her and decked her out.

The taste for simple, untamed, or at least less-conventionalised nature, which finds expression throughout the literature of the eighteenth century, reaches its most comprehensive formulation in the Sturm und Drang, and particularly in Goethe. It had many roots—among them dissatisfaction with polite society, the longing for a more subjective religion, the movement of scientific discovery. Its blossoms were often to have a poisonous sweetness, in extravagant exoticism, in the search for a refuge in the countryside from the torments of intellectual and social life, in the spiritualisation of nature, all characteristic forms of European romanticism. For the Stürmer und Dränger, for Goethe too, nature was at times a refuge from social triviality, a solace in personal entanglement, a setting for dreams, a channel for religious feeling. But all these separate emotive functions of nature are reconciled with the intellectual grasp of nature, the need to comprehend man's place in nature. Goethe's attitude does not grow from systematic thought on religion, philosophy or science, but springs from his feeling of the sustaining power of nature to which so many of his early poems give witness. In the vitality of living nature he finds the analogy, the source, the identity of his own surging feelings, which were to him the proof and justification of his existence. Nature is the source of his being, as it is the limit ; what is beyond is meaningless, is unreal. Where this surrender to nature would lead he did not know ; its dynamism was necessary and not to be denied ; it had to be followed even if tragedy were to ensue. Whether, in human or social terms, it was good or bad, was insignificant ; the goodness of nature transcended the limited judgment of man. At the bottom of this Sturm und Drang conception of nature lies its characteristic subjectivity, its search for experience at all costs ; but it turns, also characteristically, into a new realism which finds truth within the phenomena of nature, in nature's variety and process. The emotive conviction of the identity of man and nature, of the natural character of thought, work, history, and art, runs through the whole Sturm und Drang ; it was only later that Herder and Goethe, in particular, were to tackle the problem of the specific character of human activity, in practical life, in the process of history, in science and art. But their later work rises, without the props of transcendental fantasies, securely upon the basis of their early trust in nature.

CHAPTER VII

THE IDEA OF HISTORY

Philosophie der Gestalten und Veränderungen des menschlichen Geschlechts nach Maasgabe der Geschichte und
Erfahrungen.—HERDER.

ALL MODERN thinking about man is impregnated by the
idea of history, of development, and it was in the middle
of the eighteenth century that the concept of historical development was first and decisively grasped. Herder was the only
Stürmer und Dränger to grapple with the problem of social
development, and his contribution to historical thinking is
generally recognised to have been of the greatest importance.[1]
Our task here is to investigate the connections between his
historical approach and the Sturm und Drang ; our attention
must therefore be directed more to his earlier work than to
his best-known writing, the *Ideas on the Philosophy of the History
of Mankind*, which belongs to his maturity. It will appear
that not only are these connections close, but also they give
a deeper understanding of the implications and meaning of
his philosophy of history.

His antecedents are British and French, rather than German.
Montesquieu had undermined the notion of a hypothetical
social contract, and had related the character of a government
with the ' disposition ' of a people, itself moulded by its peculiar
circumstances and mode of life. He had broken away from
the rationalist and the religious type of abstract social principles
and absolute judgments. More profoundly than Montesquieu,
Vico had grasped the principle of social development as a
natural process affecting all aspects of a people's culture,
though Vico remained unknown to Herder till late in life.
With Turgot and the Scotsmen round Adam Smith the categories of social development were defined more precisely, a
law of social growth was sought, and the past was related more
firmly to the contemporary situation. Combining materials
from the history of Greece and Rome, of the modern European
nations, and from travellers' accounts of nations and tribes all

over the globe, they saw government, personal and family ties, culture, science, and language itself as products and functions of social relationships, which themselves arise out of the particular ' mode of subsistence ', be it food-gathering, hunting, stock-raising, agriculture, or industry and commerce. They explained and justified the contemporary social organisation in their own countries with an eye to further developments in accordance with the growing importance of industry and trade and the middle class.[2] Their ideas appear in fragmentary form in many works of the time, and particularly in the *Encylopédie*.[3] The Göttingen historians, Schlözer and Gatterer, adopted some of their views, notably the recognition of the importance of mechanical inventions in history, and the consequent changes in nature and social organisation ; but their pedantic works fail to give anything like a coherent picture of historical development, as Herder wrote in an angry review of Schlözer's *Conception of Universal History*.[4] Möser's *History of Osnabrück* (1768) was the nearest German approach to a ' natural history ' of society, and though its scope was limited to a small state, Möser occasionally draws illuminating parallels between local institutions and those of ancient or distant peoples like the Spartans or the North American Indians.[5]

Herder's earliest writings show the historical attitude of the Enlightenment. In *Have we still the Public and Fatherland of the Ancients* he praises his own times for their ' pure, reasonable religion ', for their patriotism, for their ' more refined and moderate freedom ', for their just and wise political constitutions, as opposed to the savagery and superstitions of earlier times.[6] In the *Fragmente* he notes with equanimity the supplanting of the poetry of earlier ages by the more prosaic, rational style of civilisation.[7] But in the second edition of the *Fragmente* of 1768, in the *Kritische Wälder* and the *Journal of my Voyage* of the following year, we can see his opposition to modern civilisation growing. He speaks with bitterness of the ' tame manners and morals ', the ' courtly pretence ', of his times, the lack of true feeling, the decay of patriotism and honour, the relaxing of personal and social ties.[8] Instead of merely showing moral indignation at the political calculation of Hobbes, Helvétius, Mandeville, Machiavelli, as in his earliest work, he now considers them as important witnesses to the characteristics of the modern age. He gives free rein to his taste for early poetry and simpler, homogeneous societies, linking up with the growing appreciation in Britain and France of medieval chivalry, folksong, Ossian or Spenser or Homer. In Montesquieu, Ferguson, Millar, he now found a theory of history which enabled him to justify the art-forms of early cultures. Working in their categories he could demolish all absolute standards of art, and reveal the beauty of the Bible, of Homer, folksong, and Shakespeare as indigenous products of a particular society and time. The introduction of historical relativism into aesthetics, most perfectly exemplified in his essay on Shakespeare, is a major contribution to the development of literary criticism.

But this relativism was not consistent, and to a large extent only a defence. In fact, Herder had a strong preference for older times and poetry, and his defence of the Bible, of folksong, and of Shakespeare is at the same time an attack on modern culture. Herder's social position was quite different from that of the well-established Montesquieu and the dignified British churchmen, academics, and lawyers who extended the range of historical feeling and understanding. He could not share their pride in modern achievements, in their great nation, nor could he feel that the German middle class was playing a significant part in shaping the world. Judging from Germany, he had no reason to believe, with Ferguson and Millar, that his own time was the apex of history. Thus it was Rousseau's passionate attack on civilised society that echoes in his bitter and enthusiastic judgments. In his review of the translation of Millar's *On the Origin of the Distinction of Ranks*, he shows his resentment at Millar's approval of the historical process he describes, his belief that everything contributes to the welfare of mankind, his lack of partisanship for pre-bourgeois times, for the feudal virtues : in fact, at Millar's ' historical, philosophical spirit '. The Scotsmen (Herder mentions Ferguson, Robertson, Gerard, Home, and Beattie) could, from the height of their social self-confidence, discuss coolly ' the philosophy of the forms and changes of the human race according to history and experience '—but Herder wanted a philosophy of history that would evaluate, pick out the good from the bad.[9] He was to call his first work on history ' Another Philosophy of History *for the Education of Mankind* '.

Herder was not able to rid himself of the contradiction in his attitude. He accepted the notion that there is no distinction between natural and unnatural in society, that all history is a natural process. He reminded himself in the *Journal* that he must not idealise the past, like Rousseau, but live in and for his own century.[10] He opposed most heartily the idea that there is a social optimum, valid for all times and peoples. Yet he could never wean himself of his predilection for early society, the pastoral or early agricultural societies reflected in the Bible or Homer, when, like Rousseau, he considered men were able to exert all their faculties in harmony. Thus, in the Ossian essay, he condemns the civilised ' art ' that ' extinguishes nature '.[11] And whenever he writes of the division of labour, as in *On Knowledge and Perception*, he does so only to describe its disastrous effects on the individual and culture.[12] It was this extravagance in him that Goethe laughed over in *Satyros*, where Herder appears as a satyr who persuades a harmless community to leave their dwellings and live on raw chestnuts.[13]

Underlying Herder's first comprehensive sketch of history we find, in addition to his social predilections, the religious polemic of the Bückeburg years. *Another Philosophy of History* was written in the same year, 1774, as the *Oldest Document*, and was also an elaboration of his religious attitude. As such, it refutes any rationalist interpretation of social development, including the theological rationalism of a Bossuet. In an indirect form it illustrates Herder's Spinozism : the principles that nature has no ends, that men in defining such ends merely substitute for reality their own prejudice and passions, that things as they are are their own perfection : ' the perfection of a thing is its reality '.[14] Chaotic and immature the work undoubtedly is ; but it is one of the most characteristic documents of the Sturm und Drang.

The scope and sequence of ' mankind ' in *Another Philosophy of History* are the same as in Bossuet's *Discours sur l'Histoire Universelle* (1681)—Hebrews, Egyptians, Phoenicians, Greeks, Romans, and modern Christendom. This is surprising in several ways. It was wilful to ignore what he had recognised in an earlier note [15] to be the earliest form of society, the hunt-

ing and food-gathering stage, an omission which can only be
accounted for by Herder's religious predisposition towards the
Hebrews, and his predilection for societies in which property,
family, and religion had already taken a civilised shape : a
predilection he shared with Rousseau.[16]   It was wilful to shut
his eyes to all cultures outside the Eastern Mediterranean and
Western Europe.   Sir William Temple had protested against
such obtuseness in the seventeenth century, and Voltaire had
effectively demolished what was in fact a Christian prejudice.
Further, Herder treats each of the cultures he discusses as a
biological entity, with its youth, maturity, and age, a conception which Ferguson and others had refuted.

In certain other respects, Herder's approach is very close
to that of Turgot or Ferguson.   He describes the Hebrew,
Egyptian, and Phoenician cultures as pastoral, agricultural,
and commercial societies, and relates their spiritual qualities
to this material source.   The peaceful labour of the shepherd,
the dependence on the rain from heaven, the patriarchal society
organised round the ownership of flocks which makes the ruler
a father : these were the material causes of the religious insight
of the Hebrew patriarchs, here all the centuries of man can
find the ' eternal basis ' of religion and morality.[17]   From this
' childhood ' mankind moved to its second stage, in the basin
of the Nile.   In these fertile lands nomadic society was replaced
by the settled forms of agriculture.   The land was divided up
and became private property, irrigation made public control
necessary, government and laws developed.   The measuring
of the land and foretelling of the seasons laid the first bases
of the sciences.   The older conception of God as a loving
father was replaced by that of Gods who represented remote
authority, law, fear.   Circumstances made this change inevitable, and it is wrong, says Herder, to judge one conception of
God against another—and he adds, in reference to contemporary speculations, it is as wrong to expect that the Egyptian
mysteries hold the key to final wisdom, as it is to condemn
Egyptian despotism by contrasting it with Greek freedom.[18]

Then mankind proceeds to its ' youth '.   First in Phoenicia,
the city-states of the seafaring merchants.   Human ties become
weaker through the development of private property in goods
and money, and the feeling for law and obedience declines.

But new virtues arise, mobility and shrewdness, international understanding, the practical sciences of arithmetic and writing. And then Greece : the full and glorious youth of mankind. In the sea-girt peninsula, favourable to commerce and enterprise, under a mild climate, freedom is paired with respect for law, the crafts turn into arts, all serious occupations and beliefs are tempered by grace and poetry. Like Shaftesbury, Lessing, and Winckelmann, Herder sees Greece only through the medium of her poets, philosophers, and artists, and idealises the grace and harmony of Greek life. He shows much less enthusiasm for the ' maturity ' of the human race, for Rome, which in conquering the known world developed to the full the human faculties for political organisation and law.

Herder's principle of selection in establishing this sequence of development is arbitrary ; he disregards chronology ; he does not discuss the development within each of the cultures he discusses. But his intention is solid and plain. Each culture he insists has its own qualities and virtues, and cannot be judged by the standards of another, least of all by the standards of his own times.

Human nature is not the receptacle of an absolute, independent, unchanging happiness, as the philosopher has defined it ; it attracts everywhere as much happiness as it can. . . . The ideal of happiness changes as circumstances and regions change—for what else is it but the sum of the fulfilment of wishes, of the purposes, and the gentle surmounting of wants, which all are transformed according to land, time and place. So at bottom all comparison is out of place. . . . Every nation has its centre of happiness within itself.[19]

This principle explains a great distinction between Herder and those contemporary historians who would not have disagreed with his relativism. It was not his final aim to describe institutions and laws ; these only tell us about the shape of a society. His essential purpose was, to reconstruct the values of a culture, the ' spirit of a nation ', the instincts and feelings which hold a people together, which are the spiritual substance of laws and manners, and which make up the ' happiness ' of a people.[20] This purpose made him less attentive to the practical activities and social organisation of cultures, and led him to dissolve

these activities into spiritual attitudes : agriculture becomes
' agricultural industriousness ', Roman law turns into ' Roman
virtue ', as Stadelmann points out.[21] But it gave him the
opportunity for sensuous seductive sketches of cultures, showing a quite new imaginative insight into the spiritual climate
and bonds of communities.

In his review of Millar's book, Herder had complained that
while Millar describes the changing forms of social relations,
he does not analyse the forces which produce change. His own
theory of change is extremely significant. The Scotsmen, by
concentrating their attention on the history of Europe or
Britain since the barbaric kingdoms, had in fact been able to
show how tribal society had merged into feudal, feudal into
monarchical, agricultural into commercial. In this process
Ferguson had discovered the proof of his assertion that no
particular culture is comparable with a biological organism,
since social structures themselves are subject to transformation.
Herder's identification of social structures with particular
peoples, each of which he treats as quite separate entities, was
a sign of a polemical intention. If each people was a biological
organism, historically detached from the others, and if, at the
same time, they were to be associated in ' universal history ' in
a purposeful order, it was necessary that this order should
appear not as the product of a natural growth, but as the
result of a metaphysical intention. The arbitrariness of his
selection served an irrational explanation.

So we find that he links the various stages of evolution by
Providence. ' Providence led the thread of development
further ' : with this phrase he passes from the Hebrews to
the Egyptians. Roman civilisation is ' the maturity of the
destiny of the ancient world '.[22] History demonstrates God's
plan to develop all the faculties of man. From a teleological
conception of this kind Herder never could completely free
himself. Its importance lies, however, more in its negative than
its positive aspect. What he intends to stress is that development is not controlled or foreseeable by man, by reason, and
that it follows an inscrutable plan ; and being good, it is
Providence that guides. Also, God adopts a purely natural
method. He does not guide mankind by arbitrary interfer-
ence, but through placing mankind in circumstances which

will quite naturally ' awaken some powers and extinguish others '.[23] Herder's biological conception of society stems from the same root. The purpose of each culture is to fulfil its own potentialities ; it grows and dies like a plant. ' Every people has its period of growth, blossoming, decline.' [24] The source of Herder's biological conception of society, which has had so mighty and baleful an influence on social thought, lies in his determination to assert that history is led by an inscrutable Providence.

The second section of *Another Philosophy of History* shows more clearly still the implications of his method. With the collapse of Rome a second ' childhood ' of the human race begins. If the Dark and Middle Ages are still looked upon essentially as a ' cure ' of humanity, a restorative after the decay of Rome, Herder also finds values in feudal times—not only in the spirit of chivalry, like Hurd, but also in the barbaric energy which colonised Europe, founded cities, and re-awakened the spirit of social freedom. In itself, his defence of the Middle Ages did not go essentially further than that of Ferguson or Hurd ; but it has an enhanced importance because of the repudiation of modern times which it introduces. When he comes to discuss the post-Reformation period, Herder loses all sense of history. He can only rage against the modern ' policed ' state, in which the individual has become the passive object of government ; he points out with indignation that the boasted freedoms of the British have resulted in the enslavement of the colonial world. ' Heart and head are separated ', freedom of thought has replaced all the substantial and emotive ties that social man needs. Fear and money are the springs of society. He quotes Millar : ' In Europe slavery is abolished,' and continues : ' Three parts of the world laid waste and controlled, and we ourselves depopulated, deprived of our manhood, sunk in luxury, exploitation (" Schinderei "), and death.' [25] Government has been turned into calculation plastered over with fine principle, religion has become a political instrument and a matter of abstract speculation. All Herder's historical principles go by the board in this sweeping condemnation of the modern state. He does not seek to find its constituting principles or specific values, but makes a scarecrow out of it, to frighten men off, back to a simpler life and to religion.

As far as historical theory is concerned, the most important part of this second section centres in Herder's treatment of inventions. His contemporaries had stressed the importance of inventions in transforming society, and had sought to show how and why the discovery of gunpowder, for instance, could so powerfully influence the course of history. Herder uses such examples in order to assert the complete unforeseeableness of history. ' Guns invented : and behold ! the ancient courage of heroes like Theseus, the Spartans, Romans, Knights and giants is gone—warfare is different, and how much has changed with this changed warfare.' With the invention of the compass there arise ' new manners, tastes, virtues, vices '.[26] He refutes both the belief that history shows a steady process of imperceptible change, and that this change is understandable in rational terms. Just as in the first section he emphasises the continual loss as well as gain incurred in historical evolution, so now he stresses the jerky, revolutionary process of change. ' A quiet progress of the human mind for the improvement of the world is scarcely anything else but a phantom of our heads, never the way of God in nature.' [27] Change takes place in sudden leaps ; using a comparison later taken up by the dialectical philosophers Hegel and Engels, he compares human evolution to that of a seed, which at each new stage of development bursts the husks of its earlier form.

But this dialectical process cannot, in Herder's view, be reduced to scientific law ; it is evidence of the mystery of God. And, appropriately enough, the beneficent Providence of the first section takes on, in the second section, the gloomy colouring of fate. Man is ' but an ant, that crawls on the wheel of fate '.

The general change of the world was guided far less by man than by a blind fate.

The education and progress of a nation is never anything but the work of fate : the result of the cooperation of a thousand causes, as it were, of the whole element in which men live.

' Chance, fate, God ' are synonyms for the inscrutable principle of historical development.[28] As Meinecke says, ' the idea of fate was one of the weapons with which Herder combated the rational conceit of the Enlightenment ' ; [29] but when it is contrasted to the middle-class self-confidence and positivism of the Scotsmen, we see too that it was the expression of Herder's hostility to the modern state, to expansionist capitalism, and also a declaration of impotence, of passivity, a ' gloomy philosophy of quiescence ', as he had called a little historical play he wrote. [30]

Another Philosophy of History is a hastily written, passionate work, arbitrary and faulty in many of its parts, unsystematic and contradictory in its method.   Merck called it an ' excretion '. [31] But its faults, like its good qualities, are not eccentric ;   the whole work is an image of the Sturm und Drang.   It brought to history all Herder's power of feeling and imagination, and in place of dry facts and analysis gave descriptions of societies which evoked the men of the past as sentient living creatures —Herder called on the historians to ' enter into the age, into the region, into the whole of history, feel yourself into everything '. [32]   His failure to pay sufficient attention to practical actions and political organisation is itself characteristic of the Sturm und Drang.   So also is his appreciation of the individuality of each culture and people, irrespective of the judgments that might be passed on them on normal moral standards.

His interpretation shook the bland optimism of Herder's time, not least of the Adam Smith school, by emphasising the conflicts in history, and their incalculable outcome.   And even in the most subjective and vulnerable parts of the work, the violent attack on post-Reformation Europe, there is a solid core of serious criticism of modern society, which, because of the class-stratification of society and the loss of the sustaining communal ties of earlier cultures, has brought about the degradation of the individual, his isolation.   Herder's recourse to the idea of fate was a step back from the achievement of Smith, Ferguson, and the rest, for their thought was bent on discovering the natural law which governs the apparently fortuitous and irrational course of history ;   Herder on the other hand calls to his aid a notion of fate which would recall the historian from scientific investigation to trembling prostration before an inscrutable God.   In the same spirit he repudiates in this work the belief in the power of men to improve society by education, a belief which the *philosophes* shared with Rousseau.   But this feeling is a profound expression of the situation of the Stürmer und Dränger, of their consciousness of being helpless in the midst of vast historical forces, and sums up their tragic dilemma. The work should have remained as the statement of a tragic situation, like *Werther* or *Faust*. Its lamest part is the *Addenda*, in which Herder asks how, in the present age, man can regain new vigour, for he can only answer, shrouding himself in mist and prophecy, that the present must have a meaning as a preparation for something better.[33]

Herder's *Ideas on the Philosophy of History* of 1784-91 was avowedly a fuller development of this early work and it is of importance to note in what respects this product of his maturity continues and corrects the Sturm und Drang interpretation. He wrote to Hamann that he had been driven to write the book by his nausea over abstract definitions of Church, State, Natural Law, and Society.[34] That is, he sought here, as in the earlier history, to demonstrate that each culture has its own excellence, and cannot be condemned by the standards of another. That this was not the outcome of mere impartiality is evident from the section on modern times, Book 9, Section iv. He says, indeed, that history no longer seems to him 'a horror of desolation on a sacred earth'; [35] but while he now writes less passionately than in *Another Philosophy of History*, he still repudiates the modern state. When he submitted the first draft of this section to the friendly perusal of Goethe, the latter told him, so Herder wrote to Hamann, that if it was to be published 'not a word could stay as it was'. In its milder final form, Herder argues that the family is the highest form of social life, and that the modern states are the outcome of force, war, and cunning.[36] The subtle, sensuous descriptions of other societies have therefore their polemical side. The object of historiography, Herder writes, is to show the different forms of human life and happiness in different circumstances and periods. Each natural organism has its own purpose, fully to realise its potentialities in its own limits. There is no single purpose for the whole human race; earlier forms of society do not simply exist for the later, as the beginnings of an ultimate perfection, but have their own perfection; the purpose of each man is to achieve 'humanity', fullness of being, happiness, in the form and degree permitted by his situation.[37]

We can recognise Sturm und Drang theses in these views ;
but the *Ideas* diverges sharply from the earlier work in its new
optimism with regard to the whole development of mankind.
Herder comes much closer to the Enlightenment in postulating
a general purpose of history, the development of ' reason and
equity ', which he considers to be evident in the past, and
which will lead in his view to a humanity which will outgrow
the limitations of nationality. The main part of the *Ideas* is
devoted, it is true, to the description of the specific qualities
of different cultures ; but Herder asserts repeatedly, in the
more theoretical sections, his belief in a converging principle
of development. Equally characteristic of his more mature
outlook is his view that all change, directed by a benign Providence, takes place as an imperceptible natural growth. Lovejoy
rightly says of the Herder of the *Ideas* that ' he does not
emphasise the fact that historic change takes place in many
instances through a series of revulsions, not to say revolu-
tions ' : [38] a remarkable comment in the light of the emphasis
on violent change in *Another Philosophy of History*, and highly
characteristic of the contrast between German ' classicism '
and the Sturm und Drang.

Borne along on the current of this optimistic teleology, the
driving force of the *Ideas* is the conception of the natural law
of social movement. The Spinozist conception of God as
immanent in nature, which is the principle of Herder's *Dialogues
on God*, is here applied to society—or rather, not to society considered as a whole, but to each particular culture he considers.
The scope of ' mankind ' is no longer restricted to Christendom
—some of Herder's finest pages are devoted to China, for
instance—and he does not now assert that human history
begins with patriarchal pastoral societies. In a broad review
of the origins and metamorphoses of human society Herder
unfolds all the richness of his generous sympathy and his love
and affirmation of life. Drawing on the scientific knowledge
of his time, he begins his history of man with an account of the
earth and its physical characteristics, then of living creatures,
and finally of man, whose existence is conditioned by the world
in which he is set, and whose spiritual powers grow out of his
physical powers and experience, according to ' a great plan of
nature '.

Thus he defines man in specifically natural terms. Created with the power of standing erect, the development of the brain has been made possible. His hands are freed, ' instruments of the finest crafts and of a perpetual groping towards new clear ideas '.[39] Language, and all his spiritual capacities, are the result of his physiological structure. His instinct for family life, for society, is based on the fact that his sexual impulses are not periodic, like those of animals, and that his young need long tending.[40] When he discusses particular peoples Herder consistently follows the method of first examining their material conditions and then describing spiritual life as the expression of these conditions. Thus he states that the great factor that made the history of Asia different from that of America was the lack of tameable animals in the western hemisphere. In all cases the aim of life is not a general one, not refinement of morals and such, but ' the use of the whole soul, in particular of its active energies '. ' Existence is its own purpose. . . . This simple, deep, irreplaceable feeling of existence is happiness.' [41] Though the emphasis on law contrasts with the dynamism of the Sturm und Drang period, this definition of man's aim, and the stress on the determining reality of the external world, link Herder's later period with his earlier.

Kant's clash with Herder over the latter's theory of history brings out its philosophical significance. In a highly suggestive little treatise, *Idea towards a Universal History from a Cosmopolitan Point of View*, Kant expounded his principles in 1784 in conscious opposition to the Herderian type of thought. After establishing on the basis of the regularities of vital statistics that social laws do exist, he proceeds to define a number of axioms which in his opinion must govern any theory of history : a theory which cannot, he asserts, be a theory of a human rational plan, but of a ' plan of nature ', or of Providence.

These theorems include the following. All potentialities of creation must be destined to be realised, otherwise there would be no meaning in life. Man's specific quality is his reason, therefore it must be his peculiar mission to develop his rational part ; and the purpose of society, education, and so forth is to further this development. The individual is not an end in himself, but exists only for the species ; and earlier generations exist as a means to the perfection of the later. Nature, in

making man ' an unsocial social creature ', has provided the
stimulus which urges man on through conflict with his associates. Man's greatest problem is, how to build a society
governed by law ; how to establish government which will not
be tyranny ; how to combine the freedom of states with a
league of nations. The historical process is completely natural
—for example, rulers are anxious to promote industry and
trade in order to increase their wealth and power, but the
growth of commerce necessarily brings with it civil liberty ; or
again, in developing the instruments of warfare, rulers ultimately must renounce warfare, since it becomes too disastrous
to be entered on. Thus the natural social process brings about
a constant advance towards enlightenment, justice, and inter-
nationalism.[42]

In the following year Kant wrote reviews of the first and
second parts of Herder's *Ideas on History*. He criticises as an
unwarrantable assumption Herder's view that nature and
natural law can be considered as an ' analogy ' of man and
social law ; the idea that man is akin to the animals, and that
reason is a product of the erect position of man, is for him a
' fearful ' thought. Equally he criticises Herder for spiritualising the world into a ' realm of forces '. Above all he opposes
Herder's view that the individual man, or the individual society,
is its own purpose. Not happiness, but ' activity and culture ',
are for Kant the aims of man, and they are realised through
the whole evolution of society, whose destiny is perpetual progress towards a final perfection.[43]

Common to both thinkers is a fundamental teleological
approach, as we find in nearly all eighteenth-century writers.
Just as Kant could believe that warfare is a Providential means
of spreading civilisation, so Herder could write that the earth's
surface was not covered with gold because man cannot eat
gold ; that men are crowded in a tiny space in order that
energy should be provoked by competition.[44] Both too defend
the principle that nature, or Providence, works only naturally,
according to natural law. But Herder sees man's mission as
the development of all his faculties, his senses and feelings as
well as his reason, while Kant draws a sharp line between
intellect and the rest of man, just as he distinguishes man
sharply from animals. And Herder asserts man's obligation

and right to fulfil all his powers, to be his own purpose, in every age, while Kant sees man only as an instrument or a stage in a process. Thus Kant sees just social institutions as the highest purpose of history, while Herder, completely in the spirit of the Sturm und Drang, demands for each man, in every period, richness of experience, the fullest possible unfolding of human powers. But there is not merely a contrast of values between the rationalist and the Stürmer und Dränger. In Herder's materialistic procedure, despite his denial of any continuous line of social development, and despite his repudiation of his own times, we are given a method for understanding the changing values of civilisation as it changes its form, and can understand that the new values ever emerging cannot be measured against the values of other societies.

We cannot speak of the historical thought of any other of the Stürmer und Dränger. Hamann's attitude to the past was completely unhistorical, and centred in his search in the past for symbols of God's power. He wrote to Herder in 1768 that he was thinking of writing something on the first chapter of Genesis : ' You need Revelation for a history of the Creation. But a witty head can manage a history of society, as this mediocrity of a Ferguson shows.' [45] In plays and novels many of the Stürmer und Dränger show their predilection for less complex societies, but usually without any feeling for particular historical situations. Goethe seems never to have been interested in the historical process, except in *Götz von Berlichingen* ; and though he successfully recaptured the spirit of the times in *Egmont*, it is evident that the work is no more an historical play than *Julius Caesar* or *Le Cid*. It is characteristic of him that he followed with the greatest interest Herder's *Ideas*, of the second part of which he wrote to Herder : ' To all of it I say Yea and Amen, and nothing better can be written on the text : God so loved the world.' [46] His own tastes drove him in this period not to history, but to natural science, to botany and anatomy and mineralogy, but he wrote that he recognised the relationship of his discovery of the intermaxillary with the theme of Herder's philosophy of history.[47] Both were establishing, but in different media, the relationship between man and the animal kingdom. By the time that Schiller began his historical studies he had left his Sturm und

Drang behind. His inaugural lecture as professor of history, *What is Universal History, and to what End is it studied?*, sees the past as a ' shaming ' childhood of the race, the present as the summation of all past ' truth, morality, and wisdom ', and the future as a perspective of higher moral progress.[48] There is little evidence that, even in his Sturm und Drang time, Schiller's view of historical evolution was different from this.

In spite of the lack of historical concern in the other Stürmer und Dränger, Herder's *Another Philosophy of History* is not a purely personal outburst ; nor is it, like Rousseau's incursions into historical theory, a mere refutation of contemporary optimism and rationalist self-adulation. In it he seeks to find a firmer social and historical basis for Sturm und Drang values, a justification of his longing for a fuller emotive life, of his delight in instinct and senses. In the exhilaration of its earlier parts, as in the gloomy expression of frustration in the later, the work is a profound expression of the glory and tragedy of the Sturm und Drang. At the same time, it has not only a subjective value. It opened up a new appreciation of the material roots and spiritual blossoms of past cultures, revealed a richer understanding of the zig-zag course of history, and contributed greatly to the historical insight, the ' historicism ', of later times.

CHAPTER VIII

THE REVOLUTION IN POETICS

Ich hatte nichts und doch genug,
Den Drang nach Wahrheit und die Lust am Trug.
GOETHE.

WE HAVE seen how, in all fields of thought, the ultimate touchstone of judgment for the Stürmer und Dränger was personal experience, impelling experience which intensified their consciousness of being alive. All thought which did not promote this vital element, all activity which was dissociated from it, all purely passive feeling, was condemned by them as inadequate and false. In the wider world of social organisation, productive activity, science, this conviction, fruitful though it was, often took an immature form ; it was a surmise rather than an achievement. It truly prospered in the enrichment of personal life and of the imaginative powers. It was above all in poetry, in imaginative literature, that they felt most surely the gushing of this ‘ cheerful fountain ’, in poetry that they succeeded in giving it shape and permanence, through poetry that they passed on to others most adequately their feeling of life. Poetry gains, in their works, a new character and function ; or rather, they restore to poetry the character and function they divine it to have with primitive peoples, with Homer and Shakespeare. It is no longer a mere embellishment or compensation ; no longer a subsidiary to morals or philosophy ; no longer attached to a separate, particular human faculty. It emerges from and concentrates the whole of their being, their experience, their truth. From this vantage-point they gain a new insight into the nature of poetry in general, and mark a decisive turning-point in the history of poetics.

Eighteenth-century poetry has been well defined as ‘ the handmaiden of polite society ’ ; [1] its poetics, whether we think of Du Bos and Batteux, or Johnson and Burke, defines the decorous cultural taste of the court, the aristocratic salon, the academy. Yet there was no lack of protest against this

decorum. From the middle of the century there was a steady
growth of taste for great emotions, for the mystery and disorder
of the Gothic, for ruins and melancholy, for the naïve vehe-
mence of folksong, for Homer and Shakespeare, for robust
passions and robust laughter. It began to be perceived that
taste was not absolute, but changed with different times and
circumstances ; that the genius makes rules, not vice versa ;
that poetry is older than prose.[2] In the novel and domestic
drama new forms and themes were developed in accordance
with middle-class interests and experience. But in poetry and
aesthetics it is characteristic of this ' pre-romanticism ' to seek
to justify both the new taste and the established aristocratic
forms, in Warton's words, ' to reconcile the willing Graces to
the Gothic pile '. Even Young, in the most far-reaching attack
on the classical rules, asserts his belief in a growing perfection
of taste, in ' correctness '. Diderot, who wrote that ' la poésie
veut quelque chose d'énorme, de barbare et de sauvage ',
respected in his own works the formal proprieties.[3]

In Germany, where aristocratic culture was sharply sun-
dered from that of the middle class, classicism had for the
latter a much weaker meaning, and appears as imitation, as
the pedantry of dogmatic rules. While the moral purpose of
poetry was more crudely emphasised than in England or France,
the problem of beauty, so unrelated to the mode of life of the
middle class, was more obscure and insistent. Thus while
Batteux and Burke could analyse beauty in terms of the actual
taste of polite society, the aestheticians of the Aufklärung (the
word ' aesthetics ' was an invention of Baumgarten) insisted on
the disinterestedness of aesthetic pleasure.[4] Aesthetic appreciation is presented as something highly intellectual, divorced
from the values of practical sensuous life ; it was in protest
against this type of approach that Herder was, late in life,
to assert that beauty arises only from interest, from ' what
raises me above myself, what sets in motion all my
powers '.[5]

Among the more practical critics and writers in Germany we
find the same dichotomy as in France and England. Wieland
translated Shakespeare, and yet remained a writer of rococo
temper and form. Winckelmann wrote the first history of
ancient art, and yet remained attached to an ideal of artistic

perfection—' a noble simplicity and tranquil grandeur '. Lessing, whose style is so vigorous and free, and who had understanding for the imaginative elements in Shakespeare, remained in general a prisoner of the old classicistic formalism.[6] Even Klopstock, who invented a new poetic idiom, shows himself in his essays to be unconscious of any new principle of aesthetics.[7]

By the time of the Sturm und Drang there was, then, a great confusion in tastes and tenets. These young men reflect in many ways the prevailing views of their time, and draw extensively on their forbears, particularly those in England and France. But they were far less acquainted with polite society than their foreign contemporaries, far more radical in their repudiation of social restraints and cultural conventions. They pick up the threads of their times, but weave them into a totally new pattern.

THE SUBJECTIVE REVOLT

In all essentials the Sturm und Drang conception of beauty arose out of a new feeling for poetry—it was only through books that these young provincials could be in touch with Europe, even with their own country. Though several of them keenly responded to music, and played instruments, their musical taste seems to have had no distinctive feature. Architecture, sculpture, and painting played an important part in the awakening of their minds, but their attitude towards the plastic arts was far more ambiguous than that to poetry. Herder's work on sculpture, *Plastik*, contains interesting psychological observations, but is of no significance in the history of taste. As a collector, Merck was a connoisseur of the conventional eighteenth-century type. Some of Goethe's most profound aesthetic views are associated with the Strassburg Minster and Rembrandt, yet he himself remained true to the classical principles of painting that he learned from Oeser in Leipzig, and his enthusiasm for the Minster did not widen into a general admiration of Gothic, of the medieval city, as with the Romantics. He failed to notice Gothic sculpture ; and when he or Merck or Herder or Lenz visited the seats of the great and museums of classical replicas, they succumbed completely to the spell of classical beauty. In their immediate environment, in the cities in which they lived, they lacked any direct contact with the Palladian or Baroque palaces of the great, with rococo sculpture and *bric-à-brac*. Their relationship to plastic art was therefore less central and decisive than that to poetry : the chief fault of theories of beauty which were based on the visual arts seemed to them to be their abstractness, their remoteness from actual experience.

Herder very forcefully pointed out how unreal and meaningless the classical conventions of art were in Germany. In a review of a translation of Batteux' *Système des beaux arts* he points out that this theory of art as ' imitation of beautiful nature ' can be accepted in France as the argument of a member of polite society, speaking to others who are surrounded by the elegant products of art and who know from their direct experience what in the argument is true and what false. But in Germany, where this whole artistic environment and experience is lacking in the middle class, Batteux' theory becomes a metaphysical dogma, his explanations of the objects he takes pleasure in turn into definitions of art in the abstract. This salon-gossip makes the German reader forget ' actuality, nature, objects, art, phenomenon, all the material side of art ', and lose himself in interminable and useless commentaries and supplements.[8]

In concentrating on the beauty which was a living source of experience the Stürmer und Dränger not only freed themselves from the artistic conventions of polite society, but also from every dogmatic approach to aesthetics. Abstract and general definitions were in their view the very antithesis of the energetic, dynamic nature of beauty. Thus Goethe turned at an early age, before he met Herder, from the philosophical approach of Mendelssohn.

Mendelssohn and others [he wrote in 1770] have tried to catch beauty like a butterfly, and to pin it down for the benefit of the curious observer ; and they have succeeded ; but that is how it is when you catch butterflies ; the poor beast flutters about in the net, shakes off its finest colours ; and even if you catch it unimpaired, yet there it is stuck, stiff and lifeless ; the corpse is not the whole animal.[9]

Mephistopheles makes the same point when he jeers at the method of metaphysicians :

> If you want to know life and describe it,
> First you must expel the spirit.[10]

Altogether, the Stürmer und Dränger are as shy of discussing the concept ' beauty ' as they are of all abstractions. The work of art exists for them as a concrete individuality, as the source of a particular exhilaration. In many ways they express this exhilaration, but extremely rarely do they seek to define what is common to all art. Just as Herder refuses to accept a rigid distinction between thinking, feeling, and willing, so they do not recognise a peculiar aesthetic sense. With an infinitely wider capacity of aesthetic appreciation than their predecessors, they scarcely attempt to find a formula which would combine the qualities of Homer and the Greek dramatists, Shakespeare, folksong, except in so far as all art stimulates in them a feeling of intense vitality. Their most important aesthetic work arises from their observation of particular works of art, of poetry ; it is criticism rather than aesthetics.

The only Sturm und Drang treatise on beauty is, in fact, an aphoristic rhapsody of Hamann's, the *Aesthetica in nuce* of 1762 ; and this work is almost as much a religious work. Like his religion, which is free of dogmatism and moralism, and rises from the intensity of his sensuous imagination, beauty is for him concrete and sensuous.

In this little treatise Hamann delivers a drastic attack upon the prevailing conception of beauty. God speaks to man, he writes, not through abstractions but through the particular individualities of his Creation. Art is then primarily religious : not in the Klopstockian sense that it is concerned with religious themes, but in the new sense that, in ' imitating nature ', it creates symbols of God's Word, symbols which speak direct through sense and feeling and thus reveal the divine force working in all life. ' Nature works through senses and passions. How can anyone feel who mutilates her instruments ? ' The artist must be the analogue of God, and his works must reveal God just as do the works of nature. In an essential sense, not merely historically, ' poetry is the mother-tongue of the human race '. The aim of the artist must be to create images as visual, as sensuously evident, as nature. ' Speak so that I can see you.' ' Senses and passions speak and understand nothing but images. In images rests the whole treasury of human knowledge and understanding.' The ideals of elegance and propriety are thrown on one side. The beautification of nature is a blasphemous folly, for all nature is God's handiwork, and God is evident essentially in vigour and life. ' If the passions are dishonourable members, does that make them stop being weapons of maleness ? ' Sexual functions may be inelegant, but they are the expression and symbol of creativeness.

Beauty then is the reproduction, through image, of the natural joy of sense-perception and of feeling. Hamann's theory is, like Blake's, the exact opposite of that of Johnson or Reynolds, who consider that generalities are more true than particulars, and who interpret the ' imitation of nature ' as idealisation of nature. But Hamann finds the justification of his opinion in his religion ; nature and beauty are not self-sufficient, but both reveal something else, God. So, in the latter part of the essay, he calls for the restoration of poetry through the imitation of Oriental poetry, primarily of the Old Testament : ' through journeys to Arabia felix, crusades to the East, and through the restoration of its magic '. And he concludes, fittingly enough : ' Let us now hear the sum of my latest aesthetic, which is also the oldest : Fear God and give Him the honour, for the time of His judgment is at hand, and pray to Him Who hath made heaven and earth and sea and the watersprings.' [11] This religious substratum of Hamann's aesthetic thought is, however, very different from that of so many of his contemporaries. In this context it frees poetry of the limitations of a particular religious content or doctrinal and moral purpose, and justifies feeling and imagination.

Many of Hamann's remarks show his contempt for the view that poetry can be contained within rules. In a letter of 1761, discussing Diderot's essay on dramatic poetry, he writes that Diderot knows the rules as well as any schoolmaster,

but this philosophe says, like a half-mystic, that it is not rules that must guide and enlighten us, but a something, that is far more immediate, far more instinctive, far more obscure and far more certain. What nonsense in the mouth of a philosopher like Diderot ! [12]

In two little essays of 1762, *Reader and Critic* and *Author and Critic*, he ridicules in the name of nature the decorative conception of art. Writers who thumb through their libraries in search of poetic embellishments, he writes, are merely making stuffed images covered in pretty rags, ' but without the essential characteristic, without scar and soul '—a typically obscure reference to the distinguishing and peculiar scar of Odysseus. So too the moralising aestheticians show only ' the bust and wardrobe ' of their characters, ' the dawn of a refreshing day which they will never experience '. ' Their ethics and their taste are based only on painted values, their mode of life and their style are a whited surface, which deceives the eye and insults the sense, their criticism is a fairy-tale of scum spooned off life.' [13] These academic legislators of art take all the life out of art : in the ' blindness and lethargy of their hearts ' they have cut off Homer's head and made the mutilated head their coat-of-arms. [14] Their theory is ' endless repetition of exhausted observations on the palette and etiquette of fine art '. [13] They make rules, and they do not see that all masterpieces are exceptions to the rules—with a characteristic comparison Hamann writes : ' No one who does not make an exception can produce a masterpiece ; for rules are Vestal Virgins, who by means of exceptions were the means of populating Rome.' [13] And he sums up his defence of originality in the notable words :

He who wants to abolish caprice and fancy from the fine arts is a quack, who knows his own rules even less than the nature of disease. . . . He who wants to abolish caprice and fancy from the fine arts is like an assassin, plotting against their honour and their life, and understands no other language of passion than that of hypocrites.

All these ' wrongheaded rules and arbitrary examples ' of the academic critics prove nothing but ' the complete lack of the most essential and fruitful principles, on which alone depend the knowledge and enjoyment, the love and procreation of fine natures '.[13]

Hamann demanded from poetry that bitter-sweet rapture that comes from surrender to emotions and sense-impressions. When Moses Mendelssohn wrote a carping criticism of the immorality of *La nouvelle Héloise*, of sentiments which he considered untrue because they conflicted with social values, Hamann jumped to the counter-attack.

If our reason has, must have, flesh and blood, and becomes a washerwoman or a siren : how can you forbid the passions the same liberty ? How can you subject the first-born emotion of the human soul to the yoke of circumcision ? Can you play with it as with a bird ? or bind it with your rules ? Do you not see, that if you did you would tear down all the lighthouses which are needed to guide you and others. . . . Who is the aesthetic Moses who may prescribe to the citizens of a free state weak and meagre laws, such as, thou shalt not attack this, thou shalt not taste that, thou shalt not touch the other ? [15]

Hamann's aesthetic doctrine is then the extreme of subjectivism. Supported by his belief that surrender to sense, to imagination, and feeling, brings contact with the Divine, he goes much further, in theory and practice, than Young in his *Conjectures*. He never shows any understanding of aesthetic form or even of the technical determinants of art, and his own style, in its waywardness and obscurity, illustrates some of the weaknesses of his theory. A genius, he writes, must shake off all rules like a fig tree its fruit.[16] These ideas obviously did not contribute much to aesthetic understanding, nor to the knowledge of artistic craftsmanship. But they were immensely valuable in that they freed his young contemporaries from respect for the conventions of their times and the pedantry of pundits, and taught them that beauty must be born within their own, personal, essential experience : that the ultimate test of art is exhilaration which thrills through sense and spirit.

The Stürmer und Dränger did not rest content with this completely subjective definition of beauty, as we shall see. But in many of their statements and works it is evident, and it can be called the rudimentary form of their revolt. It is the source of the notion of the ' original genius ', the ' Genie ', in its crudest form ; it encouraged them to disregard all conventions of artistic form and of language, and often to disregard the need for communicability. It emphasised—over-emphasised—that aspect of poetic creation which is spontaneous utterance, ' nature ', as opposed to rational intention and to the principle of form.

Like Hamann, Lavater and F. L. Stolberg could find the justification of this extreme subjectivism in the analogy they drew between the poet and God. Lavater compares poets with the God who is ' the essence of all movement, creative power and influence '.[17] Poets are the interpreters of divine power :

Human gods ! Creators ! Destroyers ! Revealers of the mysteries of God and of men ! Interpreters of nature ! Speakers of inexpressible things ! Prophets ! Priests ! . . .
Who is a poet ? A spirit who feels that he can create, and who does create, and whose creation does not only please himself as his work, but of whose creation all tongues must witness : Truth ! Truth ! Nature ! Nature ! We see what we never saw, and hear what we never heard, and yet, what we see and hear is flesh of our flesh and bone of our bone ! [18]

In the same rhapsodic tone F. L. Stolberg defines poetry as enthusiasm, inspiration, ' nature ', unqualified by any condition. The excellence of Homer, the authors of the Bible, Shakespeare, is due to their not having learnt anything from anyone.[19]

Similar expressions are found in the Stürmer und Dränger, who at times define beauty as the simple product of spontaneous creation, and exalt the poet as the analogue of God. Herder characterises the peculiar quality of Klopstock's odes as ' the feeling for nature, the whole richness of heart and soul '.[20] In his supremely important essay on Shakespeare he writes :

Step before Shakespeare's stage as before an ocean of events, where wave surges into wave. The scenes of nature ebb and flow ; work upon one another, however disparate they appear ;

give birth to one another, and destroy one another, so that the intention of the creator, who seemed to have joined them together in a plan of intoxication and disorder, may be fulfilled—obscure, small symbols like sun-cast silhouettes of a theodicy of God.[21]

Goethe also could fall temporarily under the spell of this conception of nature and poetry. Shakespeare was for him, even more than for Herder, a signal of revolt against all form.

> When I had finished the first play of Shakespeare's . . . I felt most intensely my existence enlarged by an infinity. . . . I hesitated not for a second to renounce the regular theatre. The unity of place seemed as oppressive as a prison, the unities of action and time burdensome fetters on our imagination. I leapt into the open air, and felt at last that I had hands and feet. . . . Shakespeare's theatre is a lovely raree-show, in which the history of the world moves past our eyes on the invisible thread of time. His plots are, to speak in conventional style, no plots, but his plays all turn round the mysterious point, which as yet no philosopher has seen and defined, at which the essential characteristic of our ego, the alleged freedom of our will, comes into collision with the necessary motion of the Whole. . . . Most of these gentlemen [Shakespeare's critics] niggle at his characters. And I cry Nature! Nature! nothing so completely Nature as Shakespeare's characters.[22]

The emphasis in these ecstatic ejaculations, in Goethe's style as in what he says, is entirely on the freedom of poetic creation. Shakespeare has an intoxicating effect on him, and he attributes intoxication to the artist. Like Herder, he was to make most important modifications to this view, but something of this subjectivism was to cling to him throughout his Sturm und Drang.

Very similar observations were made by Lenz in his essay on Goethe's *Werther*. How can one argue about a work that casts such a spell? he asks. It is justified because it wins our love.[23] Lenz finds a characteristically whimsical image for the freedom of the poet in his *Observations on the Theatre*. Poetry, he says, is imitation of nature,

> that is, of all the things that we see, hear, etc., around us, which penetrate through the five gates of our soul, and according to its

dimensions throw into it a weaker or stronger garrison of ideas, which then begin to live and move, to group themselves in this city under certain main principles, or also, on occasion, to wander round without a commander, orders, or discipline, as Bunyan has so pleasantly described in his *Holy War*. And they often fall asleep at their posts like drunken soldiers, and wake up at the wrong moment, et cetera. . . . We are, or at least would like to be, the first rung on the ladder of freely active independent creatures, and since we see around us, here and there, a world that is the proof of an infinitely and freely active being, the first impulse we feel in our soul is the desire to do likewise. But since the world has no bridges and we have to content ourselves with the things that are there, we do at least feel an accretion to our existence, happiness, by re-creating its Creation on a small scale.[24]

The nature of which Lenz here writes is the infinite variety of individual beings and things, not the limited, ordered, and beautified nature of Boileau or Gottsched or Johnson. Its unity lies in no pattern or law, but in the creative spirit which is always throwing up and destroying a profusion of creatures, and beauty is the evocation of this creative spirit (we are reminded of Blake's ' exuberance is beauty '). Lenz could so far disregard the problem of form as to suggest that the highest works of art have something incomplete about them.[25]

No literary genre was so encumbered by rules at this time as the drama. And even here, when the technical conditions of the stage necessarily impose certain limitations, the Stürmer und Dränger boldly sought to abandon all rules—at least for a time. The impact of Shakespeare was at first completely bewildering. In ignoring the rules of the classical theatre he seemed to them to observe no rules, to be nature naked. Herder could write, in the first draft of his Shakespeare essay, that no term could sum up the great variety of his plays but ' history '.[26] And even in the final version : ' When I read him, theatre, actors, scenery disappear ! Nothing but leaves from the book of events, of providence, of the world, blowing in the storm of time.' [27] In the course of the composition of this essay, between 1771 and 1773, Herder only slowly came to grips with the dramaturgical problem posed by Shakespeare, and when he did, he adopted in one sense the definitions of Gerstenberg, whose articles on Shakespeare were the direct

stimulus of his own essay. Gerstenberg had defended Shakespeare's disregard for the unities of time and place by giving
a new definition of dramatic illusion. As opposed to the
normal view that the purpose of theatrical illusion was to
persuade the spectator that what goes on on the stage is
modelled on normal experience and might be happening in
real life,[28] Gerstenberg asserted that dramatic illusion throws
us outside the theatre, outside the consciousness of the time
and place in which we exist.[29]

Gerstenberg himself did not seem to realise the implications
of his statement. On the one hand, he suggested that ' Shakespeare's works are not to be judged from the standpoint of
tragedy, but as copies of moral nature '.[30] On the other hand,
he still hankered after the old, conventional rules of drama,
and even tried to prove that Shakespeare in fact observes
them.[31] But Herder, much more ardent in his defence of
Shakespeare, and much more determined to find a formula
which would embrace both Greek drama and Shakespeare,
eagerly caught at Gerstenberg's suggestion. Asking, what was
the purpose of the Greek theatre, he cries :

Aristotle has defined it and there has been enough argument
about it—nothing more nor less than a certain shattering of the
heart, the awakening of the soul in a certain measure and from
certain sides, in short, a type of illusion.[32]

And by illusion (he uses the latinate word) Herder does not
mean the deception through imitation, the ' Täuschung ', of
Mendelssohn or Lessing, no more than he means the verisimili-
tude of Boileau and Gottsched. He does not mean that the
spectator is persuaded that the scene and persons on the stage
correspond with the normal experience of his life.[33] Illusion
is the power of the poet to impose on us his own world, to throw
us out of normal experience and destroy normal standards, to
subject us to his imagination. The poet, the ' dramatic God ',
has to shatter our consciousness of the time and place in which
we are.

For you, as a dramatic poet, no clock strikes on tower and temple,
but you have to create space and time ; and if you can produce

a world and it cannot exist but in time and space, lo, your measure of time and space lies within you ; thither you must bewitch all your spectators, you must impose it on them, or you are—anything but a dramatic poet. . . . It matters not how or where the dramatic poet carries you away ; if he can carry you away, there is his world.[34]

That this is a highly eccentric interpretation of Aristotle is clear enough. It expresses a violent movement of revolt against the whole traditional approach to art, a defiant self-reliance which all the Stürmer und Dränger needed if they were to justify the immense experience Shakespeare offered them. It needed to be said, to be borne in mind. But it is only the beginning of art, and only too often was asserted as its end. The less significant of the Stürmer und Dränger scarcely rose above this level of understanding. Heinse or Schubart do not get further than to say that art must ' ravish and transport ',[35] and in their critical works they seek only to express, often in stuttering ejaculations, how enraptured they are. Yet Heinse also translated the complex stanzas of Ariosto, and had a particular liking for the intricacies of Renaissance poetic forms. Klinger and Müller allowed themselves all sorts of eccentricities in their plays, disregarding the necessities of staging and of dramatic action, and at the same time took over the form of Shakespearian or even the more regular drama. In ignoring the characteristics and function of form, it was only too easy to identify the form they preferred with ' freedom ', ' nature ', and thus to fall unconsciously into a new type of imitation. In Herder and Goethe, to some extent in Lenz himself, we find, however, that this highly subjective conception of poetry is moulded, from early on, by a search for objective principles, which would both place their appreciation of Shakespeare, or Homer, or folksong on a more solid foundation, and provide a securer starting-point for the new poetry they were writing and seeking. The Sturm und Drang provides not only the formula for the rejection of conventional standards, but also the basis for a new method of literary criticism and a new principle of poetry.

THE SEARCH FOR OBJECTIVE PRINCIPLES
OF CRITICISM

The Stürmer und Dränger came nearer to objective principles of criticism first of all in the field of language. In revolt against the Aufklärung ideal of a general grammar and an abstract ' correct ' language, they delighted in the diversity of idiom. Hamann again led the way. In an essay on the reciprocal influence of language and opinions he wrote : [36]

The natural cast of mind has an influence on language. . . . If our ideas arrange themselves according to the viewpoint of the soul, and if the latter, as is commonly held, is determined by the situation of the body, the same can be said of the body of a whole people. The lineaments of its language will therefore correspond to the general cast of its mind ; and every nation reveals it through the nature, form, laws, and customs of its speech, just as through its external culture and through the drama of its public actions. The Ionian dialect has been compared with its costume, and the strict observance of the Law which made the Jews so blind at the time of the divine Visitation is evident in their language. From this cast of mind arises the relative richness in certain branches of language, and the complementary poverty in others, all of which are phenomena which derive from the misproportion of language and are sometimes reckoned as perfection, sometimes as imperfection : the peculiar quality we observe in idioms, and all that is understood by the term ' the genius of a language '. This nature of language must not be confused with grammar or eloquence. . . . My readers will readily think of the names of two scholars, Gottsched and Michaelis, who possess distinguished and estimable insight, the elder in the grammar and knowledge of German, the younger in the grammar and knowledge of Oriental languages ; but both have accepted and publicly established as the standard of their judgment on the genius of these languages many prejudices of philosophical myopia and philological quackery. . . . Since our cast of mind is based on sensuous impressions and associated feelings, we can very probably assume a consonance of the organs of feeling and the sources of human speech. So, as nature has given a people a certain peculiar colour or shape of eye, just as readily has she been able to communicate to their tongues and lips modifications which are imperceptible to us. . . . The investigation of the deaf and dumb throws much light on the nature of the oldest languages. The mere breath of a sound is sufficient to make the most subtle distinctions. . . . We can see how the character of observations and of the objects observed can enlarge and narrow the language of a people, give it this or that shade.

In this (exceptionally lucid) passage Hamann is applying the principles of Bacon and Montesquieu to language, and his conclusions are important. Instead of viewing language as the imperfect reflection in the phenomenal world of a perfectly orderly, logical ideal, he sees it as the product of circumstances and national character. Its actual appearance is its only reality, and the philosopher will take delight in every language as it is. Every language is good because it expresses the life of the people that has shaped it. Thus he relishes idioms, dialect forms ; he points out that every section and class of a people has its own vocabulary ; he would defend and presere these forms because they express the true spirit of the users. Hamann's defence of such forms is another aspect of his war on rationalist idealism and pedantry ; he is in fact establishing a theoretical basis on which one might expect a theory of poetical language to be erected, a theory which would relate the meaning of words and cadences to their origin, function, and value in active social life. But, disappointingly enough, he does not pursue these thoughts further. His discussion of the nature of poetry in *Aesthetica in nuce* treats of verbal images as products of isolated man facing God's nature, without any reference to the meaning that words accumulate historically and socially. And his own style is arbitrary and inorganic, full of images and references culled from the world of books, and without any roots in his physical or social environment.

The work with which Herder first made his mark, the *Fragments on Recent German Literature*, is to a large extent based on Hamann's view. Herder had written to Hamann in 1766 that the form of an expression determines the meaning : ' if you think in a different way you think differently',[37] and the *Fragments* are largely an extended investigation of the cultural and spiritual implications of linguistic usages in general, with particular reference to German.

The Aufklärer Sulzer had asserted the desirability of a definitive German grammar and dictionary which should establish correct usage and precise meanings. Even Mendelssohn had protested that the realisation of such a plan would be the death of poetry, which prospers on superfluity and irregularity.[38] Herder subscribes to this criticism, but he goes further and shows that Sulzer's conception of language turns men into abstract intelligences. Language is, on the contrary, the product of particular groups in particular circumstances. ' In a sensuous language there must be unclear words, synonyms, inversions, idioms.' Language has the individuality of a people—' idioms are patronymic treasures of beauty, like the palm trees round the academy of Athens which were dedicated to Minerva '. The whimsicality of the British humorists, of Shakespeare and Swift and Fielding, he points out, is so dear to the British because it is the fruit of the national genius, part of the national character. Gottsched's search for purity, for a ' watery and levelled down ' language, has deprived German of its peculiar character.[39] Each language has its own character, and its greatest beauties are untranslatable. The poetry of the Bible, or of Homer, is the product of uncivilised peoples, and cannot be truly rendered into a civilised tongue.[40]

Herder extends his investigations to rhythm. Foreign metres cannot be indiscriminately adopted, and the Alexandrine of the French is a failure in German. With great insight he shows how Klopstock, though he aimed at reproducing the Greek or Latin hexameter, has actually produced a rhythm which is not analysable in terms of classical prosody. ' When I read Homer, I stand in spirit in Greece in a thronging market place . . . where even in ordinary life men spoke in such a raised tone, with high and low pitch, that every ear could plainly judge the prosody of the rhapsodists.' How different are the cadences natural to German, in the songs of the peasants and the oldest hymns, how different German life ! [41] Similarly, he points out that both the character of the images found in the Bible or in Homer, and the function of these images, are quite different from their character and function in modern poets, even where the latter try to imitate the older styles. The Hebrews were a pastoral people, and their language is built out of the materials of their environment ; the Germans are townsfolk, and their language is made up of ' household gear ; words from the crafts ; burgher expressions ; turns of expression from social intercourse '. But the German use of images is different too.

The ancients spoke through images ; we at best with images, and the imaged language of our descriptive poets compares with that of the oldest poets as an example to an allegory, as an allegory to an image presented in one stroke. Read Homer, and then read Klopstock ; the former paints as he speaks ; he paints a living nature and a political world ; the latter speaks in order to paint, he describes . . . a totally different world, the world of the soul and thoughts—while the former clothes them in bodies and says : Let them speak for themselves.[42]

Supported by the conclusions of Du Bos, Lowth, and Blackwell, and of many philosophers of language, who had demonstrated the specific social origin of Greek and Hebrew literature, Herder is here giving direction and purpose to the disjointed ideas of Hamann. He is concerned to define the poetical potentialities of German as they can be deduced from the actual state of German life and language. So, accepting the thesis that ' every language grows, blossoms, and decays ', he defines three main ages of language—the early sensuous, poetical age ; the second, that of ' beautiful prose ' ; the third, that of correct, abstract prose. German he considers to be in the second stage, half-way between the poetical and the philosophical.[43] His main intention was to prove the fruitlessness of the attempt to imitate the Bible, or Homer, or Pindar ; and even more of the aim of imitating the ' philosophical ' language of Rome or France. Much of the third Collection of the *Fragments* is devoted to a defence of German against those who believed that only Latin was a worthy medium of expression. Such latinists as Klotz had condemned German as barbaric and clumsy, aesthetically intractable. But Herder claims that the ' barbaric ' elements in German, proper to the stage of development of the people and the language, the peculiar sound-groups, provincialisms and idioms, irregularities and ' imperfections ', are the strength of the German language, and make it susceptible of poetic expression. Let Latin remain the language of scholars ; but it lacks the ' character and life ' to be the language of poetry :[44]

> Languages that lack the living voice
> To carry meaning to the natural heart.[45]

Herder's next publication, the *Kritische Wälder*, fails to develop in any significant way the suggestions of the *Fragments*. Its sub-title is *Observations touching the Science and Art of the Beautiful*, and the task he set himself seems to have been beyond his powers. Much of this work is again taken up with a polemic against Klotz, and in concentrating on Greek and Roman literature and the aesthetic theory deduced from it Herder gets bogged down in conventional concepts. The first *silva* is the most important. It contains a long discussion of Lessing's *Laokoon*, and a refutation of Lessing's conception of the principles of poetry. Lessing had believed that Homer's mode of writing was the outcome of his conscious recognition that poetry is ' the representation of events in time ', as distinct from painting or sculpture, which is ' the representation of objects in space '. Herder asserts, on the contrary, that the art of Homer was not the result of deliberate intention, but a product of a way of life and thought. He criticises too Lessing's intellectualistic approach to poetry, and points out the sensuous qualities of words, their evocative power and musical resonance. He comes to the conclusion that poetry is ' energy '. ' The object of poetry is the energy that adheres to the inner meaning of words, the magic power which works upon my soul through fancy and memory.' [46] But this conclusion, significant as it is, is very abstract and could be no guide either for taste or for poetic creation. Herder's really decisive ideas were to spring from his reflections over works which threw him out of the conventional classical field of aesthetic argument.

It was difficult for him to discard the normal notions of beauty. Occasionally, as in the review of Gerstenberg's tragedy, *Ugolino*, we see the rush of his spirit towards a poetry which stirs and shakes him, and his readiness to abandon all the aesthetic pre-occupations and preconceptions of his time.[47] In the *Journal* of 1769 he recognises the specific character of every man's experience and therefore of every man's language, and describes how the peculiar circumstances of his voyage enable him more fully to appreciate the Nordic poetry of the Edda and Ossian. But he is still haunted by the ideal of classical harmony and balance.[48] So too, in his correspondence with his betrothed, the highest epithet he can find for her is ' my Grecian ', to define the poise, serenity, grace he saw in her.[49] At this stage in his development he wavers between two opposed conceptions of beauty—the classicistic ideal of reserve and harmony, most powerfully substantiated by Winckelmann, and the new craving for exuberance, passion, ecstasy. It is only in his two great essays in the volume *On German Character and Art* of 1773 that he at last establishes principles of criticism which justify both.[50]

Both the Ossian and the Shakespeare essays spring directly from Gerstenberg's articles, and in both Herder seeks to put Gerstenberg's championship of ancient Nordic poetry and Shakespeare on a secure and independent footing. Gerstenberg had tried to reconcile the ' Nordics ' with the conventional prejudice in favour of classical rhetoric and classical dramatic proprieties ; Herder seeks objective principles which would justify folksong and Shakespeare in their own right, without denying the artistic achievement of the Ancients. He draws upon all the new insight into the social and historical origin of art and language—the sensuous source of language, the original association of poetry with music and dance, the influence of social conditions on the content and form of art—but synthesises and focuses these new ideas with such vigour that his essays have an unparalleled force and may rightly be considered to be epoch-making.

He begins the essay *On Ossian and the Songs of Ancient Peoples* with a criticism of a German translation of *Ossian* into hexameters.[51] These Klopstockian rhythms, he asserts, completely distort the character of the original, for Klopstock's style interprets modern, sentimental, reflective man, while *Ossian* is ' songs, songs of a people, songs of an uncultured, sensuous people '. Gerstenberg himself, writes Herder, had already pointed out how important is the order of words in poetry, how meaning is affected by the accent and melody of speech ; and in this translation, what has happened to the ' tone, colour, the fleetest feeling of the peculiar identity of place and purpose ' ?—' And does not the whole beauty of a poem, all the spirit and power of speech, depend on these ? '

Fortunately Herder then escapes from Ossian, and all the pitfalls of this forgery, and quotes Shakespeare's *Come away Death.* The content of this poem, he admits, is insignificant ; its beauty lies in ' its sensuous qualities, in its form, sound, tone, melody, all those obscure and ineffable impressions that flood our soul as we hear it sung '. Herder proceeds in the course of the essay to quote many poems, Eddic lays, Lapp, Scottish, English, and German folksongs, Luther's hymns. He points out how their beauty arises from the peculiar character of the rhythm, the meaningful imagery taken from living experience, the dramatic dialogue. Quoting *Edward, Edward* (of which he gives an excellent translation) he points out how the progress of the action of this ballad is carried forward by ' leaps and sallies ' from symbol to symbol, how the very jerkiness of the narrative is its beauty, for the poem speaks to our imagination and feeling, not merely to our intellect.

All the songs of primitive peoples are woven round existing objects, actions, events, round a living world ! How rich and manifold are these circumstances, features of actuality, incidents ! And the eye has seen all ! The soul imagines them ! That imposes leaps and sallies ! There is no other connection between the parts of the song than there is between the trees and bushes in the forest, between the rocks and grottoes of the desert, between the scenes of the event itself.

We can see the connection between this appreciation of folksong and Herder's theory of the relations of mind and body. The content and form of a poem are given by the whole experience of the writer, and must, if they are to be poetic, speak to the whole man, to the imagination in which all man's senses and capacities are fused, not to a mere part of him. There is therefore no general ideal form or mode of expression ; poetry is beautiful in so far as it rises from full experience and presents ' sensuous situations ' to us, ' sen-

suous creatures ' ; form is not an absolute, but a function of a
poetic purpose.

But Herder goes further. Why, he asks, have the language
and songs of primitive peoples so peculiar and great a power,
as compared with the mass of modern poetry ? His answer
is a sociological one.

> The wilder, i.e. the more living, more freely active a people is,
> the wilder, i.e. the more living, more sensuous, freer, fuller of lyrical
> action must be its poetry. The further away from artificial,
> scholastic modes of thought, speech, and writing a people is, the
> less its songs will be made for paper and be dead literature. The
> essence and purpose of these songs depends alone on the lyrical,
> living, as it were dance-like character of song, on the living presence
> of the images, on the connection and as it were dire urgency [' Noth-
> drang '] of the content and feelings, on the symmetry of word,
> syllables, yes often even of letters, on the movement of the melody,
> and on a hundred other things which belong to the living world
> and these national songs. . . . Hence the whole magic power
> that makes of these songs the entrancement, the spur, the ever-
> lasting inheritance of joy of a people.

Herder describes how deeply he felt the power of the Edda as
he himself travelled on a ship over the ' endless element '
past the Baltic cliffs. He learned not only that this poetry
arose from an active community, interpreting its life and
experience ; but also he learnt that poetry is not mere ' amusing, interrupted reading, in the scholar's chair or the drawing
room ', but is a stimulus, a ' spring of action '. Poetry has a
vital, active function, in society as in the individual, it accom-
panies the hunter and the lover, it is a people's ' everlasting inheritance ', renewing their strength and joy in life.
It not only expresses experience, it condenses, organises,
directs it.

Herder finds poetry which fully carries out these functions
only in the Bible, in Homer, and in the poetry of earlier
cultures. But, for all his ' enthusiasm for the savages ', to
which he jokingly refers, he is not concerned primarily with
a defence of early art. In fact, he confuses folksong with
Ossian, with Shakespeare's and Goethe's lyrics, with German
post-Renaissance songs. But this confusion does not do

offence to his argument, for he is ultimately concerned to define the quality of true poetry and to find the way to its renewal.

He recognises that the difficulties for the modern creative artist are enormous. Modern society has cut off the cultured class from the active life of society. The modern writer lives in a study, his knowledge is acquired from books, his ideas are ' shadows ', his purposes are tortuous, his impulses perverted by ' slavish expectations, timidly slinking diplomacy, and confusing premeditation '. Poetry cannot be rescued by the imitation of the older songs. Gray, Akenside, and Mason show, he writes, what failure results from the imitation of Pindar ; and if folksong can help, it cannot be through imitation of ' its form, its dress, its idiom '. The modern world and modern society are different from those in which Homer and the Edda were born, and therefore modern poetry must be different from them.

What is then to be done ? Herder falters at this point, only too aware of the harm done by tyrannical aesthetic legislators. At one point in his essay he tries to analyse the quality of the best of modern poets. Some, like Milton or Haller, are primarily, he says, poets of ideas ; such a poet must grasp the whole meaning of his poem in such a way that ' all the letters are already graven deeply in his soul, and he gives his poem only the total, honest expression'. Others, like Klopstock, are primarily sentimental poets, and ' must abandon themselves to the ardour of a happy hour, write, and entrance '. That is, the character of the poet and the poem must determine the form, without respect to scholastic regulations. Herder is well aware of the vagueness of these prescriptions, and gladly confines himself to the critical analysis of folksong.

This essay was in the main composed in 1771. In this year the first collection of Klopstock's odes was published, and suddenly Herder's earlier appreciation of Klopstock ripened into the joyful conviction that here was a modern poetic genius. So, in a *Postscript*, he gives a solemn greeting to Klopstock,

gushing forth a sevenfold source, to renew the full, healthy bloom of the world's youth so that in ode and grace at table, in hymn

and love-song, the heart will speak, and no code of rules, no Horace,
Pindar or Orbilius [Orbilius was Horace's tutor] . . .
Ode ! it becomes again what it was ! The feeling of a total
situation of life ! Dialogue of the human heart—with God ! with
itself ! with all nature. Euphony ! it becomes again what it was.
Not an artificial construction of numbered harmonies ! Movement ! Melody of the heart ! Dance !

From Herder's letters to Caroline, and from a long review
of Klopstock's odes that he wrote in 1773, we know that he
made some reservations in his praise of Klopstock. He disliked his tendency to rhetoric and tirade, to a too spiritualised
etherealism, to a too involved metre. But he recognised in
Klopstock a true poet. His poems are true ' effusions of the
heart '. For every poetic theme he finds its own ' colour and
tone ', in image, period, metre, down to the choice of letters
and pauses.

It seems to the reviewer that in this respect these poems have
something unique, original, a spirit of their own ; just as nature
has given to every plant, shrub and animal its own shape, sense and
character, which is individual and cannot be compared, so in each
individual poem of Klopstock there floats a different fragrance and
moves a spirit peculiar in its nature and passion.[52]

Klopstock has not constructed his odes on a general pattern,
according to rule, but has found varied forms to express the
individuality of each of his varied themes.
   The theoretical importance of the Ossian essay lies in
Herder's search for a definition of the relationship between
art and experience, and consequently of the specific nature
and function of form. It is not a mere rhapsody on folksong.
Poetry arises in the first place from the ' dire urgency ' of
the theme. Its nature and form are moulded by the specific
character of a society which constitutes and shapes the experience of the individual writer ; and Herder concludes that
poetic form must change according to the nature of such
experience. He asserts with great emphasis that the ancient
Nordic poetry is as artistic as the Greek or Roman, that its
crudeness is only apparent, and its form the result, conscious
or unconscious, of a distinct artistic impulse ; but content,

impulse, and form, as well as function of these poems, is associated with the character of social life. And, in his eulogy of Klopstock, he points to the task of the modern poet : the creation of a poetry which must be personal and individualistic, since modern society has cut off the writer from the active community, but which must focus all the feeling and sensuous delight of which modern man is capable.

Equally significant is Herder's essay on Shakespeare. In the three versions of this little work, which fall in 1771, 1772, and 1773, we can actually follow step by step the development of his historical, relativistic approach to the great problem of the ' rules ' of tragedy.[53] The first version is essentially a panegyric of Shakespeare, an ardent confession of faith in a writer who presents nature and history direct, without the intervention of art and calculation. At the end of the second version Herder adds some rather disjointed reflections on the difference between Shakespeare and the Greeks, belatedly realising that the critic must investigate the questions : ' What advantages and disadvantages belong to the Greek and the Shakespearean drama, each considered in itself ? and then : was a Greek drama possible in Shakespeare's time, is it possible in ours ? '[54] The final version opens with general considerations on the nature of tragedy and its historically changing forms, so that the essay is no longer a mere panegyric of Shakespeare but the most profound study of the genetics of dramatic form in this century.

Drama arose in Greece, Herder begins the final version, from a particular tradition and language, and in a particular form.

In Greece it arose as it could not arise in the North. In Greece it was what it cannot be in the North. So, it is not, and cannot be, what it has been in Greece. Sophocles' drama and Shakespeare's drama are therefore two things which in a certain sense have hardly the name in common. . . . One can see the genesis of one out of the other, but at the same time transformation, so that it does not remain the same at all.

Fortunately Herder does not attempt to show that Shakespeare's drama arose from the Greek ; the essay as it proceeds

VIII. MERCK, 1772
A painting by H. Strecker

IX. SCHILLER, *ca.* 1780

asserts the totally different origins and character of the two types. Summing up the results of contemporary scholarship, Herder goes on :

Greek tragedy arose as it were out of one scene, out of the impromptu of the dithyramb, of the mimic dance, the chorus. This was enlarged, re-moulded : Aeschylus brought two characters on to the stage instead of one, invented the concept of the hero, and diminished the choral element. Sophocles added a third character, invented the stage. . . . One immediately sees that this origin explains certain things which are terribly misunderstood when gaped at as dead rules. That simplicity of the Greek action, that sobriety of Greek manners, that sustained cothurnus-like elevation of expression, the music, stage, unity of place and time— all this lay without art or witchcraft naturally and essentially in the origin of Greek tragedy. . . . All was husk, in which grew the fruit.

The Greeks did not write their tragedies according to some fixed concept of art ; their simplicity, their rules, were a natural product of their times, their religion, their cultic ceremonies.[55]

As ' the nature changed that created Greek drama ', that is, as society, manners, religion, myths, even music, expression, the ' measure of illusion ' altered, so tragedy was bound to change. Any attempt to imitate the form of Greek tragedy, to comply with the rules drawn up by Aristotle, was bound to fail, and Herder harshly condemns the whole of the French neo-classical drama. The violence of his attack is perhaps justified if we consider that he was most concerned with classicistic legislators like Batteux and their baleful influence in Germany, and that in condemning French drama he was giving expression to his abhorrence of the polite society of court and salon which imposed restraint on the expression of that ' shattering of the heart, awakening of the soul ' which he defined as the meaning of Aristotle's pity and terror. His prejudice against the French neo-classical drama was so strong that he does not even discuss its form and indigenous qualities ; yet his approach to Shakespeare might well have thrown new light on the great French tragedy too.

How is great drama to come to being ?

Let us postulate a people that desires to invent its own drama.
The first question is, it seems to me : when ? where ? in what
circumstances ? what is it to build on ? And no proof is needed
to show that the new invention will and can be nothing but the
result of these questions.

This approach is the key to Shakespeare.

Shakespeare found around him anything but that simplicity
of national customs, deeds, tastes and historical traditions, that
formed the Greek drama. . . . Shakespeare found no chorus
there ; but he did find historical and marionette plays—well
then ! out of these historical and marionette plays, such poor
clay ! he moulded the splendid creation that stands and lives
before us !

Following the character of his times and the national dramatic
tradition, Shakespeare built his plays in great complexity
round a ' great event ', ignoring the Greek notion of ' action '.
All classes of society, all modes of speech, all varieties of character are held together round this great centre.   Herder insists
that the established formal principle of tragedy, the unity of
action, which had brought all aestheticians to condemn, or at
least to shake their heads, over Shakespeare, cannot hold good
for the Elizabethan drama, because of the whole character of
Elizabethan England and its dramatic traditions.   He goes
on to review the movement of *Lear* and other plays to show
the unity and power within their apparent disparate variety.

And that is no drama ?   Shakespeare no dramatic poet ?   He,
who takes a hundred scenes of a world-event, seizes them in his
arm, orders them with his glance, and fills them with the breath
of his life-giving soul ?

Herder then proceeds to examine the meaning of the unities
of time and place.   If Shakespeare had to present a great
variety of scenes, then necessarily he had to present them in
their specific time and place.   For time and place are not
abstractions ; they are constitutive elements of experience.

Is it not place and time and fullness of external circumstances that give the whole story substance, duration, existence ? and will a child, a young man, a lover, a man in the field of activity ever suffer the amputation of one circumstance of the environment, of the how, and where, and when, without injury to the whole image in his soul ?——

He sketches the action of Macbeth, the heath and thunder-storm in the witches' scenes, the night-wanderings of Lady Macbeth in her castle, the arrival of Duncan before the castle walls, and so forth : ' just trot through all these places and times, and say whether it could have been different than it is, in view of the purpose of the author '. Shakespeare is akin to Sophocles, is ' the brother of Sophocles ', as Young had said, precisely where he is so different from him. Both are ' ser-vants of nature ', that is, of the world and society into which they were born.

In equating ' art ' and ' nature ' Herder is not asserting that there is no ' art ' in the Greeks or Shakespeare. His theme is that the character of art, its forms, must change according to the changing complex of experience and the world. At the end of his essay he even makes a movement as if to investigate the formal characteristics of Shakespeare, as Aristotle had investigated those of Greek drama.

Now the heart of my investigation should begin : ' how, and with what art and creative genius, Shakespeare was able to turn a wretched romance, tale, and fabulous history into a living whole ? What sort of laws of our historical, philosophical and dramatic art may lie in each of his steps and knacks ? '

This task, he says, has been neglected even by Shakespeare's countrymen.[56] But he too now recoils from such an under-taking—the first critic to tackle it was a German of the next generation, A. W. Schlegel.[57] Herder does ridicule Gersten-berg's attempt to take Polonius' formal definitions seriously ; but he does not get further than the reiteration :

Every play is history ! a pageant of heroes and states corre-sponding to the illusion of the Middle Ages ! or (with some few exceptions) a complete, grandiose occurrence of a world-event, of a human fate.

There are weaknesses in Herder's essay. The rhapsodic style and obscurity of phraseology were necessary in Herder's view in order to transmit to his readers the actual impression made on him by Shakespeare, but it makes his argument hard to follow and hides the logic of his approach. He over-estimates the 'simplicity' of Greek life and manners. His definition of the effect of tragedy does not distinguish the particular methods and character of tragedy from those of lyric or epic and novel. But in spite of these drawbacks the essay marks the beginning of modern dramatic criticism, and, by implication, of all modern literary criticism. Form is seen as a product of social and technical conditions and conditioning.

These conclusions are a development from those of the Ossian essay, largely because with the drama Herder was considering a literary form which comes to life only through a public presentation on a stage, and which is much more directly dependent on social forms and tastes than the more private lyric. Because of this public, social character of drama Herder is, however, unable to point the way ahead in Germany, except in the very general sense that the rules of the past and of foreign cultures may be discarded. That he certainly did not call Germans to imitate Shakespeare is clear from his whole argumentation ; and it is characteristic that he told Goethe, when the latter sent him the first version of his *Götz von Berlichingen*, 'Shakespeare has quite spoilt you.' [58] But he could be satisfied that he had fulfilled the duty of a critic in clearing the ground for a new start in Germany. He had decisively shaken the hold that the conventions of regularity and propriety still exerted on Hurd, Home, Blair, and even Young. His ardent imagination had carried him far beyond Diderot, Lessing, and Mercier, with their failure to understand the illusory character of art and its imaginative function. But equally he had gone far beyond the purely individualistic, subjective attitude of Hamann, who had merely denounced all rules and discipline and had completely failed to understand the meaning and function of form. [59]

Though it was only in the final version of the *Shakespeare* essay that Herder gave due prominence to his new historical and relativistic approach to art, it was evident in many of his utterances before 1771. Thus it was that Goethe and Lenz express similar views on the drama in essays that were written before the publication of Herder's manifesto. In *Zum Schäkespears Tag* of 1771, a speech in honour of Shakespeare's birthday, Goethe too asserts that the Greek drama was originally ' an intermezzo of religious worship ', and produced for Greeks, so that imitation of Greek drama cannot be more than a parody. But Goethe's ejaculatory address does not apply any similar measure to Shakespeare, who is ' nature ', a ' lovely raree-show ', ' history of the world '.[60]

Lenz's *Observations on the Theatre* are more ambitious. He too points out the cultic origin of Greek tragedy, but mainly, like Home in his *Elements of Criticism*, in order to demonstrate that the conception of fate that rules Greek tragedy is unsuitable for modern, Christian times.[61] The major part of the treatise is devoted to a discussion of the rules of Aristotle. He asserts that the unities correspond to the feeling of the Greeks, but not to the modern German taste. The Germans are not content with a simple action and a single place and limited time in Aristotle's sense ; they need individuality, colour, variety. ' What a greater, more divine pleasure it is, to observe the movement of a world, than that of a House ! '[62] The Germans demand in drama not ' action ', but ' a series o actions '.[63] Shakespeare's *Julius Caesar* is infinitely greater than Voltaire's *Mort de César* because man is there represented not as a silhouette, but in his fullness.[64] Modern man demands a different type of tragedy from the Greek :

And so I find that the popular taste of our time, in face of tragedy or historical show (it's all the same), violently insists on feeling, ' That is a colossal fellow [" Kerl "] ! Colossal fellows ! ' . . . The chief feeling in a tragedy is the character, which creates its events.[65]

There are no rules in art.

When Lenz's weak comedy, *Der neue Menoza*, was criticised for its shapelessness, he wrote a review to defend it. His arguments cannot reconcile one to the play, but they show how aware he was of the social determinants of literary form. He distinguishes tragedy and comedy according to the audience to which they are directed, not primarily according to the emotions they arouse. Tragedy is ' for the more serious part of the public '. Comedy is not merely a vehicle for laughter, but ' a show for everybody '.

> The distinction between laughter and weeping is only an invention of later critics, who did not see why the greater part of the common people is more inclined to laughter than to tears. . . . Comedy is a picture of human society, and when the latter becomes serious, the picture cannot rouse laughter. . . . Therefore our German writers of comedy must be comic and tragic together, since the people for whom they write (or at least should write) are such a hotch-potch of culture and coarseness, of good manners and savagery. Thus the comic poet creates a public for the tragic writer.[66]

We can detect in Lenz's views the impulse from Herder's historical insight. It did not lead to dramatic theory, but made writers aware of the general, social determinants of their art, and encouraged them to build a new, meaningful poetry out of the elements of their experience, as communication between them and the society in which they were placed.

These new principles of poetry gave a new direction to the perennial endeavour to create a German literature which should be at least the equal of classical, or French, or English literature. This was the primary intention of Opitz and Gottsched, who had both asserted that the way forward was through the imitation of neo-classical French or Italian or Spanish or English works, and through the adoption of neo-classical principles as defined by Scaliger, Malherbe, Boileau, and the rest. Even Lessing, though introducing a more vigorous, personal style and themes appropriate to his outlook and times, had built his works and principles largely on the model of the Classics and the modern English and French like Richardson, Lillo, and Diderot. The essential error in all these endeavours was the belief that there is an absolute ideal of artistic form. The effort of the Stürmer und Dränger was of a totally different character. Though they occasionally fell into imitation, for instance of Shakespeare, the historical insight of Herder helped them to free themselves from the whole idea of imitation and to seek in their own selves for a true German poetry. The shallow superficiality of pretentious imitation made them furious :

German Sophocles, German Plautus, German Shakespeares, German French, German Metastasio. . . . How it's all mixed up, Cluver's *orbis antiquus* with modern heraldry, and the tone all through so little German, so critically quavering, so successfully beautiful—he who has ears to hear, let him applaud, the people is accursed.[67]

In their personal mode of life, in their social philosophy, the Stürmer und Dränger rejected outright the ideals of behaviour and of art of their British and French contemporaries, and felt the inward strength to build a poetry òn their own intimations. There were dangers looming from their closest allies. Klopstock and his disciples felt a similar urge, and Klopstock forged a poetical language which was highly individual and original. Though Klopstock believed that he was composing, even in his odes, along the lines of classical metrical forms, Herder could point out how original his handling of metre was, how little his odes could be scanned by classical measures.[68] But Klopstock, Voss, and the Stolbergs fell also into the seductive error of believing that a national poetry involves, or even demands, national themes, and that patriotic enthusiasm suffices to establish the originality of a work. Thus Klopstock inserted, in new editions of early poems, ' Nordic ' names in place of classical, in later poems often took Nordic themes as the subjects of his odes, and wrote patriotic plays on Arminius ; his disciples and associates wrote odes extolling the ancient German virtues. But *Die Hermanns Schlacht* was written in an Ossianic prose interspersed with choruses in classical metre, and the scene does not change throughout the meagre action. The odes of Voss and the Stolbergs follow classical patterns, and the language they use is archaic and academic. So, too, Klopstock thought to give a peculiarly native German stamp to his poetics by putting it in the form of laws debated and issued by a Witanagemot —the *Republic of Scholars*.

But the true, indigenous art that the Stürmer und Dränger sought was not of this type ; it was not based on a belief that Germany represented a superior culture, and it was not associated with any political conception of Germany. It is significant that Herder's review of Klopstock's odes emphasises their high quality as ' a complete effusion of an enthusiastic imagination or an agitated heart ', but shows some uneasiness about the patriotic ' tirades of fantasy '.[69] Goethe's glowing recommendation of the *Republic of Scholars* ignores the antiquarian trappings, about which he shared the doubts of most of his contemporaries, and emphasises alone the inner substance. It is ' the only poetics for all times and peoples ' for here poetry is discussed not as a deduction from an ideal but as ' history of feeling, as it bit by bit grows firm and pure, and as with it expression and language take shape '.[70]

It is true that the Stürmer und Dränger often expressed a violent distaste for French culture. Herder, Goethe, and Lenz all condemned neo-classical French drama and poetry, which did not excite their imagination and reflected in their view a polite, restricted, drawing-room or ante-chamber world. But at the same time they appreciated highly the work of Rousseau or Diderot or Mercier, not to speak of Rabelais. Equally, while they were enraptured by Shakespeare or Fielding or Sterne, they were highly critical of much in the modern English tradition, Pope, Gray, Akenside, and the rest. That is, their judgment was based not on a national principle, but on a particular attitude to art. They repudiated the modern French conventions because, as Goethe says in *Poetry and Truth*, they felt French culture to be ' aged and aristocratic '.[71] ' German ' was for them not primarily a national conception, but denoted a principle of youth, candour, simplicity, sensuous feeling, vigour, which they rejoiced in wherever they found it. So they never lose their love of Homer, or Pindar, or the Greek dramatists, and never denigrate the Mediterranean culture as compared with that of the North, of Germany, except in so far as it failed in later times to produce what in their feeling was true poetry.

Goethe's essay on the Strassburg Minster is as important in this connection as Herder's essay on Shakespeare. Like Herder, he criticises classicistic French architecture because it is not ' characteristic ', not the expression of a people. It is clear that he, like Herder, failed in this period to understand

French art ; but he is on surer ground when he criticises those aestheticians who would reduce all good architecture to certain measurable proportions, valid in every time and place. It is necessary, he asserts, to abandon the pretentious claim to judge all art on the basis of pre-conceived notions. Every people, savages as much as different civilised nations, can create its own beauty if it surrenders to the inborn feeling of form which grows within its character and experience. The columns and proportions of classical art have perhaps their historical origin in the primitive hut based on four pillars, but earlier still, Goethe suggests, is the hut made of two pairs of crossed poles, joined by a ridge-pole : that is, Goethe is seeking a basic functional structure from which Gothic has developed. The wall is the essential component of the northern dwelling, he says, not the column ; and the beauty of the Strassburg Minster arises from the fact that the architect has developed this functional wall ' so that it rises like a sublime, wide-spreading tree of God, with its thousand branches, millions of twigs, and leaves like the sands by the sea, announcing the glory of the Lord, its Master, to the region round about '.[72]

Just as the central achievement of Herder's Shakespeare interpretation is the definition of the principles governing all great tragedy, ancient and modern, so that of Goethe's Strassburg essay goes far beyond the rescue of the idea of Gothic architecture.

The only true art is characteristic art. If its influence arises from deep, harmonious, independent feeling, from feeling peculiar to itself, oblivious, yes, ignorant of everything foreign, than it is whole and living, whether it be born from crude savagery or cultured sentiment.[73]

The manifesto *On German Character and Art* contained in fact essays on the English Shakespeare and the supposedly Celtic bard, Ossian, as well as that on the ' German ' architecture of Strassburg Minster. Herder in any case continued to associate the term ' Gothic ' with artistic confusion—

Certain forms of beauty must appear in sculpture like the proportions in architecture, or art will again become Gothic, i.e. elements are attached where there should be none, elements are confused where the movement of the eye demands a smooth succession.[74]

The Stürmer und Dränger were far from admiring poetry or art simply because it belonged to a German tradition, though they asserted that true artistic form could arise only if it was grounded in a native tradition. Goethe's argument in favour of Gothic was directed against all abstract, inorganic principles of art, against ' the Frenchmen in all nations '.[75] The Stürmer und Dränger did not share the predilection for German or Gothic of the later Romantics ; the ' romantic ', congested, walled-in medieval German cities oppressed them because of their lack of ' form ', of clear line and proportion. Nothing could be more misleading than the thesis that the Sturm und Drang founds a ' German movement ' which culminates in the rabid nationalists Lagarde, H. S. Chamberlain, Rosenberg, and Hitler.[76]

At the same time Herder, and Goethe even more, did renew a German tradition. Götz von Berlichingen is a true German knight in an historical German situation. The language he uses, blunt and vigorous, the simplicity of the relations between him and his wife and retainers, the virtues of loyalty and independence, are shown as belonging to a German tradition, in contrast to the contemporary perversion of these virtues. The delight Herder and Goethe took in Luther's obstinate personality and vigorous and sometimes drastic idiom leads them to acclaim him as a true German. The figure of Faust rises from German history and a deep-seated popular delight in the folk-play. Even more deliberately, Goethe resurrected the figure of Hans Sachs, the sixteenth-century shoemaker and poet. He sometimes adopted, and his example inspired Merck and Herder and Lenz to adopt, the mode of expression of Hans Sachs, and deliberately reproduced the clumsy rhythm of his rough doggerel as a protest against the smooth ' licked ' metres of his contemporaries. He delighted to re-create the narrow, old-world atmosphere of the sixteenth-century burgher and home, in *The Wandering Jew*,[77] the farces, in *Götz* and *Faust*. *Götz* was in fact the forerunner of the historical drama and novel in Europe. In all this he was recalling Germans to a consciousness of their own cultural and poetic traditions, and giving a practical demonstration of the poetical potentialities of forms and a language which were normally despised.

But this restoration of the dignity of old German speech and forms of life was never associated with a belief that German culture was in any way higher than that of other peoples. Werther discovers a real German household in the ' Deutsches Haus ' where Lotte lived ; but his response to these values is associated with, even intensified and condensed, by his spiritual communing with Homer. If Goethe wrote lyrics in the style of German folksong, like *Heidenröslein* or *Der König in Thule*, he also translated Pindar and the Song of Songs. His *Wandrer*, like other odes, is Pindaric in inspiration, and is set in Cuma, in Magna Graecia. The architecture the wanderer marvels at is Greek ; the peasant mother is no German. Herder could properly admire this poem as ' genuinely old-German ' ; [78] the phrase indicates the scope of the meaning of the word German, for it means an attitude, a group of values without a particular national limitation. Goethe was obsessed in this period, as later in life, not only by German myths, but also by figures like Mahomet, Prometheus, Caesar ; the form of his *Prometheus* drama is more that of a lyricised Aeschylean drama than anything else. Herder responded more ardently to the poetry of the Old Testament, of Homer, Shakespeare, the Scottish ballads and Spanish romances, Ossian and the Edda, than he did to ancient or medieval German poetry. Lenz and the others rarely treat of German themes in any precise national sense, and Lenz found nothing incongruous in adapting Plautus to the German scene.[79]

The essential principle of the new poetry of the Sturm und Drang was in fact that enunciated by Herder in his essays in *On German Character and Art* : that is, the demand for a literature that should fully express the experience, the ' living world ', of the writer. Goethe put it very plainly in his review of a volume of poems by a Polish Jew. He writes that he opened the book with keen anticipation, in the hope of finding the specific feelings of a Polish Jew. But alas, here is the usual devotee of the ' fine arts ', with his fashionable clothes, powdered hair, and hairless chin ! Everything about his girl and his feelings is generalised and abstract. Let a poet arise,

Goethe cries, who will live fully and joyously in his circle,
however restricted it be, who will tell us of his experiences as
they are : ' Then there will be truth in his songs, and living
beauty, not iridescent soap-bubble ideals such as float about
in a hundred German songs.' [80]

The Stürmer und Dränger were the founders of modern
German poetry because they insisted that poetry is not an
abstract self-contained activity, but a function of living individuals in a concrete situation.   In a little work published
when the Sturm und Drang was over, Justus Möser grasped
many of the essentials of their attitude.   His *On German
Language and Literature* of 1781 was an answer to Frederick
the Great's condemnation of German literature as provincial
and formless. [81]   Möser considers that the inadequacy of
German was due to its bookish, academic character, and he
holds up English as an example of good language.

The English language, like the nation itself, is the only one
that is afraid of nothing, but lays its hands on everything. . . .
It is the only folk-language which is written in Europe, a provincial
dialect raised to the throne, which stands upon its own lush soil,
and does not, like our book-languages, wither in the barn.

He praises Lessing for having introduced provincial turns
of speech into literature, and goes on to commend the Sturm
und Drang for having shown Germans as they really could be
(he is referring to *Götz* in particular).   And with this realism
he associates the subjectivism of the Sturm und Drang.   This
healthy grasp of reality, he says, can be acquired only by
following the principles of Rousseau and Klopstock, ' one must
create out of oneself and only express one's feelings '.   Even
if this subjectivism leads to extravagance, it is the only way
to grasp the external world as it really is, the only way to true
poetry. [82]

Of course, the unity in the natural and social circumstances
of a nation gives a unity to its culture ; but at the same time
there is continual change in a national cultural tradition,
corresponding to the changes in outer life and social constitution.   Cultural affinities can be sought according to the
feeling of any particular generation, and forms will necessarily

develop and change. The affinity in spirit that Herder found between Greek and Shakespearian tragedy was possible, he asserted, only through the total dissimilarity of their form, since each form won its validity from its relationship to the total experience of the poet. And this principle must be valid within all national cultures and languages. Thus the Sturm und Drang did not even discuss any supposedly indigenous characteristics of Germanic art, except in the sense that, in order to be true art, it must reflect the inner nature of the poet and the external nature and society in which he is placed. But though this insight was of profound truth, and of profound significance in freeing them from outworn formulas of art, it left them, as creative artists, with a great dilemma. How was subjectivism, inner feeling, to be associated with realism, as Möser claimed? How were imagination and true experience to be combined? The Klopstockian surrender to feeling often led to ' tirades ', to an etherealism and unrealism that irritated them ; the realism of a Diderot, Mercier, or Lessing, or Nicolai, was without wings, without poetry. Not all the Stürmer und Dränger saw this problem ; but some did, and their efforts to solve it again sound a peculiarly modern note.

IMAGINATION AND REALITY

Eighteenth-century poetry shows many signs of discontent with the prevailing temper of sobriety and rationalism. Gray and Mason in their ' Pindaric ' odes, Smart in the *Hymn to David*, find pleasure in sublime feelings and obscure, grandiose expressions. The growing taste for the world of chivalry, for Tasso and Spenser, was largely based on a delight in the sublime, exotic, fantastic, and finds an extreme form in Warton's discovery of the charm of ruins and decay, in the ' romanticism ' of Strawberry Hill. But this taste was recognised to be only ' poetical ', and did not constitute a challenge to the normal values of intercourse and life. Hurd could define the poet's world as ' marvellous and extraordinary ', a frank admission that poetry is a separate activity of the mind, dissociated from the truths that we gain from experience. The first book of *La nouvelle Heloïse* constituted a serious challenge to this equanimity, for the lonely reveries of St.-Preux are weighed against the wise conclusions of common sense and sober social experience ; but even Rousseau's ultimate purpose was to show that the exalted imagination was the product of a diseased temperament in a harsh society. Klopstock transplanted the taste for sublime feelings into Germany, but he and his disciples were conscious that they were often giving way to expressions and feelings that were not true, neither as they were related to the external world nor to themselves.

Despite the debt that Herder owed Klopstock, he always felt uneasy about the idealising trend of the latter's poetry. He corrected his betrothed's adoration of the ' sweetness and grace ' of Klopstock, the attraction of which he admitted, because it transported the reader beyond the human sphere into unearthly regions.[83] Goethe expressed the same unease, but more drastically, referring particularly to the bardic odes of the Klopstockians : ' Noise and shouts instead of pathos . . . Tinsel and that's all. . . . The most unbearable thing about a picture is untruth.'[84] Bürger wrote to Boie, criticising a bombastic Klopstockian ode of Schönborn : ' In poetry, in spite of all divine sublimity, everything must be tangible and visual ; if not, it is no poetry for this world, but perhaps for a different world which, however, does not exist.'[85] And the same strain is heard in the mature Schiller, for while he deplores the moral effects of Klopstock's ' everlasting straining of the emotions ', he also points out its aesthetic failings—' he always leads us out of life . . . without refreshing the mind with the tranquil presence of an object '.[86]

But poetry for the Stürmer und Dränger was a realm neither of pastime nor of sublime unearthliness. It expressed their deepest subjective need, their deepest truth. They therefore protest continually against an attitude to poetry which would segregate feeling and imagination in a separate compartment of the mind. They felt that Homer and Shakespeare and folksong expressed fundamental values, the nature of life in its deepest sense and highest dignity ; the truth of poetry was something infinitely more necessary to man than the indifferent conclusions and wisdom of common sense and reason. Were they merely to revel in feeling and imagination at odd times, in their leisure hours, but at other times behave 'seriously' like the rest ? This was what Nicolai suggested in his *Joys of Werther the Man* ; and this they repudiated. Shakespeare was one of their guides, for in his plays they found true man and true history. But Shakespeare could also be a danger, for his power of illusion, of which Herder wrote, might be understood as the power to transport into a world of imagination attractive just because it was different from the sober world of real experience. Herder clearly recognised this attraction. He wrote to Merck: ' In my frenzy for Shakespeare I had long ago settled down specially to [translate] the scenes where he opens up his new world of ghosts and witches and fairies.' [87] It was this side of Shakespeare that particularly appealed to Bürger, who thought it a special merit that the witches of Macbeth belong ' to fancy and feeling, not reason and wit '. [88] The poets of the Sturm und Drang all succumb at times to the fascination of the unreal, the fantastic, for its own sake ; in this respect they anticipate the extravagance and morbidity of the later German romanticism that Wordsworth found so distasteful. Bürger's ballad, *Lenore*, which had so great a success, is an exercise in the macabre. He told his friends that it would scarify like the ghost in *Hamlet*, and recommended them to read it at twilight in a ghostly room, with a skull on the table. [89] In *Fausts Leben*, Maler Müller takes over much of the terrifying trappings of the puppet-play, the ludicrously awesome antics of the devils. The stage directions of the first scene are : ' Midnight. Tempest. Ruins of a decaying Gothic church, overgrown with debris ' (*sic* !). The last setting is a cross-roads before a dark forest, with a bell tolling midnight in the distance. Ghosts and premonitions play their part in many plays, which borrow from Shakespeare the thrill of the supernatural, of storms and the blackness of night. Goethe has a gruesome scene in *Götz*, the sitting of the secret court, the ' Vehme ', at which Adelheid is condemned with solemn and mysterious rites. The last act of *Clavigo* uses to the full the tension of a midnight setting, with torches and cloaked men. In Klinger's *Otto* there is a wild mixture of all such macabre elements, and it may be considered to be the first of the lugubrious extravaganzas which were later such popular German exports.

It must be emphasised, however, that settings of this kind,

and the use of the supernatural, are rare in the works of the Stürmer und Dränger. It is one of the extraordinary achievements of Herder in his essay on Shakespeare that he treats the supernatural elements of the plots, the witches in *Macbeth* and the ghost in *Hamlet*, in the same way as he does the blasted heath and the midnight battlements, not as ' pleasures of the imagination ', but as constituents of the real human scene. His, and Goethe's, love for folk-ballads did not lead them to revel in hallucinations, like Bürger, to whose *Lenore* Herder took up a somewhat critical attitude. The folk-ballads Goethe collected, and his own compositions, are essentially, in this period, songs of human feeling and human relationships, like the *König in Thule* ; ballads like *Erlkönig* and *Der Zauberlehrling* belong to later periods—though, of course, for all their evocation of supernatural beings and weird or macabre situations these too are securely anchored in real experience. Goethe's works are the living evidence of his Strassburg habit of utilising nocturnal expeditions to lonely spots, churches and graveyards, for the purpose of hardening himself against ' the attacks of imagination '.[90]

But even when fantastic means are employed in the works of the Stürmer und Dränger, they are rarely used arbitrarily for the mere purpose of thrilling the reader or audience with a feeling of mystery and horror. In Maler Müller's *Fausts Leben* it is necessary that scenes of devilry and exorcism should have a mysterious, abnormal setting. The ghost that the hero of Klinger's *Die Zwillinge* sees is justified as an emanation of a diseased and guilty mind. The masked figures of *Clavigo*, the midnight burial, are not arbitrarily introduced and belong legitimately to the theme. It is perhaps most surprising that, in Goethe's *Urfaust*, the product of his Sturm und Drang, there are scarcely any of the supernatural elements that belong to the traditional story. The Earth-Spirit is an emanation of nature, and speaks as ' nature '. The Mephistopheles we see is the most human devil imaginable, an evil and subtle, malicious and sarcastic fellow, whose magic does not go further than helping Faust to conjure up wine, and providing him with treasures as gifts for Gretchen. If he can help Faust to break into prison, he has no power over Gretchen. When we consider Goethe's task in face of the legend and puppet-play, it

is clear that he denudes the story almost entirely of its supernatural, fearsome aspects, and concentrates all his attention on
the human tragedy. It was a later Goethe who showed
Faust's exorcism of the poodle, the Witch's Kitchen, the
Walpurgis Night—and, of course, not in order to bemuse or
scarify, but in order to show the barrenness of Mephistopheles'
world and its inherent incapacity to satisfy Faust's yearnings.
Of all the Stürmer und Dränger, Lenz comes closest in this
respect to the mystifications of German romanticism. In his
plays there is a plentiful admixture of fanciful elements, castles
and arbours, moonshine and twilight, particularly in *Der
Engländer* and *Henriette von Waldeck*. In those works which
directly express his own spiritual torment he often yields to the
temptation to find solace in unreality ; nothing in these two
plays is in perspective, nothing clear, but all vague, blurred.
But he had a bad conscience about the ' capricious aberrations of fancy ' of such plays.[91] The works of which Lenz was
most proud, *Der Hofmeister* and *Die Soldaten*, are full of realistic
observation of persons from his own environment—he told
Herder emphatically that the latter play was ' true history, in
the strictest sense of the word '.[92] When Lenz succumbed to
the charm of imaginations which seemed to compensate the
harshness of the real world, he was aware that he was failing
in his poetic mission, and betraying the very spirit of poetry.
The imagination, he writes in his *Observations on the Theatre*, must
serve to reveal the characteristic individuality of scenes and characters, not the ideals of the poet which are real only to him.[93]

From Shakespeare the Stürmer und Dränger received the
confirmation of their own experience that feelings and imagination acquire their substance from actual situations, and can
be expressed in poetry only through the evocation of this
sensuous environment and source. There is an individuality
and particularity in the settings of their works, their lyric
poems, their novels, and their plays, which is new in German
literature. Goethe's poems nearly all reflect the very scene in
which his feelings were formed, the nocturnal ride and sunlit
departure in *Willkommen und Abschied*, the lake, sky, mountains,
and ripening grapes in *Auf dem See* ; or, in a transposed sense,
the noble ruins and fruitful earth of *Wandrer*, the actual movement and sound of the spinning wheel in Gretchen's *Meine*

Ruh ist hin. As he was to say, much later, his poems reflect
'the particular character of some state and circumstance'.[94]
The Lotte of *Werther* comes to life in the midst of the tasks of
the home, and Werther himself is understandable only in
relation to the thronging world around him, the countryside,
the peasants, Lotte's home. In the normal sentimental novel,
like Gellert's *Schwedische Gräfin*, the characters flit across the
vaguest backcloth, and even in the more precise *Fräulein von
Sternheim* of Frau von la Roche, the court and country mansion
and 'Scottish lead-mines' are at best background, just sufficient
to indicate the moral struggles and stresses of the heroine.
With *Werther*, however, the setting is not mere background, it
enters into the substance of the hero's soul, it constitutes his
experience. Lenz achieved the same substantial quality in his
Liebe auf dem Lande, and, not quite so successfully, in his tales,
Zerbin and *Der Waldbruder*. Müller's idylls *Das Nusskernen* and
Die Schafschur owe their charm to the reality of the peasants
and activities described, as do the earlier parts of Jung-
Stilling's autobiography, when he does not seek to do more
than describe the circumstances of his early life and
development.

In comedy the realistic tradition was established, since even
Gottsched had asserted that comedy is the representation of
the 'vices' of the middle class. But while neo-classical
comedy had sought to confine the setting to one scene, a
drawing-room, or as in Lessing's *Minna von Barnhelm* an inn,
Lenz allows himself in his comedies much greater freedom of
action. The plot of *Der Hofmeister* moves through many
milieux, the tutor's home, the mansion of his employers, a
student's lodgings, a village school-house, a hovel, etc., so that
we see the characters in the actual environment which interprets, and partly determines, their ideas and feelings. But this
is one of the very few Sturm und Drang works which can rank
as comedies. Their satire is usually interwoven with a sentimental theme, and 'comedies' like *Die Soldaten* are better
described as plays of common life. In this play, the characters
again move through different milieux, and as tragedy begins to
envelop Marie, we are thrown with bewildering rapidity
through the scenes of her downfall, which as they change
interpret her abandonment. One of the chief weaknesses of

plays like *Der neue Menoza* or *Die Freunde machen den Philosophen* arises from Lenz's failure to give any precision or real relevance to the situations in which he places his characters.

The Sturm und Drang polemic against French tragedy had its roots in a protest against the flatness of characters assembled against an indifferent or unchanging background. They resented this background in so far as it always reflected the environment of polite company ; but even more because it deprived the characters of the substantiality that individual settings give. This is the burden of their frequent criticism of the sentimental novel. ' What is Grandison, the abstract figure of a dream, compared with a partridge that stands there before us ? ' [95] Thus an essential characteristic of the literature of the Sturm und Drang is its realism, the concrete substantiality of its figures, scenes, and language ; a realism which, as Auerbach has pointed out, surpasses anything before it or since in German literature.[96] Yet this realism is not the opposite of imagination, of poetry, as is the realism of Diderot's or Lessing's plays. It is imaginative ; it is poetic. The fusion of imaginative experience and reality is one of the great achievements of the Sturm und Drang, through which it is the spiritual parent of both the romanticism and the realism of the nineteenth century.

Often enough the Stürmer und Dränger fail. The characters of Klinger are rootless and abstract, their language rhetorical. Leisewitz's and Schiller's characters too often slip into impersonal discourses. Some of Goethe's smaller works, like *Stella* or *Erwin und Elmire*, lack the substantiality of a real background and existence. At times the world of fancy attracts them as more seductive, more beautiful, than the real world. Merck wrote in sympathetic criticism of Herder : [97]

Ewig wirst du Träume jagen, fangen,
Dürstend an dem Kelch der Liebe hangen,
Dich äfft Wiederhall der Sympathie,
Doch als Zephyr küsset sie Dich nie.

You will for ever hunt and catch dreams, hang thirsting on the cup of love ; the echo of sympathy will mock you, yet never kiss you like a zephyr.

Goethe also felt the comfort of dreams.[98]

> Als ich noch ein Knabe war,
> Sperrte man mich ein.
> Und so sass ich manches Jahr
> Ueber mir allein,
> Wie im Mutterleib.
>
> Doch du warst mein Zeitvertreib,
> Goldne Phantasie ;
> Und ich ward ein warmer Held,
> Wie der Prinz Pipi,
> Und durchzog die Welt.
>
> When I was a lad
> They'd lock me in my room,
> And I sat for many a year
> Close within my lair,
> As within the womb.
>
> Yet thou wert my pastime,
> Golden fantasy ;
> I became an ardent knight
> Like the Prince Pipi,
> Journeying far and wide.

So Goethe could contrast, in the poem *An Belinden*, the richness of his dream-world with the vexations of polite amusements.[99] But far more characteristic of him and Herder is the effort to overcome the seductions of dreams, to grapple with reality, and find self-fulfilment in experience and activity. ' Away, thou dream, golden as thou art ; here also is love and life.' [100] In *Werther* Goethe describes the tragedy of a young man who ' loses himself in dreams ', as he wrote.[101] But before the tragic turning-point in Werther's life, when he succumbs to his dreams, his imagination leads him to appreciate in a new intensity the reality of simple and vital forms of existence, nature, the children and the peasants, Lotte in her home.

With the Stürmer und Dränger, despite their aberrations, we find the imagination restored to the function which they recognised it had in Homer or Shakespeare : not a means of escaping from reality, of beautifying reality, but a means of penetrating to its innermost truth and meaning. Merck was always prompt to criticise them when they surrendered to unreal fancies. Of Maler Müller's *Situation aus Fausts Leben* he wrote vexedly that few writers ' feel the detail, the character in every work of nature with sufficient respect', and that Müller, like other young dramatists [of the Sturm und Drang], had taken his material ' from obscure dreams of poetic desire, and not from the market of life '.[102] He often corrected Goethe's tendencies in this direction, and Goethe reports him as telling him :

> Your endeavour, your unswerving tendency, is to give reality a poetic form ; the others seek to turn. the so-called poetic, the imaginative, into something real, and that produces nothing but stupid stuff.[103]

So the highest praise he gives to *Faust* is that it is ' stolen with the greatest faithfulness from nature '.[104]

This phrase has a totally different meaning from the traditional ' imitation of nature '. It is not a question of a mechanical observation of reality, but an imaginative grasp of reality, which synthesises in an intense experience the complex and successive factors of reality, and presents it in a specific poetic form. Lenz discusses this poetical process in his *Observations on the Theatre*. He begins with the subjective purpose of poetry, the feeling of ' an accretion to our existence ', which results from poetry. Our experiences of normal life are successive : the poet has to turn these successive experiences into something instantaneous, into a single, all-embracing experience. ' We would like to penetrate with one glance into the innermost nature of all beings, to absorb with one feeling all the joy that is in nature and combine it with ourselves.' Analysis and synthesis go hand in hand : ' It is our constant endeavour to unwrap all our collected ideas and see right through them, and make them visual and present.' The supreme achievement of the artist is ' to grasp firmly all our knowledge until it has become visual [" anschaulich "] '. This operation is neither mechanical nor arbitrary—' the true poet does not combine in his imagination according to his own whim . . . He takes a standpoint and then he has to combine accordingly.' [105]

It is not surprising, in view of the difficulty of the problem, that we find little theoretical discussion of the relation between imagination and reality. The Sturm und Drang restoration of the imagination to its vital function is largely an intuitive assertion, expressed in occasional criticism and in their poetical works. Poetry for them must be impregnated with reality, the poet must be, in Herder's phrase, ' the interpreter of nature ', but his tools and methods have their own characteristics and speak to the imagination. Words are not objective descriptions of a material or intellectual reality, as the Aufklärung thought, but statements of a relationship between man and nature ; they are ' energetic ', active, interpreting vital impulses in man and a process in nature. Thus, in place of the flat prosaism or conventional rhetoric of contemporary poetry, they love the earthy idiom and plastic phrase of the peasantry— not because it is more ' realistic ' in the simple sense, but because of its evocative, sensuous power. [106] They grasp the function of rhythmic speech, anticipating Coleridge's criticism of Wordsworth's view that the language of poetry is that of ' ordinary men '. [107] Through rhythmic speech, ' the dark stream of melody ', through image, the poet recaptures the total significance of an experience, and transmits it to the ' inner sense ' of the hearer. Herder's emphasis on song, on actual music, in his essay on folksong indicates how fully he recognised that poetry, while arising from a concrete situation and interpreting in sensuous imagery the peculiarity of this experience, speaks in specific imaginative terms. The imagination is the instrument which collects all the elements of experience, sensuous, emotive, and intellectual, and condenses them into a unity which sets the whole man tingling.

Willey has pointed out how dependent Coleridge's conception of the imagination was on his metaphysics. [108] With Hamann and Lavater we find indeed the imaginative impulse justified as a link with a supersensual reality. For the chief Stürmer und Dränger, as for Wordsworth, the imagination places us ' in the presence of truth ', of deepest reality. But their conception of reality is far less mystical, less metaphysical than that of the later Wordsworth or Coleridge.

Imagination gives insight into reality because it issues from the ultimate identity of the poet, of man in general, with the observed world. It does not point, for Herder and Goethe, to a transcendental realm of reality opposed to that of experiential ' appearance ', it is not evidence of a dualism of Reason and Understanding such as Coleridge and the German Romantics postulated. It establishes the correspondence of inner and outer life. It is the expression of that mysterious and fundamental sympathy of man with nature, to which Goethe and Wordsworth often give the name love, and which is the kernel of Herder's and Goethe's pantheism. In the framework of this general pantheistic interpretation of the universe they can justify the most mysterious function of imagination, what Goethe calls ' anticipation ', and which may variously be described as intuition, surmise, foreboding. It is the specific poetic quality to anticipate reality, to grasp it imaginatively. Goethe commented in later life on the truth of his *Götz von Berlichingen*, in which he ' anticipated ' the knowledge of human relations which he did not as yet ' possess '.[109]   When his friend Zelter wrote to him, in 1831, to say that near Naples he had identified the place and person of the poem *Wandrer*, Goethe answered that he had written the poem long before he had visited Italy—' but that is the advantage of the poet that he can anticipate and value in imagination what those who seek reality must doubly love and delight in, when they find it in real existence '.[110]   The young Goethe was not distinguished from his contemporaries by a wider experience or knowledge, but by the intense vividness with which his imagination turned experience into general symbols.

Mysterious as are the workings of imagination, it is given no mystical character by the Stürmer und Dränger. It is for them the key to real experience, as anticipation or as synthesis. Quite logically it guided Herder to his new understanding of history, of man in the varied circumstances of the past, as it did Goethe in his study of nature, in his scientific work. When Goethe wrote that ' a fairy-tale too has its truth ' [111] he was asserting the fundamental identity of intuitive and experiential knowledge which he associates in the ' Prologue on the Stage ' in *Faust* :

I had nothing, yet profusion,
The urge for truth and joy in delusion.

Imagination is thus, for the Stürmer und Dränger, the
counterpart in the individual of the creative force in the
universe, operative in all essential human energies as in
the process of nature. It is, in Herder's word, an ' inward
sense ', which synthesises all the outward senses, which grasps
what is meaningful in the world of daily experience and
behaviour, and presents it ' through a burning-glass '.[112]
Poetic imagination thus has more truth than the most punc-
tilious description in the naturalistic manner. The language
of poetry is therefore not that of everyday life, its truth is not
tested by its rationality ; it is necessarily imaged, rhythmic, for
it has to evoke a truth which is both on the surface, sense-given,
and a truth under' thc surface, which links the poet and the
world outside him ; it links inner knowledge with that given
by experience. Imagination is not a substitute for reality, but
penetration of reality in its fullest form. Wordsworth's words
are not far from the belief of the Sturm und Drang : [113]

This spiritual Love acts not nor can exist
Without Imagination, which, in truth,
Is but another name for absolute power
And clearest insight, amplitude of mind,
And Reason in her most exalted mood.

POETIC FORM

In relating poetry to inward and outward experience, the
Stürmer und Dränger necessarily placed the whole problem
of poetic form in a new context. When Herder wrote in the
Ossian essay of the ' dire urgency ' of the content of poetry,
and when he asserted that he was not concerned to ' excuse
or slander ' Shakespeare, he was implicitly condemning as
frivolous every purely formalistic approach to poetry.[114] Thus,
in all the Stürmer und Dränger, we find continual indignation
with critics who carp at their works in the name of general
rules and abstract critical principles. Hamann led the way
in deriding such pedants, who ignore all the effect of art in
order to chatter about indifferent formalities. Goethe, in his

customary manner, wrote farcical little poems on such ' connoisseurs '.   In one of these he describes how he offers a guest the best fare he can provide, and how, after eating his fill, the ungrateful fellow goes next door and complains to his neighbour that the soup might have been tastier, the roast browner, the wine more mature.   And Goethe concludes :   ' Devil and damnation !   Strike him dead, the dog, it's a reviewer ! ' [115] ' You don't look a gift-horse in the mouth ! ' [116]   Equally derisive is his poem *The Connoisseur*.   He takes the connoisseur to meet the girl he loves, but the expert does not notice her ' fresh, young, warm life ', he merely comments that she is too thin and has too many freckles.   When they go to a picture gallery, the connoisseur can only make pedantic objections while Goethe is transported by the ' ardour of the human spirit '.[117]

Herder had defined literary criticism as something quite different.   The task of the critics is not to judge all art by a dogmatic system of rules, to make the poet their servant ;   it is their function to serve the poet and the public.[118]   His insight into poetry had brought him to an historical and relativistic conception of form, and his criticism of dogmatic pedantry arose from his conviction that the critic must seek for ' the concrete qualities and modes of the beautiful in history '.   The critic must be able to empty himself of preconceived dogmatic notions, must be able, as he defined his own purpose in the Shakespeare essay, ' to expound, to feel how the poet is '.   ' Feel yourself into everything ', he charged the historian, and this is also the principle of his literary criticism.[119]   The traditional relationship of critic and poet is reversed ;   the critic, instead of claiming to be the instructor of the poet, becomes his interpreter.   His task is, not to show where the poet's work corresponds to his own taste, but to reveal the spirit and purpose of the poet, to show the inner structure of the poem and the experience in it, to make it easier of access to others, perhaps too to make the poet more conscious of his own purpose and intention.   Klopstock indeed sent Herder a striking tribute, telling him that Herder was the only critic of whose comments he took note, ' because you are a critic through your own very strong feeling ', that is, not a critic by theory and rules.[120]

Goethe wrote some verses which assert that nature and art can be appreciated only if the observer, the critic, himself feels within himself the creative power that drives to form : [121]

> Was frommt die glühende Natur
> An deinem Busen dir ?
> Was hilft dich das Gebildete
> Die Kunst rings um dich her ?
> Wenn liebevolle Schöpfungskraft
> Nicht deine Seele füllt,
> Und in den Fingerspitzen dir
> Nicht wieder bilden wird.

> What avails your heart the glow of nature, what use to you is art, the shapely forms all round you, if loving creative power does not fill your soul, and if it does not drive your finger-tips to mould and form.

These expressions, ' creative power ', ' mould and form ', are extremely characteristic of the Sturm und Drang, and were so often repeated that they called down the ridicule of rationalists like Lichtenberg. The conception of form that is involved is totally different from the traditional one of writers of poetics. Just as the lyrics of Goethe or Lenz burst the framework of the traditional lyric, so the Stürmer und Dränger felt uneasy even about such relatively clear terms as tragedy or comedy, and prefer other names. Herder would prefer to call Shakespeare's tragedies ' plays ', ' dramas ', ' histories '. Goethe called *Götz* ' a dramatised history ', *Stella* a ' play '. Lenz uses the looser term ' Trauerspiel ' for tragedy, and says that his *Soldaten*, which was published as a ' comedy ', should properly have been called a ' play ' [' Schauspiel '].[122] Bürger attacked the whole division of plays into comedy and tragedy and suggested that all should be called ' Schauspiele '.[123] Indeterminacy and mixtures of form are characteristic of the works of the Sturm und Drang, and indicate their unwillingness to admit any absolute validity to established forms. Form they felt to be merely a function of a peculiar experience and personality ;

or, in the widest sense, of a particular historical and social situation. Therefore it must vary accordingly.

To some extent, this new insight into the character of form encouraged the Stürmer und Dränger to disregard the need for communicability, and some of their works are deliberately rank in form and obscure in diction—Nicolai and Lichtenberg charged them repeatedly with wilful esotericism. But such extravagances, which may be found even in Goethe, are only incidental to their main purpose, the discovery of a principle of form which would be applicable to all the great literature of the past, and serve as well as a guiding principle for their own times. Gerstenberg had already drawn their attention to statements in Shakespeare which associate nature and art : [124]

> This is an art
> Which does mend nature—change it rather ; but
> The art itself is nature.

It was along these lines that their thought ran—not without disturbance from the Rousseauistic derogation of art in favour of nature.

Herder's Shakespeare essay is essentially an exposition of the dependence of dramatic form on the changing nature of society and man. He had attributed the peculiarity of Homeric song to the circumstances in which it was sung and the nature of the Greek language. He had compared the unity of folksongs and the form of Klopstock's odes with that of a plant, an animal, a natural landscape. Goethe defined the unity of the Gothic structure of the Strassburg Minster in similar terms. In contrast to Herder's criticism of ' the artificial, gloomy, and monstrous vaults of Gothic ', to which he prefers ' the free Greek temple, with its lovely, regular colonnade ',[125] Goethe discovered the harmony of Gothic. ' All these masses ', he wrote in face of the minster, ' were necessary. . . . As in works of everlasting nature, down to the least fibre, all is form, all a purpose in a whole.' This form is as justifiable as that of the Greek temple ; and Goethe continues :

In man there is a formative nature, which actively asserts itself as soon as his existence is secured. As soon as he is free of anxiety and fear, the demigod, active in his repose, stretches out his hand for matter into which he may breathe his spirit.[126]

Goethe is not comparing the formative power of the artist with that of the gardener who beautifies nature, but with that of nature herself, as evident in all her parts. In the same way, in the poem *Connoisseur and Artist*, he compares artistic creation with physical procreation : [127]

> O rathet ! Helft mir !
> Dass ich mich vollende !
> Wo ist die Urquell der Natur,
> Daraus ich schöpfend
> Himmel fühl' und Leben
> In die Fingerspitzen hervor !
> Dass ich, mit Göttersinn
> Und Menschenhand,
> Vermög' zu bilden,
> Was bey meinem Weibe
> Ich animalisch kann und muss !

> O counsel ! help me !
> That I fulfil myself !
> Where is nature's primal source,
> Drawing at which I may
> Feel heaven and life
> Right into my fingertips !
> That I, with sense divine,
> And a human hand,
> May have power to form,
> What, with my wife,
> In the flesh I can and must !

On his third visit to the Strassburg Minster, when returning from his first visit to Switzerland, Goethe was again overpowered by the feeling of the kinship between the formative process of nature and art, and humorously admitted that it seemed to be his fate ' to stammer poetically about the proportions of masses '. Again he apostrophises the minster :

Thou art one and living, begotten and evolved, not pieced together and patched. Before thee, as before the foam of the rushing fall of the mighty Rhine, as before the radiant crown of the eternal snow mountains, as in the sight of the serene expanse of the lake, and, gray Gotthard, of thy cloud-rocks and desolate valleys : here, as before every great thought of Creation, there stirs in the soul whatever of creative power it possesses. It stammers over in poetry, in scrawling lines it hurls on to paper adoration to the Creator, eternal life, all-embracing, inextinguishable feeling of what is and was and is to come.

But this creative feeling is not chaotic ; it has within it the principle of organic form. As he climbs the steps of the tower with Lenz he reflects :

The creative power in the artist is this swelling, soaring feeling of proportions, of masses, and what belongs to them, and only through these can an independent work, like other creatures, spring into being through its individual germinal force.[128]

Each work of art is then, for Goethe, individual ; individual in its source and setting, individual in its form. The task of the artist is to feel the specific individuality of each experience, and to establish its inner structure and proportion, as it is grasped in the ' inward world ', the imagination. He wrote to F. H. Jacobi : [129]

The beginning and end of all writing is the reproduction of the world around me, through the inward world which lays hold of everything, combines it, re-creates it, and kneads it, and reproduces it in its own form and manner—that remains for ever a mystery, God be praised, and one I shall not reveal to the onlookers and gossips.

Compelling experience, the impact of the outer world, goes hand in hand with the inward effort to grasp and shape it.

The good spirit has revealed to me the source of my being. It came to me as I thought over Pindar's ἐπικρατεῖν δύναϑθαι. When you stand boldly in the chariot, and four fresh horses rear up wild and distracted at the reins, and you guide their strength, whip in the one who's kicked over the traces, force the other to stop rearing, and you gallop and guide them and turn, whip them, and stop, and then dash off again until all the sixteen

feet keep time as they bear you to your goal. That is mastery,
ἐπικρατεῖν, virtuosity. But I have only just sauntered around,
only taken a peep here and there. Nowhere really set to. To lay
hold, get a firm grasp, that's the essence of mastery.[130]

Bürger wrote something apparently similar, yet characteristically different. To write poetically one must have, he
says, ' courage and strength enough to feel, to lay hold of a
thing, to hold it, to hurl it and toss it into the air '.[131] Here
the arbitrary character of his own poetry is evident, he can
play with the ' thing '. For Goethe ' the world around him ',
the ' wild horses ', have to be mastered, but they have to be
mastered in a form which they themselves impose. Mastery
is not merely an assertion of will, but a product of understanding, of self-identification and self-fusing with the outer
stimulus or experience.

Like Herder, then, Goethe repudiates the notion of absolute
form, but at the same time is aware that what distinguishes the
artist is not only emotive and imaginative power, but also
feeling for form, for proportion, for measure. In unconscious
refutation of his own earlier interpretation of Shakespeare's
plays as a ' raree-show ', in 1775 he distinguishes the artist's
feeling for form from the formless impressions of normal men,
for whom ' the world is a raree-show, whose illusions flit past
and disappear, leaving shallow and isolated impressions on
the soul '.[132] His comments on Mercier's *Du théâtre*, which were
published in 1776 as an appendix to Wagner's translation, are
extremely interesting in this connection. Mercier's work was
a scathing attack on the formalistic neo-classical theatre, and
a defence of the modern realistic social drama. Goethe
sympathised with the theme of the book, but found that though
Mercier asserted that style is the expression of the individuality
of an author, the real problem of form was not really dealt
with. After recommending the book he goes on :

It is time that people stopped talking about the form of dramatic
plays, their length or shortness, their unities, beginning, middle and
end, and all the rest of it. And our author goes pretty direct
to the question of content, which as a matter of fact seemed to
follow of itself.

Yet there is a form, distinct from that other sort of form as much as the inner sense from the outer, which cannot be caught in one's hands, and must be felt. Our head must survey what another head can hold, our heart must feel what can fill another's. . . . If this feeling of inner form, which embraces all forms in itself, were more widespread, we should have fewer distorted products of the mind. One would not get the idea of turning every tragic event into a drama, or breaking up every novel into a play ! I wish some wit would parody this doubly vexatious error and turn, say, Aesop's fable of the wolf and the lamb into a five act tragedy.

All form, even the most deeply felt, has some untruth about it, but it is once for all the glass through which we focus the holy beams of dispersed nature into a fiery ray on to the heart of man. But the glass ! Those who have not got it won't get it by hunting, it is like the mysterious philosopher's stone. . . .

And if you do really want to write for the stage, be sure to study the stage, the effect of paint in the distance, of the lights, make-up, glazed canvas, and tinsel, leave nature in her own place, and take careful thought to contrive nothing but what can be carried out on the boards, between laths, cardboard and canvas, through puppets, before children.[133]

These remarks indicate a much deeper understanding of the problem of art than his earlier statements, in which Goethe had emphasised above all the need to subject oneself to experience and master it. He recognises that art must have a significant content, but is here mainly concerned with the ' mystery ' of form, the process by which art is produced. Form he still calls something ' untrue ', unnatural, but it is the means by which nature, experience, can be focused in the poet's mind as in a burning-glass, and communicated to the hearts of men. The artificiality of this medium is stressed as he enumerates the properties of the theatre ; it is the problem of the artist to work through these trivial, unnatural means, to accept these conditions, as a means to present nature in its essential quality :

> So in this narrow wooden mansion,
> Pace out the circle of creation.[134]

The rest of these jottings are concerned mainly with pictorial art, and circle round the same theme. Art, Goethe writes,

cannot come into being in the frivolous salons of the great,
nor in frigid academic institutions. ' Poetry dwells only where
dwell intimacy, need, inward feeling.' The artist must love,
and describe the world as he loves it. Goethe cuts across the
great controversy of his times over the relative merits of
Rembrandt, Raphael, and Rubens, by asserting that in this
all are alike, all are true artists. That Rembrandt confined
himself to a particular group of articles, ' old household gear
and strange rags ', does not limit his power, but ' leads him
into the mysteries through which the thing presents itself to
him as it is '. ' Start from domestic concerns, and then spread
yourself, if you can, over the whole world.' These great artists
are not to be criticised for their one-sidedness ; it is the
peculiar character of their minds that ' magically ' transforms
their themes into ' true human sympathy and participation '.
The harmonies of nature are everywhere, and they are the
inspiration of the artist ; but he must reproduce them in
his art according to the character of his material and his
individuality.

The artist does not only feel the influences [of nature], he pene-
trates to their very source. The world lies before him as before
its Creator, who in the moment when he rejoices over his creation
enjoys also the harmonies by which he has produced it and in
which it consists. Therefore do not think you can so quickly
understand what it means to say : feeling is harmony and vice
versa. And it is this that weaves through the soul of the artist,
that in him presses on to the most understood expression, without
having gone through the intellect. . . . The eye of the artist
sees these harmonies everywhere. He may enter the workshop
of a cobbler, or a stable, he may gaze upon the face of his beloved,
his boots or antique statues, he sees everywhere the holy vibrations
and subtle tones, by which nature links all objects. At every
step a magic world is revealed to him.

These comments of Goethe are the profoundest commentary
on poetry to be found in the Sturm und Drang, and at the
same time they indicate Goethe's emergence from his Sturm
und Drang. Here once again the unity of nature and art is
asserted, and yet in a way which distinguishes them sharply.
Art is the reproduction of nature, whose energy can be recog-

nised more easily in the work of art ' because of the simple and strong effect ' ; but the emphasis is not so much on the chaotic creative force of nature as on the unity, the ' wondrous harmonies ' of nature. The poet is ' the interpreter of nature ', as Herder called Shakespeare, but in a medium totally different from nature, with its own specific conditions. The environment and inner feeling, impact from outside and energy from within, are necessary conditions of the structure of aesthetic experience and poetical production, but the main problem of art appears as the problem of form, the process by which experience is turned into art—the very problem which Herder avowedly shirks at the end of his Shakespeare essay.

Goethe's little essay was written when he was composing *Faust*, and it seems to be the very definition of this play. Its form is a development of the popular folk-play, built therefore, as Herder demanded, on the myths and ' theatrical illusion ' of a popular tradition. It is an historical play, yet interpreted in a way specific to Goethe, so that we forget its historicism and think of it essentially in terms of its present, immediate relevance. It starts ' from domestic concerns ', from the inward and outer knowledge which was the stuff of the author's experience, and is universal, as Goethe said of Rembrandt's paintings. It struck all its contemporary readers, Merck, Boie, and the rest, as being overwhelmingly true and real, yet it is poetic, unrealistic in form. Its language is full of the idiom and variety of natural speech, yet it is unnatural, poetic, rhythmical. Its construction is like that of a ballad, springing from scene to scene, without the detail and complex transitions of real events. It is, indeed, nature focused in a burning-glass ; nature intensified, nature transformed : art.

THE FUNCTION OF POETRY

It can be seen that, for the Stürmer und Dränger, poetry had a dynamic function of which the eighteenth century before them had little or no inkling. Their predecessors pursued poetry as a reputable conventional activity, and justified it in the main either as an intellectual recreation, or as a pleasant means of moral instruction. For the fashionable poets of the 1760s, like Gleim, Ramler, Uz, Georg Jacobi, poetry was a

U

graceful game. They chose their themes without reference to any significant personal experience, and they even assured their readers that, if they wrote about wine and women, their sentiments were not to be taken seriously. Their poetry was appreciated as an agreeable relaxation, and they themselves judged poetry on purely formal grounds, according to its smoothness of metre, neatness, its conventional imagery, its ' propriety ' of diction. In folksong men like Ramler saw only vulgarity of theme and clumsiness of form ; and in Batteux' formalism they found the highest statement of poetics. At times the Stürmer und Dränger confessed to a liking for these graceful nothings. Herder sometimes praised Ramler's poems, and was always a friend of Gleim ; Goethe and Lenz composed little poems, even operetta-like texts, in the anacreontic vein. But they were aware that this sort of poetry was at best a minor matter, an agreeable pastime. When they were writing seriously about poetry they tended to explode in gusty ridicule of all this frivolity, as Lenz did in *Pandämonium Germanicum,*[135] and Wagner in *Prometheus, Deukalion und seine Rezensenten.*[136]

The formalist poets were in no sense aesthetes ; that is, they did not consider art to be an end in itself, and in fact, when in serious mood, they fell back on a moralism little different from that of Goeze or Nicolai. But they tried to find an aesthetic justification for the pleasures of art. Sulzer, their magistral spokesman, asserts that nature has fashioned men so that they find aesthetic delight in pleasant scenes, and that men are thus intended to be educated to gentle and humane sentiments. Art has the duty of presenting this pleasant side of nature and of human relationships ; its principle is not imitation of nature but beautification of it. Thus, in his extremely pedantic review of the fine arts, Sulzer indicates the formal rules for presenting the agreeable sides of nature and love, etc.[137] Both Merck and Goethe exploded at this conception of art, which completely ignores all the subjective necessity of art, as it distorts the character of life. Merck wrote :

If only Herr Sulzer were himself a practising artist, his system of art would be not gloomy zealotry, but serene faith, that never reviles.[138]

And Goethe :

> If a man has no sensuous experience of art, better leave it alone.
> Why should he occupy himself with it ? Because it is the fashion?
> Let him bear in mind that all this theory bars the way to real enjoy-
> ment, and that a more harmful inanity has not been invented.[139]

The great mass of criticism in Germany was religious or moralistic in character. Klopstock asserted that the highest poetry was religious in character, and that all poetry must have a moral purpose ; [140] the most serious criticism of his *Messias* came from writers, like Lavater, who considered his work primarily as a religious document. Mendelssohn condemned Rousseau's *La nouvelle Héloise* for its immorality. Nicolai, the leader of a great group of Aufklärung critics, wrote very frankly to Herder : ' A certain part of poetry, the imagination, in so far as it does not directly improve or impair the intellectual forces and society, is off my path.' [141] Lessing was far more sensitive towards poetical expression than most of his contemporaries, and sought to define in *Laokoon* and the *Hamburgische Dramaturgie* the specific technique of artistic forms. But his own works, and his evaluation of others, were largely shaped by moral considerations, even though his outlook was much broader, more humanitarian, than that of his rigid, dogmatic, utilitarian contemporaries. It is not an accident that his plays all bear a definite moral lesson. In the best of them there is evident a delight in human personality and tensions which goes beyond his theory, but there is no doubt that he, like all his associates, would have subscribed to the view of the Hamburg zealot, Goeze, who wrote in indignant horror at Goethe's *Stella* : ' I thought that the stage had the aim of showing virtue to be charming, and vice abominable and disastrous.' [142]

The publication of Goethe's *Werther* marshalled the forces of the moralists of all camps. Goeze led with a review that condemned the book as being a defence of suicide, and called for its confiscation. His criticism was supported by quotations from the Bible to prove how immoral and irreligious Goethe's work was.[143] He carried the attack further in his review of *Stella*, where he repudiates the distinction drawn by another

critic between poetic and moral ethics. The *Reichs-Postreuter,*
which attacked sentimental novels because ' they make young
folk incapable of becoming useful members of society ', called
Goethe's *Erwin und Elmire* a ' damnable ' play because it
ridiculed religion, and dismissed *Werther* as ' a school for
suicides ', *Stella* as ' a school of abduction and polygamy '.[144]
Nicolai put the crown on this type of criticism by giving
Werther a new and moral ending. Others ' rescued ' *Stella*
by adding a sixth act in which the hero is punished for his
bigamous frivolity.

Some of the fellow-travellers of the Sturm und Drang shared
this attitude, though not in quite so simple a form. Klopstock had asserted that poetry, in order to achieve ' moral
beauty ', must ' set the soul in motion ' and represent the
passions in their truth, but he and his followers believed that
only noble, moral themes were susceptible of poetic treatment. Lavater and F. L. Stolberg succumbed to the charm of
Goethe's poetry and personality, and championed poetry as
the expression of feeling. But they convinced themselves of
the ultimate coincidence of feeling with moral goodness and
the Christian religion. Bit by bit, as they discovered the
implications of the new poetry, they turned from it. Stolberg's ecstatic essay, *On Fullness of the Heart,* which has been
defined by Ermatinger as a paraphrase of Goethe's ' Feeling is
All ',[145] is on the contrary a moralising distortion of Goethe's
view, for Stolberg insists here that feeling is and must be
noble and good, and must lead to ' admiration of the good,
horror of the bad ' ; feeling for nature and the Christian
religion are identified.[146]   Such men did not share the narrow-
minded moralism of clergymen like Goeze and deny to Goethe
outright any poetical worth. But they were puzzled and
worried, like Fritz Jacobi, by the contradiction between his
immoralism and his poetical achievement, and tried to suggest
some way in which poetry could be brought back to the
fold.

To this doubt the Stürmer und Dränger answered with the
assertion of the necessity of truth in the representation of
nature and passion, irrespective of its goodness. Heyne,
Herder's good friend at the university of Göttingen, was
alarmed at Herder's ' obstinate determination to ban morals

outright from the fine arts '.[147] Heinse anticipated the criticism of the moralists when he wrote, in the preface to his translation of Petronius :

> Poets, painters, and novelists have their own morality. It would be very inappropriate to demand of them that they should bring to birth nothing but Grandisons, Madonnas and crucifixes and Messiads. The morality of the fine arts shows men as they are and always were, in outstanding actions, for the pleasure, instruction, and admonition of all men. A genius is therefore allowed to describe and paint everything that has happened or may happen. He is permitted to relate and paint in the most expressive words the fairest and ugliest actions and thoughts of men. He is in the wrong only when he praises the most abominable vices as good.[148]

Thus Heinse answered all the criticism of *Werther* by saying ' it is just the description of the sorrows of young Werther '.[149] In an essay on the ' Goethe-school ', *Über das Göthisiren*, a writer asserts :

> The ideal of poetry is the impassioned man. Its matter is action, and the sum of the energies that produce the action is the measure of its perfection. Othello, the throttler of the chastest woman that ever lay in the arms of a man, is poetically more perfect than the whole of that divine Grandison.[150]

The Stürmer und Dränger do not, however, deny a moral function to poetry. Some of their works are indeed centred on social or moral problems, as we have seen. Schiller's essay *On the Stage as a Moral Institution* of 1784 considers the drama entirely as a supplement to the pulpit and the legal code. But in general their conception of nature and man is infinitely more complex than that of their contemporaries, just as they make many more demands on social life. Poetry is for them not a means by which human feelings and relations are arranged into a pattern corresponding to the demands of the dominant religion and morality, but it is the expression of things ignored and combated by the moralists, it asserts new values, and by its actual being it moulds personality anew. It is not a means of arguing about the known, but the discovery of the unknown, and with this the re-creation of personality.

At the bottom of their poetical activity and theory lies the fundamental discovery of the supreme joy of aesthetic experience. This is the theme of Herder's essays on folksong and Shakespeare, in which he finds rhapsodic expression for the tumultuous rapture that poetry brings, for ' those obscure, ineffable impressions that flood our soul '.[151] This aesthetic experience is not separate from the moral part of man ; through it one becomes enlarged, fuller, richer in total personality. So Goethe could write that, on reading Shakespeare, ' I felt my existence enlarged by an infinity.' [152] In almost the same words Lenz wrote that poetry brings ' an accretion of our being '.[153] This joyous response to poetry is not due to any moral theme or intention of the poet's, but simply to his poetic activity, to the character of poetry. This is the meaning and justification of poetry, its essential function.

How closely related this new response to poetry—or this new awareness of its permanent character—was to the narrowness and deprivations of German social life is made clear by K. P. Moritz's account of his reading of Shakespeare and *Werther*. A sensitive and intelligent child, he was oppressed by the poverty of his parents, the humiliations he had to suffer at school and at the hands of his betters, the narrowness of the pietistic beliefs and practices of his relatives and patrons. At school he discovered Shakespeare.

After and as he had read Shakespeare, he was no longer an ordinary and everyday man—before very long his spirit worked its way up out of its external oppressive circumstances, out of the derision and contempt to which he was succumbing. . . . Through Shakespeare he was led through the world of human passions— the narrow circle of his ideal being was enlarged—he was no longer so isolated and insignificant as to be lost in the crowd— for in reading Shakespeare he had experienced the feelings of thousands.

And further :

After reading Werther, as with Shakespeare, he felt himself elevated above all his circumstances ; the intensified feeling of his isolated existence, which brought him to consider himself a being in whom heaven and earth are mirrored, gave him pride in his humanity, and he felt himself no longer to be the insignificant outcast he thought he was in the eyes of other men.

It is an interesting comment on the comparative poetic quality of Klinger's *Die Zwillinge* that, after seeing this play, which fascinated and harrowed him, Moritz describes how conscious it made him of his own humiliations and spiritual suffering, and how it intensified his melancholia, his ' horror of himself '.[154]

If we compare this psychological analysis of the effect of poetry with Herder's rhapsodic utterances on folksong, we can see how closely linked, for the Stürmer und Dränger, are the two aspects of the function of poetry—the inner expansion of being that it brings, and the communion it establishes between men, between men and nature. Herder attributed the power of primitive poetry to the community of life of primitive peoples, whose poetry expresses the common basis of their experience and, binding them imaginatively together, is a ' spur ' to activity. He demanded for his own time a poetry which would inspire modern men to joyous existence in the same way as the ' songs of war, heroes, and ancestors ' inspired ancient peoples.[155] This is the theme of Goethe's criticism of the *Love Songs of a Polish Jew* in 1772, where he links the true poet's capacity for deep and ' hallowed ' feeling with that for friendly, gay, social intercourse in his own circle.[156] Lenz even proposes a new test for poetry. In his little essay on *Götz von Berlichingen* he writes that a literary work must be judged not by its formal qualities, but by its power to stir the reader to a new way of life : [157]

So, qui bono ? what effect do the products of all the thousands of French geniuses have on our mind, our heart, our whole being ? Heaven forfend that I should be unjust. We take a nice, blissful, sweet feeling home with us, as if we had emptied a bottle of champagne.—But that is all, too. Sleep on it, and it is all blotted out. Where is the living impression, which expresses itself afterwards in convictions, deeds, and actions, the Promethean spark which has stolen so imperceptibly into our inmost soul and inspires our whole life—unless we let it die away through complete lethargy. . . . And now give your opinion on *Götz*. I would like to shout to the whole German public : All of you, first behave like Götz, first learn how to think, feel, act, and then, if you like the change, give your opinion on *Götz*.

This function of poetry, to change men inwardly and establish new relationships between men, was defined most clearly by Herder in his essay on folksong. But how could it be fulfilled in a time when there was no German nation and no national purpose, when the social classes were separated by occupation, custom, even language, and when the literary class was divorced from practical life ? This was a problem the Stürmer und Dränger could not solve. Thus Herder's Ossian essay closes with a panegyric of Klopstock's odes, poems which lack any tangible social function and are, in his words, ' meditations of the human heart with God, with itself, with the whole of nature '. Though the Stürmer und Dränger could see that the re-invigoration of man through poetry was at the same time the re-establishment of man's communal nature, for their own times they could only assert the subjective side of this function, the psychological restoration that poetry brings. The community that poetry strengthens is a spiritual, not an actual community : it is made up of a few like-minded individuals, not a whole society.

But even with this restriction—a restriction imposed on them by the character of their times—the Stürmer und Dränger give poetic production a significant function in personal life. Poetry must well up from inner experience, imaginative or actual ; it is not the result of intellectual intention, shaped by a moral or formal purpose. But it also reacts back upon the poet, it is a deep and necessary function in his moral existence. Goethe, the greatest poet of the Sturm und Drang, insisted on this inward necessity of his imaginative writing. When he met Kestner's reproaches with his ' Werther must must be ', or when he got furious with critics who said he should not have written in the way he did, he was not only asserting that something within him drove him to write, but also that his poetry was the means to an inner ' purification ' [' Läuterung '], a word he often uses in 1775 and afterwards. He describes himself to a correspondent he had not met :

ever living in himself, striving and working, seeking to express according to his measure the innocent feelings of youth in small poems, the pungent spice of life in many sorts of dramas, the figures of his friends, his circumstances, and his beloved house-gear in chalk on gray paper—and asking neither to right nor to left, what people think of what he is doing ; for as he works he always rises a step higher, because he does not want to jump after an ideal, but let his feelings develop into capacities, through struggle and play.[158]

His attentiveness to his feelings, to his inner tensions and joys, was not morbid, but a means to self-development.

An early review of Goethe's expresses in a more general form the same appreciation of the function of art. It was written before *Götz* had appeared or *Werther* was thought of, and has some obvious immaturities of expression, but it is highly characteristic. Goethe was expostulating against the conception of nature as a kindly mother, who leads man only to agreeable experiences, and against the conception of art as the reproduction of the pleasant aspects of nature :

What we see of nature is force that swallows up force, nothing present, all transitory, a thousand seeds crushed, every moment a thousand born, great and significant, manifold to infinity ; beautiful and ugly, good and evil, everything existing side by side with equal right. And art is its very counterpart, it arises from the endeavour of the individual to preserve himself against the destructive force of the whole. Animals themselves define themselves, preserve themselves by their artistic instinct ; man in all his circumstances affirms himself against nature, to avoid its thousand-fold evils, and to enjoy his measure of good ; until he manages in the end to enclose the circulation of all his true and invented wants as far as is possible in a palace, to lock up all dispersed beauty and happiness in his glass walls, where he can become more and more mild, can substitute the joys of the soul for the joys of the body ; and thus his energies, no longer braced as in the natural world to resist vexations, may be resolved into virtue, benevolence, and sentiment.[159]

The ideal of resistance to the ' pains and evils ' of life interprets *Götz* rather than *Werther* or *Faust*, and Goethe was in other jottings to emphasise the need for unreserved experience of the process of nature ; the ideal of ' virtue, benevolence, and sentiment ' was to be replaced by a much more complex conception of man's purpose. But this early definition of the intimate relation between nature and art, and of the profound psychological function of art as a mental restorative, anticipates his later development and thoughts.

In his autobiography Goethe found the classic formulation for this function of poetry as he himself experienced it. Reflecting on the imperious inner necessity which drove him to write *Werther*, and the effect the composition of this work had on him, he writes :

> By this work I rescued myself more than by any other from a stormy element, upon which I had been tossed to and fro in the most violent manner, through my own and others' fault, through accident and deliberate choice, through intention and over-haste, through obstinacy and acquiescence. I felt, as after a general confession, cheerful and free again, and entitled to a new life. My old specific had this time done its work excellently.[160]

This ' specific ' was his innate instinct to turn reality into poetry, to objectivise his own stresses in poetical, imaginative form. And in this passage he not only claims as a function of poetry the declenching of almost unbearable tensions, but, because of this, its function as releasing the poet for ' new life ' —leading him out of ' murk and mist' into clarity, out of tortured feeling into serenity, out of isolation into society, out of introspection into activity. The theme of self-education, which is ever-present in Goethe's later works, in *Iphigenie*, *Tasso*, *Wilhelm Meister*, in *Faust* itself, continues on an ever-widening scale the earliest experience of self-education through art, and Goethe distinguishes himself from all earlier thinkers through his appreciation of the educative function of beauty.

Whether considering poetry from the point of view of the reader or the poet, then, the Stürmer und Dränger introduce totally new conceptions of its function. They see it as a subjective necessity, but one that in enriching the personality links it up with the community ; they see it as arising from internal stresses, as subjectively determined, and yet as liberating the personality from encumbering experience, and freeing it for living. It mirrors the experience of the writer, and reproduces the world ' according to his measure ', and yet at the same time gives the truth of existence. It is seen, not as pastime or morals or philosophy, but as a dynamic and necessary function of the totality of man, arising out of vital experience, and modulating his being, preparing him for life and work.

CHAPTER IX

THE ACHIEVEMENT

Die Natur bildet den Menschen, er bildet sich um, und diese
Umbildung ist doch wieder natürlich.

GOETHE.

THIS STUDY of the Stürmer und Dränger has reviewed their
personal and social situation, their social and philosophical
outlook, their approach to poetry and the principles of their
poetic work. It will be completed by an analysis of their
literary works, which must be reserved for another volume.
The order in which their work has been presented corresponds
as far as possible to the actual historical succession of their
experience and thought, and care has been taken to show the
historical development of personalities, ideas, and works.
But at the same time the arrangement of this investigation
was determined by an evaluation of their work, which has
given their insight into poetry pride of place as their supreme
achievement. In this they most evidently pass beyond their
contemporaries, both in the appreciation of poetry and in the
creation of imaginative literature : in their understanding of
the quality of the great poetry of the past, their appreciation
of the aesthetic problems of their own times, and their ability,
through their own works, to reinstate poetry as a significant
human function. In the history of European literature the
Sturm und Drang represents the conscious emergence of a
new mode of poetry, full of latent potentialities, as characteristic of the society of the following hundred and fifty years
as the poetry of Homer, Dante, or Shakespeare was of theirs,
and with its own peculiar themes and principles of style.

This new poetry was rooted in the forms of life and the
philosophical outlook of the times, and like them it was not a
sudden, spontaneous growth. It drew sustenance from the
poetry of simple, unstratified societies, such as Homer and the
Edda, and from the poetry of the common people. To
Shakespeare it owed its most powerful single inspiration, and
Herder ascribed the power of Shakespeare to the diversified

unity of a vigorous national community. In conscious hostility to the social and literary forms of aristocratic culture, it was the outcome of a complex movement towards a middle-class society and culture which in the eighteenth century had already become the conscious purpose of many writers. Thus in religion it linked on to the whole tradition of undogmatic, non-institutional belief, of mystics, pietists, pantheists. In philosophy it found its allies in the empiricists and sensualists, in Bacon, Locke, Diderot, in all thinkers who accepted the reality of the world of the senses. It is a modern form of humanism, embodying the essential Renaissance trust in human energy and activity, the belief that the world is not definable in fixed terms but is an evolving process, to be investigated and re-shaped by human endeavour to which no bound is set. The Sturm und Drang is a marked stage in the transformation of the feudal-aristocratic conceptual world through the bourgeoisie, and its members recognised gratefully their debt to the great figures of this movement.

The Stürmer und Dränger contribute nothing positive to social and political theory and activity. At best they define the tragic situation of a middle class which is powerless in the hands of an absolute prince and a privileged nobility, or engaged in insignificant trade. Destruction, flight, or resignation are the lot of their ' titanic ' heroes, who themselves almost always owe their boldness to their aristocratic birth. They are tempted to idealise primitive or feudal times, even serfdom itself, in contrast to their own ' policed ' states. In this respect they fail even to understand the thought and efforts of their French and British contemporaries, and see only the negative sides of national power and constitutionalism. They show no signs of having grasped the importance of Turgot's or Adam Smith's economic theories. They even represent a step back from some of the principles of social reform of their elder German contemporaries. But in spite of these failings, and perhaps just because of the pettiness of German circumstances, they threw down a challenge to the State and its purposes in the name of personal and social culture, a challenge that succeeding generations could not ignore.

Their greatest achievement lies in the cultural sphere, though here too they were deeply indebted to the thinkers and

poets of Britain and France. It was in these countries that
nature was first given a divine halo, that man's struggle with
nature was given its true dignity, that energy and activity
were enthroned as his highest qualities, that reason and
scientific experiment were freed from dogmatic and conventional fetters, that it began to be understood that history
itself is a man-made process. It was in France and England
that the first efforts were made to create a literature of the
middle class, circling round bourgeois institutions, bourgeois
feelings and virtues, bourgeois activities. But within these
societies, these ideas and purposes were held in check. In
England the new secular and scientific philosophy was
obstructed by an uneasy accommodation with established
religion, even with the Established Church. In France, as
in England, the conflict between the new and old ideas was
glossed over by a pervasive optimism, a belief in the irresistible
march of reason and civilisation under the protection of
Providence. Shaftesbury could assert that ' nature has no
malice '. ' The eighteenth century on the whole thought well
of human nature, and it was generally believed that men were
" by nature " sociable, sympathetic, and benevolent.' ¹ Even
in France, where the philosophical struggle with the Church
was much sharper, the same optimistic belief prevailed, and in
D'Alembert's *Discours Préliminaire* of the *Encyclopédie* found its
most eloquent exposition. ' Le premier principe des philosophes est un optimisme réfléchi.' ² Though laws of progress
and development were beginning to be perceived, the notion
of challenge and struggle was either avoided or put in so
abstract a way that the ideal of the full development and
engagement of the whole personality, entailing the possibility
of a total clash between personality and social forms, was
ignored. The imaginative self-projection of the middle-class
writers allowed for feelings only in so far as they chimed in with
domestic and civic virtue ; or, as a compensation, they
constructed sublime and heroic attitudes which were not meant
to make any impact on actual forms of living.

Nearly all these writers submitted to the cultural manners
of polite society, in which the aristocracy predominated, and
were held in check by them, believing that these manners
provided an immutable framework for civilised progress. ' It

was one of the most important functions of the eighteenth
century [English] writers to maintain and cherish the standards
of polite society, not only in matters of taste and manners,
but also in morality and religion.' ³ The greater centralisa-
tion of cultural life in France and the cultural predominance
of the aristocratic salon had an even profounder effect on the
manners and taste of the French writers of the middle class.
In both countries the aristocratic patron was a subtly effective
cultural force. The satire of a Voltaire or Swift was contained
within these limits ; the robust realism of a Fielding did not
shake the foundations of aristocratic manners or bourgeois
self-idealisation ; and the individualism of a Mandeville or
Vauvenargues was too paradoxical to carry much weight.

The light from abroad filtered darkly into Germany. The
German Enlightenment turned reason into an abstract principle and adopted the dualism of Descartes rather than the
empiricism of Bacon and Locke. The struggle with the
Church turned into an abstract argument, and Providence
appears in German thought less as the justification of effort
than as the solace for impotence. English bourgeois confidence
was transformed into an affirmation of the *status quo*, an acquiesc-
ent belief in the inevitability of ' perfection '. Only Lessing
protested with vigour, and he himself was driven more and
more into theological disputes : the supreme effort of the
German Enlightenment was the demand for religious toler-
ation. Against the abstractness and supineness of German
thought the Stürmer und Dränger lifted their voices, inspired
in the first place by the movement abroad. But they carried
this movement further—not in all respects, for they lacked
the experience to grasp the full significance, for instance, of
Diderot's theory of nature and science, or of Turgot's and
Adam Smith's conception of historical development. But
they added essential principles, and in so doing came into
conflict with their teachers.

The point at which they joined issue with their century had
already been defined by Rousseau. He had challenged the
whole idea of social advance and had asserted that the highest
culture was that of peoples in the earliest stages of civilisation.
He sought circumstances in which personal and social values
would not be at variance, and in which man could find room

for the essential longings and powers of his nature. Rousseau
would not believe that the gap between the individual and
society was unbridgeable, and found a reconciliation in *La
nouvelle Heloïse* as in *Du Contrat social* and *Emile*. The Stürmer
und Dränger, inspired by him, were to start on his problem
afresh.

Rousseau's antithesis of individual and society was felt by
them with peculiar force. Even in the free cities the dominant
sections of the bourgeoisie were traditionalist and rigid, and
deserved little admiration, while the ideological sections of the
middle class constructed theories very much out of contact
with reality—as Voltaire rudely told them in *Candide*. The
German nation did not exist, and patriotism like that of the
Klopstockians was too forced and false to have any real
meaning. All the states were governed by despots, and the
more efficiently they were managed, the more despotic was
government. In addition, the nobility affected a French
culture alien to the reality and requirements of burgher life,
in home and church and social relations. In such circumstances Rousseau's theses struck home. The established social
and cultural values, of courts as of the bourgeoisie, could be
discarded as meaningless, as utterly irrelevant to the needs of
the individual. The cautious spirit of Diderot or d'Holbach,
the efforts at reconciliation of Rousseau, the shrewd common
sense of Hume or Ferguson, lacked in Germany the essential
basis of a strong middle class, and could find a parallel only
in the social acquiescence of Schlözer, Nicolai, and Mendelssohn. The German situation provoked a revolution in values,
a radical new start.

This new start was, in some respects, convulsive and immature. Most of the Stürmer und Dränger were impulsive and
unstable in character ; it was Hamann's very instability and
social irresponsibility that allowed him to claim, as Goethe put
it, that ' everything man undertakes must spring from his
whole united powers '. His temperament, his pietist leanings,
allowed him to ignore social and practical necessities. Herder
and Lenz had something of the same irresponsibility, Goethe
was lucky enough to be able to take his profession lightly,
Bürger despised his petty office, Maler Müller and Heinse
were completely unpractical. At the same time, the Sturm

und Drang was a movement of young men, who, with the excusable disregard of youth for practical obligations, sometimes claimed to be voicing only the needs of youth. Johanna Fahlmer reports an illuminating conversation with Goethe, whom she had been reproving for his resentment of the criticism of Wieland. Wieland is wrong, cried Goethe ; perhaps he is right for his age, but he has no right to expect a young man to think like him—' That paternal tone ! That's what made me so furious. That's just how my father talks.' [4]

Temperament and youth encouraged the Stürmer und Dränger to be radical and extreme, and there are many examples of juvenile exaggeration and wilfulness in their works and ideas. This wilfulness was in part the cause of the lack of popularity of their plays on the stage. Bruford has shown how rarely their plays were performed—Goethe's weaker middle-class dramas, *Clavigo* and *Stella*, were by far the most popular.[5] But the deeper cause was the challenge they delivered to the values of the contemporary middle class, who wanted above all compassionate tears, high-flown ideals, and an ultimate reconciliation, not bitter satire and tragedy.

From the beginning the theme is the rights of the inward needs of man, at first, with Hamann or Klopstock, dependent on the sanction of religion, but liberating itself rapidly to a characteristic trust in natural feeling. Love, feeling for nature, the vague longings of youth, which convention hitherto had ignored and stifled, assert a validity superior to all else. Inward activity is given priority over all external standards, all practical and moral achievement : ' We often find that with our drifting and veering we get further than others with their sails and oars,' says Werther, the symbol of Sturm und Drang subjectivism.[6] In plays and novels this conflict between inner values and outer forms (the State, society, profession, family, religion, morality) is presented, in which the hero tragically asserts his subjective values rather than renounce and submit to standards which are meaningless for him. What distinguishes them from Klopstockians and sentimentalists is that they do not blind themselves to outer reality, to the inevitable conflict between their inward urge and reality, but in the main present their problem as a tragic one, in which the impassioned individual must perish. They

x

affirm the inward energy they felt, in its richness and its torment, despite the catastrophe it brings.

But, equally characteristically, they do not ascribe a transcendental origin or purpose to their inward drive. It was for them a principle linking them with the energies of the universe, energies they asserted to be present in matter as in spirit, in nature, in the historical process. Their subjectivism led them to a new grasp of reality, or rather of those aspects of reality in which they thought this fundamental energy was not deadened and destroyed. Thus they see nature with new eyes and establish a new feeling for nature in its elemental character, as growth, organic form, decay. They enlarge human sympathy for past civilisations where vigour and activity prospered in communities whose thought and values were not divorced from sensuous activity, where theory was not divorced from practice. They describe in their literary works people and an environment where the same qualities thrive, with vivid local and individual realism : the family in the productive social classes, children and young people, artisans and peasants, who hitherto had been depicted, if at all, either with superior condescension or with idealising sentimentality.

In all this consciously opposing the standards of their own times, they were at the same time recapturing elements in the long Renaissance tradition. The Faust-myth, which was a characteristic product of the Renaissance, is treated not only by Goethe and Maler Müller, but by Lenz and (later) Klinger. It symbolises the theme of human contest with the barriers imposed by authority and custom, the modern Prometheus. It stands not merely for emotive or moral protest, but also for activity ; for that human restlessness, Locke's ' uneasiness ',[7] that seeks to transform the outer world. In the Sturm und Drang period these young Germans could not define the way in which they could direct their energies to the outer world. The emphasis is all on the powers within them that demanded action, and the inward and outer contradictions which obstruct these energies. Their conception of the great man of action is often juvenile, equating feeling with achievement ; but they are haunted by the ideal of practical achievement in the warrior, the national leader, the scientist, the home-builder. And if, as a rule, they themselves feel the irreconcilability of inner demands and the discipline demanded by practical achievement, there are signs that they recognise that the two are not only compatible but mutually conditioning : ' Man's environment does not only act upon him, he again reacts upon his environment, and as he lets himself be modified, so again he modifies the world around him. Nature forms man, he transforms himself, and this transformation too is natural.' [8]

In the Sturm und Drang, all the emphasis is laid on the subjective factor in this dialectical, dynamic interaction of nature (or society) and the individual. It is from the individual that comes the impetus towards action. But the completed version of *Faust Part 1* interprets the Sturm und Drang outlook without any essential modification. To Faust's despair over the impossibility of joyous experience, Mephistopheles answers : ' We'll just clear out.' [9] The first step in Faust's spiritual progress is to leave his study, to get into the wide world : ' In the Beginning was the Deed.' [10] Activity is not conceived as something opposed to inward development, but as the means to it. Later in life, very much in the spirit of Bacon, Goethe was to emphasise ever more strongly the interdependence of activity, knowledge, and inward enrichment, the theme of Herder's *On Knowledge and Perception*.

The conflict between the Sturm und Drang system of values and that prevailing in normal social life was so sharp that their works were consistently condemned as immoral. The violent attacks on Goethe's *Werther* and *Stella* were taken up again when *Faust* was published, and were echoed in England, even by such admirers as Crabb Robinson. Later generations slurred over their moral challenge, but there was a deep truth in it, and Coleridge and others were not so far wrong when, writing after the French Revolution, they indignantly asserted that the Sturm und Drang works they knew were not only immoral, but revolutionary in tendency. In actual fact, very few of the writings of the Sturm und Drang are concerned directly with political doctrine. Only Schiller, writing at the beginning of the next decade, sketched new political principles based on inner values—Karl Moor, in *The Robbers*, tries to build a society based on fraternity, equality, love, and the theme of *Kabale und Liebe* is the rottenness of a society which throttles natural feeling. That Karl Moor fails and recants did not lessen, for his contemporaries, the appeal of his ideals. Otherwise, the criticism of particular social evils to be found in Sturm und Drang works is not of great moment—the criticism of courtiers and pedants, of abstract education, the plea for sympathy with the unmarried mother who commits infanticide, and such. Their social conscience was far less stirred than that of Burns, Blake, Wordsworth, who knew and were appalled by the evils of the modern state and modern industrial society.

Their peculiar moral ' revolutionary ' significance lies not in an attack on particular social evils, but in the depiction of the unease of man in modern society, of the contradiction between inner values and social forms. The heroes of their works are caught in a web from which there is no escape ; we admire and love them, yet they must perish. The Stürmer und Dränger may point to past times or primitive societies where such contradictions do not exist, they may suggest here and there that a law or conventional custom should be changed. In essence, however, they point to an irreconcilable antagonism between the deepest qualities of man and society. This is the theme, more or less profoundly expressed, of Herder's essays, of Lenz's dramas and novels, of Klinger's *Das leidende Weib* and *Die Zwillinge*, of Leisewitz's *Julius von Tarent*, of Maler Müller's *Fausts Leben*, of Schiller's early plays. It is the theme of *Götz von Berlichingen*, *Werther*, of *Faust* in respect to both Faust himself and Gretchen. In their deepest works it is understood not as a mere conflict between a ' good ' individual and a bad society, but as a conflict within the individual too, which forces him, in responding to his best intimations, to destroy himself and what he holds dearest, even to be false to himself. They can say, like Faust himself, that the God who ' stirs them in their innermost parts ' cannot move the outer world ; or like Lenz in his vehement *Hymn* : ' Must I burn for evermore ? '—

> No, I cry—o Saviour ! Father !
> My heart's yearning must be stayed,
> Must be sated ! If not, rather
> Smash the image thou hast made !

This conflict between man and society, between the values of the individual and of social morality (and therefore of established religion), appears to arise at times from a particular social condition, or a perverse pathological streak in the individual. In such cases, its general relevance is limited, as with Guelfo of *Die Zwillinge*, Evchen Humbrecht of *Die Kindermörderin*, Lenz's *Der Engländer* or *Der Waldbruder*, even Goethe's temperamental Weislingen in *Götz* and Fernando in *Stella*. Its full bearing can be recognised only in such characters as Prometheus, Faust, and Gretchen, whose problems arise out of the very fullness and richness of their characters. The Gretchen tragedy, the only fully developed theme of the Sturm und Drang *Faust*, shows the unfolding of the rich feeling of this young girl in all its beauty, and as she herself is fulfilled, so she comes unconsciously into conflict with society. There is here no polemic against social morality ; in her conscious thought Gretchen fully accepts the morality of her neighbours and her church. But her instinct carries her in the opposite direction, and causes her to fall into deceit, immorality, and crime. Unable to understand and master the process of which she is the victim, half out of her wits, she still does not indict an unjust morality but clings repentant to hope in the grace of God. Gretchen's love is not thereby condemned—her repentance is her own judgment, not ours, and is in no sense the dramatist's summing up, as Karl Moor's recantation largely is. We are left with that fundamental ambiguity :

> Yet—all that drove me on
> God ! was so good ! alas, was so dear !

It is the same with Faust, whose intensity of feeling brings him to destroy the girl he loves. Similarly, Klärchen has become the mistress of Egmont not because she is the pitiful victim of the seducer's arts, the unfortunate innocent of so many contemporary works, but because she is high-spirited and independent, because she is in her way heroic.

In these works Goethe reveals, with infinite subtlety, fundamental antagonisms within modern man and modern society ; antagonisms he cannot resolve, but which he displays in all their stark truth. For this reason he was charged with

immorality. Of course, he was no immoralist, certainly no
amoralist. The main works of his later life show how he
wrestles with the problems he had earlier posed. He shows
the conflict between man's powers, or better, his potentialities,
and the practical and theoretical forms the times have established. His heroes rebel against practical occupations, social
conventions, religious sanctions, against the state, the study,
the family ; this rebellion is their glory, though it is often
impure and unclear, a composite of good and bad, egoism
and selflessness. A solution which might be more than a
sentimental reconciliation was clearly not possible without a
reconstruction of social relations, and precisely in this sphere
Germany could not offer the Stürmer und Dränger the experience from which to construct positive ideas.

If this is the most significant aspect of their thought, its
supreme expression is found in their poetic, imaginative
works. Not that their treatises and essays are without philosophical importance. But it is evident that they could not
grasp clearly all the bearing of their attitude nor express it
logically and consistently. All their essays have something
' poetical ' in their style, they abound in personal, even
whimsical expressions, and appeal to the emotive responses
of the reader as much as, if not more than, to his reason.
Their values are an ' obscure urge ', a ' dunkler Drang ', rather
than a formulated principle ; their knowledge presents itself,
like Werther's, ' more in surmise and obscure desire than in
clear shape and living force '. They more easily find symbols
to express their attitude than arguments to explain or defend
it. In all but the shortest of their essays—and it indicates
Goethe's sense of fitness that all his essays in this period are
hardly more than jottings—they cannot get free of normal
formulations and normal terminology, philosophical or religious, however much they strive to find a new tone and new
expressions. Their mode of apprehension of life was so new,
so challenging, that its rational expression was extremely
difficult ; while in imaginative works, in poetry, drama, and
novel, they were able to grasp their situation and their problem
most adequately.

Only too often their poetry (the word is here used in its
widest sense of imaginative literature, ' Dichtung ') has been

considered to be mere subjective statement, effusion of the heart. It does include, as a most important constituent, the expression of intense experience, a new ardour in love, love of persons and nature. But it has been pointed out above that in their lyric poetry feeling itself is shaped and matured, collected ' as in a burning-glass ', made fruitful and serene. Their lyrics—and above all Goethe's—arise from intense experience, but also release tensions and restore wholeness, restore them to the social world. In nearly all their work that ' ille ego ' of which Wieland spoke shines through, sometimes clumsily, sometimes with ' infinite delicacy '. Goethe stressed in innumerable variations the dependence of poetry on urgent feeling : ' Poetry dwells only where dwell intimacy, need, inward feeling.' [11]

This element of feeling drowns at times everything else. At times, in theoretical essays as in imaginative works, they equate genius with excess of feeling, with a creativeness that is chaotic, formless. We have seen evidences of this attitude in the treatises of Lenz, of Bürger, and here and there in the others. But Lenz himself was aware of the fatality of his excessive subjectivism, and he sought to school himself ; his best imaginative works show indeed a very sharp observation of external reality. The permanent significance of Sturm und Drang literature arises from the alliance between intense feeling and a realistic grasp of the outer world, through which their inner promptings acquire shape and substance. Through a new capacity for feeling, or at least through a new evaluation of the fundamental significance of feeling, they were able to grasp their specific environment more firmly than their contemporaries. Thus their works offer brilliant examples of satirical realism when they are dealing with men and circumstances perverted, in their view, by harmful or trivial convention—for example, the scenes of garrison life in *Die Soldaten,* the tradesmen's interiors in that play and *Die Kindermörderin,* the student scenes in *Fausts Leben,* the vivid sketches in Goethe's humorous playlets and poems, the doctor and noble bureaucrats in *Werther,* Marthe, Lieschen, Valentin in *Faust.*

But this realism appears not only in satirical form. Equally characteristic is the grasp of those elements in social reality where the profound and permanent substance of human life thrives. In their sketches of the bourgeois family the Stürmer und Dränger do not hide those factors which cause distortion of natural feeling, particularly the misplaced rigour or foolish indulgence of parents. But at the same time they show what stores of profound contentment, of self-realisation, the family engenders and preserves. It was the vivid realism of *Werther*, not only its morbid passion, that appealed to Goethe's contemporaries, and was fixed in the engravings that were stuck up in sitting-rooms all over Europe. ' *Faust* is stolen with the greatest faithfulness from nature,' wrote Merck. Commenting on Rembrandt, Goethe insisted that art must start from the particular, from a workshop, a stable, antique statues, or a pair of boots ; in these the artist may discover ' the mysteries through which the thing presents itself as it is '. ' Start from domestic concerns, and then spread yourself, if you can, over the whole world.' [12] It is the same principle as we find in Blake and Wordsworth, a realism which is highly selective since it arises from the particular ' domestic concerns ' and the particular feeling or vision of the poet, but which is throbbing with meaning and which gives reality a new, unimagined significance. This combination of realism with inner meaning is the signal achievement of Sturm und Drang literature ; it links the Stürmer und Dränger not so much with the metaphysical and irrationalist Romantics as with the whole tradition of imaginative realism, whether it is in Blake and Wordsworth and Pushkin, or in the realistic novelists like Balzac, Stendhal, and Tolstoy. [13] This realism is the aesthetic counterpart of the philosophical realism, the dynamic monism expounded in Herder's philosophical essays, which is to be contrasted with the idealism and dualism of the leading German philosophers of the time, and even more with the ' magic idealism ' of the German Romantics.

The Sturm und Drang poetic idiom shows the same fusion of subjectivism and realism. Their language interprets a new intensity of experience. It is not statement of fact, nor of abstract idea, but communication between living men, urgent, compelling, full of energy. But they were conscious that all experience is moulded by the specific time and place, the specific circumstances in which it comes into being, as Herder wrote in his interpretation of Shakespeare. Thus their poetic idiom—and indeed much of their prose in essays and letters —has a highly complex, dual character. On the one hand it is extremely free, in word as in rhythm, and elements in it may be traced back to Homer or Pindar, Shakespeare, Luther's Bible, folksong ; on the other it is full of the words and phrasing of the actual, purposeful, practical speech of unsophisticated classes.

The poetry of the Stürmer und Dränger expresses a new human situation, and with it new human values and potentialities. In their theoretical works they formulate the interconnection of the social environment, the world of sense and activity, and the inner powers of man which are nurtured by certain aspects of the environment and hindered by others. Confident in the goodness of these inner powers and of nature, they accept the tragic inevitability of conflict with a deep feeling of exhilaration. Their consciousness of being part of a process, as members of a changing society and as young men developing towards maturity, leads them to avoid all final definitions of a human or personal goal, and present their feeling of life in a provisional, even problematical, form, that is, in a form appropriate to their time and situation in Germany, to their own personal experience. There is a dynamic tension in their whole way of thought, which drove the best of them, Herder, Goethe, and Schiller, to a perpetual struggle for solutions which, as Goethe said about his completed *Faust*, ' like the history of the world and of man give rise to a fresh problem that needs to be solved '.[14] Beneath all the formulations of their problem, whether in ecstatic, tragic, or satirical mood, lies the effort for all-sided and full experience, embracing feeling, activity, knowledge. Romanticism, especially German romanticism, only partially fulfils their promise. In their dynamic naturism, their imaginative realism they set the tone for the nineteenth century ; they open up the richness not only of the romantic imagination, but also of the teeming outer world of the great realists.

NOTES

CHAPTER I.—*THE PERSONALITIES*

1 See A. M. Wagner, *H. W. von Gerstenberg und der Sturm und Drang*, 2 vols., Heidelberg 1920–4.
2 In *Frédéric Soret*, ed. H. H. Houben, Leipzig 1929, 349.
3 Jacobi to Dohm, 20 June 1818. Morris iv. 121.
4 Heinse to Wieland, 2 January 1774. Heinse, *Werke* ix. 180–4.
5 Goethe to Schönborn, 4 July 1774 and to Fr. Jacobi, 21 August 1774. Morris iv. 29 and 133. Jacobi to Goethe, 21 October 1774. *Briefwechsel zwischen Goethe und Jacobi*, 39 ff.
6 Nicolai to Herder, 6 September 1773. *Von und An Herder* i. 353–4.
7 *Aphorismen*, passim.
8 *Teutscher Merkur* 1774. No. 8. 174–84.
9 To Herder, October 1771. Morris ii. 116–17.
10 To Herder, 20 November 1775. *Briefe* i. 146.
11 Hamann gives a frank account of his childhood in *Gedanken über meinen Lebenslauf* (*Schriften* i) and an interesting letter to Bucholtz of 1784, published in the periodical *Goethe* vii. 141–5. Many new facts have been given in J. Nadler, *Hamann*, Salzburg 1949.
12 Hegel, *Ueber Hamanns Schriften*, 1828. *Werke* xvii. Berlin 1835, 44.
13 ibid. 78, 74.
14 *Dichtung und Wahrheit*, Book 12. *Werke* x. 563.
15 Hamann, *Lettre perdue d'un Sauvage du Nord*. *Schriften* iv. 151.
16 To Herder, 3 June 1781. Hamann, *Schriften* vi. 193–4.
17 W. Michel, *Der Kriegsrat J. H. Merck*, Darmstadt n.d
18 Goethe's *Tagebuch*, 13 July 1779.
19 *Faust*, l. 3488.
20 To Wieland, Spring 1776. Merck, *Schriften* ii. 76.
21 Reported by Goethe, *Dichtung und Wahrheit*, Book 15. *Werke* x. 724.
22 *Metakritik* 1799 and *Kalligone* 1800. *Werke* xxi and xxii. See C. Siegel, *Herder als Philosoph*, Berlin 1907 ; A. Tumarkin, *Herder und Kant*, Bern 1896.
23 To Caroline, 20–22 September 1770. *Briefwechsel* i. 51–5.
24 18 December 1771. *Briefwechsel* i. 410.
25 *Journal meiner Reise*. *Werke* iv. 438–9.
26 ibid., 446–7.
27 To Caroline, 28 December 1771, 23 May 1772. *Briefwechsel* i. 414, ii. 119.
28 To Merck, October 1772. Merck, *Schriften* ii. 29.
29 To Zimmermann, 8 July 1773. C. Janentzky, *Lavaters Sturm und Drang*, Halle 1916, 57.
30 *Dichtung und Wahrheit*, Book 10. *Werke* x. 453.
31 To Merck, 13 June 1777. Merck, *Schriften* ii. 92.
32 *Dichtung und Wahrheit*, Book 10. *Werke* x. 451.

[33] Preface and Postscript to *Volkslieder*, 2ter Teil. *Werke* xxv.
[34] 7 November 1772. Merck, *Schriften* ii. 30–1.
[35] 28 August 1774. op. cit. ii. 42–3.
[36] To Höpfner, July 1775. op. cit. ii. 59.
[37] Herder to Hamann, 9 February 1783, reporting a conversation with Wieland. *Herders Briefe an Hamann*, 190.
[38] See the description of Frau Professor Höpfner, Morris ii. 321–2.
[39] To Nicolai, 19 January 1776. Merck, *Schriften* ii. 67–8, Morris v. 472.
[40] To Caroline, 21 March 1772. *Briefwechsel* ii. 68.
[41] Morris v. 299–304.
[42] 3 August 1775. Morris v. 291.
[43] 18 October 1775. Morris v. 308.
[44] To Frau von Stein, 10 December 1777.
[45] *Fragment eines Romans*, 1771. Morris ii. 54.
[46] To Herder, July 1772. Morris ii. 294.
[47] *Einfälle und Notizen*. Morris v. 461.
[48] G. F. E. Schönborn to Gerstenberg, 12 October 1773. Morris iii. 389.
[49] To Hennings, 18 November 1772. Morris 315–16. Goethe to Herder, *c.* July 10, 1772, Morris ii. 294, where Goethe, quoting Herder's statement, says that he is trying to give a plastic quality to his poetry.
[50] Morris ii. 104.
[51] To Wieland, 27 August 1774. Morris iv. 118.
[52] Carl August von Meiningen, 20 August 1775. Morris v. 275.
[53] E. Stoeber to a friend, July 1772. Morris ii. 103.
[54] To Wieland, 8 June 1774. Morris iv. 78.
[55] To Lavater, 10 June 1774 and 17 October 1773. Morris iv. 82 and iii. 390.
[56] To Lerse, 1780. Quoted W. Bode, *Goethes Leben—Am Bau der Pyramide*, Berlin, 1925, 440–1.
[57] To Zimmermann, 20 October 1774. Morris iv. 114.
[58] To Sophie von la Roche, 10 August 1774. Morris iv. 118.
[59] To Wieland, 8–9 November 1775. *Goethe als Persönlichkeit* i. 127.
[60] Kestner to Hennings, 18 November 1772. Morris ii. 315, 325.
[61] 21 November 1774. Morris iv. 147.
[62] To Schönborn, 1 June 1774. Morris iv. 26.
[63] Morris v. 32.
[64] *Lilis Parck* and *An Belinden*. Morris v. 312 and 34.
[65] Knebel to Bertuch, 23 December 1774. Morris iv. 371.
[66] 19 January 1776. Merck, *Schriften* ii. 67–8 ; Morris v. 472.
[67] *Collected Papers*, 1925, iv. See my *Goethe's Autobiography and Rousseau's Confessions*.
[68] To Kestner, October 1774. Morris iv. 142–3. To Jacobi, April 1775. Morris v. 25–6.
[69] *Heinrich Stillings Lebensgeschichte*. The relevant passages are printed in Morris ii. 98–102.
[70] To Nicolai, 11 September 1773. Morris iii. 388.
[71] Caroline to Herder, 9 March 1772. *Briefwechsel* ii. 49.
[72] K. von Lyncker. 46 ff.

[73] To Auguste zu Stolberg, 30 January 1775. Morris v. 8.
[74] 13 February 1775. Morris v. 10.
[75] To Auguste Stolberg, 7 March 1775. Morris v. 16.
[76] Morris v. 299–304.
[77] 11 August 1781.
[78] See my *The Novels of F. H. Jacobi and Goethe's Early Classicism.*
[79] To Merck, 22 January 1776.
[80] Oberlin's account of his illness is given in A. Stöber, *Der Dichter Lenz,* Basel 1842, 11–31 ; it was the basis for the moving fragment *Lenz* of Georg Büchner.
[81] *Tagebuch* and *Moralische Bekehrung eines Poeten. Schriften* v.
[82] *Notizen. Schriften* iv. 285.
[83] May 1775. *Briefe* i. 103.
[84] July 1775. *Briefe* i. 114.
[85] 9 September 1776. Merck, *Schriften* ii. 83.
[86] To Herder, 28 August 1775. *Briefe* i. 124.
[87] May 1776. *Briefe* i. 262.
[88] 14 March 1776. *Briefe* i. 203.
[89] October 1772. *Briefe* i. 59.
[90] Some of the papers Salzmann read before his circle are published in his *Kurze Abhandlungen,* 1776.
[91] H. Kindermann, *Lenz und die Romantik,* Wien 1925, 194.
[92] This is the theme of Kindermann's book.
[93] *Letters of a Russian Traveller.* Quoted M. N. Rosanow, *Lenz, Der Dichter der Sturm- und Drangperiode,* Leipzig 1909, 427–8.
[94] M. Rieger, *Klinger in der Sturm- und Drangperiode,* Darmstadt 1880, 63, 83, 154 passim.
[95] To Klinger, December 1777. Heinse, *Werke* ix. 365–7.
[96] Goethe to Lavater, 16 September 1776.
[97] Autumn 1774. Rieger, op. cit. 372.
[98] August 1777. Rieger, op. cit. 409.
[99] To Kayser, 23 April 1779. Rieger, op. cit. 423.
[100] *Schillers Persönlichkeit* i. 150 passim.
[101] ibid. ii. 39–40.
[102] ibid. i. 164, ii. 39.
[103] *Zur Erinnerung an das Publikum,* 1784. *Werke* xv. 233.

CHAPTER II.—*THE STURM UND DRANG AND THE STATE*

[1] A. Dock, *Der Souveränitätsbegriff,* Strassburg 1909. G. P. Gooch, *German Views of the State,* in *The German Mind and Outlook,* 1945.
[2] See C. Justi, *Winckelmann und seine Zeitgenossen,* Leipzig 1898, i. 188 ff.
[3] To Nicolai, 25 August 1769. *Briefe* i. 297–8.
[4] *Ueber die deutsche Sprache und Litteratur. Werke* ix. 139.
[5] See in particular A. L. Schlözer's periodical, *Briefwechsel meist politischen und statistischen Inhalts,* 1775–82, continued later as *Staatsanzeigen* ; and

F. C. von Moser, *Der Herr und der Diener*, 1759 and *Von dem deutschen National-Geist*, 1765.

6 e.g. in his ode, *Delphi*, 1782.

7 See Klopstock, *Die Hermanns Schlacht*, a play of 1769, and his ode *Mein Vaterland* ; M. Claudius, *Ich bin ein deutscher Jüngling* ; F. L. Stolberg, *Freiheitsgesang aus dem zwanzigsten Jahrhundert* ; Voss, *An Goethe* (a characteristic misunderstanding of *Götz von Berlichingen*) ; Schubart, *Ein Gesicht*.

8 His poem, *Karl der Grosse*, *Werke* xxix. 335–7, and comments, *Werke* xviii. 150–1, and to Caroline, July 1772, *Briefwechsel* ii. 169–70.

9 Herder, *Werke* v. 355, and to Caroline, 9 November 1771, *Briefwechsel* i. 369 ; Goethe to Friederike Oeser, 13 February 1769, Morris i. 322–3.

10 To Höpfner, 23 August 1777. *Briefe* ed. Wagner 1847, 149.

11 See Bode, *Goethes Leben* iii. 164.

12 Möser, *Patriotische Phantasien. Werke* i. 115.

13 e.g. M. Claudius in 1794. *Werke* ii. 173–217.

14 See Goethe's comments in *Dichtung und Wahrheit*, Book 15. *Werke* x. 702–3.

15 An anonymous reviewer in *Frankfurter Gelehrte Anzeigen*, 1772, ed. Bergsträsser, 585 ; and Schubart, *Deutsche Chronik*, 1 January 1777. *Gesam. Schriften* vi. 267.

16 *Die Soldaten*, Act iii, Sc. 10.

17 J. Nadler, *Hamann*, Salzburg 1949, 71–81.

18 Nadler, op. cit. 205–6, 370–85 passim ; R. Unger, *Hamann und die Aufklärung*, Halle 1925, 170–80.

19 *Au Salomon de Prusse. Schriften* viii (1). 191–8.

20 Merck, *Schriften* i. 202.

21 Caroline von Herder, *Erinnerungen aus dem Leben Herders*. In Herder, *Werke*, ed. Müller, Erster Teil, xx. 32–3.

22 *Auch eine Philosophie der Geschichte. Werke* v. 577–82.

23 *Ursachen des gesunknen Geschmacks. Werke* v. 625–32, 653–5.

24 *Ephemerides*. Morris ii. 40. See, for Goethe's political attitude, W. Mommsen, *Die politischen Anschauungen Goethes*, Stuttgart 1948.

25 To Kestner, Christmas 1773. Morris iii. 73.

26 See G. Lukács, *Wilhelm Meisters Lehrjahre* and *Fauststudien*, in *Goethe und seine Zeit*, Bern 1947 ; B. Fairley, *A Study of Goethe*, 1947, Chapter xix ; and my essay, *Faust*, in *Essays on Goethe*, ed. Rose, 1949.

27 In *Sturm und Drang*, ed. Freye, i. 111–14.

28 *Ammerkungen übers Theater. Schriften* i. 248–9.

29 *Werke* xxviii. 11–27 and 52–68.

30 Morris v. 333–6.

31 Bodmer to Schinz, 15 June 1775. Morris v. 269.

32 *Werke* vi. 522 and *Werke* xviii. 208–16.

33 To Lindau, March 1776. *Briefe* i. 201.

34 To Kayser, 23 April 1779. M. Rieger, *Klinger in der Sturm- und Drangperiode*, 423. *Sturm und Drang*, Act i, Sc. 1.

35 *Ursachen des gesunknen Geschmacks. Werke* v. 613–17.

[36] *Idcen zur Philosophie der Geschichte der Menschheit,* 1784–91, Book 9, Chapter 4. *Werke* xiii. The first draft of this chapter, rejected by Goethe because of its violence, is published in this volume as an appendix. Rousseau expresses similar views in Chapter 2 of *Du Contrat Social*, but draws different conclusions.
[37] See A. Jolivet, *Wilhelm Heinse,* Paris 1922, 266–9.

CHAPTER III.—*THE STURM UND DRANG AND THE SOCIAL CLASSES*

[1] *Frankfurter Gelehrte Anzeigen,* 27 October 1772, ed. Bergsträsser, 569–71. On the German nobility, see W. H. Bruford, *Germany in the Eighteenth Century,* 1935, Part ii.
[2] To Lenz, 17 March 1776. *Briefe von und an Lenz* i. 207–8.
[3] To Wieland, 9 July 1777. Merck, *Schriften* ii. 93.
[4] See for instance the memoirs of K. F. von Klöden, *Jugenderinnerungen,* 1874.
[5] *Teutscher Merkur,* 1778. Merck, *Schriften* i. 110.
[6] *Dichtung und Wahrheit,* Book 17. *Werke* x. 774.
[7] *Adrastea,* 1801. *Werke* xxiii. 188.
[8] See W. H. Bruford, *Germany in the Eighteenth Century,* Part iii.
[9] 29 January and 14 February 1774. Merck, *Schriften* ii. 41–2.
[10] *An Belinden,* 1775. Morris v. 34.
[11] *Anton Reiser,* 60–1.
[12] See S. E. Schreiber, *The German Woman in the Age of the Enlightenment,* New York 1948.
[13] *Faust,* ll. 3109–48.
[14] Morris iv. 293–4.
[15] Möser, *Patriotische Phantasien. Werke* i. 203.
[16] *Erwin und Elmire,* 1775. Morris v. 41–3.
[17] Möser, *Abgerissene Gedanken. Werke* v. 37.
[18] *Ueber die deutsche Sprache und Litteratur. Werke* ix. 142, 150.
[19] *Werke* v. 181–2.
[20] *Zwischen Lavater und Basedow.* Morris iv. 95.
[21] *Prolog zu den neusten Offenbarungen Gottes.* Morris iv. 45–7.
[22] *Werther.* Morris iv. 291–2.
[23] *Dichtung und Wahrheit,* Book 10. *Werke* x. 473.
[24] Particularly that in *Unzeitgemässe Betrachtungen.*
[25] See for instance the preface to Arnim and Brentano's *Des Knaben Wunderhorn.*
[26] In Goethe's *Satyros* and *Erwin und Elmire,* more seriously in Lenz's *Der Waldbruder* and *Die Kleinen.*
[27] Hölty, *Werke* i. 34–7.
[28] 28 October 1770. *Briefwechsel* i. 116.
[29] See K. Stavenhagen, *Herder in Riga,* Riga 1925, 20.
[30] *Réponse,* in *Briefe aus dem Freundeskreis,* ed. Wagner 1847, 73–83.
[31] To his wife, 20 January 1791. ibid. 301–2.

[32] *Eine Landhochzeit.* Merck, *Schriften* i. 115.

[33] *Faust*, ll. 921–2.

[34] See *Die Erziehung des Menschengeschlechts.*

[35] *Der Hofmeister*, Act v, Sc. 9.

[36] *Die Kleinen. Schriften* iii. 327–8.

[37] *Der Waldbruder. Schriften* v. 109–10.

[38] The idylls are published in *Sturm und Drang*, ed. Freye, Part iv.

[39] See for instance his description of the parson's visit to the peasant homestead, *Lebensgeschichte* (Reclam), 33–4.

[40] *An Prediger, Provinzialblätter*, 1774. *Werke* vii. 265.

[41] *Ueber Ossian und die Lieder alter Völker*, 1773. *Werke* v. 185.

[42] See the draft prefaces to his collections, *Werke* xxv. pp. 7, 9, 83 passim.

[43] In the preface to Volume 2 of his anthology, *Lyrische Bluhmenlese*, 1778 —'lyrical botching', Herder called this anthology to Gleim, 6 December 1778. *Von und an Herder* i. 59.

[44] To Herder, 10 January 1779. Lessing, *Briefe* ii. 302–3. Herder's letters, ibid. v.

[45] *Von Aehnlichkeit der mittlern englischen und deutschen Dichtkunst. Werke* ix. 522–35.

[46] 22 December 1777. *Von und an Herder* i. 51.

[47] All the prefaces, introductions, and postscripts to his collection of *Volkslieder* are to be found in *Werke* xxv.

[48] *Adrastea* 1803. *Werke* xxiv. 226.

[49] *Herzensausguss über Volkspoesie. Sämmtliche Werke* vi. 179–94.

[50] *Werke* vii. 5–19.

[51] ibid. 29.

[52] ibid. 266–76.

CHAPTER IV.—*RELIGION*

[1] See H. Schöffler's study, *Protestantismus und Literatur*, Leipzig 1922.

[2] The fullest account of pietism is A. Ritschl's *Geschichte des Pietismus*, 3 vols., 1880–6.

[3] *Teutscher Merkur*, 1779. Merck, *Schriften* i. 201.

[4] *Die Dichtung von Sturm und Drang*, Leipzig 1928, 23.

[5] *Werke* x.

[6] *Gedanken über meinen Lebenslauf*, 1758. *Schriften* i. 211–12.

[7] *Biblische Betrachtungen*, 1758. *Schriften* i. 148.

[8] *Aesthetica in nuce* (*Kreuzzüge des Philologen*, 1762). *Schriften* ii. 280–3, 283–4.

[9] *Des Ritters von Rosencreuz letzte Willensmeinung*, 1772. *Schriften* iv. 27.

[10] *Sokratische Denkwürdigkeiten*, 1759. *Schriften* ii. 35.

[11] To Lindner, 11 September 1759. In the periodical *Goethe* vii. 115.

[12] To Herder, Whitmonday 1768. Hamann, *Schriften* iii. 381–2.

[13] Wieland, *Teutscher Merkur*, 1774, viii. 174 ff.

[14] *Dichtung und Wahrheit*, Book 12. *Werke* x. 563–4.

[15] To Hamann, 23 April 1785. *Herders Briefe an Hamann*, 213–16.

[16] To Caroline, 24 January and 21 March 1772. *Briefwechsel* ii. 12, 68.

[17] To Herder, 12 November 1772. *Von und An Herder*, i. 339.
[18] A. L. Schlözer, *Herrn J. G. Herders Consistorial-Raths zu Bückeburg Beurteilung der Schlözerischen Universalhistorie*, Göttingen 1773.
[19] Caroline von Herder, *Erinnerungen*. Herder's *Werke*, ed. Müller, Erster Teil, xx. 241.
[20] To Hamann, 20 July 1776. *Herders Briefe an Hamann*, 110–11.
[21] To Hamann, 13 January 1777. ibid. 123.
[22] To Herder, 15 January 1776.
[23] A. Gillies, *Herder*, 1945, 62.
[24] May 1774. Hamann, *Schriften* v. 70–6.
[25] 1773. *Briefe an Hamann*, 72.
[26] *Uebers Erkennen und Empfinden in der Menschlichen Seele*, 1774. *Werke* viii. 236–62.
[27] *Hamanns Sprachtheorie*, München 1905, 181.
[28] Korff, *Geist der Goethezeit* ii. 23.
[29] *De sacra Poesi Hebraeorum*, 1753.
[30] To Herder, 24 August 1772. *Von und An Herder* i. 336.
[31] *Aelteste Urkunde des Menschengeschlechts*. *Werke* vi. 206.
[32] ibid. 219, 225.
[33] In the essays on Ossian and Shakespeare, *Werke* v.
[34] *Werke* v. 270.
[35] *Auch eine Philosophie der Geschichte zur Bildung der Menschheit*. *Werke* v.
[36] *Werke* v. 565, 559–60 passim.
[37] *Provinzialblätter* No. 4. *Werke* vii. 242.
[38] ibid. 243.
[39] ibid. 244.
[40] *Provinzialblätter* No. 7. *Werke* vii. 261–4.
[41] ibid. No. 8. *Werke* vii. 265.
[42] 28 August 1774. Merck, *Schriften* ii. 42–3.
[43] To Schönborn, 8 June 1774. Morris iv. 27.
[44] To Herder, c. 12 May 1775. Morris v. 30. ' Castor ' is a joke on the theme of Herder's *Letters of Two Brothers of Jesus*, *Werke* vii. 471–560.
[45] *Lebensbild* iii. 111.
[46] Herder to Jacobi, 6 February and 20 December 1784. *Aus Herders Nachlass* ii. 251–4, 263–5. Reprinted, together with Jacobi's and Mendelssohn's contributions on Spinoza, in *Hauptschriften zum Pantheismusstreit*, ed. Scholz, 1916.
[47] 15 February 1775. *Von und An Herder* i. 36.
[48] *Gott. Einige Gespräche*, Vorrede. *Werke* xvi.
[49] See for instance his criticism of the metaphysical and speculative approach of Jacobi in Herder's letters to Hamann, October 1785 and 2 January 1786. *Briefe an Hamann*, 219–26.
[50] E. Hoffart, *Herders ' Gott '*, Halle 1918, distinguishes four different conceptions of God in this work.
[51] To Merck, 12 September 1770. *Herders Lebensbild* iii. 110–11.
[52] *An Prediger*. *Provinzialblätter* No. 13. *Werke* vii. 301.
[53] *Erläuterungen zum Neuen Testament*, 1775. *Werke* vii. 355–7.
[54] ibid. 417–23.

[55] To Langer, 24 November 1768. *Der Rokoko-Goethe*, ed. Kindermann, Leipzig 1932, 345–6.
[56] To Langer, 17 January 1769. ibid. 347–8.
[57] 30 November 1769. ibid. 350.
[58] 26 August 1770. Morris ii. 12.
[59] Professor Metzger to Elias Stüber, 1771. Morris ii. 103–4.
[60] Cf. to Herder, 12 May 1775. Morris v. 30.
[61] Kestner to Hennings, 18 November 1772. Morris ii. 316.
[62] *Dichtung und Wahrheit*, Book 12. *Werke* x. 560. To Lavater, 20 February 1776.
[63] Morris iii. 36.
[64] *Dichtung und Wahrheit*, Book 14. *Werke* x. 671.
[65] To Betty Jacobi, December 1773. Morris iii. 72.
[66] *Dichtung und Wahrheit*, Book 14. *Werke* x. 670.
[67] ibid. Book 9. *Werke* x. 407–9.
[68] Lavater to Wieland, 8 November 1775. Morris v. 275. See also Heinse to Klamer Schmidt, 13 October 1774. Heinse, *Werke* ix. 229–30.
[69] *Urfaust*. Morris v. 422.
[70] *Brief des Pastors zu *** an den neuen Pastor zu ***, 1773. Morris iii. 110–21.
[71] *Zwo wichtige bisher unerörterte Biblische Fragen*, 1773. Morris iii. 122–31.
[72] Jung-Stilling, *Lebensgeschichte*, (Reclam), 298–303 ; Hasenkamp's *Tagebuch*, July 1774. Morris iv. 117–18.
[73] To Kestner, November 1772. Morris iii. 8.
[74] *Ein Fastnachtsspiel vom Pater Brey*, 1773. Morris iii. 157–70.
[75] *Götter, Helden und Wieland*, 1773. Morris iii. 329–47.
[76] *Satyros* 1773. Morris iii. 283–306.
[77] *Die Leiden des jungen Werthers*, 1774. Morris iv. 222.
[78] ibid. 296–7.
[79] Morris iv. 38–41.
[80] Morris v. 422–4.
[81] June 1776. J. Janssen, *F. L. Graf zu Stolberg*, Freiburg 1877, i. 70.
[82] To Johanna Schlosser (formerly Fahlmer), 10 November 1779. *Jahrbuch der Goethe-Gesellschaft*, i. (1914).
[83] *Wilhelm Meisters Lehrjahre*, Book 6.
[84] Reported by Bodmer, 3 August 1775. Morris v. 275.
[85] Review in *Frankfurter Gelehrte Anzeigen*, 1772. Morris iii. 94–7.
[86] See Lichtenberg's crushing satire *Timorus*, 1773.
[87] See O. Guinaudeau, *Lavater*, Paris 1924.
[88] Letter to Goethe, 1 May 1774. *Goethe und Lavater* 25–8.
[89] *Physiognomische Fragmente* 1775–8, i. Abschnitt 1, Frgt. 5. *Werke* ii. 128.
[90] ibid. Frgt. 13. *Werke* ii. 148.
[91] *Phys. Fragmente* ii. Vorrede. *Werke* ii.
[92] ibid. iii. Abschnitt 10, Frgt. 1. *Werke* ii. 1.
[93] cf. Herder's *Johannes*, 1774, *Werke* vii, and other exegetical works in the same volume ; Lavater's *Jesus Messias*, 1780.
[94] To Goethe, 30 November 1773. *Goethe und Lavater* 9–10.

[95] 1 May 1774. ibid. 26.
[96] Quoted by Lavater in his letters to Goethe, 30 November 1773 and 4 January 1774. ibid. 9 and 12.
[97] 26 April 1774. Morris iv. 15–16.
[98] *Dichtung und Wahrheit*, Book 14. *Werke* x. 672.
[99] To Lavater, 28 October 1779.
[100] 22 June 1781.
[101] 29 July 1782.
[102] 4 October 1782.
[103] 9 August 1782.
[104] 14 November 1781.
[105] The poem *Vermächtnis*, 1829.
[106] To the Duchess Luise of Saxe-Weimar, 29 May 1788. *Goethe und Lavater*, 365–7.
[107] Rosanow, *Lenz* 118.
[108] *Versuch über das erste Principium der Moral. Schriften* iv. 17.
[109] *Meinungen eines Laien. Schriften* iv. 81–128.
[110] *Vom Baum der Erkenntnis Guten und Bösen. Schriften* iv. 31–78.
[111] *Brief an einen Freund, der Theologie studiert. Schriften* iv. 23.
[112] H. Kindermann, *Lenz und die Romantik*, 317 ff. Kindermann's whole approach to Lenz seems to me mistaken.
[113] *Catharina von Siena. Schriften* iii. 284–6.
[114] *Vom Baum der Erkenntnis. Schriften* iv. 71.
[115] *Meinungen eines Laien. Schriften* iv. 160–86.
[116] *Ueber die Natur unseres Geistes. Schriften* iv. 25–9.
[117] e.g. *Ideen zur Philosophie der Geschichte der Menschheit*, Part 1, 1784. *Werke* xiii. 165–6.
[118] *Dichtung und Wahrheit*, Book 11. *Werke* x. 537.
[119] *Eduard Allwills einziges geistliches Lied. Schriften* i. 185–6. This edition has wrongly, in the second line of the penultimate stanza, ' wird ' for ' will '. I have followed the reading in *Tiefurter Journal*, No. 31, 1781, ed. von der Hellen, 256–7.
[120] Quoted *Tiefurter Journal*, ed. von der Hellen, 385.
[121] *Dichtung und Wahrheit*, Book 11. *Werke* x. 537–9.

CHAPTER V.—*THE CREATIVE PERSONALITY*

[1] *Dichtung und Wahrheit*, Book 12. *Werke* x. 563.
[2] To Mendelssohn. *Lebensbild* ii. 108.
[3] *Idee zu einer allgemeinen Geschichte in weltbürgerlicher Absicht*, 1784. *Werke* iv.
[4] To Caroline, 9 January 1773. *Briefwechsel* ii. 325.
[5] *St. Johanns Nachtstraum.* To Caroline, 11 July 1772. *Briefwechsel* ii. 161–5.
[6] To Caroline, 20 September 1770. *Briefwechsel* i. 51.
[7] *Auch eine Philosophie der Geschichte. Werke* v. 537.
[8] ibid. 523–5.
[9] ibid. 508–9.

[10] *Uebers Erkennen und Empfinden in der Menschlichen Seele*, 1774. *Werke* viii. 244.

[11] ibid. 258.

[12] ibid. 259.

[13] ibid. 252.

[14] *Ideen*, Book 8. *Werke* xiii. 337.

[15] *Frankfurter Gelehrte Anzeigen* 1772. Morris iii. 94–7.

[16] *Physiognomische Fragmente*, 1775–8, Abschnitt 2, Frgt. 2. *Werke* iv. 205.

[17] ibid. Abschnitt 1, Frgt. 10. *Werke* iv. 198.

[18] 1773. Morris iii. 138–41.

[19] 1773. Morris iii. 307–23.

[20] Morris iv. 40–1.

[21] *Die Leiden des jungen Werthers*, 1774. Morris iv. 222.

[22] ibid. 226.

[23] cf. *Prelude*, Book xii, ll. 248 ff.

[24] *Werthers Leiden*. Morris iv. 230.

[25] ibid. 293–4.

[26] *Urfaust*. Morris v. 364.

[27] ibid. 394.

[28] ibid. 410–11.

[29] ibid. 418.

[30] *Masuren oder der junge Werther*, 1775. *Auswahl* ed. Schüddekopf, 155–6.

[31] To Schleiermacher, August 1777. Rieger, *Klinger in der Sturm- und Drangperiode*, 409.

[32] Dedication of *Fausts Leben*. *Sturm und Drang* ed. Freye, iv. 225.

[33] To Gotter, 10 May 1775. *Briefe* i. 104.

[34] To Merck, September 1770. Merck, *Schriften* ii. 6.

[35] *Dritte Wallfahrt nach Erwins Grab*, 1775. Morris v. 262.

[36] *Ueber Götz von Berlichingen*. *Schriften* iv. 222–7.

[37] To Gleim, 15 February 1776. Heinse, *Werke* ix. 261.

[38] *Freuden des jungen Werthers* . . . 1775.

[39] An outburst of H. L. Wagner's *Prometheus, Deukalion und seine Recensenten*, 1775, had annoyed Merck.

[40] To Nicolai, 6 May 1775. Merck, *Schriften* ii. 52–3.

[41] To Schönborn, June 1774. Morris iv. 26.

[42] 1775. Morris v. 32.

[43] D. Mornet, *Origines intellectuelles de la Révolution française* 93.

[44] The two novels were later expanded and appear in Jacobi's *Werke*, i and v, as *Allwills Briefsammlung* and *Woldemar*. See my paper *The Novels of F. H. Jacobi and Goethe's Early Classicism*.

[45] Morris iv. 242–3 and 248–9.

[46] *Auch eine Philosophie der Geschichte*. *Werke* v. 544.

[47] *Journal meiner Reise*. *Werke* iv. 370–401.

[48] *Shakespear*. *Werke* v. 209.

[49] *Dichtung und Wahrheit*, Book 14. *Werke* x. 673.

[50] Quoted Jolivet, *Heinse*, 262.

[51] See Th. Ziegler, *Geschichte der Pädagogik*.

[52] See *Das leidende Weib, Der Hofmeister, Fausts Leben*.

[53] To Fr. Jacobi, 21 August 1774. Morris iv. 133.

[54] Morris iii. 322–3.

[55] Morris v. 426.

[56] Morris v. 421.

[57] Morris iii. 178.

[58] *Tagebuch. Schriften* v. 1–49.

[59] *Schriften* i. 77–89.

[60] Rothe in *Der Waldbruder* and Gangolf in *Henriette von Waldeck* are thinly disguised portraits of Goethe.

[61] Klopstock's letter 8 March 1776, *Goethe als Persönlichkeit*, i. 157–8. Goethe answered 21 May 1776.

[62] To Kanzler von Müller, 16 March 1824.

[63] *Faust* II, l. 7488. See my article on *Faust* in *Essays on Goethe*, ed. Rose.

[64] Helvétius, *De l'Esprit*, Discours iv.

[65] *Werke* viii. 256–9.

[66] ibid. 260–1.

[67] ibid. 295, 308–13.

[68] ibid. 314–24, 329–30.

[69] ibid. 331.

[70] ibid. 214–31.

[71] ibid. 308.

[72] ibid. 201–2.

[73] ibid. 202.

[74] *Ideen*, Book 1. *Werke* xiii. 27.

[75] *Ideen*, Book 5. *Werke* xiii. 154–65.

[76] *Vom Erkennen* . . . *Werke* viii. 324.

[77] *Allwills Briefsammlung* (originating 1775–6). *Werke* i. 178.

[78] For English views, see F. W. Stokoe, *German Influence in the English Romantic Period*, 1926.

[79] *Goethe und seine Zeit*, particularly 176–90.

CHAPTER VI.—*THOUGHT AND REALITY*

[1] Lenz, *Ueber die Natur unsers Geistes. Schriften* iv. 25–9. See above, pp. 124–7.

[2] J. Sully. Quoted by R. A. Wilson, *The Miraculous Birth of Language*, 56.

[3] *Essay concerning Human Understanding*, Book iii, Chaps. 1–3.

[4] *Nouveaux essais sur l'entendement humain. Schriften* v. 253–64, 316–18.

[5] Maupertuis, *Réflexions philosophiques sur l'origine des langues et sur la signification des mots*, 1755. Mendelssohn, *Sendschreiben an Herrn Magister Lessing in Leipzig*, 1756 ; D. Tiedemann, *Versuch einer Erklärung des Ursprungs der Sprache*, 1772.

[6] Condillac, *Essai sur l'origine des connaissances humaines*, 1746. *Œuvres*, 1798, i. La Mettrie, *Histoire naturelle de l'âme*, 1745. *Œuvres philosophiques* 1774, i. Diderot, *Lettre sur les Aveugles*, 1749. *Œuvres*, 1875, i. Turgot, *Discours en Sorbonne*, 1750, and *Deuxième Discours sur l'histoire universelle*, 1750. *Œuvres*, 1844, ii. Rousseau, *Origine de l'inégalité*,

1754 and *Essai sur l'origine des langues. Œuvres*, 1825, i. J. C. Gatterer, *Einleitung in die synchronistische Universalgeschichte*, Göttingen 1771, 91 ff. For Adam Smith's school, see Chapter vii.

[7] J. P. Süssmilch, *Beweis dass die Sprache göttlich sei*, 1766.

[8] *Ueber die neuere Deutsche Litteratur, Fragmente*, Erste Sammlung. *Werke* ii. 65–8.

[9] *Essai sur l'origine des connaissances humaines. Œuvres* i. 78 ff., 262 ff.

[10] *Abhandlung über den Ursprung der Sprache*, 1772. *Werke* v. 5–47.

[11] ibid. 48–69.

[12] To Hamann, 1 August 1772. Hamann, *Schriften* v. 8.

[13] G. Révész, *Ursprung und Vorgeschichte der Sprache*, 95.

[14] Hamann's comments were published in 1772 in reviews in *Königsberger gelehrte und politische Zeitung*, Nos. 26 and 37 ; and in the booklets *Des Ritters von Rosencreuz letzte Willensmeinung* . . . ; and *Philologische Einfälle und Zweifel* . . . All are contained in the fourth volume of his *Schriften*, 6–72.

[15] To Nicolai, 2 July 1772. *Von und An Herder*, i. 334.

[16] To Hamann, 1 August 1772. Hamann, *Schriften* v. 7–14.

[17] See above, Chapter IV.

[18] See A. O. Lovejoy, *Monboddo and Rousseau. Essays in the History of Ideas*, 1948, 38–61.

[19] Herder's Preface to the translation of Monboddo, 1784. *Werke* xv. 179 ff.

[20] Review of the translation of James Beattie's *Essay on the Nature . . . of Truth. Frankfurter Gelehrte Anzeigen*, 1772. *Werke* v. 456–62.

[21] *De l'Esprit*, Discours 1, Chap. 1.

[22] e.g. Herder's *Plastik, Werke* viii.

[23] e.g. Herder's essay on Shakespeare, *Werke* v. 226–9.

[24] *Nouveaux essais sur l'entendement humain. Schriften* v. 131–2.

[25] ibid. 101, 400–2, 358–60.

[26] See the histories of science by A. Wolf, W. Dampier-Whetham, and Charles Singer. In particular E. Nordenskiöld, *History of Biology*, 1946 ; and E. Guyénot, *Les Sciences de la Vie*, 1941.

[27] See H. Metzger, *Newton, Stahl, Boerhave et la doctrine chimique*, 1930.

[28] Diderot, *De l'Interprétation de la Nature*, 1754. *Œuvres complètes*, ii. 11. Herder and Goethe would know this, as they knew Diderot's *Principes philosophiques sur la matière et le mouvement* (1770). They knew d'Holbach's *Système de la Nature* (1770). It is very unlikely that they knew, in this period, the boldest dialogues of Diderot, *Entretien entre d'Alembert et Diderot* ; *Rêve de d'Alembert* ; and *Suite de l'Entretien*, which were not published till 1830. For the relations between d'Holbach's philosophy and natural science, see P. Naville, *Paul Thiry d'Holbach*, 1943.

[29] See the list of Goethe's reading, Morris ii. 48.

[30] Herder, *Werke* viii. 196. Bürger, *Aus Daniel Wunderlichs Buch*, Preface. *Werke* vi.

[31] To Merck, 13 June 1777. Merck, *Schriften* ii. 92.

[32] *Schriften* iv. 223.

[33] To Friederike Oeser, 13 February 1769. Morris i. 319.
[34] To Merck, September 1770. Merck, *Schriften* ii. 6.
[35] *Fragmente*, Zweite Sammlung 1767. *Werke* i. 256.
[36] *Uebers Erkennen und Empfinden. Werke* viii. 238–9.
[37] ibid. 246–54.
[38] *Vom Erkennen und Empfinden*, 1778. *Werke* viii. 169–71.
[39] ibid. 171–80.
[40] ibid. 185–93.
[41] ibid. 193.
[42] ibid. 178.
[43] ibid. 291.
[44] ibid. 197–8.
[45] *Gott. Einige Gespräche. Werke* xvi.
[46] *Gefundene Blätter . . . Werke* v. 269.
[47] To Herder, May 1774. Printed in the periodical *Goethe* vii. 135–6.
[48] See Priestley's edition of Hartley's *Observations on Man*, 1775 ; his *Disquisitions relating to Matter and Spirit*, 1777 ; and *Free Discussions of the Doctrines of Materialism*, 1778. Hartley's *Observations* and Priestley's *History of Electricity* were translated into German in 1772.
[49] *Signs of the Times*, 1829. Centenary edition, ii.
[50] *Marx-Engels Gesamtausgabe*, I. v. 533.
[51] *Sämmtliche Werke*, iv. 169–81.
[52] *Ideen*, Book 9. *Werke* xiii. 361. Herder wrote two works against Kant, the *Metakritik* of 1799 and the *Kalligone* of 1800. *Werke* xxi and xxii.
[53] *Anmerkungen übers Theater. Schriften* i. 229.
[54] *Von der Physiognomik überhaupt*, 1775. Morris v. 322.
[55] *Faust*, ll. 1224–37. Usually the word ' Sinn ' is understood in its other signification of ' mind ', but this translation misses the whole point of the movement of Faust's thought. In this short passage Goethe is summing up the predominant philosophies of his time, idealism, sensualism, and Herder's solution. Faust's conclusion is not dissimilar from Fichte's, though the latter's ' Tathandlung ' is characteristically abstract.
[56] *Faust*, ll. 1754–5.
[57] *Urfaust*. Morris v. 373–7.
[58] *Maximen und Reflexionen. Werke* ix. 650.
[59] Schiller, *Ueber den Zusammenhang der tierischen Natur des Menschen mit seiner geistigen. Werke* xv. 87–131.
[60] *Spectator*, No. 414.
[61] See D. Mornet, *Le Romantisme en France au xviii siècle* and *Le sentiment de la nature de J. J. Rousseau à B. de Saint-Pierre*, 1907.
[62] *Briefwechsel über Ossian. Werke* v. 169.
[63] Herder to Caroline, July 1772. *Briefwechsel* ii. 169–71.
[64] To Caroline, 11 May 1771. *Briefwechsel* i. 209–10.
[65] Müller, *Fausts Leben*, Dedication. *Sturm und Drang*, ed. Freye, Part 4, 223–4.
[66] September 1776. *Briefe* ii. 29–30.
[67] To Sarasin, November 1777. *Briefe* ii, 118.

[68] To Salzmann, October 1772. *Briefe* i. 62–3.

[69] *Der Waldbruder. Schriften* v. 109, 111.

[70] To Merck, 4 December 1774. Morris iv. 150–1.

[71] Maybe the reference is to Cook's first voyage round the world, in which Banks and Solander took part. See Leitzmann's notes to Morris, *Zum jungen Goethe. Ztschr. für deutsche Philologie* LVIII (1933), 343–9.

[72] *Mayfest*, 1771. Morris ii. 60–1.

[73] *Wandrers Sturmlied*, 1772. Morris ii. 124–7. See the excellent interpretation of this poem by E. M. Wilkinson, *German Life and Letters*, January 1948.

[74] Morris v. 312–16.

[75] *Erwin und Elmire*. Morris v. 59.

[76] *Reisetagebuch* 1775. Morris v. 257. (Later altered, and entitled *Auf dem See.*)

[77] *Zum Schäkespears Tag*, 1771. Morris ii. 140.

[78] *Wandrer*. Morris, ii. 130–5.

[79] Morris iv. 40–1.

[80] *Werthers Leiden*, first version. Morris ii. 264–6.

[81] ibid. 303.

[82] ibid. 295.

[83] To Goethe, 26 August 1774. *Briefwechsel zwischen Goethe und Jacobi*, 32 ff.

[84] *Die Natur. Gedichte der Brüder Stolberg*, 23.

[85] To Merck and to Lavater, December 1774. Morris iv. 151–2 and 153–4. There are slight differences between the two versions.

[86] Morris v. 366.

[87] *Faust*, Part 1. ll. 3278–9.

[88] *Dritte Wallfahrt nach Erwins Grab*, 1775. Morris v. 262.

[89] *Auf dem See*. Morris v. 257.

[90] *Gesang der Geister über den Wassern.*

[91] Letter to Kanzler von Müller, 24 May 1828. Printed with the essay, *Natur*, in *Werke* xvi. 921–6. See R. Hering, *Der Prosahymnus ' Die Natur ' und sein Verfasser, Jahrbuch der Goethe-Gesellschaft* xiii (1927), 138–56.

[92] To Kanzler von Müller, 24 May 1828.

[93] Diderot, *De l'Interprétation de la nature*, 1754. *Œuvres* ii. See particularly the *Prière*, 60–1 ; D'Holbach, *Système de la nature*, 1770 ; Buffon, *Histoire naturelle*, from 1748.

[94] It is clearly a mistake to believe that nature, in Goethe's view, appears in her destructive aspect only to the ' unhappy and unhealthy heart ' (E. A. Runge, *Primitivism in Sturm und Drang Literature*, Baltimore 1946, 20). The vigorous, healthy heart, unlike Werther, accepts the idea of death as nature's means ' to have much life '.

[95] *Auf dem See* (revised form).

[96] *Das Göttliche*, c. 1781.

[97] Goethe's Essay on Spinoza, c. 1785. *Werke* xvi. 841–4.

[98] W. Dilthey, *Weltanschauung und Analyse des Menschen seit Renaissance*

und Reformation. Schriften, Berlin 1914–17, ii. Goethe's essay on
Spinoza is here reprinted in full, pp. 392–4.

⁹⁹ To F. H. Jacobi, 9 June 1785. Jacobi's book is his *Über die Lehre des
Spinoza in Briefen an Herrn M. Mendelssohn.*

¹⁰⁰ See B. Willey, *The Eighteenth Century Background*, 1940. B. Suphan,
Aus der Zeit der Spinozastudien Goethes, Goethe-Jahrbuch 1891 ; *Zu Goethes
Philosophie der Natur, Archiv für Geschichte der Philosophie*, ii. Ernst Cas-
sirer, *Schiller und Shaftesbury*, English Goethe Society Publications,
1935.

¹⁰¹ *Maximen und Reflexionen. Werke* ix. 574.

CHAPTER VII.—*THE IDEA OF HISTORY*

¹ See E. Fueter, *Geschichte der neueren Historiographie*, München 1911.
W. Sulzbach, *Die Anfänge der materialistischen Geschichtsauffassung*,
Karlsruhe 1911. F. Meinecke, *Die Entstehung des Historismus*, 2 vols.,
München and Berlin 1936. J. W. Thompson, *A History of Historical
Writing*, 2 vols., New York 1942. R. G. Collingwood, *The Idea of
History*, 1946. R. Stadelmann, *Der historische Sinn bei Herder*, Halle
1928.

² Montesquieu, *Considérations sur les causes de la grandeur des Romains . . .*,
1734 and *De l'Esprit des Lois*, 1748. Vico, *Scienza nuova*, 1744. Turgot,
Plan de Discours sur l'Histoire Universelle ; *Deuxième Discours* ; *Remarques
critiques sur . . . Maupertuis* and *Réflexions sur la Formation et Distribution
des Richesses.*

  Adam Smith, *Lectures . . . 1764*, ed. Cannan, 1896. Adam
Ferguson, *An Essay on the History of Civil Society*, 1766. W. Robertson,
History of the Reign of Charles V, 1769, and *History of America*, 1777.
John Millar, *The Origin of the Distinction of Ranks*, 1771. Henry
Home (Lord Kames), *Sketches of the History of Man*, 1774. Monboddo,
Of the Origin and Progress of Language, Vol. i, 1773. See W. C.
Lehmann, *Adam Ferguson and the Beginnings of Modern Sociology*, New
York, 1930, and his forthcoming study of John Millar. See also my
articles, *Property and Society—The Scottish Historical School*, 1938 ; and
Herder and the Scottish Historical School, 1939.

³ See R. Hubert, *Les sciences sociales dans l'Encyclopédie*, 1923.

⁴ J. C. Gatterer, *Handbuch der Universalhistorie*, Göttingen 1761, and
Einleitung in die synchronistische Universalgeschichte, Göttingen 1771.
A. L. von Schlözer, *Vorstellung der Universal-Geschichte*, Göttingen 1772,
and *Weltgeschichte*, Göttingen 1785. See E. Schaumkell, *Geschichte der
deutschen Geschichtsschreibung*, Leipzig 1905. Herder's review of
Schlözer's *Vorstellung* appeared in *Frankfurter Gelehrte Anzeigen*, 1772
—Herder, *Werke* v. 436–40.

⁵ *Osnabrückische Geschichte*, from 1768.

⁶ *Haben wir noch jetzt das Publikum und Vaterland der Alten*, 1765. *Werke* i.
13–28.

⁷ *Ueber die neuere Deutsche Litteratur, Fragmente*, 1766–7. *Werke* i. 151 ff.

⁸ *Kritische Wälder*, 1769. *Werke* iii. 37.
⁹ *Frankfurter Gelehrte Anzeigen*, 1772. *Werke* v. 452–6.
¹⁰ *Journal meiner Reise*. *Werke* iv. 364.
¹¹ *Ueber Ossian und die Lieder alter Völker*. *Werke* v. 182.
¹² *Vom Erkennen und Empfinden*. *Werke* viii. 217 ff.
¹³ *Satyros oder der vergötterte Waldteufel*. Morris iii. 283–306.
¹⁴ Spinoza, *Ethics*, i. Introduction and iv. Preface.
¹⁵ *Plan zum Unterricht des jungen Herrn von Teschow*, 1772. *Werke* xxx. 395–402.
¹⁶ See Lovejoy, *Essays in the History of Ideas*, 14–37.
¹⁷ *Auch eine Philosophie der Geschichte zur Bildung der Menschheit*, 1774. *Werke* v. 480–7. See also *Aelteste Urkunde des Menschengeschlechts. Werke* vi.
¹⁸ ibid. 489–92.
¹⁹ ibid. 509.
²⁰ *Gedanken bei Lesung Montesquieus*, 1769. *Werke* iv. 466–8.
²¹ R. Stadelmann, *Der historische Sinn bei Herder*, 133.
²² *Auch eine Philosophie*. *Werke* v. 487, 500.
²³ ibid. 505–7.
²⁴ ibid. 588.
²⁵ ibid. 550.
²⁶ ibid. 533. The term ' giants ' is probably a reflection of Hurd's belief that the giants of legend are the poetical form of ' oppressive feudal lords '. *Letters on Chivalry*, 1762, No. 4.
²⁷ *Werke* v. 532.
²⁸ ibid. 531, 530, 539, 531.
²⁹ F. Meinecke, *Die Entstehung des Historismus*, München and Berlin 1936, ii. 425.
³⁰ To Caroline, May 1772. *Briefwechsel* ii. 116 and 118.
³¹ To Nicolai, 28 August 1774. *Briefe aus dem Freundeskreis*, ed. K. Wagner, 106. The letter is incomplete in Merck, *Schriften* ii. 42–4.
³² *Auch eine Philosophie*. *Werke* v. 503.
³³ ' Zusätze '. *Werke* v. 554–86.
³⁴ To Hamann, 23 August 1784. *Herders Briefe an Hamann*, 195.
³⁵ *Ideen zur Philosophie der Geschichte der Menschheit*, Book 9. *Werke* xiii. 353.
³⁶ *Ideen*. *Werke* xiii. 375 ff. The first draft is printed in the same volume, p. 448 ff.
³⁷ *Ideen*, Book 9, Section i. *Werke* xiii. 343 ff.
³⁸ Lovejoy, *Herder and the Philosophy of History*. *Essays* 181.
³⁹ *Ideen*, Book 4. *Werke* xiii. 137.
⁴⁰ *Ideen*, Books 2–4. *Werke* xiii. Herder is indebted to the method and ideas of Buffon and many other natural historians. Other historians, e.g. Gatterer, introduce their study of man by an account of the structure of the earth. But Herder is the first to link human history so firmly with the order of nature, though in several of the Scots and French philosophers we find similar suggestions on the physiological roots of human nature.

[41] *Ideen,* Part 2. *Werke* xiii. 333–42.
[42] *Idee zu einer allgemeinen Geschichte in weltbürgerlicher Absicht. Werke* iv. 141–57.
[43] Kant, *Werke* iv. 171–81, 184–91.
[44] *Ideen. Werke* xiii. 50, 61, 347 passim.
[45] To Herder, Whitmonday 1768. Hamann, *Schriften* iii. 381.
[46] To Herder, 20 February 1785.
[47] To Herder, 27 March 1784. Goethe was not the first to discover the intermaxillary in man (Nordenskiöld, *History of Biology,* 1946, 280), but the purpose and principle of his investigation are highly significant.
[48] *Was heisst und zu welchem Ende studiert man Universalgeschichte? Werke* viii. 9–30.

CHAPTER VIII.—*THE REVOLUTION IN POETICS*

[1] J. Sutherland, *A Preface to Eighteenth Century Poetry,* 1948. 39, 50 passim.
[2] e.g. R. Hurd, *Letters on Chivalry,* 1762 ; T. Blackwell, *Enquiry into the Life and Writings of Homer* ; R. Wood, *Essay on the Original Genius of Homer,* 1767 ; E. Young, *Conjectures on Original Composition,* 1769 ; P. Brumoy, *Le Théâtre des Grecs,* 1730, enlarged 1763 ; L. Jacquet, *Parallèle des Tragiques grecs et français,* 1760. See D. Mornet, *Origines intellectuelles de la Révolution française* and *Le Romantisme en France au xviii siècle* ; A. Monglond, *Le Préromantisme français,* 1930 ; P. van Tieghem, *Le Préromantisme,* 1924.
[3] Diderot, *De la poésie dramatique,* 1758. *Œuvres complètes* vii. 370–1.
[4] M. Mendelssohn, *Ueber die Hauptgrundsätze der schönen Künste und Wissenschaften,* 1758 (later revised), and *Rhapsodie über die Empfindungen. Philosophische Schriften,* 1771, ii. Kant, *Kritik der Urteilskraft,* 1790. Schiller adopts a very similar view in *Ueber Anmut und Würde,* 1793, and *Briefe über die aesthetische Erziehung des Menschen,* 1795.
[5] Herder, *Kalligone,* 1800. *Werke* xxii. 96–7.
[6] See my *Shakespeare in Germany,* Introduction.
[7] Klopstock, *Von der Sprache der Poesie,* 1758 ; *Gedanken über die Natur der Poesie,* 1759 ; *Von der heiligen Poesie,* 1760. *Werke* x.
[8] Herder, *Allgemeine Deutsche Bibliothek,* 1772. *Werke* v. 278–82.
[9] Letter to Hetzler, 14 July 1770. Morris ii. 7.
[10] *Urfaust.* Morris v. 374.
[11] *Aesthetica in nuce (Kreuzzüge des Philologen). Schriften* ii. 255–308.
[12] To Lindner, 5 May 1761. *Schriften* iii. 81.
[13] *Leser und Kunstrichter,* 1762. *Schriften* ii. 395–412.
[14] *Schriftsteller und Kunstrichter,* 1762. *Schriften* ii. 377–94.
[15] *Chimärische Einfälle (Kreuzzüge des Philologen). Schriften* ii. 196–8.
[16] *Fünf Hirtenbriefe das Schuldrama betreffend,* 1763. *Schriften* ii. 430–1.
[17] Lavater, *Physiognomische Fragmente,* Vorrede. (The phrase is a quotation from Herder's *Aelteste Urkunde.) Werke* ii. 116.

[18] ibid. iv. Erster Abschnitt, Frgt. 10, and iii. Neunter Abschnitt, Frgt. 1. *Werke* ii. 198, 178.

[19] *Die Insel*, 1788,

[20] Review of Klopstock's *Odes*, *Allgemeine Deutsche Bibliothek*, 1773. *Werke* v. 350.

[21] *Werke* v. 220.

[22] *Zum Schäkespears Tag*, 1771. Morris ii. 137–40.

[23] *Briefe über die Moralität der Leiden des jungen Werthers*, 1775, ed. Schmitz-Kallenberg, 1918. The work is not included in Lenz, *Schriften*.

[24] *Ammerkungen übers Theater. Schriften* i. 226–7.

[25] *Das Hochburger Schloss. Schriften* iv. 228.

[26] *Werke* v. 235–6.

[27] ibid. 219.

[28] Home, *Elements of Criticism.* Diderot, *Entretiens sur le Fils Naturel.* Home was defining the classical conception of the unities, Diderot his adaptation of them to the realistic ' genre sérieux '.

[29] Gerstenberg, *Rezensionen in der Hamburgischen Neuen Zeitung*, 1767–71, ed. Fischer, 103.

[30] Gerstenberg, *Briefe über Merkwürdigkeiten der Litteratur*, 1766, ed. v. Weilen, No. 15. See my *Shakespeare in Germany*, where some of the most important passages are reprinted.

[31] ibid. Nos. 17, 18.

[32] *Shakespear. Werke* v. 215.

[33] See J. G. Robertson, *Lessing's Dramatic Theory*, 1939. Chapter xv— ' Imitation and Illusion '.

[34] *Shakespear. Werke* v. 226–8.

[35] Heinse, *Ricciardetto, Teutscher Merkur* 1775. *Werke* iii. 453–72.

[36] Hamann, *Vom Aristobulus (Kreuzzüge des Philologen)*, 1762. *Schriften* ii. 122–5.

[37] To Hamann, 1766. *Herders Briefe an Hamann*, 30–1.

[38] *Briefe die neueste Litteratur betreffend*, No. 62, 1759. *Schriften* iv. a 573–5.

[39] *Fragmente*, Erste Sammlung. *Werke* i. 159–65.

[40] *Fragmente*, Zweite Sammlung. *Werke* i. 258–61, 307–17.

[41] ibid. 173–8.

[42] *Fragmente*, Erste Sammlung. *Werke* i. 166–9.

[43] ibid. 151–5.

[44] *Fragmente*, Dritte Sammlung. *Werke* i. particularly 400–14.

[45] Wordsworth, *Prelude*.

[46] *Kritische Wälder*, 1. *Werke* iii. 139.

[47] *Allgemeine Deutsche Bibliothek*, 1770. *Werke* iv. 308–20.

[48] *Journal meiner Reise*, 1769. *Werke* iv, see 438–40, 457.

[49] Letters to Caroline, August–September 1770. *Briefwechsel* i. 15, 29, 92.

[50] *Von deutscher Art und Kunst.* Besides Herder's essays on Ossian and Shakespeare, the volume contained Goethe's essay *Von deutscher Baukunst*, and two less important articles, one by Justus Möser.

[51] *Briefwechsel über Ossian und die Lieder alter Völker. Werke* v. 159–207.

[52] *Allgemeine Deutsche Bibliothek*, 1773. *Werke* v. 350–62.

⁵³ The three versions are published *Werke* v. 208–53.
⁵⁴ ibid. 249–50.
⁵⁵ Hurd, Home, and Blair had all shown that Greek tragedy was founded historically on the chorus, and owed its form to this circumstance.
⁵⁶ The same criticism in his review of Eschenburg's translation of Lady Montagu's *Essay on the Genius and Writings of Shakespeare.* *Allgemeine Deutsche Bibliothek*, 1773. *Werke* v. 314.
⁵⁷ See my *Shakespeare in Germany.*
⁵⁸ Goethe to Herder, 10 July 1772. Morris ii. 295.
⁵⁹ See Hamann, *Fünf Hirtenbriefe das Schuldrama betreffend*, 1763. *Schriften* ii. 430–1.
⁶⁰ Morris ii. 138–9.
⁶¹ *Anmerkungen übers Theater*, published 1774. *Schriften* i. 251.
⁶² ibid. 237.
⁶³ ibid. 238.
⁶⁴ ibid. 248–9.
⁶⁵ ibid. 252.
⁶⁶ *Rezension des neuen Menoza. Schriften* ii. 333–4.
⁶⁷ Lenz, *Anmerkungen übers Theater. Schriften* i. 225.
⁶⁸ In the review of the odes, *Allgemeine Deutsche Bibliothek. Werke* v. 355–60.
⁶⁹ ibid. 350, 355.
⁷⁰ To Schönborn, 8 June 1774. Morris iv. 28.
⁷¹ *Dichtung und Wahrheit*, Book 11. *Werke* x. 532.
⁷² *Von deutscher Baukunst.* Morris iii. 104.
⁷³ ibid. 107.
⁷⁴ *Werke* v. 359.
⁷⁵ *Dritte Wallfahrt nach Erwins Grab.* Morris v. 263.
⁷⁶ Kindermann, in the introduction to *Deutsche Literatur in Entwicklungsreihen, Irrationalismus*, Vol. 6.
⁷⁷ Morris iv. 48–57.
⁷⁸ To Caroline, 13 or 17 June 1772. *Briefwechsel* ii. 140.
⁷⁹ *Lustspiele nach dem Plautus. Schriften* ii.
⁸⁰ *Frankfurter Gelehrte Anzeigen* 1772. Morris ii. 308–11.
⁸¹ *De la littérature allemande*, 1780.
⁸² *Ueber die deutsche Sprache und Litteratur. Werke* ix.
⁸³ 20 September and 28 October 1770. *Briefwechsel* i. 51 and 116.
⁸⁴ To Friederike Oeser, 13 February 1769. Morris i. 323.
⁸⁵ Bürger to Boie, 29 September 1777. *Briefe* ii. 144–5.
⁸⁶ *Ueber naive und sentimentalische Dichtung*, 1795–6. *Werke* vii.
⁸⁷ 28 October 1770. Merck, *Schriften* ii. 12.
⁸⁸ *Herzensausguss über Volkspoesie, Deutsches Museum* 1776. *Sämtliche Werke* vi. 187.
⁸⁹ Bürger to Boie, 12 August 1773. *Briefe* ii. 132.
⁹⁰ *Dichtung und Wahrheit*, Book 9. *Werke* x. 410–13.
⁹¹ To Herder, 9 October 1776. *Briefe* ii. 39.
⁹² 28 August 1775. *Briefe* i. 124.
⁹³ *Anmerkungen übers Theater. Schriften* i. 235.

[94] *Bedeutende Fördernis durch ein einziges geistreiches Wort.* *Werke* xvi. 881.

[95] Lenz, *Anmerkungen übers Theater.* *Schriften* i. 235.

[96] E. Auerbach, *Mimesis.* Bern 1946.

[97] To Herder, October 1770. *Schriften* ii. 14.

[98] *Der neue Amadis*, 1774. Morris iv. 164–5. The poem may be of an earlier date—see Leitzmann, *Zum jungen Goethe. Ztschr. für dt. Philologie*, LVIII (1933), 343–9.

[99] Morris v. 34.

[100] *Auf dem See.* Morris v. 257.

[101] To Schönborn, 1 June 1774. Morris iv. 26.

[102] Merck, *Schriften* i. 288–9.

[103] *Dichtung und Wahrheit*, Book 18. *Werke* x. 787.

[104] To Nicolai, 19 January 1776. Merck, *Schriften* ii. 69.

[105] *Anmerkungen übers Theater.* *Schriften* i. 226–30.

[106] Merck, *Ueber den Mangel des Epischen Geistes in unserm lieben Deutschland*, 1778. Merck, *Schriften* i. 188–94.

[107] Wordsworth, Preface to *Lyrical Ballads.* Coleridge, *Biographia Literaria*, Chaps. xvii and xviii.

[108] B. Willey, *Nineteenth Century Studies*, 1949, 31.

[109] To Eckermann, 26 February 1824.

[110] From Zelter to Goethe, 7 May 1831 ; Goethe to Zelter 28 June 1831. See the observations of Strich, *Homunculus*, Publications of the English Goethe Society, xviii. 1949.

[111] To Friederike Oeser, 13 February 1769. Morris i. 323.

[112] *Aus Goethes Brieftasche.* Morris v. 344–5.

[113] *The Prelude*, Book xiv.

[114] *Werke* v. 164 and 208.

[115] *Ein Gleichnis*, 1774. Morris iv. 31–2.

[116] *Der Welt Lohn*, 1773. Morris iii. 86.

[117] *Der Kenner.* Morris iv. 162–3.

[118] *Vorläufiger Discours* to the second collection of *Fragmente.* *Werke* i. 24.

[119] *Werke* v. 380, 208, 503.

[120] To Herder, 5 May 1773. *Aus Herders Nachlass* i. 202–3.

[121] *An Kenner und Liebhaber.* Morris iv. 163.

[122] To Zimmermann, March 1776. *Briefe* i. 191.

[123] *Aus Daniel Wunderlichs Buch.* *Werke* vi. 182.

[124] Gerstenberg, *Merkwürdigkeiten der Litteratur*, 16ter Brief. ed. von Weilen, 135–6.

[125] Review of Klopstock's *Oden.* *Werke* v. 359–60.

[126] *Von deutscher Baukunst.* Morris iii. 101–9.

[127] *Kenner und Künstler.* Morris iv. 163–4.

[128] *Dritte Wallfahrt nach Erwins Grab im Jahre 1775.* Morris v. 261–3.

[129] 21 August 1774. Morris iv. 132.

[130] To Herder, 10 July 1772. Morris ii. 293–4.

[131] *Aus Daniel Wunderlichs Buch.* Bürger, *Werke* vi.

[132] *Dritte Wallfahrt nach Erwins Grab.* Morris v. 263.

[133] *Aus Goethes Brieftasche.* Morris v. 344–50. These jottings are composed of two groups, entitled *Aus Goethes Brieftasche* and *Nach Falconet und*

über Falconet. They were first published in Wagner's translation of Mercier's *Du Théâtre* along with *Dritte Wallfahrt nach Erwins Grab* and five of Goethe's poems on the artist.

[134] *Faust,* ' Vorspiel auf dem Theater '.

[135] *Schriften* iii.

[136] *Stürmer und Dränger,* ed. Sauer, ii. 359–80.

[137] J. G. Sulzer, *Allgemeine Theorie der schönen Künste,* 1771, and *Die schönen Künste in ihrem Ursprung . . .,* 1772.

[138] Review of Sulzer's *Allgemeine Theorie* in *Frankfurter Gelehrte Anzeigen,* 1772, ed. Bergsträsser, 80.

[139] Review of Sulzer's *Die schönen Künste* in *Frankfurter Gelehrte Anzeigen,* ed. Bergsträsser, 665. Morris vi. 221.

[140] *Von der heiligen Poesie* and *Von dem Range der schönen Künste. Werke* x.

[141] 18 March 1773. *Von und An Herder* i. 350.

[142] *Freiwillige Beyträge zu den Hamburgischen Nachrichten,* February 1776. Reprinted in *Goethe im Urteil seiner Zeitgenossen,* 244.

[143] ibid. April 1775. *Goethe im Urteil* 94–103.

[144] *Goethe im Urteil* 47, 109, 229.

[145] E. Ermatinger, *Die deutsche Lyrik,* Leipzig and Berlin 1925, i. 66–7.

[146] *Ueber Fülle des Herzens, Deutsches Museum* 1777. Reprinted in *Sturm und Drang, Kritische Schriften,* 791–800.

[147] Heyne to Herder, 2 June 1772. *Von und An Herder* ii. 135.

[148] *Begebenheiten des Enkolp,* 1773. *Werke* ii.

[149] *Iris,* 1774. *Goethe im Urteil,* 65.

[150] *Deutsches Museum,* 1776. *Goethe im Urteil,* 304–7.

[151] *Briefwechsel über Ossian. Werke* v. 163.

[152] *Zum Schäkespeurs Tag.* Morris ii. 138.

[153] *Anmerkungen übers Theater. Schriften* i. 227.

[154] K. P. Moritz, *Anton Reiser,* 1785–6, ed. Geiger, 233–5 ; 259–60 ; 302.

[155] *Ueber Ossian . . ., Werke* v. 200–1.

[156] Morris ii. 308–11.

[157] *Ueber Götz von Berlichingen. Schriften* iv. 224–5.

[158] To Auguste zu Stolberg, 13 February 1775. Morris v. 10.

[159] Review of Sulzer's *Die schönen Künste in ihrem Ursprung . . ., Frankfurter Gelehrte Anzeigen,* 1772. Morris vi. 223.

[160] *Dichtung und Wahrheit,* Book 13. *Werke* x. 642.

CHAPTER IX.—*THE ACHIEVEMENT*

[1] B. Willey, *The Eighteenth Century Background,* 95. Of course, the term ' eighteenth century ' is here, as with Sutherland, used in a particular and rather limited way.

[2] Mornet, *La Pensée française au 18e siècle,* 37.

[3] Sutherland, *A Preface to Eighteenth Century Poetry,* 39.

[4] June 1774. Morris iv. 78–82.

[5] Bruford, *Theatre Drama and Audience in Goethe's Germany,* 1950, 170–205.

[6] *Die Leiden des jungen Werthers.* Morris iv. 274.
[7] Locke, *Essay concerning Human Understanding,* ii. Chap. 20.
[8] Goethe, *Von der Physiognomik überhaupt,* 1775. Morris v. 322.
[9] *Faust,* l. 1834.
[10] *Faust,* l. 1237.
[11] *Aus Goethes Brieftasche.* Morris v. 347.
[12] ibid. 345–50.
[13] See G. Lukács, *Goethe und seine Zeit,* Bern 1947.
[14] Goethe to H. Meyer, 20 July 1831.

BIBLIOGRAPHY

A list of works consulted would run to many hundreds of titles. I therefore give below only the titles of the editions of the German texts used, to many of which reference is made in the Notes in an abbreviated form. A list of my own shorter studies on the period is attached.

CONTEMPORARY TEXTS

Bürger, G. A. *Sämmtliche Werke*, ed. Reinhard, 7 vols., Berlin 1824.
Briefe von und an Bürger, ed. Strodtmann, 4 vols., 1874.
Claudius, M. *Werke*, ed. Adler, 3 vols., Weimar 1924.
Gerstenberg, H. W. *Gedicht eines Skalden*. Kopenhagen 1766.
Ugolino, 1768 (in *Sturm und Drang*, ed. Freye).
Briefe über Merkwürdigkeiten der Litteratur, 1766.
Rezensionen in der Hamburgischen Neuen Zeitung, 1767–71.
    (Both the latter are reprinted in *Deutsche Litteraturdenkmale des 18 und 19 Jahrhunderts*, Nos. 29–30 and 128.)
Gleim, J. W. *Sämmtliche Schriften*, 6 parts, 1773.
Briefe von den Herren Gleim und J. G. Jacobi, Berlin 1768.
Briefwechsel zwischen Gleim und Heinse, ed. Schüddekopf, Stuttgart 1894.
Briefwechsel zwischen Gleim und Uz, ed. Schüddekopf, Stuttgart, 1899.
Briefwechsel zwischen Gleim und Ramler, ed. Schüddekopf, Stuttgart 1906.
Goethe, J. W. *Werke*, 24 vols., Zürich 1949–52.
Der junge Goethe, ed. Morris, 6 vols., Leipzig 1910–12 (referred to in the text as ' Morris ').
Goethe als Persönlichkeit, ed. Amelung, Vol. I, München 1914.
Goethe im Urteile seiner Zeitgenossen, ed. Braun, Berlin 1883.
Goue, A. S. von. *Auswahl*, ed. Schüddekopf, Weimar 1917.
Hamann, J. G. *Schriften*, ed. Roth and Wiener, 8 vols., Berlin 1821–43.
Neue Hamanniana, ed. Weber, München 1905.
Briefe in the periodical *Goethe*, vii. 1943.
Heinse, W. *Werke*, ed. Schüddekopf, 11 vols., 1907–13.
Herder, Caroline. *Erinnerungen aus dem Leben J. G. Herders*. (Herder's *Werke*, ed. Müller, Stuttgart 1827. Zur Phil. und Gesch. xx.)
Herder, J. G. *Sämmtliche Werke*, ed. Suphan, 33 vols., Berlin 1877–1913.
Briefwechsel mit Caroline Flachsland, ed. Schauer, 2 vols., Weimar 1926–8.
Von und An Herder, ed. Düntzer and F. G. Herder, 3 vols., Leipzig 1861–2.
Herders Lebensbild, ed. F. G. Herder, 3 vols., Erlangen 1846.
Aus Herders Nachlass, ed. Düntzer and F. G. Herder, 3 vols., Frankfurt 1856–7.
Briefe an Hamann, ed. Hoffmann, Berlin 1887.
Hippel, T. *Sämmtliche Werke*, 11 vols., Berlin 1828.
Hölty, L. H. C. *Sämtliche Werke*, 2 vols., Weimar 1914.
Jacobi, F. H. *Werke*, ed. Jacobi and Roth, 6 vols., Leipzig 1812–25.
Die Hauptschriften zum Pantheismusstreit, ed. Scholz, Berlin 1916.

Briefwechsel zwischen Goethe und Jacobi, ed. Max Jacobi, Leipzig 1846.
Briefe, ed. Hecker (in the periodical *Goethe* vi, vii, viii, 1941–3).
JUNG, HEINRICH. *Lebensgeschichte* (Reclam), Leipzig 1908.
Briefe Jung-Stillings an seine Freunde, ed. Vömel, Berlin 1905.
KANT, I. *Sämmtliche Werke*, ed. Hartenstein, 8 vols., Leipzig 1867.
KLETTENBERG, S. K. VON. *Die schöne Seele. Bekenntnisse etc.*, ed. Funck, Leipzig 1911.
KLINGER, F. M. *Dramatische Jugendwerke*, ed. Berendt and Wolff, 3 vols., Leipzig 1912–13.
Ausgewählte Werke, 8 vols., Stuttgart 1878–80.
(See *Sturm und Drang*, ed. Freye.)
KLOPSTOCK, F. G. *Sämmtliche Werke*, 10 vols., Leipzig 1855.
LAVATER, J. C. *Ausgewählte Werke*, ed. Staehelin, 4 vols., Zürich 1943.
Goethe und Lavater (Correspondence), ed. Funck, Weimar 1901.
LEIBNIZ, G. W. *Die philosophischen Schriften*, ed. Gerhardt, 7 vols., Berlin 1882.
LEISEWITZ, J. A. *Sämmtliche Schriften*, Braunschweig 1838.
(See *Sturm und Drang*, ed. Freye.)
Briefe an seine Braut, ed. Mack, Weimar 1906.
Tagebücher, ed. Mack and Lochner, 2 vols., Weimar 1916–20.
LENZ, J. M. R. *Gesammelte Schriften*, ed. Blei, 5 vols., München 1909–13.
Briefe über die Moralität . . . des jungen Werthers, ed. Schmitz-Kallenberg, 1918.
Briefe von und an Lenz, ed. Freye and Stammler, 2 vols., Leipzig 1918.
(See *Sturm und Drang*, ed. Freye.)
LESSING, G. E. *Sämtliche Schriften*, ed. Lachmann-Muncker, 23 vols., Stuttgart 1886–1924.
Briefe von und an Lessing, ed. Muncker, 5 vols., Leipzig 1904–7.
LICHTENBERG, G. C. *Aphorismen*, ed. Leitzmann, 3 vols., Berlin 1902–6.
Briefe, ed. Leitzmann and Schüddekopf, 2 vols., Leipzig 1901.
LYNCKER, K. VON. *Am Weimarischen Hof*, ed. Scheller, Berlin 1912.
MENDELSSOHN, M. *Schriften*, 7 vols., Leipzig 1843–5.
(Correspondence, see Lessing, above.)
MERCK, J. H. *Schriften und Briefwechsel*, ed. Wolff, 3 vols., Leipzig 1909–11.
Briefe an Merck von Goethe, Herder etc., ed. Wagner, Darmstadt, 1835.·
Briefe an und von Merck, ed. Wagner, Darmstadt 1838.
Briefe aus dem Freundeskreis von Goethe, Herder, Merck, ed. Wagner, Basel 1847.
MILLER, J. M. *Siegwart eine Klostergeschichte*, 3 vols., Leipzig 1777.
MORITZ, C. P. *Anton Reiser*, ed. Geiger. (*Deutsche Lit-denkmale des 18 und 19 Jahrhunderts*, No. 23.)
MÖSER, JUSTUS. *Sämmtliche Werke*, ed. Abeken, 10 vols., Berlin 1842.
MOSER, F. C. *Der Herr und der Diener*, Frankfurt 1759.
Treuherziges Schreiben . . . an den Magus in Norden, Frankfurt 1762.
Von dem deutschen National-Geist, Frankfurt 1765.
Ueber Regenten, Räthe, und Regierung, Frankfurt 1784.
Politische Wahrheiten, 2 vols., Zürich 1796.

MÜLLER, J. F. (MALER). *Werke*, 3 vols., Heidelberg 1811.
(See *Sturm und Drang*, ed. Freye.)
NICOLAI, F. *Freuden des jungen Werthers* . . ., Berlin 1775.
   Das Leben und die Meinungen . . . *Sebaldus Nothankers*, 3 vols., Berlin 1773–6.
   Eyn feyner kleyner Almanach voll schönerr . . . *Volckslieder*, ed. Bolte, 2 vols., Weimar 1918.
   (Correspondence, see Herder, Lessing, above.)
RAMLER, K. W. *Lyrische Bluhmenlese*, 2 vols., Leipzig 1774–8.
LA ROCHE, SOPHIE VON. *Geschichte des Fräuleins von Sternheim*, ed. Wieland, 1771. (*Dt. Lit-denkmale des 18 und 19 Jahrh.* No. 25.)
SALZMANN, J. D. *Kurze Abhandlungen*, Strassburg 1776.
SCHILLER, F. *Werke*, ed. Bellermann, 15 vols., Leipzig n.d.
   Schillers Persönlichkeit, ed. Hecker and Petersen, 3 vols., Weimar 1904–8.
SCHUBART, C. F. D. *Gesammelte Schriften*, 8 vols., Stuttgart 1839–40.
STOLBERG, C. and F. L. *Gedichte der Brüder Stolberg*, ed. Boie, Leipzig 1779.
   Gesammelte Werke, 20 vols., Hamburg 1821.
SULZER, J. G. *Allgemeine Theorie der schönen Künste*, Leipzig 1771.
   Die schönen Künste in ihrem Ursprung . . ., Leipzig 1772.
SÜSSMILCH, J. P. *Versuch eines Beweises, dass die Sprache göttlich sei*, Berlin 1766.
VOSS, J. H. *Lyrische Gedichte*, 5 vols., Königsberg 1802.
WAGNER, H. L. *Prometheus, Deukalion und seine Rezensenten*, 1775 (in *Stürmer und Dränger*, ed. Sauer).
   Die Reue nach der Tat, Frankfurt 1775.
   Die Kindermörderin, Leipzig 1776 (in *Sturm und Drang*, ed. Freye).
   Mercier—Neuer Versuch über die Schauspielkunst, Leipzig 1776.
WIELAND, C. M. *Sämmtliche Werke*, 42 vols., Leipzig 1794–1802.
WINCKELMANN, J. *Werke*, 2 vols., Stuttgart 1847.

SELECTIONS OF TEXTS

Stürmer und Dränger, ed. Sauer, 3 vols. (*Deutsche National-Litteratur*, Nos. 79–81).
Sturm und Drang, ed. Freye, 4 vols., Berlin and Leipzig (Bongs Klassiker).
Sturm und Drang. Kritische Schriften, ed. E. Löwenthal, Heidelberg 1949.
Von deutscher Art und Kunst, ed. Purdie, 1924.
Shakespeare in Germany, 1740–1815, ed. Pascal, 1937.

PERIODICALS

Briefe über den itzigen Zustand der schönen Wissenschaften, Berlin 1755. (Nicolai.) ed. Ellinger, Berlin 1894.
Briefe die neueste Litteratur betreffend, Berlin 1759–65. (Lessing, Nicolai, Mendelssohn.)
Bibliothek der schönen Wissenschaften, Leipzig 1757–65. (Nicolai.)
Allgemeine Deutsche Bibliothek, Berlin 1765–. (Nicolai.)
Der Wandsbecker Bote, Wandsbeck 1771–5. (M. Claudius.)

z*

Musenalmanach, Göttingen 1770–5. (Gotter and Boie.)
Frankfurter Gelehrte Anzeigen (Deinet). The numbers for 1772, which include many contributions from Merck, Goethe, and Herder, have been reprinted by Bergsträsser, Heilbronn 1883.
Iris, Düsseldorf 1775–6. (Heinse.)
Der Teutsche Merkur, Weimar 1773–. (Wieland.)
Deutsche Chronik, Augsburg 1774–8. (Schubart.)
Deutsches Museum, Göttingen 1776–8. (Boie.)

EARLIER STUDIES BY THE AUTHOR ON THIS PERIOD

Shakespeare in Germany 1740–1815, 1937.
Property and Society—The Scottish Historical School. (*Modern Quarterly*, i, 1938.)
Herder and the Scottish Historical School. (*English Goethe Society Publications*, xiv, 1939.)
Nationalism and the German Intellectuals. (*The German Mind and Outlook*, ed. Farquharson, 1945.)
The Novels of F. H. Jacobi and Goethe's early classicism. (*English Goethe Society Publications*, xvi, 1947.)
Goethe's Autobiography and Rousseau's Confessions. (*Studies presented to Professor Ritchie*, 1949.)
Faust. (*Essays on Goethe*, ed. Rose, 1949.)
Lenz as Lyric Poet. (*Studies presented to Professor Willoughby*, 1952.)
J. M. R. Lenz—A Bicentenary Lecture. (*Publications of the English Goethe Society*, xxi, 1952.)
The Sturm und Drang Movement. (*Modern Language Review*, xlvii, 2, 1952.)

INDEX OF NAMES

referred to in the Text

341

Printed in Great Britain by
Butler & Tanner Ltd.,
Frome and London

I

F